# SILLS OF BOWDOIN

*The Life of Kenneth Charles Morton Sills, 1879–1954*

President Sills of Bowdoin. Portrait by Leopold Seyffert, N. A.

# SILLS OF BOW[

### THE LIFE OF

### KENNETH CHARLES MORTON

### 1879–1954

## HERBERT ROSS BROWN

COLUMBIA UNIVERSITY PRESS

New York and London 1964

TO

# E. L. K. S.

*"Doctor of Ease and Graciousness"*

# PREFACE

Upon his retirement as president of Bowdoin College in 1952, Kenneth C. M. Sills read with quizzical amusement a sketch of his career in *Time*: "A former Latin instructor famed for his fidgets (he used to tear whole handkerchiefs to shreds while teaching), 'Casey' Sills mellowed into a pleasant, paunchy 'ex-scholar,' famed for his love of Dante, for eating (so goes the legend) eleven lobster stews at a sitting, and for liking to run his piny campus just as if Longfellow were still there—'Excellent teaching in wooden halls is much better than wooden teaching in marble halls.'"

Had the author of this news magazine item been a Bowdoin undergraduate, he would have received a familiar Sillsean come-uppance: "What reporters have to say to us is always interesting, sometimes important, but not necessarily conclusive." The president acknowledged that as a young administrator he may have fussed unduly with his handkerchief, but his campaign as a Maine Democrat for the U.S. Senate in 1916 had taught him to speak without conspicuous embarrassment. As for the tradition of his fondness for lobster, he conceded that repeated denials had not prevented the legend from becoming a campus myth. He demurred, however, at the intimation of wanting to run a nineteenth-century college. To critics of the requirement of Greek or Latin or mathematics for twentieth-century Freshmen, he replied, "A first-rate thing is never dead." And, at the end of his presidency of thirty-four years, he continued to regard excellent teaching, whether in halls of wood, brick, or marble, as Bowdoin's chief distinction. "In so many postwar plans," Kenneth Sills remarked in 1945, "the teacher is the forgotten man. We do not intend to forget him at Bowdoin."

This biography of President Sills is, in some respects, the portrait of an anomaly. Primarily a scholar-teacher, he trained himself to become an able executive. Never a fluent speaker, he often gave seventy-five formal addresses and scores of informal talks in a single academic year. Despite increasingly heavy and complex demands upon him, he found time annually to teach a large course in comparative literature and to correct all the papers himself. A stanch Democrat in a state which often viewed such political loyalty as a mild form of insanity, he worked harmoniously with Governing Boards whose membership was overwhelmingly Republican. Although he considered his position to be "a very high one," he was so indifferent to the trappings of official status that for a long time after his election he seemed content to conduct college business without a private office or telephone.

These anomalies might easily be multiplied. President Sills was an Episcopal layman without formal theological training, yet none of the seven ordained Congregational ministers who had preceded him in office was more devoted to the Church. Although he faced the difficult experience of following a "giant," and believed William DeWitt Hyde was "the greatest president Bowdoin ever had or is ever likely to have," he immediately proved his fitness by relying on the momentum generated by his predecessor while quietly initiating an educational program of his own. Perhaps few college presidents possessed less of the managerial temperament or had more impatience with modern gadgets to increase efficiency, yet even fewer achieved his detailed mastery of the operation of his institution. Never entirely happy as a fund-raiser, he nevertheless recognized the truth of President Robert Hutchins' dictum that a college which is not short of money has run out of ideas. The fivefold increase in Bowdoin's endowment during his administration is evidence not only of Kenneth Sills's persuasive statements of the needs of the college but also of the generosity of donors when a president exemplifies as well as endorses the values of a liberal education.

It will hardly tempt a prospective reader to turn the pages of this book if he is warned at the outset that its subject doubted whether an adequate biography of a college president is ever likely to be written. His own life, he told a colleague, had been full and exciting, but he felt that its drama would seem pale within the covers of a book. When his friend, Dana Ferrin of Appleton-Century Crofts, urged him to write his memoirs, he protested that the subject was altogether unpromising. His habitual reticence shrank at the prospect of making critical comments which might seem invidious or malicious. The responsibilities of a college presidency had too often required the giving and receiving of pain for him to wish to run the risk in his retirement. His lifelong habit of calculated speech could not be easily abandoned, yet he knew that only by "speaking out," by naming names, and by identifying situations could the emotional intensities of the inner drama of his career be conveyed. A dozen fragmentary manuscript pages found among his papers indicate that he had made the attempt. When he read them to his wife, she objected that what he had written seemed strangely impersonal and that the protagonist rarely appeared in the center of the stage. Finally, despairing of forcing himself to say what he felt should remain unsaid, he laid the project aside.

"Blessed is the college," Kenneth Sills once remarked in a chapel talk, "whose annals are uneventful." Certainly the Bowdoin of his day knew no such beatitude. He was destined to guide his Alma Mater through two world wars, a major depression, the dislocations caused by the conflict in Korea, and the ensuing armed truce. As he neared his seventieth birthday in 1949, he saw clearly that the Second World War marked a great divide in Bowdoin's history. He realized that his successor could not return to the earlier simplicities which had enabled him virtually "to carry the college in his head," to move easily from reading financial statements in his office, to lecturing in the classroom, and to conducting daily chapel.

Amid the present complexities, such a concept of the college president—omniscient and omnipresent—is seen by President Emeritus Henry M. Wriston of Brown as surrounded by the aura of a myth: "He is at once the illuminating teacher, the great inspiration, the awful disciplinarian, and the kindly, warm-hearted friend who loans students money, forgives academic deficiencies because of profound faith in youth."* In *Academic Procession*, a report of his experiences of more than thirty years, Dr. Wriston encountered only two men in this century who might be said to approach the image: Ernest Martin Hopkins of Dartmouth and Sills of Bowdoin. It is the purpose of this biography to tell the story of Kenneth Charles Morton Sills and of the college whose ideals he embodied as professor, dean, and president for forty-six years.

This is a Bowdoin book, and it is a measure of the personal impression Kenneth Sills left on Bowdoin men that all of Bowdoin was eager to have a share in fashioning it. Since few biographies have owed so much to so many collaborators, I cannot begin to name all those who have assisted me. Scores of them who are mentioned in the text have already received my thanks, but it is pleasant to thank them again on the threshold of what is the result of a joint and friendly enterprise.

Of those who died before the manuscript reached the printer, I owe the heaviest debt to Professors Emeriti Wilmot Brookings Mitchell, William Witherle Lawrence, and George Roy Elliott. The first of these was a member of the faculty when Kenneth Sills entered college in 1897 and knew the Bowdoin scene intimately for seventy-six years. His remarkable memory enabled him to enliven the prosy minutes of countless faculty minutes and to salvage many details which otherwise would have been unremembered. It was Professor Lawrence who first

---

* Henry M. Wriston, *Academic Procession: Reflections of a College President* (New York, Columbia University Press, 1959), pp. 174-75.

urged the need of a full-length biography and graciously furnished me with reminiscences of the years he shared with Kenneth Sills in Portland, Cambridge, and New York. To Professor Elliott I am grateful not only for a critical and sympathetic reading of the manuscript but for personal kindnesses far too numerous to recount. Grateful homage is also due to the memory of Paul Nixon, Kenneth Sills's incomparable dean, who allowed me to draw upon his recollections of almost daily association with the president for twenty-nine years. Debts such as these are a pleasant duty to acknowledge, even though they can never be repaid.

Without the help of members of the Governing Boards and faculty colleagues, past and present, this biography could not have been undertaken. The president and Trustees opened all college records to my scrutiny, and the administrative and library staffs went far beyond the line of duty to facilitate their use. A committee of Trustees and Overseers, which did me the welcome honor of suggesting that I write *Sills of Bowdoin,* has been unfailingly and continuously helpful from the beginning. Its members and a faculty representative (Messrs. Earle S. Thompson, William D. Ireland, Philip G. Clifford, Clement F. Robinson, and Professor Thomas A. Riley) gave the manuscript a careful reading and have encouraged me at every stage of its progress. Nor may I omit mention of my gratitude to President James S. Coles, whose knowledge of the habits of at least one member of his faculty prompted him to arrange for a generous leave of absence to enable me to write a major part of the book.

A few other friends, whose help was so extensive that it would be churlish of me not to cite it here, include Professor Emeritus Thomas C. Van Cleve, whose Bowdoin tenure spans the last years of the Hyde administration and all of Kenneth Sills's presidency. Almost every page of this book bears witness to his counsel. My thanks also go to Glenn R. McIntire, former bursar and now assistant treasurer of Bowdoin, whose helpfulness belies the myth that financial officers sometimes forget that a college has a heart as well as a head. Particular acknowledgment is due to Professor Nathan Dane II, a successor of President Sills in the Winkley professorship of Latin, who supplied valuable information about "Casey's Lit.," to Mr. Harry G. Shulman and to the late Kosti Ruohomaa, who provided the photographs, and to Miss Mabel Matthews, who typed the manuscript with skill and unfailing cheerfulness.

Indebtedness of a personal kind is owed to the Percolators, a coffee club whose members began teaching at Bowdoin as young instructors under President Sills's benign direction. Their wide hospitality permitted me to read the entire manuscript, chapter by chapter, at successive meetings. The lively and informed criticism of these loyal colleagues—Edward S. Hammond, Cecil T. Holmes, Fritz C. A. Koelln, Athern P. Daggett, Reinhard L. Korgen, Samuel E. Kamerling, and George H. Quinby—saved me from many blunders. Their suggestions, and those from a patient Griselda who refuses to be named, deserved to bear fruit in a better book. I am also grateful to the far-flung family of Bowdoin alumni and friends who responded to appeals for information. Perhaps nothing is more characteristic of Kenneth Sills's humanity than the fact that many letters, often from men and women in humble walks of life whose words are too intimate to be quoted, described acts of such rare thoughtfulness that each writer believed his experience must have been unique.

Mrs. Sills, with the graciousness that all Bowdoin has come to associate with 85 Federal Street in Brunswick and 134 Vaughan Street in Portland, entrusted me with her husband's letters, papers, and—most important—her memories of a blessed life. My deepest debt of all, however, save for the dedication, must remain unexpressed.

H. R. B.

Brunswick, Maine
February 21, 1964

# CONTENTS

*A group of photographs appears after page 142.*

# SILLS OF BOWDOIN

*The Life of Kenneth Charles Morton Sills, 1879–1954*

# I

## A PORTLAND BOYHOOD

### 1880-1897

Portland in 1886 was a dignified dowager of a town, but for the three days beginning with the Fourth of July, she was prepared to let herself go a bit. Ordinarily she would have blinked incredulously at the sight of hawkers of pink lemonade and vendors of toy balloons on State Street. Yet now she approved the gay banners hanging from Greek porticoes and garlands festooning the columns of prim doorways. Up the street, near the corner of Congress, at numbers 173 and 175, the wrought-iron balconies of both the John Neal houses were alive with flags, and down toward Spring, the sedate mansions of the Danas, Paysons, and Shepleys were blossoming with rosettes. So festive a departure from the usual decorum was not to be explained by an ordinary holiday. In July, 1886, Portlanders were not merely preparing for another Independence Day—they were about to celebrate their city's centennial.

Even the Reverend Charles Morton Sills, the new Canon of St. Luke's Cathedral, had caught the carnival spirit and was flying the Stars and Stripes from every one of his windows at 135 State Street. As a loyal British subject, who had recently arrived from Canada, he may have felt some misgivings at the absence of the Union Jack. But he was now in the United States, and the city of his adoption was primping for her one hundredth birthday. The Canon's six-year-old son Kenneth, torn by no such divided allegiances, was an excited observer of the gala proceedings. Just the day before, the boy had watched admiringly as the firemen in Falmouth Engine House 4, around the corner on Spring Street, put the finishing touches on the brasswork of their engine for the parade. His father had promised that he would be allowed to see the entire two-and-one-half-mile procession of floats, bands, soldiers, and sailors—and perhaps even to stay up late enough to enjoy the fireworks from the Western Promenade.

The Reverend Canon and Mrs. Sills had arrived in Portland from Halifax, Nova Scotia, in the summer of 1880, bringing with them their infant son. Although they loved St. Andrews, New Brunswick, where Mrs. Sills's father was the rector of All Saints Church, and would always have affectionate memories of Halifax where their boy was born on December 5, 1879, the Sillses were delighted to be in Portland. With the birth of a daughter Mary, in 1882, the happiness of their household seemed complete. As Canon and Mrs. Sills looked ahead to the education of their children, they were gratified to learn of the excellent reputation of the Butler Grammar School on nearby West Street. Since his fifth birthday the boy had been attending Mrs. Alice Carter's kindergarten on Spring Street. The following September he would enter the Park Street Primary School.

Indeed, the more Canon Sills and his wife saw of Portland, the more pleased they were with the position at St. Luke's which had induced them to leave the curacy in Halifax and settle in the United States. In Nova Scotia they had been told that Boston was the most British of all the cities in "the States," but they now doubted that there could possibly be a friendlier place than Portland. When the Canon looked at the façades of the four-story brick houses on the west side of Park Street, he felt almost as though he were in London itself. The Park Street block, a row of twenty gracious dwellings, had been spared in the Great Fire of 1866 which destroyed 1,800 of the town's most substantial buildings and left nearly 10,000 people homeless. The Reverend Mr. Sills marveled at the way Portland had recovered her aplomb in so short a time. Lincoln Park, now a green oblong in the heart of the community, had been laid out in the center of what, only twenty years before, had been a desolate wilderness of gaunt

chimneys and blackened walls. The flames, he had been told, had
charred many huge elms and maples, and he heard his parishioners
speak nostalgically of the days when Portland was known as
the "Forest City,"—but he thought enough noble trees had survived to justify the old title. The Canon enjoyed walking down
State Street, still lined with arching elms, toward Deering's
Oaks. Carpeted with thick grass and heavily timbered, the spot
seemed as fresh and fair as when young Longfellow wandered
in its dappled shade to dream the long, long thoughts of youth.
The poet had remembered his birthplace as "the beautiful city
that is seated by the sea," and the present inhabitants continued
to see it through his eyes.

By the time of the centennial, Canon Sills had lived in Portland
only six years, but his rambles through the older parts of the
town had shown him that its pride in the past was not unfounded.
He had taken his son to see the burial place of the victims of the
Indian Massacre of 1690 on the southern slope of Munjoy Hill
in the Eastern Cemetery. He told his boy how Sir William Phipps
had interred their bleached bones two years later when the Royal
Governor stopped at the ruins of the settlement on his voyage
to Pemaquid. The Canon also visited the graves of Captains
Burrows and Blythe, of the American brig *Enterprise* and His
Majesty's ship *The Boxer*, who had lost their lives in a sea fight
off Monhegan on September 5, 1813, while anxious Portlanders
crowded the tiny Munjoy Observatory to watch the smoke of
battle 40 miles away. Even if the centennial had not happened
to fall on the Fourth of July, Canon Sills would soon have learned
that the city cherished its heroes of the Revolution. He showed
young Kenneth the gentle, grass-covered curves tracing the line
of earthworks thrown up as a defense against the British fleet,
behind the Settlers' Monument in Fort Allen Park. In October,
1775, four enemy vessels under Captain Henry Mowat opened a
bombardment, burning the settlement then known as Falmouth,
an outrage which General Washington called a "flaming argument for independence." The Reverend Mr. Sills, who knew

some of Captain Mowat's descendants in St. Andrews, could only regret the rupture between the mother country and her colonies, but he rejoiced that neither this conflagration, nor the later Portland fire in 1866, had broken the spirit of the citizens.

In the spring of 1886, at the request of the Centennial Committee, Canon Sills was engaged in some of his own research into Portland's past. He had accepted an invitation to prepare an historical essay, not only as a welcome honor to a newcomer, but as a means of learning more about the town while becoming familiar with the annals of his own parish. Although his discourse was concerned primarily with church history, it had been based upon enough reading to enable him to share the local pride in Portland literary traditions. To be sure, Longfellow had lived most of his creative years in Cambridge, but his family home on Congress Street was fast becoming a national shrine. Portlanders might ask confidently whether any American city had been as lovingly evoked as were their own wharves, streets, and groves in "My Lost Youth." The name of Longfellow had been familiar to the Canon from his boyhood days in the 1850s in Hertfordshire, England. He had not known, however, that the poet's Bowdoin classmate, Nathaniel Hawthorne, had lived for several happy years in Raymond, on Sebago Lake, and had been tutored for college by Parson Caleb Bradley in a house still standing in Stroudwater, in the western section of town. Perhaps Portland might claim a modest share in the novelist's glory.

In addition to these stars of first magnitude, Canon Sills learned of a galaxy of lesser lights deserving remembrance. There was Portland's intrepid Madame Wood who had had the temerity, as early as 1800, not only to defend the deplorable habit of reading fiction but to write several novels herself. Some reflected glory also came from a surprising number of local writers who left Portland to gain fame elsewhere. The first of these, the novelist John Neal, had scattered his undisciplined talents, but remained to the end a passionate champion of a native literature which he insisted, prophetically enough, should speak to the world in accents unmistakably American. Another Portlander, Seba Smith, from his house on Back Cove, began in 1830 the series of Jack Downing letters for the *Portland Courier* which was destined to beget a progeny of crackerbox philosophers and popular wiseacres. Portland could also boast of Nathaniel Parker Willis, whose dandified *Pencilings by the Way* caught the popular fancy in the mid 1830s, and of his no less celebrated sister, Sara, upon whom he had conferred the pen name "Fanny Fern." Her *Fern Leaves from Fanny's Portfolio* had inspired a host of other scribbling females in the feminine fifties. Even after making proper allowance for the enthusiasm aroused by the centennial, Canon Sills was ready to believe that Portlanders had earned their right to celebrate.

As if all these honors were not enough for one town, Judge William LeBaron Putnam, the Canon's friend and State Street neighbor, reminded him that Portland's political traditions were equally impressive. William Pitt Fessenden, Lincoln's secretary of the treasury, who later braved the wrath of his constituents by voting in the Senate against the impeachment of Andrew Johnson, read law in Portland, and lived and died on State Street. An ardent Democrat, Judge Putnam was proud to point to another Democratic Portland lawyer, Nathan Clifford, the only Maine jurist to sit on the U.S. Supreme Court. There was also that fiery Southern orator, Seargent Prentiss, Portland native and Bowdoin graduate, who studied law in Maine before embarking on his tempestuous political career in Mississippi and Washington, D.C. Little wonder, the Judge remarked, that still another senator and secretary of the treasury, later to become chief justice of the United States, the Honorable Salmon Portland Chase, should have considered it an honor to bear the name of so famous a city.

Such distinctions, however impressive they may have been to the Reverend Mr. Sills, were not likely to have dazzled his son Kenneth. The boy's current heroes were not in Washington, but in Falmouth Engine House 4. He had discovered the gray granite building on his very first exploration of the neighborhood and soon made friends with Gus Griffiths, the foreman, who wore a shiny badge embossed with a gigantic "4." It was not the least of the merits of Mrs. Carter's kindergarten that it was located diagonally across the street from the engine house where the pupil could look in to pay his respects every day going to and from school. Gus initiated the youngster into the mysteries of the fire alarm signals and allowed him to clamber all over the Amoskeag steamer. Tom Williams, the engineer, and Henry Towle, the hoseman, also welcomed their daily visitor and explained the virtues of rubberlined cotton hose. And there were the drivers, Billy Lord and Ben Libby, who promised an occasional ride when the four-wheeled hose cart was taken out each week to exercise the horses. Being an unofficial mascot of Engine House 4 carried fully as much prestige among the children at Mrs. Carter's as being the son of a canon of the cathedral.

But if the boy's world was bounded by the fire station on one side and the cathedral on the other, there is no doubt where his heart belonged. Next to his parents and sister and his grandfather Ketchum in New Brunswick, Bishop Henry Adams Neely of St. Luke's was the best person in the whole world and St. Luke's Cathedral was a miracle of beauty. His portrait had the place of honor in Kenneth's scrapbook, which bulged with pasted-in pictures of a generous assortment of theologians, ranging from the Archbishop of Canterbury to Bishop Crowther of Nigeria.

There were any number of reasons why Doctor Neely should rank high in young Kenneth's hierarchy of dignitaries. After all, a real bishop living next door was worth a dozen in remote parts, especially since he was never too busy to listen to the boy's account of the lightning speed with which Falmouth's steamer responded to the fire bell. It was not hard to please his father by loving Bishop Neely, the dear friend of his parents and the godfather of his sister "Muffet" who had been christened Mary Neely Sills. The gate to the Bishop's garden at 143 State Street was always open whenever Rip Dana, Robert Boyd, or Dana Pendleton came to play soldiers. "Pitched battles" were fun, but "Waterloo" was even better because it lasted longer. First there must be a full-dress review of the lead soldiers carefully lined up on the floor of the Canon's study. When the other boys, Rip Dana and Dana Pendleton, brought their own "men," the reenforced "massed troops" made a brave show. Protocol next demanded that they study the colored battle map which Colonel Robinson sent to his "comrades-in-arms," all the way from Fredericton, New Brunswick. With these preliminaries over, the Bishop's hummocky garden was transformed into the field of Waterloo. The boys took turns being the Duke of Wellington, but they had the Colonel's assurance that Field Marshal von Blücher was also a good tactician. Kenneth invariably despatched a gravely written report on the action to his military friend in Canada, announcing the end of Napoleon's power. On more than one occasion he was rewarded by a "citation" embellished with the colors of the retired Colonel's old regiment addressed to "Colonel Sir Kenneth Sills of the Most Honorable Order of the Garter" commending him and his troops for "devotion and heroism." Mrs. Neely also deserves to be cited—she always left a full cookie jar in the pantry for the hungry officers.

In the summer months there were real soldiers to admire in St. Andrews, where the Sillses spent their vacations. Kenneth Sills was unable to remember a time when he had not spent at least part of July and August in the large, square rectory of his maternal grandfather, Dr. William Quintard Ketchum, on Parr Street, overlooking the Bay of Fundy. Kenneth was only eighteen months old on the occasion of his first trip to New Brunswick in July, 1881; he was admired as the Sillses' "true-born British subject," an honor to be denied his sister Mary, who had the misfortune to be born in Portland. The meaning of this distinction became clearer with each successive summer in the Loyalist town, as the boy was told more and more about his ancestors. On his mother's side all were Tories: the Heads, the Ketchums, the Peterses, and the Quintards—well-known Loyalist families who had moved to New Brunswick in the 1780s from Long Island and Connecticut, leaving the "rebels" to glory in their victory after Cornwallis' surrender at Yorktown. One of Kenneth Sills's earliest memories was of his grandfather pointing to the beautifully carved royal coat of arms over the west door of All Saints Church on King Street. The emblem, Dr. Ketchum said, had been brought to New Brunswick in 1786 by the first rector, Reverend Samuel Andrews, from his old parish in Wallingford, Connecticut. It had been a parting gift of his parishioners who had barely saved it from the rebels bent on destroying all vestiges of British origin.

Kenneth Sills was to owe much of his knowledge of the family's history to his grandfather. He knew by heart the story of Jonathan Ketchum, his great-great-grandfather, who celebrated his arrival in Woodstock, New Brunswick, in 1783, by kicking George Washington's picture down the stairs and out of the house. And later, when he discovered that some china he had ordered from Boston was made up of pieces adorned with views of Faneuil Hall and Bunker Hill, the irate old gentleman smashed every bit of it, even before he could import a set of less revolutionary ware from London. Dr. Ketchum told his grandson that it was not a deprivation to be ineligible for membership in the Sons of the American Revolution as long as he could join the Sons of Colonial Wars. But as summer followed summer, Kenneth Sills could see the lines dividing Canadians and Americans becoming more and more dim. On the golf links and tennis courts at the gay Algonquin Hotel he noticed that British and Americans rarely alluded to the past. Indeed, loyalties were strangely mixed. "I remember," Kenneth Sills recalled, "when I was a youth at St. Andrews, hearing Mr. David Forgan, the Chicago banker, say to Sir Thomas Shaughnessy, president of the Canadian Pacific Railway, 'It's a strange thing, Sir Thomas,—here are my children, all born in Fredericton, New Brunswick, always taking up for the Americans, and here all your children, every one born in Milwaukee, always on the Canadian side.' "

These annual summer visits meant fun and freedom from school, but they were also excursions into the background of his family. It was like playing a genealogical game by fitting pieces together to form a family tree, or like learning snatches of history by remembering the St. Andrews streets named after the provincial governors and the twelve children of George III. Young Kenneth soon had the royal children down pat. To reach his favorite swimming place at Katy's Cove, he had to cross Edward and Elizabeth, climb the hill by way of Adolphus or Harriet to Prince of Wales on the ridge. Living in the house of his mother's parents, it was natural for the boy to hear most about his maternal ancestors. His grandmother, Elizabeth Head Ketchum, was the granddaughter of Thomas Wetmore, attorney general for New Brunswick in 1809, and members of her family had always been prominent in the affairs of the province. His grandfather, Dr. William Quintard Ketchum, All Saints' beloved rector, was also something of a personage. He was a cousin of Bishop Quintard of Tennessee who, prior to his consecration, had fought through the Civil War in the Confederate Army, and he was related to the Canadian authors, Bliss Carman and Charles G. D. Roberts. If the rector's library was small, it was a good one, and he continued to study Shakespeare and read the Greek tragic poets in the original language long after his 80th birthday. On occasion Dr. Ketchum represented the Church of Canada at general conventions, and it was on one such errand, in New York City, that he was made a doctor of divinity by Columbia University.

It was also at St. Andrews that Kenneth Sills gradually came to learn about his father's family. His father's father, James Payn Sills, was a full-blooded English gentleman who loved horses, hunting, and outdoor life. His enthusiasm for horse-racing was so keen that he actually named his son after Voltigeur, a famous winner of the Doncaster Cup in 1850, a sporting appelation which the young man discreetly dropped before his ordination as a priest in 1874. The elder Sills came out to New Brunswick in the 1860s, living near Fredericton on a large tract of wild land he had bought in what proved to be an unfortunate speculation. His son, who was born in Colney, Hertfordshire, in 1850, studied for a time at Hurstpierpont College in Sussex but, emigrating to Canada with his father, was graduated from the University of New Brunswick in 1870. Shortly after his ordination four years later, he came to St. Andrews as master of the local grammar school and missionary to the Anglican Church at Campobello, positions which gave him opportunity to see enough of the rector's daughter Elizabeth to fall in love with her. For two years he had full charge of the parish on Campobello, a post he was happy to resign when Miss Ketchum warned that she would never marry a man content to spend his life on an island. Since this was apparently her only objection to accepting his proposal of marriage, the young priest's cup of felicity was filled to overflowing when he was offered a curacy in the Episcopal Church in Halifax in 1876.

The Reverend Mr. Sills inherited his father's ardent love of all sports and was an excellent athlete. In his youth in England he played cricket well enough to be groomed for the county team, was a good tennis player, and later developed into a better than average golfer. In the 1890s, it was Canon Sills's enthusiasm which helped organize the Portland Country Club and plan its golf course on Falmouth Foreside. Although his son strove manfully to achieve a decent competence in all these games, he never succeeded in beating his father at any of them. As late as 1910 Kenneth Sills was still trying, with the usual results. "You will pardon me for saying," Professor Henry Leland Chapman wrote, "that I am glad there is still one father who can beat his son in the noble game of golf." It was an old, old story. In 1953 Kenneth Sills recalled his chagrin as a boy in the nineties when he was sent on an errand to the printing shop of the *Beacon* on Water

Street in St. Andrews. "Are you Charley Sills's son?" the foreman asked as he looked the boy over critically from head to foot.
"Your father excels in all kinds of sports and games: cricket,
tennis, croquet, battledore, and golf. He is one of the finest of
men. And you're not a bit like him."

As a youngster, Kenneth Sills's life continued to swing pleasantly between school in Portland and vacation at St. Andrews.
It was like having the best of two cozy worlds. When he left
kindergarten, he was sure there could never be another teacher
like Miss Rosa E. True, the principal of Park Street Primary
School. Large and friendly, she nevertheless let it be known
there would be no nonsense in her room. She was also a stickler
for what she called "slate work" in penmanship, beginning with
the thirteen easy, short letters, and then moving to the more
extended "loop characters" as the year wore on. After a year or
so, Miss True, with the help of *Harper's Primary Writing Book
No. 2*, managed to produce something like legibility in Kenneth
Sills's handwriting. Penmanship was, however, destined to be
the one subject in which her pupil's work never progressed. "I
wish, my dear boy, you would be more careful," Dr. Ketchum
warned his grandson, then in the fourth grade. "It is a bad
thing to get in a blind way of writing. It is not too late to mend."
Similar admonitions from his father, uncles, and godfather were
duly acknowledged, but always in the same marvelously un-
readable scrawl. Later, when he was in college, his friends accepted the phenomenon as an inexplicable quirk, much like his
strange loyalty to the Democratic party. The amused protest
of his classmate Roland Bragg was to be repeated by all his
correspondents. "When I got the letter out of the envelope,"
Bragg wrote in 1902, "I knew at once from its utter illegibility
that it must be from my great and good friend, Kenneth Charles
Morton Sills."

Harrington's *Speller* held no terrors for the youngster in fifth
grade, but even here he received correction from both sides
of the Canadian border. "I am afraid you will never get to be a

priest while you spell *Reverend* as you did on the envelope of
your letter," Bishop Neely warned him in 1889. "And when
you have learned a little Latin, you will understand why *Reverend*
couldn't possibly be spelled *Reverand*." The delight Canon Sills
took in his son's account of how Rip Dana called at 5:45 to share
the morning of "the *glorius* 4th" in 1891 by snapping firecrackers
for two hours before breakfast did not prevent him from remarking that the holiday might have been even more glorious with an
extra "o." Such gentle lessons began to have their effect on the
orthography of Kenneth's youthful diary, but any improvement
in its legibility was not perceptible.

The name of Rip occurs in the entries almost daily. The son
of Dr. Israel Dana, whose house at 181 was less than two blocks
away on the same side of the street, was young Kenneth's best
and earliest friend. The inseparable companions had entered
Park Street School together and seemed to be forever running in
and out of each other's houses or waiting for each other and Dana
Pendleton, another State Street neighbor, at the fence on the
corner of Spring Street. It was Kenneth who proposed allowing
his hair to grow until it "caught up" with Rip's so that both
might have theirs cut on the same visit to Mr. Sherry's shop at
475 Congress Street. The youngsters always giggled delightedly
at the sign over the door: "Mr. John F. Sherry, Hair-dresser &
Wig-maker." As an ultimate acknowledgment of their friendship, Kenneth took Rip to meet "the boys" at Engine House 4,
but was careful to introduce them with grave formality as "Mr.
Augustus Griffiths, Foreman" and "Mr. Henry Towle, Hoseman." Try as they might, the companions could not imagine a
future without each other within hailing distance. From Park
Street and Miss True, they had proceeded to Butler Grammar
and Miss Moxcey where, in turn, they looked forward to entering Portland High as classmates. And when Rip's older brother
Francis was preparing to go to Bowdoin in the fall of 1890, old
Bowdoin seemed to be the only college. Yet whatever the college, they vowed it would be the same college, and the same

fraternity, too, although they needed no abracadabra to make them brothers.

If vacations as perfect as those at St. Andrews had any flaw, it was the separation of the friends, but this could be remedied by letters and visits. In the summer of 1895 when Rip was taken to New York City by his uncle, he reported the sights of the city to his friend. "I saw Steve Brodie's saloon on the Bowery and heard Souser's band," he wrote on July 13, "and I went to Coney Island where we saw the Streets of Cairo, shot the chutes, went into the Cabinet of Death, and saw the Houchi-Couchi, though I haven't told you half of my experiences. You bet I was weary when I got home." Canon Sills rejoiced in the friendship. "One makes many acquaintances but few real friends," he told his son. "I fancy that you and Ripley may grow up to be such loyal and true friends." Dr. Ketchum added his own invitation to bring Rip to St. Andrews, where there was always plenty of room in the rectory. The guest always cherished memories of his hospitality and saw in the saintly character of the grandfather the same trait which drew him to the grandson. "He always picked out what little good there was in any one," he wrote after Dr. Ketchum's death in 1901, "and overlooked, as much as possible, the bad."

When Rip finally did come to St. Andrews, Kenneth showed him all his old haunts. The fun was doubled when he could share it with his friend. Now they could play soldier and plan strategy in what had once been a real fort, Fort Tipperary on Barracks Hill, which had bristled with Redcoats during the Fenian Raid in 1866 when ships of war patrolled the St. Croix River. Since then the old fort had been dismantled to make room for the summer home of Lord Shaughnessy, but the ramparts were still there. So were the immense cannons commanding both sides of the peninsula. For all its virtues, Bishop Neely's garden lacked real guns, and the toy soldiers couldn't stand up against the moustachioed officers and men of the 67th Battalion of Canadian Militia encamped at St. Andrews in July, 1889. When Kenneth's martial

ice-cream parlor on Congress Street, a mecca for the enviable
high school boys and girls who could talk so carelessly about
dances and the prospect of beating Bangor in November. Rip
agreed that it was funny just how much there was to see at night
on the brightly lighted streets. A few years ago in his centennial
oration, Thomas Brackett Reed had boasted: "Any girl can go
at night from Munjoy to Bramhall dryshod, lighted on her way
by the blaze of electric lights." Now almost everybody took electricity for granted, and since 1889 the Bishop's house had been
lighted by Edison's lamps instead of the old-fashioned gas jets and
Welsbach mantles. Kenneth Sills's diary indicates that he was
staying up later, often past eleven o'clock, reading or helping his
father paste up the dummy of the diocesan paper, the *Northeast*.
On January 7, 1891, he accompanied his parents to John L. Stod-
dard's illustrated lecture on Vienna, and less than two weeks later
he heard Sir Henry Stanley's thrilling account of his rescue of
Emin Pasha. The boy liked both talks "very much," but he could
find room only for the picture of Sir Henry in his scrapbook. In
the midst of new interests, he still dropped in to see "the boys" at
the Engine House, and kept a conscientious record of all the
alarms to which his favorites responded. To his delight, Ben
Libby now included Rip on hose-cart rides to exercise the horses.
Other diversions were also attracting his attention. He was
thrilled by seeing Joseph Jefferson in "Rip Van Winkle" at the
Jefferson Theater, and heard the celebrated actor make a graceful
curtain speech acknowledging the honor of playing on a stage
named after him. Early in 1891 he was invited to listen to the
phonograph owned by Mr. Alexander Stephenson on State Street.
That invention heightened his interest in Jules Verne's *Around
the World in Eighty Days*.

All in all, 1891 was a memorable year. During the spring he
had been taking music lessons with Mrs. Carter, and by June was
ready to take his place in the choir of the cathedral. "My first
Sunday in the choir," he noted on June 28. "I am now a choir
boy. What an important event!" Even more important, if space

in his diary is a criterion, was his first visit to Bowdoin College earlier in the spring. Rip's older brother Francis offered to put the boys up in his room in 10 Appleton Hall and to give them a taste of college life. He was as good as his word. On April 30, Francis met the boys at the Brunswick station, escorted them about the college grounds, and took them to the Delta to see his Freshman class team play the varsity. "Went to see the baseball game between freshmen and *varceys*. Later on, slept in Frank's room," Kenneth noted in his journal, in a fashion not likely to gratify Miss Moxcey. It was a memorable weekend. Next morning they breakfasted at the D. K. E. table, attended chapel, and were mystified by a class in mathematics taught by a Professor Moody, before returning to Portland on the 11:30 train. Kenneth Sills had gained his most vivid first impression of a Bowdoin professor in action during the previous winter, in Butler Grammar School. Suddenly, in the midst of a recitation, the door opened and a strange looking man with long arms strode in and began to demonstrate what was then known as "Swedish gymnastics." The performance was so startling that the interlude was remembered more than sixty years later. "His vitality filled the room," Kenneth Sills recalled in 1953, "and we youngsters followed the physical gyrations with wide open eyes." The spare but lusty demonstrator was Dr. Frank Nathaniel Whittier, director of the college gymnasium, and later to become Bowdoin's revered physician.

The boy's broadening interests in the early 1890s included politics. His first memory of preelection excitement was of a torchlight procession of bands and partisans swirling by his house during the Blaine-Cleveland campaign in 1884. They chanted derisively, "Blaine, Blaine, James G. Blaine; The continental liar from the State of Maine!" His beloved Bishop Neely was a firm Democrat, but Mrs. Neely and their son Albert were ardent Republicans. The good Bishop had been highly indignant a few nights before when he returned home to see his house illuminated from cellar to attic in honor of the Republican candidate. On the evening of the parade for Cleveland, Dr. Neely took no chances, and went all over the house himself, lighting the gas jets in every room. Then, chuckling confidently, he sat down in his favorite chair to ponder a teasing chess problem. Later, when he asked a visitor whether he had observed the house lighted in support of the Democrats, he was told the place was as black as Erebus. To his dismay, the Bishop learned that his Republican spouse and son had tiptoed through every room and pulled down all the shades. Not a glimmer had been visible from the street.

Presumably, Canon Sills and his son sympathized with their discomfitted Bishop, but the incident is not likely to account for Kenneth Sills's early attachment to Maine's minority party. The youngster's political loyalties, like Topsy, "just grow'd." Although a few of his father's influential friends, the Bishop, Judge Putnam, and John F. A. Merrill were Democrats, the Canon himself did not vote until after 1901. He took out his citizenship papers only after the death of Queen Victoria, for he could not bring himself to take an oath which might compel him to take arms against his beloved queen. A more plausible explanation of the boy's devotion to the Democrats was the influence of his regular reading of Judge Putnam's favorite newspaper, the New York *Evening Post*. "It is not usual for an ordinary lad to be interested in editorials," Kenneth Sills conceded in 1953, "but I early formed the habit of regarding the editorial page as the most interesting of the whole paper."

His avid interest in politics and his respect for Edwin Godkin's editorials in the *Post* were probably not shared by many of the 206 boys and girls who entered Portland High School for the first time on September 10, 1893. The Freshman class began their studies in what Henry Seidel Canby has called "The Age of Confidence," when "what to know had been made to seem more important than how or why to know it." As Kenneth Sills and his classmates trooped into the newly renovated building on Cumberland Street, they doubtless shared their generation's belief that all facts were important and that the learning of them

would somehow transform their lives. Principal Albro E. Chase
subscribed to their romantic faith, but ruled his school with a
rod of iron. Kenneth Sills was later to remember him gratefully
for maintaining high standards, but in 1893 his students regarded
him as a cast-iron disciplinarian who strove to enforce the same
respect for order that he commanded as head of the high school
cadet battalion. The Principal invariably wore a tall silk hat
which he doffed only when talking to "females," and he strode
through the corridors in his Prince Albert coat with eyes straight
ahead as though he were wearing blinders to prevent him from
looking to the right or left. Trained at Harvard, Mr. Chase felt
himself competent to fill in during the absence of his teachers,
but it was apparent to his best students like William Lawrence
and Kenneth Sills that his knowledge of Greek was a trifle
shaky. Both boys remembered him resorting to the old dodge,
"let's skip it," when he was confronted with a difficult passage.

Fortunately, instruction in the ancient languages was only an
occasional responsibility of the Principal. Kenneth Sills was delighted with his teacher of Greek, Mr. Leroy L. Hight, a Portland attorney and author of operettas, who had a lively appreciation of the literary value of the classics. He often treated his
classes to samples of his own charming light verse, like his "Bal-
lade of the Old School Book," which Kenneth Sills later published in the *Racquet*. Of all his teachers he owed the greatest
debt to the formidable Miss Sara Gilpatrick, in Latin. Quite unlike the easygoing and casual Mr. Hight, Miss Gilpatrick, "stern
and sixtyish," put all her students through a stiff course in Brus-
sels sprouts. Impatient with the current "heresy" that her real
subject was "the child," not Latin, she waged a relentless rear-
guard action against all "progressive innovations" in education.
She also resented the interruptions for such "frills" as the recently introduced calisthenics period, which brought a visiting
teacher to her room for brief periods three times each week.
Miss Gilpatrick scowled and skulked in her enormous gray
sweater while the advance of Caesar's legions was halted and the

class obeyed commands thoroughly un-Roman: "Now will everybody please stand? Extend both arms out as far as you can. Now try to stretch an inch further. Now loosen all fingers and let them droop. Now shake the fingers while relaxing the arms. Now clench the fists hard. Now take three deep breaths and exhale slowly. Now arms back to sides. Twist arms, palms front. Reverse twist." Miss Gilpatrick was not herself until such "nonsense" was over. She not only knew Latin, but made her pupils feel it was good to know Latin too. An old battle-axe of a teacher, she required rather than talked about hard work, believing that nothing could toughen the mind like declensions and conjugations. And since every construction had its exact meaning, she settled for nothing less. Kenneth Sills never forgot Sara Gilpatrick or ceased to be grateful to her for starting him on the road to scholarship. Almost sixty years after he entered her class in second-year Latin, he recalled her as "the best teacher I ever had in school, college, or university."

In 1893 he enrolled in the classical or college preparatory course which provided four years of Latin, English, and mathematics, and three years of Greek, a domain which Miss Gilpatrick ruled as her own. She approved the spartan program which Albro Chase prescribed for those less hardy souls who wanted a few pleasant oases in the Sahara of "disciplinary" subjects. "It has been found," Chase told a group of rebels in Kenneth's senior year, 1896, "that after an hour of studying Latin, the best rest is not found in mental inactivity. You actually get more rest from the complete change found in turning to the study of algebra. And your other studies rest your minds after Latin and algebra. . . . If extra time is needed, it can easily be found by dropping the various social activities not absolutely obligatory." The incident became known as "Albro's Mutiny," but the insurrection was quelled, and the Gilpatrick-Chase axis remained firm.

Although Kenneth Sills led his class in each of his four high school years, he seems to have found time for activities which the redoubtable Albro might not have deemed "absolutely obligatory." His diary shows that he had discovered the attractions of the trolley park in Riverton near the Presumpscot River bridge. There, on January 1, he helped his classmates celebrate the advent of their graduation year by dining and dancing until after midnight. Even the embarrassment of being called on for "a short speech" did not mar his fun. As a member of the cadet battalion, he drilled and danced at the annual military ball on March 5, an affair described by the *Racquet* as "Venus uniting with Mars in the consummation of a royal spectacle." By his senior year he had yielded to the mysterious charm of "mixed parties." Journal entries tell of merry skating parties at Red Water, snowshoe expeditions to Stroudwater, and cycling trips to Riverton, whose manager provided a shed "where those who came on wheels can leave their silent steeds." Kenneth's grandfather Ketchum presented him with a new bicycle on April 14, a Victor model 30, and it presumably found safe shelter there during the merry-making.

For the first time, the names of young ladies begin to appear in the intermittent listing of his social engagements. Significantly enough, they usually appear in groups, like those of "Mary's crowd," or the "Deering Street bunch," or the members of his favorite, "The Girls' Cooking Club." The club specialty was bubbling hot Welsh rarebit served from a chafing dish, but a party on February 27, 1897, may have had an even more tasty menu, for the collation was singled out as "worthy to be marked with a silver star." The names of his hostesses are sprinkled on the pages of his journal: Edith Woodbury, Bessie Whipple, Eleanor Wright, Louise Allen, Julia Bolster, Jane Morse, and Florence Hinckley. The high school senior always paid his social debts conscientiously by making party calls on every member of the club. On these shy visits he was usually accompanied by his friend John Small, who was never at a loss for words when conversation threatened to lag. On the comparatively rare occasions when he went alone, he showed a fine impartiality by making several calls of equal length on the same afternoon.

In the spring of his senior year, Kenneth Sills sorely missed the companionship of Rip, who had withdrawn from high school to be tutored privately for his Bowdoin entrance examinations. Often, in the whirl of school affairs, he mourned for his old playmate Dana Pendleton, whose death from typhoid fever the year before was the first break in the circle of boyhood friends. "I want you to have lots of friends," Mrs. Pendleton wrote, "but I can't feel that I want you to love any of them more than Dana. He was always so fond of you. I cannot seem to imagine him anywhere but at the house on the corner where you boys used to wait for each other." Young Pendleton, a winner of the Brown medal for scholarship at Portland High School, had just passed his college entrance examinations when death struck. Kenneth Sills, who sensed how much the bereaved mother had looked forward to her son joining his old friends at Bowdoin, was never too busy in school or later in college to write her a thoughtful note on each anniversary of his friend's death.

After his graduation, if he ever looked into the scrapbook of clippings and trophies assembled during his high school days, they would not have evoked memories of a long, extracurricular binge. "The primary motive of school life is often lost sight of," he wrote in the *Racquet* for November, 1896. "We come to learn. . . ." And, like a good editor, he followed his own injunction to put first things first. For all his pleasure in the company of his classmates, he knew no substitute for the pleasure of being alone with his books. Yet despite Miss Gilpatrick's daily assignment of 300 lines and the other demands of his preparatory course, Kenneth Sills found time to identify himself responsibly with a number of outside activities. He rose to the rank of sergeant major in the cadet battalion, helped organize a debating club, joined with Rip in promoting interest in interscholastic tennis competition, and edited the high school magazine. Of all these activities, he enjoyed most keenly his editorship of the *Racquet*. It enabled him to preserve his detachment while commenting upon, and occasionally attempting to direct, the pageant of student life. He also used his editorial column to remind his fellow students that "A school is judged . . . not by the football games its team wins, not by the school paper its scholars edit, not by the drills of its military battalion, but by the characters of the pupils in the school, and their ability to do the work set forth for them."

He was excited by the "free silver" issue in the presidential campaign in the fall of 1896, and followed Godkin's lead by favoring the "Gold Democrats" led by Palmer and Buckner, but he maintained a nonpartisan tone in his *Racquet* editorials. After failing to uncover a single Democrat among his primary and grammar school classmates, he was prepared to find the high school overwhelmingly Republican. Instead he encountered an almost total apathy, and proposed forming a debating society to discuss political issues. He was in the throng at Union Station on September 24 who heard the Democratic candidate, William Jennings Bryan. He followed the editorial comments upon the campaign. After the landslide for McKinley, he marched like a good soldier when his cadet battalion was ordered to take part in the Republican victory parade. What his thoughts were on this occasion, he discreetly kept to himself. In the *Racquet*, a week following the election, he urged his readers to prepare themselves for the time when they would help to elect a president. "If all study carefully the results," he wrote on November 11, "in the future they will be better qualified to settle the great questions that will be sure to agitate the Republic." He wryly advised "the ardent silverites" that "Bryan's speeches are not in order for declamations now."

Meanwhile, the students' lack of interest in national affairs was equaled by their passionate concern for athletics, an anomaly over which Kenneth Sills was to puzzle in the autumn of 1896 for the first, but not the last time. "We regarded Bangor as our mortal enemy," he wrote, and hopes ran high in September with the appointment of Charles McCarthy, a former Brown University star, as coach of the Portland team. The real disaster of that dismal season was not early defeats by Hebron and Thornton or even the loss of both the Bangor games. "It is unpleasant to record the fact," the *Portland Transcript* noted on November 11, "that not less than four of the eleven representing Portland are not entitled to represent the school in any capacity." Although the *Transcript* demanded an immediate "reconstruction of the team," a week later it charged that objectionable men were still playing and that "a graduate of several years standing was added to the Portland eleven." When the disillusioned editor of the *Racquet* was convinced of the truth of the charges, he refused to find comfort in the general opinion that Bangor was equally guilty. Nor would he allow the coach, manager, and captain to be made the only scapegoats. "It is generally recognized," he wrote on December 16, "that grievous mistakes have been made by those in charge of the team." Yet he felt himself to be tainted by the scandal. Recalling his father's remark that "It is never a good plan to beat anything with more feeling than a carpet," he saw clearly that every student had been at least tacitly willing to sacrifice sportsmanship for the hope of victory. "The whole school should feel its responsibility in the matter," he declared flatly in a *Racquet* editorial. "If ever again such methods as have been in vogue the last season are thought of, let every honest scholar 'arise in his might' and not allow the question to be considered for a moment." There was a barb in his renewed pleas for more support of debating and school publications: "If more of the students realized that it is just as important that the literary *talent* of a school be developed as that its *athletic* interests should not be allowed to flag, there would be no difficulty in forming a debating society."

With the coming of spring, the editor of the *Racquet* reminded his classmates of the approach of examinations for college. "Only three months more!" he warned on March 24. "Yet the three months may settle the fate of many a son of the High School. To work then!" In subsequent issues he cited as encouraging examples the scholarly records of former Portland students in various colleges, especially the many honors won by Henry Pierce and William Lawrence at Bowdoin. But he was of two minds about the value of college entrance examinations. Why, he asked, should not a certificate of satisfactory work done in school be sufficient? Is it not true, he declared in the *Racquet*, that entrance examinations when set by a college "prove in many cases, not the ability, but the luck of the candidate?" Such apprehensiveness, however, was dictated by editorial rhetoric rather than any actual fear on the part of the first scholar of his class, whose four-year average was 98.1. In any event, he showed himself quite ready to accept philosophically a stunning bit of good luck in his own entrance examination in Greek. One evening, while browsing in his father's library, he chanced upon an edition of all seven books of Xenophon's *Anabasis,* and read a passage in the fifth book which was not in Kelsey's text used in Mr. Hight's class. A few weeks later, when he found the identical passage as the "sight" test on his Greek paper at Bowdoin, he was almost apologetic about the speed and accuracy of his translation.

Kenneth Sills always assumed that he would go to college and had taken the Bowdoin entrance examinations in June as a matter of course. Portland, after all, was a "Bowdoin town," and many of his older acquaintances like Rip's brother Francis, William Lawrence, Henry Pierce, and Percival Baxter were full of Bowdoin lore and songs when they came home for their vacations. Most persuasive of all was his knowledge that Rip, whose heart had always been set on Bowdoin, had passed his entrance examinations. The two friends recalled with a pang how often Dana Pendleton had anticipated their college days together. Kenneth Sills's decision to go to Bowdoin was not so much a conscious choice as a developing conviction born out of countless unremembered boyhood commitments, solicitudes, and loyalties, a conviction no less strong because it had not been formally voiced.

His sister Mary, sensing intuitively the strength of these involvements, was sure all along that her brother would end up at Bowdoin, even though she had heard her parents speak of the advantages of several Episcopalian institutions. Long before Canon and Mrs. Sills made up their minds, she gave him her private blessing in advance: "Don't drink, dear, and do look out for the electric cars, for little sister's sake."

College men in the 1890s were a small minority, popularly believed to inhabit a utopia of charmed irresponsibility. Less than one-third of the eighty-nine members of Kenneth Sills's high school class were enrolled in the "classical" course, and of this number only fourteen were boys. In the presidential campaign of 1896, when Bryan told a boisterous rally in New Haven that virtually all Yale undergraduates were "sons of the idle rich," he was voicing a prevailing prejudice. Doubtless a majority of Kenneth Sills's privileged student contemporaries went to college as the socially respectable "thing to do" or as an escape from the rigid conformities of a utilitarian world. The high school senior was to feel the force of this view of college life as an escape in a letter from his godfather, G. C. Coster, of St. John, New Brunswick. Mr. Coster, a beef-and-iron British businessman, had accompanied a present of Whyte-Melville's *Gladiators* with a blunt question to his godson: "Are you going to college or start the real work of life?"

To this uncomfortable inquiry, Kenneth Sills made the best reply in his power. He would not concede that all "the real work of life" was done outside college halls, as Mr. Coster seemed to think. Even in high school the work and pressures had been "real" enough. One always had to decide for himself whether or not he would cut corners and follow the beckoning of the crowd of "good fellows." While others were winning immediate popularity for "doing something for the school," it took courage to see beyond the monotony of daily tasks and to strive patiently for remote ends. The high school corridors buzzed with cliques, tolerated petty snobberies, and condescended to those from the unfashionable sections of town. Surely one did not escape the push and pull of "real" life by going to high school. The collapse of idealism in organized athletics had at least taught him that much. Nor could he believe, remembering Dana Pendleton, that students were immune to sorrows, blighted hopes, and death.

The high school senior had gratified his family by winning valedictory honors as the ranking student of his class, but he was only made uncomfortable when the *Racquet* described him as "a scholar and a ripe one." Long hours in his father's library had shown him how hard it was to reach a truly disinterested opinion on any subject. Whatever else he may have wished for in college, it was an opportunity to strive for excellence among his peers. And for that he knew he would need all the stamina he could muster. Like so many of his generation, he saw college life through the sentimental mists of song and story. But he had sensed that the unique offer of the college was something more than a means of attaining social status. He yearned above all to live the life of the mind and spirit in an hospitable environment. Four years later he found the things he was trying to tell Mr. Coster set forth incomparably by Bowdoin's President Hyde in his "Offer of the College." But in 1897 Kenneth Sills could only promise, whatever Bowdoin offered, he would do his best to be loyal to his aspirations.

# 2

## UNDERGRADUATE AT BOWDOIN
### 1897-1901

"Who is that thoughtful-looking boy with a freshman cap?" asked Professor Wilmot Mitchell as he and a colleague, William Houghton, walked from Memorial Hall on the first day of the fall term of 1897. "Why, that's Kenneth Sills, the son of Dean Sills of Portland," his friend replied. "He was the valedictorian of his high-school class." The object of this attention had arrived in Brunswick only the afternoon before. He and Rip Dana had come down on the two o'clock train on September 13, and by nightfall both had been pledged to Delta Kappa Epsilon. They had shared too many good times since they entered Butler Grammar School together to think of going separate ways now that they were in college.

Although many of their Portland friends who had preceded them to Bowdoin in the last few years—Billy Lawrence, Howard Ives, and Tom Pierce—were members of Psi Upsilon, Rip's brother Francis was a Deke, and the Dekes had shown the sub-freshman a wonderful time on June 25 when he visited Brunswick to take his entrance examinations. After three hours of mulling over a Greek test on the hard benches of the Classical Room, he found a band of brothers waiting for him at the door. And before he could catch his breath, he was on an open electric car jouncing toward the New Meadows Inn with Percival Baxter '98 and some new friends. That night, when he returned to Portland on the late train, he noted in his diary: "Shore dinner by D. K. E. Had a great time." During the following summer at St. Andrews, whenever he thought of the college, Bowdoin and the Dekes seemed almost synonymous.

Now, three months later, after the opening chapel exercises, he felt as though he had always been destined to go to Bowdoin. Yet this was not quite true. In St. Andrews, his maternal grandparents had been enthusiastic about Columbia, which in 1869 had conferred a cherished D.D. upon his grandfather, the Reverend William Quintard Ketchum. Hobart College also had strong Episcopalian affiliations to recommend it. Only last January, the Reverend Charles Hayes of Geneva, who preached at St. Luke's Cathedral, had remained in Portland for a day to speak to the high school senior about Hobart's advantages. Although a graduate of Hobart, Bishop Henry Neely preferred Trinity, and, for a time, persuaded Dean Sills to consider it as a likely place for his son. In April, an emissary from Brown University, a persuasive Mr. Smart, called at the deanery to urge no end of plausible reasons why a devoted churchman could feel at home in a Baptist institution. Dean Sills, however, was an admirer of President William DeWitt Hyde from whose hands he had received an honorary D.D. in 1887, and he had been studying the Bowdoin catalogue. "You are all right about Bowdoin," he assured his son, "for I am more and more convinced that the course there is as good as that in any of the smaller colleges."

The tuition fee of $75 a year and the other modest charges were also points in Bowdoin's favor. Room rent in 10 Appleton Hall where Kenneth Sills was to live was only $42, and board cost less than $4 a week. The average cost of a Bowdoin education in 1897–98 was $330, and many boys, as President Hyde had said, lived in decent comfort on as little as $250. The small legacy which Dean Sills had received from an aunt in England made it possible for him to see his son through four years without too much strain. All things considered, Bowdoin seemed an ideal choice. General John Marshall Brown and Judge William LeBaron Putnam, Bowdoin trustees and members of the cathedral vestry, had been urging all along that there was no place like it, and no president—not even the great Eliot of Harvard—could hold a candle to Prex Hyde. The household at 135 State Street readily agreed. With Brunswick only twenty-eight miles from Portland, Mrs. Sills could look forward to seeing Kenneth on weekends. It was almost like going away to college and being at home at the same time. Mary rejoiced at the prospect of exciting visits to the campus and, perhaps, "spreads" in her brother's room. Even Aunt Catherine, who would have preferred an Episcopalian college, could not see how Bowdoin's Congregationalism would defeat her ambition to have her nephew become an Anglican priest. When the virtues of other colleges were talked over by the family, Mrs. Sills's emphatic remark often ended the discussion. "But at Bowdoin," she said, "there is President Hyde."

When Kenneth Sills entered Bowdoin in the autumn of 1897, President Hyde had been in office twelve years, although he was then only thirty-nine, and physically and intellectually vigorous. The greatness of the president and the remarkable stability of the college might not have been immediately apparent to an eighteen-year-old Freshman, but they were to have a strong influence upon his undergraduate and later life. Of the fifty-nine members of the class of 1901 who signed the registration book on September 14, virtually all were to be graduated four years later. Kenneth Sills's fraternity mates did even better. All eleven of the D. K. E. Freshman delegation received degrees with their class. The faculty, too, exhibited the same stability. Between 1897 and 1901, the only break in the professorial ranks occurred at the end of Kenneth Sills's Junior year with the resignation of Henry Crosby Emery who, at the age of twenty-eight, was called to the chair of political economy at Yale. The Governing Boards appeared to be equally resistant to the whirligigs of time. There was not a single change in the Board of Trustees, which numbered among its thirteen members two distinguished generals of the Civil War, a former governor and an active chief justice of Maine, a U.S. senator, and the chief justice of the United States. In the larger body of Overseers, there were only three changes among the forty-five members, and none of these was an officer of the Board. Such continuity of tenure gave the sons of the college a common experience and a common memory. Kenneth Sills and his classmates enrolled together, shared their intellectual-coming-of-age, and were graduated together. Their sense of community was heightened by the similarity of their geographical background. Nearly all were graduates of public high schools in Maine. Of the 243 students registered at Bowdoin in the fall of 1897, only twenty-one were from outside the state. Of these, only six came from homes outside New England. So invincible was President Hyde's faith in the stamina of Maine boys, especially those from small towns and villages, and so firm was his belief in the strength of a small, tightly knit college, that he had once almost persuaded the Boards to restrict attendance at Bowdoin to boys from Maine. More than forty years later, in the dark days of the Second World War, when a Bowdoin undergraduate wrote from a chaotic battlefield in Europe, imploring the president to keep the college just as he had known it—"Don't change a single thing!" he begged—Kenneth Sills knew exactly what the lad meant.

The curriculum also contributed effectively to the unity of the college. In the fall of 1897 it was a bastion built solidly upon Greek, Latin, mathematics, and modern languages. This program of studies was yielding with glacial slowness to the first cautious reforms of President Hyde, who believed a college should offer something more than a continuation of secondary school subjects. To this end he had created in 1894 a chair of economics and sociology, and, in the following year, he urged the Boards to adopt a substitute for Greek for admission. By Kenneth Sills's Senior year, Spanish had been reintroduced to take its place beside French and German, and the number of electives was increased in the upper-class years. However, the catalogue for 1897 –98 put the matter flatly: "The course of study is adapted solely and strictly to students desiring a liberal education." And a liberal education meant studies leading to the degree of Bachelor of Arts. Even though students without Greek in fitting school or in college might enroll for the degree of Bachelor of Science, only one of Kenneth Sills's classmates, his fraternity brother Donald Snow, elected to take this option. Indeed, in the years between 1897 and 1901, only one other college contemporary, Royall Cleaves '99, became a candidate for the B.S. degree.

Although the college year was divided into fall, winter, and spring terms, President Hyde had devised a program to avoid what he deplored as "the scrappy and haphazard study of isolated subjects by single terms." In his Freshman year, Kenneth Sills studied Greek, Latin, French, and mathematics for four hours each week consecutively through the entire year. To these subjects were added one hour each week of hygiene in the autumn, followed by elocution for an hour each week during the winter and spring. There was no course in English composition. The only required study of English was to come later in the fall term of his Sophomore year, as a four-hour course in rhetoric. "Thank heaven we did not have to write daily themes, nor indeed 'themes' of any sort," he recalled. "We learned our English from Latin and Greek, from reports in history and other social subjects." Later experience as an instructor of English composition at Harvard and Columbia only confirmed his distaste for themes as a royal road to mastering a serviceable English style. Throughout his long career as a Bowdoin teacher and administrator, he continued to lament as one of the deplorable trends in American collegiate education that "which ran away from the classics and put great confidence in themes."

His teachers in Freshman year were all full professors of ripe experience: William Houghton in Latin, Frank Woodruff in Greek, William Moody in mathematics, Frank Whittier in hygiene, Henry Johnson in French, and Wilmot Mitchell in elocution. He was later to note at Harvard, where Freshmen were often taught by inexperienced and languid graduate students, how much richer his own instruction had been in his first year at Bowdoin. Of these early teachers he recalled with especial vividness the redoubtable Professor Buck Moody for his course in mathematics. It was in Buck's classroom on the last day of the spring term in 1898 that Kenneth Sills learned a lesson in intellectual honesty he was to remember for the remainder of his life. All through the fall and winter he had done his daily assignments in Wentworth's *Algebra* and in solid geometry with his accustomed conscientiousness. For his efforts he was rewarded with an "A" at the end of each term. And now, at the very last meeting of the course in trigonometry, in June, after having been called upon to recite for three days in succession, he came to class confident he would be passed by. But Buck was as inscrutable as he was just. To the dismay of the totally unprepared Freshman, he was called upon, and, when he tried to bluff, was promptly rebuked with a well-known formula of dismissal: "That will do, Mr. Sills, sit down!" Professor Moody invariably treated Tyrians and Trojans alike. The two lowest grades on Kenneth Sills's Bowdoin transcript are shaky "A's" in Mathematics 3 and in Elocution 2.

The latter course was taught to the entire Freshman class by Professor Wilmot Mitchell, youngest of the full professors, who had just been advanced from an instructorship in June. The shy Freshman, who as one of his contemporaries, Billy Lawrence, noted, "was always a little awkward with his hands and feet and never learned how to type," found standing on the stage in Memorial Hall to declaim in orotund tones and with appropriate gestures declamation classics like Kellogg's "Spartacus to the Gladiators" a terrifying ordeal. More than sixty years later, his instructor remembered Kenneth Sills's manly fervor and decorum, although frequently his manner was self-deprecatory, as if he wished to apologize for his very presence. Professor Mitchell's memories also include impressions of the steady improvement of his student when he recited Senator Hoar's oration "Against Imperialism" in a Junior competition, and in his Senior year when he won the Class of 1868 Prize with an oration on "The Sea in English Poetry."

Kenneth Sills owed the heaviest debt to his teacher of French, the scholarly poet Professor Henry Johnson who, along with President Hyde, was destined to have the most abiding influence of all his instructors in college or university. Almost equally at home in Latin, French, and Italian, Johnson was the second member of the Bowdoin faculty to earn the doctorate in philosophy, proceeding to his degree in 1884 at the University of Berlin. "In season and out of season," Kenneth Sills recalled gratefully, "he taught the virtue of fidelity." The Freshman was to remember his teacher's invariable query when confronted with a glib translation in class: "Yes, but is that exactly what the French says?" Professor Johnson's textual scholarship in his editions of *A Midsummer Night's Dream* and *Macbeth* won the acclaim of his peers here and abroad. Literature for him was a passion as well as a discipline. He exemplified President Hyde's ideal in the teaching of letters, not alone for philological information or aesthetic delight, but as a criticism and interpretation of life.

It was as a poet that Frenchy Johnson made his deepest impression. Kenneth Sills discovered in his master's translations of portions of the *De Rerum Natura,* the sonnets of Heredia, and *La Divina Commedia* poignantly true expressions of the moving and mysterious ideas that haunted him in his own readings of the classics. No other faculty home in Brunswick, not even Prex Hyde's study, came to mean so much to Kenneth Sills as "the booky house" on Maine Street near the southwest corner of the campus. There Professor Johnson was always ready to read with gentle understanding the boy's own verse translations from Latin and Italian. Johnson recognized a kindred spirit behind the youth's shy advances, and the Freshman friendship deepened with each passing year. It was to Henry Johnson that Kenneth Sills later turned for counsel in his graduate school years, and it was to him he dedicated his book of early verse, *The First American*, in 1911. Out of their long and intimate friendship grew the younger scholar's interest in comparative literature and his devotion to Dante. The association was ended only by Professor Johnson's death. As he lay dying in early February, 1918, he made Kenneth Sills his literary executor. "I love the boy," he told his daughter Helen. "If he were my own son, I could not love him more."

In greater measure than for most of his Bowdoin comrades, the life of the college for Kenneth Sills was the life of the mind and the spirit. No entries appear more often in the skimpy and fragmentary diary he kept in his Freshman year than "Went to room and plugged," or "Studied and thought, I suppose," or "Read in library and room." His resources were interior, yet there was an external college life to be enjoyed as well, and he savored it keenly. He had not been on the campus a week before he was known to his fraternity and later his college mates as Casey. The affectionate nickname he was to bear for the rest of his life was bestowed by Thomas Marble '98, a D. K. E. Senior who, noting the inviting first two initials of the signature of the neophyte from Portland, exclaimed, "Let's call him 'Casey.' "

It was Tom Marble, too, who invited the Freshman to contribute to the *Quill* and the *Orient*, although the former editor of the *Racquet* needed little coaxing. His sketch of a hero under the Duke of Wellington, based upon a sentimental tale he had heard in St. Andrews, was printed in the October issue of the *Quill*, his first appearance in print in a Bowdoin publication. On December 8 he was elated by the printing of another of his sketches—this time in the college newspaper. His second *Orient* article, a biographical essay on Nathaniel Hawthorne, may have betrayed his own feelings about Professor Mitchell's course in elocution, which he had just begun in the winter term. At any rate, he sympathized with Hawthorne's reluctance to "declaim" in public. "Although fairly studious," he wrote, "nothing on earth could induce him to declaim." The issue of the *Orient* for March 16 must have had especial interest for him. It not only included his short story, "Quits," with an O. Henry surprise ending, but an announcement of his election to the staff. Casey's contributions to the campus publications, as well as his occasional poems read at the literary portions of his fraternity meetings, won for him a college reputation as a promising writer. "Sills scribbles," noted the 1898 *Bugle*, "as if he were head clerk to the Fates."

Scribbling and studying were not the only occupations of his Freshman year. Thanks to his sound training at Portland High School under Mr. Abbott and Miss Gilpatrick, the Bowdoin courses held no terrors for him. He had plenty of time to prolong the dinner hour for good talk at the eating club which Mrs. Stetson maintained for the Dekes on Page Street. And it was an unusual week in which he did not enjoy at least one "spread" in the "Ends" or a "feed" at Jake's on the Bath Road. He found it agreeable, too, to spend an evening every month or so, playing whist or "500" at Miss Fanny McKeen's hospitable house. But there were times, especially in the long, rainy autumn of 1897, when he was homesick for Portland. Brunswick social life seemed a trifle thin and provincial when he compared it with the gay times he knew were waiting for him on State Street. The "sociables, so-called" which he dutifully attended at St. Paul's rectory were not in the same class with the meetings of "The Girls' Cooking Club" at Eleanor Wright's house or the dancing parties which Edith Woodbury seemed able to arrange so easily at a moment's notice. At these affairs he could always count on seeing his old friends in "Mary's crowd," like Louise Harris, Bessie Whipple, and Florence Hinckley. And there was no Brunswick equivalent of the Western Promenade or Deering Oaks where he and John Small loved to "go perambulating" on Saturday nights. The "ten-cent shows" which sometimes drew him to the Brunswick Town Hall were amusing enough, but a paltry substitute for the plays at the Jefferson Theater where he could see *The Prisoner of Zenda* or *The Circus Girl* or *Way Down East*. The pull of Portland was hard to resist, and so back he went for no fewer than fourteen weekends during his first year. "Back on the late train" became a constant refrain in his diary. Always, of course, with his parents' blessing—a difference Kenneth Sills may have remembered when as dean he later took a dim view of weekend exoduses.

Brunswick was more habitable in the spring. March 15 brought an end to the detested dumbbell drills and Indian club swinging in the badly ventilated gymnasium. "Hurrah!" he exulted in his diary, "No more gym." His father helped him celebrate by sending down his "new bike" for excursions to Merrymeeting Bay, Mere Point, and Bath. He resumed his tennis by advancing three rounds in the college tournament before losing to Walter Came '99 in the quarter finals, 4–6, 3–6. Paired with Rip, he reached the semifinals of the doubles. In the intercollegiates in Waterville, on June 6, after he and Rip were put out in the first day's play, they found solace by "inspecting Colby" and "going to a show." The two friends were more successful at the Freshman Banquet two weeks later, when they shared honors, with Rip as toastmaster and Casey as the closing speaker. They had, as the latter noted in his diary, "a great time." The class chartered a special "1901 Car" for the railroad trip to Portland, and they marched from Union Station to the Falmouth Hotel with the solemnity of a royal procession. After three hours of dining, singing, and cheering, it is not likely that Kenneth Sills's classmates gave him their undivided attention as he announced as his theme "the homely adage" that "Everyone is a good fellow when you get to know him." But they were listening to the trumpet of a prophecy. "Therein lies a deal of philosophy," he told his classmates. "And, if you care to think long enough, more or less religion." It was the closest he came to a philosophy. His religion was ever to be of faith and charity compact. The longest memory in the Falmouth banquet room that night has never been able to recall an instance in which Kenneth Sills failed to believe that all men would live up to the high opinion he held of them.

His Sophomore and upper-class years seemed to pass with incredible swiftness. The second-year program was less of a strait jacket, although he continued to study Greek and Latin for each of the three terms. German in place of mathematics and rhetoric as a substitute for elocution were welcome changes. He invariably chose literary topics for the required themes in Rhetoric 1. Professor Mitchell remembers him modestly blushing at praise for his essay on "Pippa Passes," and then graciously thanking his teacher for having introduced him to the poem. After a steady diet of the annals of Greece and Rome, he found Professor William MacDonald's course in English history strangely exciting. "Willie Mac fine today," he wrote in his diary, and then he was off to the library for material about England's treatment of the Boers. His new interest in history led him to join the history club and prompted his taking MacDonald's survey of American history in his Junior year. History in the making was even more exciting, and he pasted into a huge folio everything he could clip from newspapers and magazines about the Spanish-American war. Aunt Catherine thought he sounded quite authoritative when he assured her there was no danger of a naval attack on Portland. His zeal for history left him little time for the *Quill;* only one of his items appeared in the 1899 volume. His intellectual curiosity did not, however, extend to the other social sciences or to any natural science. There is no evidence that he ever set foot in the Searles Science Building as an undergraduate, although he did take a hurried look into Adams Hall, the bleak home of the Maine Medical School, source of so many grisly campus myths. Later he was to lament his lack of training in the disciplines of the laboratory. "I have always regretted," he wrote in 1953, "that I had no science of any sort in college." In 1950 when the Governing Boards wished to honor him by giving his name to a new chemistry laboratory, the present Cleaveland Hall, he was moved, but blushed at the inappropriateness of the gesture.

Literary studies continued to absorb him the most fully. After the flinty, required courses in elocution, rhetoric, and Jevons' *Logic,* he rejoiced in the green fields of English letters as taught by the courtly Henry Leland Chapman. Not content to be a

rhetorician, although no man of his generation was a more polished occasional speaker, and in no sense of the word a technical
scholar, "Prof. Harry" possessed a generous knowledge of all
good literature. His lectures were felicitous essays, less concerned
with dates and sources than with the brain stuff and spirit of the
masterpieces he loved to read to his classes. At his touch, authors
became men and literary periods took on color and life. When
Kenneth Sills first encountered Chapman's teaching in the fall
term of his Junior year, he had earned the privilege. He had come
to Milton with a mind saturated in the classics, and his teacher
made him see that the poet's religion was more music than dogma,
and that to understand him was to come close to the very essence
of poetry itself. Later, as a graduate student at Harvard and
Columbia, and then as a teacher and administrator at Bowdoin,
Kenneth Sills witnessed the gradual disappearance of professors
of Chapman's qualities. With the rise of specialists produced by
the demands for a scientific study of literature, the "old-fashioned" professor of English became extinct. Yet in considering
candidates for Bowdoin appointments, he always sought those
who knew and loved literature itself rather than facts about it.
Professors Johnson and Chapman had schooled him to prefer
teachers who embodied in themselves the culture they taught and
to suspect those who merely preached about it. He chiefly prized
those who, as Robert Frost once remarked, "had a weakness for
poetry." If this was an old-fashioned virtue, he would strive to
keep Bowdoin an old-fashioned college. Whenever he discovered
a young instructor able to communicate a sense of the excitement
of literature and to encourage students to read widely on their
own, he tried to grapple him to the college with hoops of steel,
even though the teacher lacked the Ph.D.

Frenchy Johnson and Prof. Harry were giants whose presence
would have conferred distinction upon any college, but their
influence was limited to those wise enough to seek them out.
President Hyde's sovereignty, however, extended into every
nook and cranny of college life. It was to Prex that Kenneth Sills

applied for admission to Bowdoin in the spring of 1897, and it was from him that he received a long-hand letter of acceptance. The president also took personal charge of all scholarships and loans, performed the duties of a guidance and placement officer, and, until 1910, handled the multifarious details which later became the responsibility of the dean. Those students who occasionally complained of President Hyde's aloofness were almost always startled to learn that he knew more about them than they had thought. It was, however, not as an administrator, but as a teacher, that Hyde first impressed Kenneth Sills.

In company with virtually all his classmates, he elected Prex's course in philosophy in his Senior year. Bearing the catalogue label of psychology in the fall term, ethics in the winter, and the history of philosophy in the spring, the offerings actually formed a consecutive course in which Hyde took all of life for his province. Here the president was in his true element. At 8:30 A.M., immediately after morning chapel, every Tuesday, Wednesday, Thursday, and Friday, Kenneth Sills heard the president expound the principles of great thinkers, from Aristotle and Plato to his own Harvard teachers, Royce and James. He soon forgot the authors of the texts he had used—Stout's *Manual of Psychology*, Mackenzie's *Ethics*, and Weber's *History of Philosophy*—but he was always to remember the steady stream of lucid expositions, surprising analogies, and provocative questions which made the 8:30 hour the climax of his Bowdoin education. The questions, curiously enough, although presumably addressed to the whole class, often seemed meant for him alone. Prex's answers, phrased sweepingly and dogmatically so as to invite opposition and discussion, often spilled over from the classroom in lower Memorial to fraternity dining rooms and midnight debates in the "Ends."

Kenneth Sills was not in the habit of recording the remarks of his teachers in his diary, but so forcibly and concretely did Hyde touch life at so many points that the Senior often hurried back to his room in Appleton to jot down some of the memorable sayings. "President Hyde today compared the nervous system to a bank on which checks can be made out but accounts must not be overdrawn," he noted after a lecture in the fall term. Other entries served as guides to his own reading and writing: "Always read by subjects; go to a book with a question to be answered"; "Men do not accept abstract ideas"; "In writing an essay be selective; it is not what you put in that counts as much as what you leave out." It was Hyde, even more than his beloved Frenchy Johnson, who gave Kenneth Sills the most convincing illustrations of the drama of the class hour, of the primary importance of what goes on in a classroom. In the spring term, as the Senior paused to watch masons at work on the new Hubbard Library, he may well have reflected that great teachers and great books are the essential stuff in the building of a college. President Hyde himself was, first and last, a teacher. Officers of administration best justified their existence when they brought books, students, and teachers together in an atmosphere hospitable to learning.

As a Sophomore Kenneth Sills began to consider plans for his career after graduation. Before he reached his twentieth birthday, he was advised by his godfather, C. G. Coster, to try law or civil engineering. "I believe in a profession," Mr. Coster wrote in January, 1899, "for if a man is knocked out in mercantile business, his whole stock in trade may be gone, whereas a professional man generally retains the capacity for making a living as long as he has any head at all." Civil engineering had a dull sound to this student, who avoided all the sciences and was only mildly interested in mathematics; law, however, was not without its attractions. Professor Willie Mac made it seem exciting enough to inspire the organization of a club "for those who intend to adopt law as a profession," and, at the urging of Don Snow and Rip, Casey duly enrolled as a member. His godfather was pleased. "There are worse professions than the law," he wrote from St. Johns, "if you can work up any interest in it." No "working up" was needed for his interest in a possible career in the Church. It was generally assumed that the son and grandson of ministers would be headed for the ministry himself. His Aunt Catherine's birthday letter in 1899 reminded him again of her hopes: "I should like you of all things to be a priest, if you feel any vocation for it." Others felt the same way. From far-off Shanghai, Dr. Charles Lincoln '91, a medical missionary at St. John's College, wrote in the fall of 1900: "Are you going to study for the Church? . . . I should be only too happy to see you in the American Church Mission in China." His Deke friend, Roy Marston '99, was only half-bantering when he urged in senior year, "Come to New York and study to be a bishop! We need more blood and less damned *religiacs* in the world. You can practice on me when you are in gear." With so many members of his own family in the Church, it was natural for Kenneth Sills to give much thought to following them. "But by the time of my senior year," he wrote in 1953, "I had made up my mind definitely that, since the ministry was not the only calling in which I could be happy, it certainly was not the calling for me."

With the shining examples of President Hyde and Frenchy Johnson before him almost daily in the classroom, it is not surprising that the Senior's thoughts turned to a possible career in teaching and scholarship. Other influences had been at work. At St. Andrews during the summer he had gained the friendly interest of several vacationing Harvard professors, Barrett Wendell, Charles Copeland, and Jefferson Butler Fletcher, all of them members of the English department at the university. They and an enthusiastic young Harvard instructor, Henry Rideout, had assured him, if he came to Cambridge, of an assistantship which would enable him to support himself while taking three courses in the graduate school. The fastidious Copey had delighted Dean and Mrs. Sills by praising an essay which their son had submitted for criticism. "It was very gratifying to me to know that your work was approved by so good a judge as Mr. Copeland," the Dean wrote. "It is very good for you to have such literary acquaintances."

Columbia's graduate faculty also had its champions. Professor

Henry Emery, who had taken his doctorate there in 1896, urged the advantages of applying for a fellowship which would involve no teaching, and volunteered to write in his behalf to Professor George Rice Carpenter, chairman of the English department. His endorsement was seconded enthusiastically by President Hyde and Professor Johnson. Such compelling recommendations had their effect on Morningside Heights. The Columbia department ranked Kenneth Sills as the most promising of the candidates, even though university fellowships were rarely awarded to men just graduating from college. The application was not, however, immediately successful. "I was exceedingly disappointed by the action of the University Council," Professor Carpenter wrote to Henry Johnson in June, 1901. "We recommended Mr. Sills and another candidate, thinking that we should get two scholarships. As it turned out, only one was placed at our disposal and the Council assigned it to the candidate second on our list on the ground that he had already been a Fellow in English." Although Columbia tried to make amends by offering a scholarship to the Bowdoin Senior, the stipend was insufficient without other means of support, and he was reluctant to ask for further financial help from his parents. Professor Emery wrote to soften the disappointment. Why not, he suggested, reapply after a year or two? His own experience had shown the Harvard-Columbia combination to be an ideal one. "It might be well for you to adopt my scheme and try both," he wrote. "Harvard is the bigger university and New York is the bigger town." Professor Carpenter was also encouraging when he learned of the candidate's decision to accept the Harvard assistantship: "You will, of course, be as well off at Harvard as you could be anywhere in the world. I shall not, however, give up the hope that you may perhaps find it worthwhile to continue or to complete your studies here."

So it was to be Harvard in the fall. Kenneth Sills would, as Prex advised, murder the alternatives and conduct no post-mortems. In any event, there would be no time for might-have-beens.

The Bowdoin Senior's spring term was too crowded for anything but the daily excitement and wonder of his last days as an undergraduate. He enjoyed his role as elder statesman to the *Quill* and the *Orient* boards, having relinquished his editorships but still continuing to contribute. He and Rip moved from their old room in 10 Appleton to share the Dekes' glory in their new chapter house, the second of the fraternities to have its own home. The long hours of "plugging" now paid off in a shower of academic distinctions: the Sewall premiums in Greek and Latin, the Class of 1868 prize in oratory, the Pray English Essay prize, and the Brown prize in extemporaneous composition. These and other honors kept coming so fast that his friend John Clair Minot '96 protested that he was kept busy merely sending congratulations, and "the occasions seem to multiply as your course advances." From Harvard, his Freshman roommate, Percy Baxter, boasted, "You didn't surprise me at all, the way you took everything. . . . Your family and friends are unusually proud of you, and I can crawl in for a little of the reflected glory, for did I not guide you through Freshman perils?" Ivy Day brought additional recognition as Class Poet, and when Rip, as class president, referred to the "honest pride" of 1901 in having "among us such scholars as 'Casey' Sills," he was interrupted by applause.

Amidst all these felicitations, the first scholar of his class succeeded in looking as uncomfortable as if he had just been told, on the eve of Commencement, that his marks were not up to graduation standard. He seemed almost apologetic at having plugged so hard, but he faced another ordeal of congratulations on Class Day, when he was called upon to give the farewell address. There, under the Thorndike Oak, surrounded by his classmates and their families, the Senior spoke of the bright but brittle college honors, soon to be forgotten in the swiftly passing generations of students: "Today we are the lords of the campus; tomorrow these very trees, those very halls will look down on us with gentle indifference. For the college belongs to the student body rather than to the trustees; to the undergraduates rather than to the alumni." This was not the last time he would remind members of the college that the president and other officers are but a row of moving shadow shapes, while the students are eternal.

More golden opinions poured in on Commencement Day, when he received his degree *summa cum laude*. He and Rip had two of the four commencement "parts" at the exercises in the First Parish Church. Later, at the Commencement Dinner in Memorial Hall, when Prex announced that the award for the best essay had gone to Kenneth Sills for his speech, "The Shortcomings of Stoicism," his loyal roommate was the first to reach his side with congratulations. If there were any exultation in the heart of the gifted graduate, it was a pride in the thought of his father and mother. Dean and Mrs. Sills, whose lives were sorely troubled by differences with the new Bishop of the Maine Diocese which culminated in the Dean's leaving the deanship, found in the triumphs of their son a needed solace and, perhaps, justification. He was, President Hyde told them, the first student, not only of his class, but of generations of Bowdoin classes. "In all my fondest hopes for you," his mother wrote later that evening, "I did not dream that you would do more than Harry Emery or William Lawrence. It was the height of my ambition that you would equal them in your work and marks, but I never dreamed you would surpass them. It was the supreme day of my life."

teachers in their off-hours at the Colonial Club, but it was their lectures which impressed him most. He trooped into Harvard Hall, along with what seemed like the entire membership of the graduate school, to marvel at Professor Kittredge's lucid explications of the text of Shakespeare's great tragedies. With his fiery power and his vast linguistic and historical erudition, Kitty seemed fully to deserve Santayana's praise as one who could "trace e'en Hamlet's silence to its source." Yet Kenneth Sills learned there was more than one Kittredge. Thanks to Fletcher's introduction, he noted that the imperious scholar who at ten o'clock in the morning appeared to have "an eye like Mars" and "the front of Jove himself," was all courtesy and deference when he received his guests at his home on Hilliard Street. Of the younger professors, he found Lewis Gates the most stimulating. "Gates struck me as an admirable critic," he wrote Stanley Chase '05. "I think he could have risen as high with us as did A. C. Bradley were it not for his tragic breakdown." Of his senior teachers, it was Professor Grandgent who was most memorable. His course in Dante not only covered but illuminated the Middle Ages and the Renaissance. He could thank Frenchy Johnson a thousand times for teaching him the importance of the Italian language and literature.

Kenneth Sills's second year in Cambridge proved to be richer than the first. He had learned how to order his work and, without neglecting his assistantship, find more time for his own scholarly interests, which were now centering in comparative literature. Socially, the year was also more rewarding. His duties as proctor in Weld Hall were not onerous, and the lively conversation made up for the dull food at an instructors' table in Memorial Hall where a group of the younger men met for their meals. Among them were scholars whose names have since become familiar in academic history: William Allan Neilson, later to become president of Smith College; Schofield and Fletcher, later professors of comparative literature at Harvard and Columbia; Chester Noyes Greenough and George Chase, who were to become the deans of Harvard College and of the Graduate School of Arts and Sciences; and William Lawrence, whose brilliant doctoral dissertation gave notice that as early as 1903 he was on the threshold of a distinguished career as a medievalist.

Of these contemporaries, Casey saw his Bowdoin friend, Lawrence, most frequently, but he also formed a close friendship with Chase and Greenough who often gathered in the proctor's room at 35 Weld Hall for after-dinner coffee and cigars. They were further united by an enthusiastic distaste for Professor Edward Sheldon's course in Romance philology, a repugnance heightened by their dislike of the thorny textbook which constituted the bible of the course, Dietrich Behrens' edition of *Grammatik des Altfranzösischen von Dr. Eduard Schwan*. "I need only say," Kenneth Sills reported to Henry Johnson, "that it is so far quite the dreariest stuff I have yet met." It was Chase who devised a safety valve to release their feelings about Behrens and Schwan. After especially dull sessions over Old French, and no less desperate bouts with the *Grammatik des Altfranzösischen*, the foursome was divided into two teams: Sills and Lawrence, representing the detested Schwan, and Chase and Greenough, the loathed Behrens. At a signal they advanced from opposite sides of the room toward their host's sofa cushions, with the aim of determining which team could kick the cushions through the wide transom over the entrance to the room. One evening, in the midst of vigorous pummeling and kicking, they were interrupted by a persistent knocking on the door; when the disheveled proctor opened it, he was greeted by a bashful Freshman seeking advice on the improvement of his themes. Lawrence recalls peeping through a crack in the bedroom door while the graduate assistant gravely admonished the surprised lad to be "a trifle less bookish in his writing," a criticism Kenneth Sills was never permitted to forget. "I don't wish to seem *bookish*," Lawrence once wrote to his friend after he had become a Bowdoin professor, "but would beg to observe that *woolly* is spelt with two (2) l's." The scrimmages in Weld were the beginning of a distinguished friendship.

From that time forward, Kenneth Sills was known to his Harvard contemporaries as "Schwan," and when later honors were conferred upon him, he sometimes received suitably inscribed resolutions of respect signed by Behrens of the Weld Pillow-kicking Association of 1903.

Although he had expected to remain at Harvard until he completed his studies for the Ph.D., he was quite ready to interrupt his graduate work to accept an invitation from President Hyde to return to Bowdoin for the academic year, 1903–4. As instructor in classics and English, he had charge of the class in elementary Greek, and assisted Professors Woodruff and Houghton in intermediate Greek and Latin. He also taught the elective course for Sophomores in English, consisting of a term of exposition and argumentation, followed by a study of nineteenth-century prose. It was his additional task to read the themes required of all Juniors and to confer with each author about his writing. Formidable as this schedule was, it enabled him to watch at first hand President Hyde's educational philosophy: a shrewd compound of financial necessity and sound academic policy. Believing that a multitude of courses was nonsensical and too often merely reflected the vanity of professors eager to cultivate their own private gardens, the president encouraged each department to offer an elementary course followed by a general course in the subject and culminating in a smaller, specialized seminar for Seniors. After his experience at Harvard under Eliot's elective system, Kenneth Sills found the Bowdoin curriculum an excellent program for a small college of liberal arts. In later years, when faculty members came to the president's office to propose new courses, they were destined to hear a good deal about the virtues of teaching a comparatively few courses thoroughly.

The Bowdoin curriculum of 1903–4, however, held no foreseeable promise of his own advancement. The department of English seemed to be placing more emphasis upon rhetoric and argumentation than upon literature, an imbalance which Kenneth Sills feared would scarcely be redressed by the appointment in 1904 of Professor William Trufant Foster to strengthen the work in debating. William Lawrence, to whom he had deplored the situation, shared Casey's alarm at the growth of forensics at the expense of courses in literature. "The idea of a college with the splendid literary traditions of Longfellow and Hawthorne going to pot in a literary way, as you say it is, is more than disquieting." "But," Lawrence added, "I don't see anything to do about it. . . . Nor do I see how you can do anything to mend matters." If the unexpressed but lively hope of ultimately being able to teach comparative literature at Bowdoin made it easy for Casey to leave graduate school, the chances of such a course now seemed slim indeed. Yet a return to Harvard to resume his studies would mean a discouragingly heavy infusion of philology. Literary courses, it seemed, were encroached upon by forensics in Brunswick and hedged about by Old French and Gothic in Cambridge. "Sometimes it seems very monastic," he complained to Henry Johnson, "and absolutely separated from the aid that literature should give to life." Meanwhile, Professor Carpenter at Columbia had not forgotten his promise to keep Kenneth Sills in mind for a suitable appointment. "We really want very much to get hold of a young man with the right temperament and intellectual character," he wrote in January, 1904, "and I have somehow come to imagine you are pretty much the man we need." Even more exciting was Carpenter's assurance of a release from all teaching in the second year with an opportunity to complete his work for the doctorate.

Academic history has its own ways of repeating itself. The rival claims of Harvard and Columbia which had confronted Kenneth Sills three years before as a Bowdoin Senior now presented no less of a dilemma to the Bowdoin instructor in the winter of his discontent. His father was all for Columbia. "Suppose you returned to Harvard for two years more," he wrote on January 10, "you should at the end of that time be glad to accept a position in such an institution as Columbia. Why not get these two years of experience there in the meanwhile. Of course your

Harvard friends will advise against Columbia but I believe President Hyde will give an unbiased judgment." The Reverend Doctor Sills was soon to learn that he had underestimated Columbia's influence on the banks of the Charles. Prex, as it turned out, urged the advantages of the Columbia offer, but so did his Harvard friends, some of whom had been themselves regarding Morningside Heights with interest. William Allan Neilson received Casey's appeal for advice just after he had decided to accept a Columbia professorship in English. His reply on January 14 was emphatic: "I feel Columbia is well worth accepting. . . . Moreover, you have already got a large part of what Harvard has to give, and a year would tell you whether you can find anything at Columbia worth your while. It is a bigger game than you are likely to be offered a hand in elsewhere."

The same mail brought the same advice from Jefferson Fletcher. "You know my feeling about our philological emphasis," he wrote. "It is wise for us to lay stress there because we have the men there. But that is another matter than saying that *you* should subject yourself to the stress. Indeed, I think it altogether possible that you would find Columbia the more tonic to your interest. . . . I should accept Carpenter's offer and think myself a lucky fellow. Needless to say, alas, this letter is a self-denying ordinance: I shall count it one more heavy loss to us—and me—if you follow Neilson."

Kenneth Sills's interest in comparative literature which had been aroused by Professor Johnson's Bowdoin lectures and confirmed by the zeal of Fletcher at Harvard was also a determining factor. At Columbia, George Edward Woodberry and Brander Matthews had created a tradition of humanistic literary studies in which comparative literature and criticism outweighed the scientific philological disciplines dominant in the German universities and widely imported by their American counterparts. James Plaisted Webber, Casey's Bowdoin contemporary who was studying for his M.A. at Columbia, added his testimony to the vitality of the teaching on Morningside Heights. His letter was filled with praise for Carpenter's selfless devotion to his students, for Trent's pioneer teaching in American literature, for George Philip Krapp's unpedantic courses in philology, and for the brilliant lectures of "that likeable freak," Brander Matthews. By all means, Casey must come to Columbia and see for himself. Although Rip Dana would have preferred his former roommate to remain at Bowdoin in spite of the overemphasis upon speech, he hailed Columbia's invitation as "the best I ever heard of for a fellow of your age." "Possibly the chance of losing you may spur Prex to make some definite proposition," he wrote late in January, "and don't let any of Prex's snap judgments have too much weight with you."

While Kenneth Sills was still making up his mind, Jefferson Fletcher himself was called to Columbia to succeed Woodberry as professor of comparative literature. "When I wrote you so urgently to accept Carpenter's offer," he explained in February, 1904, "I was totally unexpectant of any such offer coming to me. . . . At Columbia they are bent on advancing comparative literature; here, in spite of a general kindly sympathy, it has seemed to promise a stunted growth. . . . I am counting much on your interest in the subject. Who knows what a nucleus of friendly enthusiasts, given an open field and a fair field, may not accomplish?" There could be no question by this time about the attractiveness of Columbia, and when Lawrence, the third of his Harvard friends, cast his vote for Morningside Heights, the trend must have seemed like a stampede. Lawrence's advice, of course, was entirely disinterested, but within a year he, too, was destined to accept a Columbia professorship. Casey had no reason to hesitate any longer, and when President Hyde gave the venture his emphatic blessing, the die was cast.

Professor Carpenter hoped that his new tutor would "make himself a rather important factor in our undergraduate work" by teaching the required Sophomore class in composition and literature. Fifty years later Kenneth Sills could still recall the anxiety with which he faced his first class in Hamilton Hall. "At

Harvard," he wrote, "I had a very minor position; at Bowdoin I knew many of the students personally and was known by them. But the name of Columbia was quite formidable and to manage that class of sophomores was quite a challenge." He was soon to discover, however, that Columbia undergraduates did not differ perceptibly from those at Harvard and Bowdoin. At any rate, they seemed fully capable of making the same errors on their papers. Their tutor had spent part of his summer at St. Andrews devising, under Carpenter's friendly direction, a syllabus which provided enough provocative reading to serve as points of departure for frequent compositions. "My present chore includes reading a great many themes which is not much fun," he wrote Henry Johnson early in the fall term, "and lecturing six hours a week which is very good fun." By the end of October he reported to Frenchy that he felt almost like a New Yorker and "everything else that's bad; I have heard the archbishop, seen *Romeo and Juliet,* been up the Hudson, heard some political spellbinders, shaken Nicholas Miraculous Butler by the hand, played three times at golf, and ridden in the subway. What more can life offer?"

Whatever hours he could spare from his teaching were put in on reading for his thesis on Dante's influence on English literature. The subject, he soon came to realize, was tremendously big and rather intangible, and demanded a knowledge of the worst as well as the best things in English. Fletcher saw that it would probably be too broad, but counseled wide preliminary reading. "It's difficult, of course," Casey confessed to Henry Johnson, "and perhaps requires a better trained mind than I have to handle it." Yet he was confident that the advantages of his topic far outweighed the possible drawbacks. It avoided what Johnson had feared might involve "too much linguistic study," and, above all, it had the merit of being "a literary subject—one that would give back far more than I take to it." "I shall get to know my Dante thoroughly," he told his Bowdoin teacher gratefully, "and the reading of Dante is one of the best things I have ever done." Wise in the ways of doctoral dissertations, Professor Johnson qualified his enthusiasm by urging Casey to consult Carpenter about reducing the dimensions of the project to one of more manageable size. "After a few years," he wrote, "you will regard your dissertation with mixed feelings. . . . The *real* reason for taking up the task at all, this love of the noble Dante, will come to its rights." Meanwhile, Kenneth Sills plugged away furiously at his subject. In May he felt the graduate student's fierce joy at seeing the galley proof of his first substantial learned article, and he celebrated the close of his first year at Columbia by mailing out reprints of "References to Dante in Seventeenth Century English Literature" which had appeared in the June issue of *Modern Philology*.

Morningside Heights had provided a congenial atmosphere for his studies. "Professionally it is good to be where some scholarly work is going forward," he wrote Johnson, "and the people I work under are certainly considerate and cordial." He was also cheered by Professor Carpenter's assurance of "a permanent place of some sort" in the department if he wished to remain at Columbia, and he was encouraged by Jeff Fletcher to look forward to offering a course of his own in comparative literature after completing the requirements for the degree. Late June also brought a flattering invitation from Prex to return to Bowdoin in the autumn of 1906. With so pleasant a variety of prospects to contemplate, he was confident that the second year at Columbia would be even more rewarding than the first. His appointment as Lecturer in English for 1905–6 meant a release from the burden of incessant theme reading and an opportunity to register for a full graduate program. He found himself enjoying his work in Romance philology under Professor Henry A. Todd, who carried his technical erudition more lightly than did Sheldon of Behrens-Schwan memories. The courses in comparative literature were a delight. He was stimulated by the lectures of Professor Joel E. Spingarn whose recent *History of Literary Criticism in the Renaissance* was one of the brilliant products of

Woodberry's teaching. Spingarn's course proved helpful as an introduction to the more specialized work of the seminar conducted by Fletcher. The courtesy and scholarship of this friend of St. Andrews and Harvard had already put the graduate student deeply in his debt. Now, at Columbia, Fletcher's seminar in the Renaissance was the high point of Kenneth Sills's graduate school years. He was always to count it as a chief blessing of his intellectual life that in Fletcher he found a scholar and translator of Dante worthy to walk in the same company with his beloved Henry Johnson.

The arrival of William Lawrence to join the Columbia faculty as a specialist in Anglo-Saxon and medieval literature was another happy omen at the opening of the fall term in 1905. At Lawrence's invitation, Casey jumped at the chance to leave his dreary room near St. Luke's Hospital to join his friend and three young instructors who clubbed together, rented an altogether royal apartment at 157 West 105 Street, hired a cook, and lived in comfort. The other members were George Philip Krapp, later professor of English at Columbia; Charles M. Baker, head of the Latin department at the Horace Mann School; and John G. Bowman, later to become president of the University of Iowa and chancellor of the University of Pittsburgh. The apartment was a walk-up, but, as Lawrence recalled, its "lift" was a moral one. If Casey still had any lingering misgivings about leaving Harvard, they were forgotten in this pleasant fellowship. With such compatible company it should be possible, he thought, to make great headway on his dissertation, and perhaps stake out an undisputed claim to the subject by publishing a few more articles in the scholarly journals. Jeff Fletcher had been prophetic in saying he should count himself a lucky fellow to be in New York.

The term which had opened so brightly was soon to be darkened by serious illness. Early in November Kenneth Sills noticed that he grew tired easily and was unable to work with his accustomed intensity. Disregarding these ominous signs, he resolved to press on with his reading rather than accept Rip's tempting invitation to spend Thanksgiving in Newton with the Dana family. A week later he was stricken with pleurisy which galloped fast into a dangerous case of double pneumonia. "There was no need of your crawling into bed just to emphasize the fact that you could not come to Massachusetts," Rip wrote before learning of the gravity of his friend's illness. Thoroughly alarmed, Lawrence telegraphed Dr. and Mrs. Sills in Geneva, New York, where the former dean of St. Luke's had become rector of Trinity Church. The message brought Mrs. Sills hurrying to the city, where she engaged a nurse and remained until after the crisis was safely passed. Under the devoted care of Dr. John Blake White, a New York friend of the Sillses, the patient recovered sufficiently to be able to travel to Geneva for Christmas and a convalescence with his family. The close call alarmed his friends. John Small covered his concern by writing cheerful warnings from Portland about the perils of female nurses: "Ripley and I have decided to take a short course in nursing . . . we have already ordered our checkered gingham suits and we hope to look very fetching. Ripley will take care of you nights and I the daytime." "Schwan's" old opponent in the pillow-kicking scuffles, George Chase, wrote from Harvard, "We were all much worried about Neilson's letter which told of your sickness. . . . How is it going to be with your work for the degree? I hope you will be able to pull it off, but for heaven's sake don't knock yourself out." Ripley Dana told his former roommate, "I don't think I have ever quite accustomed myself to living without your being in the same apartment. . . . You had every one's hair standing on end."

Kenneth Sills's Columbia teachers showed their concern in ways which belied the popular myth of the impersonality of a large university. There were cheerful letters from Professors Todd and Spingarn with assurances that their assignments could be made up by the end of the term, and with cautions not to resume work until it was perfectly safe to do so. Professor Carpenter saw the illness as "a sort of blessing in disguise" in providing a vacation with the opportunity of completing the requirements for the degree at a more leisurely pace. He suggested a trip to Italy in the spring, some reading in the Vatican library, and later at the British Museum. "You could then finish your work next year," he concluded, "with colors flying and without the feeling of great pressure." This proposal had its charms, but Kenneth Sills was eager to get as much of his graduate work behind him as possible. President Hyde had already intimated the strong likelihood of a permanent place at Bowdoin next autumn, and such a chance might not come again. As for his health, long walks in the purer air of Geneva and the loving care of his parents and sister had restored him to his usual vigor. A visit to the rectory in early January had convinced William Lawrence of the completeness of the recovery. "Your room has been cleaned and polished," he wrote on his return to New York on January 7, "and I think there will be few reminiscences of the late unpleasantness when you return. Possibly a slight odor of liniment, that is all, save a row of bottles on the *chiffonier*." These, Lawrence promised, would not be there to greet him on his arrival.

Lawrence was aware of other reasons which made Professor Carpenter's proposal of less haste seem inexpedient. There were disquieting rumors that a book on Dante's influence in England was being readied for publication by Paget Toynbee in London. The doctoral candidate's nightmare of the threat of prior publication by another scholar now seemed sufficiently real. It was well enough for his friends to describe the retaliatory joys of tearing a rival's book to shreds in a lethal critical article, but it was poor solace to review a work which one had wanted to write himself. Clearly there was no time to lose. There were no less alarming reports from Brunswick, where President Hyde was watching the painful case of the growing disability of a member of his faculty slowly develop into what was ultimately to become a major crisis of his administration.

The increasing deafness of Kenneth Sills's old teacher of Latin, the urbane and widely traveled William Addison Houghton, had led the Governing Boards in 1905 to authorize the president to seek the services of another scholar to begin his work in 1906. There was no secret about the trying situation. For some time it had been apparent that Professor Houghton was not fully able to perform his duties as the Winkley Professor of the Latin Language and Literature. Kenneth Sills had noted the demoralization of the instruction in Latin during his interlude of teaching at Bowdoin in 1903–4. Professor Houghton himself, aware of his growing infirmity, had assured the president in writing of his readiness to resign his chair at the end of the next academic year, 1905–6. Armed with this assurance, and supported by a vote of the Boards, Hyde had asked Casey after the Commencement of June, 1905, whether he could accept the professorship in Latin a year hence. Even under the tortuous circumstances, the offer was too good to refuse. Prospects of a permanent position at Columbia were, at best, fairly nebulous and would depend upon his degree. He had no reason to doubt Carpenter's promise to find a place for him, but the appointment might be in composition. To be sure, the Bowdoin professorship was in Latin, but it might eventually lead to a chair in comparative literature or in English. Had not Henry Leland Chapman begun his Bowdoin career as a teacher of Latin and later shifted to English literature? Dr. Sills urged his son to accept the flattering offer. "It will give you opportunities for immediate advancement," he wrote from Geneva, "and it will put a higher value upon your services should Columbia desire to call you to her faculty at some later time." With Professor Houghton seemingly willing to resign, it seemed generally understood that the matter was settled, and Kenneth Sills had already received the congratulations of several of the trustees and overseers. He was confident that the Boards would handle the situation with equity to all concerned.

Then suddenly in January, 1906, while still convalescing at Geneva, he learned that Professor Houghton, rescinding his earlier agreement to resign, had served notice on the president that he would not retire unless forced to do so by a vote of the Boards. The situation was still clouded with uncertainty when Kenneth Sills returned to Columbia in late January. Fearful that his friend would withdraw rather than risk any possible ill-will from Professor Houghton's supporters, Ripley Dana was emphatic in his advice. "Don't back down an inch," he wrote, "don't worry about the thing, nor about your Ph.D. *either.* . . . I don't believe any of the faculty have any ill-feeling toward you. I'll let you know anything I can find out." From Portland came word from John Small that Professor Houghton would resign after all. "Everybody knows," he wrote, "that you're coming back." The same counsel came from Harry deForest Smith '91, professor of Greek at Amherst, who, as a Bowdoin alumnus and classical scholar, was watching the tempest in the Brunswick teapot with more than professional interest. "Like many other young alumni, I want you and not Houghton in the Latin chair," he wrote on April 4. When Kenneth Sills suggested that the rumpus might affect his popularity with the students or faculty, Smith's reply was emphatic: "Any row between Hyde and Houghton will not affect you. I don't agree with you when you say that 'it would not pay' to have the matter brought to a head in such a way as to cause a row. A good row may bring good results when other measures fail. I really think it is up to Prex to do the worrying if there is any to be done, and not you." At Columbia, Professor Carpenter counseled a waiting game. President Hyde, he was confident, could manage to get along for a year or two and keep the position open. In the meantime there would be a blessed interval in which to finish the dissertation.

Back at Bowdoin Prex was showing visible signs of strain under the mounting pressure. The social prominence of the Houghtons in Portland as well as in Brunswick, the activities of their friends, the bruiting about of rumors of the president's ruthless and tactless treatment, and the chance to embarrass the president for those who were critical of his policies combined to make it possible that the Boards might reverse their decision. President Hyde, who had always warned an administrator to avoid controversy as he would avoid poison, maintained with firmness that the weakness in the instruction in Latin had reached a point at which remedial measures were necessary. In his view, neither Professor Houghton's twelve years of service nor his present convenience should be allowed to outweigh the demand for effective teaching in an important department. He would not sacrifice Bowdoin's tradition of vital teaching, which he regarded as the distinction, if not the main function of the college. Having made up his mind on the basis of the available evidence, the president refrained from taking part in the controversy. He even absented himself from the meeting on Commencement morning, June 27, 1906, when the issue was considered; he had, however, submitted his own formal resignation to a trustee, Edward Stanwood, to be read in the event his position was not sustained. Beneath the windows of Hubbard Hall where the Boards were in session, the Commencement procession was delayed for two hours. The venerable Chandler's Band played through its entire repertoire while the debate continued and the Seniors and their guests milled around the campus. The president's resignation was destined to remain unread in Mr. Stanwood's pocket. By a narrow margin of several votes, the Boards upheld President Hyde's recommendation, although there was a certain amount of face-saving. Professor Houghton was granted another year's tenure in the Winkley professorship to expire in June, 1907, but the Boards authorized the president "to assign the duties of the chair." Even Barrett Potter, the attorney who served as secretary to the trustees, confessed that he "would not undertake to say exactly what this authorization means." Kenneth Sills was elected adjunct professor of Latin.

There was no elation when the news reached the new adjunct professor in New York. "I am not at all sure," he wrote Henry Johnson on June 30, "that the most dignified course for me to follow would not be to say flatly that I had better not accept the proposition and begin to look for a job elsewhere. The president informs me that Professor Houghton is to stay only one year more, but it seems to me that I heard *that* about a year ago. As it is, most of the honor and pleasure of going back has been taken away." While waiting to receive Professor Johnson's answer, he sought his father's advice in Geneva, although he was sure that practical considerations would weigh most heavily with the rector. His surmise was correct. The lateness of the academic year, the difficulty of finding a satisfactory place at another institution, the friendship and confidence of President Hyde and of many influential members of the Boards, and the certainty of succeeding to the Winkley professorship within twelve months—all these were advanced to show the folly of refusing so handsome an offer. But Casey resolved to talk over the problem with Ripley Dana before deciding. His old friend was bristling with arguments when they met the next day in Boston: The opportunity was the chance of a lifetime. He could count on the sympathy and interest of the most powerful members of both Boards. The faculty was looking forward eagerly to his return. He must let everything else go hang—even the Ph.D. He must not let Prex and the college down. After all, Bowdoin was Bowdoin. In the midst of their discussion, a letter arrived from Judge Putnam with a more formal but no less urgent plea to accept the president's offer. "Professor Houghton's case is a very hard one," the judge wrote. "The Boards are disposed to help him out all they can. I have no doubt you sympathize with our efforts in that direction." Rip leaped on the judge's concluding sentence as a confirmation of his own opinion: "From any point of view, for a graduate of 1901 the promotion is and will be a very rapid one." Professor Johnson's words, however, were the most compelling of all. When his old friend and master said he must come back because he was needed at Bowdoin, Kenneth Sills knew in his heart of hearts there could be only one response.

Summer in St. Andrews brought time for reflection and with it a slowly mounting confidence. He would swallow his pride about the *adjunct* professorship. Judicious compromise was a law of life. A scrutiny of his own conduct in the affair convinced him he had done nothing for which he could reproach himself. If, as the Methuen Company had informed him, Toynbee's book "would not be published until early next year," he would keep plugging and await the appearance of the volume. There were plenty of other subjects to write about. Comparative literature was a broad and rich field to plow. Fletcher once suggested that he develop the idea of *virtu* and *fortuna* in the Middle Ages and the Renaissance. This hint would certainly bear careful investigating; he would get Frenchy's opinion about it as soon as he returned to Brunswick. Almost daily his mail brought encouraging messages. From his friend Charles Clifford Hutchins, the Bowdoin physicist who shared a love of Dante, came a jubilant letter after he had heard about the appointment in England where he was enjoying a sabbatical. "Mrs. H. and I executed a war-dance" to celebrate, he wrote from Lincolnshire in July. The notes from President Hyde were filled with enthusiastic plans for the work of the Freshman year. The new adjunct professor, Prex said, was just the man to make elementary courses inspiring as well as thorough. The best cheer, as always, came from Henry Johnson, who welcomed him back as a devoted friend and comrade. With such high comradeship awaiting him, Kenneth Sills returned to Bowdoin in the fall.

# 4

## BOWDOIN PROFESSOR AND
## FACULTY SECRETARY, 1906-1910

Coming back to Brunswick in the fall was hardly a novel experience for Kenneth Sills, but his return in mid-September, 1906, smacked of pleasant permanence. He felt strangely excited at the station as he watched the baggage man unload the cases of books marked for delivery to 31 Federal Street. After living in five different lodgings in the last five years in Cambridge, Brunswick, and New York, it was fun to be coming home. His life as graduate student and instructor had been rootless, and K. C. M. S. always cherished a strong sense of place. Now that his parents and sister were settled in the rectory in Geneva, Portland no longer seemed quite the same old place. He was to think of Brunswick as home for the rest of his life.

He counted himself lucky in being able to return to the living quarters he had enjoyed in 1903–4, during his interim appointment as instructor in Latin and English. There, in the Wheeler house on lower Federal Street, his rooms had included a study in the northwest corner of the ground floor with a bedroom above it. The windows looked out upon an elm-shadowed street which reminded him, especially in the golden light of autumnal afternoons, of his beloved State Street. The rest of the yellow, clapboarded house was occupied by Mrs. Mary Wheeler and her son Edward, who had attended Bowdoin with the class of 1898 and was now a rising young lawyer and moderator of the Town Meeting. The Wheelers, who were pleased to have had the quiet and considerate instructor in their house two years before, were happy to welcome him back. From his point of view the arrangement was ideal. It provided the privacy of his own apartment along with the friendly atmosphere of family life. The house, only a few minutes walk from the campus, would be convenient for students to drop in for conferences. There was also a fireplace. As Casey scuffed his way to classes that autumn through the fallen leaves on the unpaved sidewalk, he had no reason to regret having left his walk-up apartment on 105 Street in New York, where he had never quite accustomed himself to the clang of trolley cars on Amsterdam Avenue.

The new adjunct professor of Latin had allowed himself a fortnight in which to arrange his books and papers and plan for the first recitations on September 27, but now he found the time all too short. The college bell, he reflected, summons adjunct professors just as imperiously as it does the students. Giving courses on one's own was likely to prove more arduous than being a mere section hand at a university. Frenchy Johnson called to assure him that no professor worth his salt ever really felt fully prepared to face any class. Professor Hutchins, who was catching up on college gossip after a sabbatical year in Germany, remarked cheerfully that from all reports Bowdoin was moving pretty much in the same old grooves. "There is some kicking on the part of the students against the new men," he said, "on the claim that too much work is given out, and some responsive kicking by the new men against the students on the ground that they are preoccupied and lazy. Probably both are right." Casey agreed that much might be said on both sides.

Since length and continuity of service were prized at Bowdoin, there were few new men for the students to kick against. With three exceptions, the faculty was the same as the one Kenneth Sills had known in 1903-4. He missed the lively intellectual companionship of Albert L. P. Dennis, who had resigned his chair in 1904 to teach history and political science at the University of Chicago, but he soon came to admire Dennis' successor, the able Allen Johnson, at whose Federal Street house he often stopped for a chat after dinner. Of the teachers who had been appointed since 1904, William Trufant Foster in English and argumentation and Charles Theodore Burnett in philosophy and psychology, it was Burnett who attracted him at once. Six years Sills's senior, he was a graduate of Amherst, where he had been a classmate of Dwight Morrow and Calvin Coolidge, and had taken his doctorate at Harvard in 1903. Although he and Kenneth Sills had been contemporaries in graduate school, their paths had not crossed in Cambridge. Now, in the self-contained life in Brunswick, they began an intimate friendship which lasted until the older man's death forty years later.

Each shared the other's faith in the abiding values of small colleges, each possessed a deeply spiritual nature, maintaining with no outward show of piety such old-fashioned practices as grace before meat, regular attendance at church, and personal study of the Bible. Early in their friendship they discovered a common loyalty to the principles of the Democratic party, an active interest in town affairs, and an enthusiastic admiration for the leadership of President Hyde. They were inseparable companions at The Octopus, a dining club at 15 Cleaveland Street for unmarried members of the faculty, and both were pleased to learn that the ladies of the Saturday Club considered them to be the town's most eligible bachelors. Since Casey was destined to become the sole surviving bachelor of The Octopus, his single state put a strain on the solicitude of many Brunswick matrons. Their continuing concern might have been less zealous had they heeded a quip of Mrs. Henry Johnson, a perceptive faculty wife. "Kenneth adores our sex," she said, "but he loves us *en masse*."

During the summer in St. Andrews, K. C. M. S. had some misgivings about his relations with Professor William Houghton, the senior member of the Latin department, whose appointment was to terminate at the end of the year, and whose chair, the Winkley professorship, was to be assigned to his junior colleague and former student. Happily, such fears proved groundless, although lesser men might have found the situation painfully awkward. For a dozen years Professor Houghton had done practically all the teaching in the department himself, including the required courses for Freshmen. Somewhat distant and reserved in dealing with students, he was more effective with advanced classes, and doubtless was ready to have his younger colleague assume the burden of the introductory work. Never in robust health, and aware of his deafness, he may have become at least partially reconciled to the prospect of early retirement. Meanwhile, Kenneth Sills treated his old teacher with unfailing courtesy and respect, and Houghton himself showed his Horatian spirit by an ironic appreciation of the caprice of fortune in which he knew his associate had played no selfish part.

The work of the department was divided about equally: the senior professor offering elective courses in Roman comedy, satire, and epic, while his junior colleague taught Latin prose and poetry to three sections of Freshmen. Unlike the smaller courses for Sophomores and upperclassmen meeting three times each week, the elementary classes met four times as a means of easing the transition from school to college. Kenneth Sills welcomed the extra hour as an opportunity to give informal lectures on literature, and to suggest the relations between Latin and English. In the first semester he was able to teach the first five books of Livy and about twenty-five of the best known letters of Pliny the Younger, as well as Cicero's *De Senectute*. The second semester was devoted to reading all the odes and epodes of Horace.

As he began his teaching, K. C. M. S. knew that his biggest job was not merely to cover his subject but to enliven it. An increasing number of Freshmen were coming to college with a distaste for Latin; more and more candidates for admission, especially from small schools in rural Maine, were offering three rather than four years of preparation. Still others, after struggling with Caesar's *Commentaries*, flatly refused to go on with Cicero and Virgil and were seeking colleges which required only two years of Latin in high school. Kenneth Sills, unlike some of his faculty friends, was not entirely willing to attribute the plight of the classics to a weakening of the fiber of the younger generation. As always, there was something to be said on the other side. In looking back at his own preparation in Greek and Latin, he could recall a good deal of languid teaching in which the instructor did little more than saw wood grammatically, but joylessly. Behrens and Schwan had their dry-as-dust prototypes in many schools and colleges. To expect students to love Latin literature after boiling them in oil in Caesar's Gallic Wars was as foolhardy, he thought, as to introduce them to American literature by requiring them to plow through the life and letters of Ulysses S. Grant.

During his undergraduate years he had often heard older members of the faculty speak wistfully about their efforts "to save Greek in the fitting schools," but they acknowledged it had been a losing fight. As early as 1892, President Hyde had recommended that Greek be discontinued as a Bowdoin admission requirement, and the Governing Boards, after resorting to a delaying action, finally yielded three years later. Louis Hatch '94 remembered the pall of gloom which shrouded the Commencement dinner in his Senior year when Prex announced that three years of French or German or two years of physics and one of mathematics might be substituted for Greek as an entrance requirement. The dinner, he recalled, was like a funeral, the public burial of Greek, "at which man after man arose to describe the virtues of the deceased." By 1902, however, only a year after Casey's own graduation, Bowdoin was granting degrees to men who were without Greek either in school or college. One needed no gift of prophecy to foresee another struggle in the offing, this time "to save Latin in the schools." Forty years later, when that battle had become a memory of far-off, old, unhappy things, Kenneth Sills remarked grimly to a theme-weary young instructor sweating over a pile of clumsily written Freshman papers, "I suppose *your* generation will soon try to save *English* in the schools!"

In the fall of 1906, however, all things seemed possible to the twenty-seven-year-old adjunct professor of Latin. He vowed to carry the fight to school boards and teachers' clubs; he would visit high schools and address student assemblies; he would write for the professional journals. First of all he would begin the campaign on the home front by making his own courses worth a student's time. He would teach Livy as a master of narrative prose. Pliny's letters could be made to open the door to the private life of the Romans under the Empire. He would compare Cicero's *De Senectute* with the thought of Bacon and other Elizabethans as well as with the ideas of modern essayists on youth and age. He would hold his students to a knowledge of the principal Horatian meters, but he would also teach them to relish Horatian phrases. A great lyric poet should be read and appreciated as a poet. To this end he would assign short papers in which his students could compare their favorite odes with the work of modern and contemporary poets. K. C. M. S. winced when he remembered hearing Professor Hutchins say that he had studied Latin and Greek without being told that the ancient languages were ever spoken. He also recalled the great Kittredge's remark that "the ancients did not know they were ancients." Perhaps forays into the high schools might help "to save Latin," but first of all he must not lose the battle in his own classroom in 103 Memorial Hall. There, at least, he could try to make the study of Latin a delight as well as a discipline. And each class hour would bring its daily payoff in victory or defeat.

Kenneth Sills soon discovered, however, that Bowdoin professors have rarely enjoyed the luxury of being free to devote their full energies to their classrooms. In a small college which contrived to get along with only such administrative responsibilities as could be shared between the president and faculty at their weekly meetings, all problems were of immediate, personal concern to every member of the college family. President Hyde, who believed that inspiring teachers are rarer than efficient administrators, was reluctant to assign administrative chores to teachers. With Prex himself teaching philosophy to virtually the whole senior class, and his faculty serving as class officers or advisers, Bowdoin had precious little internal administrative machinery. It was not until 1900, with the appointment of Professor George Taylor Files as registrar, that some semblance of organization was effected. During Files's administration of this new office, school records, reports of entrance examinations, election of courses, the recording of ranks, and the other details of academic bookkeeping were put on a businesslike basis. Formerly, the laborious process of tabulating absences and granting excuses had been handled by the faculty class advisers. These duties were added to the burdens of the registrar, who was also expected to teach his full complement of courses in German. Although Professor Files and, after 1905, his successor, Professor Burnett, did their work faithfully, their real interest was in their teaching. The faculty continued to be plagued by the vexatious problems arising from infractions of college rules, especially of the regulations governing attendance at class exercises. It was becoming apparent, even to those who feared the multiplication of administrative officers, that a perilous but vital administrative no man's land needed to be filled.

The new adjunct professor listened to a lengthy report on the situation at his first faculty meeting on September 25. In the previous June, dissatisfaction over the administration of college rules had become sufficiently acute to induce President Hyde to appoint a committee headed by the most articulate of the critics, Professor William Foster, to study the whole problem and to bring appropriate recommendations to the faculty in the fall. Now, at the opening of the new term, Foster's cogent report urged that the sole power of granting excuses for absences be vested in a new officer to be known as the secretary of the faculty. The title of secretary seemed innocuous enough, but the duties of the office called for a man with the highest qualities of tact and executive ability in what was perhaps the most delicate aspect of administrative work. In many colleges of the size and resources of Bowdoin, such an officer bore the title of dean, but Foster, a shrewd teacher of argumentation, did not wish to provoke the opposition of his more conservative colleagues by seeming to propose a startling innovation. He would settle now for the office of secretary. The deanship was an academic chick that could be hatched later. Those who disliked Foster's "Harvard manner" were sure that he hoped to be in the egg.

As Kenneth Sills listened to the discussion which followed the report, he may have been thankful that he would not have to face the responsibilities of the secretaryship. If, as it seemed likely, Professor Foster wished to gain administrative experience, he was welcome to the opportunity. The position certainly was not without pitfalls. Members of the Bowdoin faculty were proud of their prerogatives and sensitive to any invasion of their rights. The older professors who had become accustomed to a minimum of administrative interference or control would doubtless resent the placing of too much "power" in the hands of any one of their number, especially an "outsider." There were those, like the stalwart Professor Franklin Clement Robinson and the conservative Professor Wilmot Brookings Mitchell, who were eager to preserve the autonomy of the faculty in administrative matters. Their feelings, Casey was reasonably sure, would also be shared by such influential colleagues as Henry Leland Chapman, Charles Hutchins, and William Moody. Yet absences and excuses were bothersome enough to call for some sort of action which would provide for a uniform and efficient enforcement of the college rules. The whole matter, it was agreed, needed further consideration, and the meeting was adjourned to the following evening.

If left to his own devices, President Hyde would probably have appointed his energetic professor of argumentation to the new post of secretary. Prex admired Foster's rigorous training of Bowdoin's debating teams and had been favorably impressed by his keen analysis of the weaknesses inherent in the casual methods of maintaining student discipline. In the previous spring it was Foster who organized a board of proctors which had succeeded in keeping reasonable order in the dormitories. Prex, however, had learned quite early in his administration that in advocating

changes in "the Bowdoin way," one must never spell evolution
with an "r." Experience had taught him to proceed cautiously
by first taking counsel with his faculty, many of whose members
were older than he. He may have sensed that their choice for
the secretaryship was Professor Chapman, a conservator of custom, who respected Bowdoin's tradition of faculty autonomy.
It was Chapman who had served as acting head of the college in
1884 while the Boards were seeking a successor to President
Chamberlain. He was the favorite choice of many of the older
alumni. Now, at sixty-one, he was the oldest teacher in years of
service, revered by the graduates, and popular with the students.
His urbanity delighted the undergraduates, whose favorite phrase
of approbation was "as smooth as Harry Chap." Professor Chapman, however, refused to consider the secretaryship when he was
approached informally by his colleagues before the evening
meeting. The cogency of Foster's report, however, was sufficiently compelling to induce them to approve a resolution to fill
the position, "even though Professor Chapman decline."

The faculty next voted "to cast ballots for the office of secretary" and "to ballot on the names presented." The first results
were indecisive and scattering, but, much to his surprise, Kenneth Sills found that his name had been proposed, along with
those of Dr. Whittier, professor of hygiene, and Professors
Mitchell and Foster. Doc Whit, whose voracious appetite for
work was a campus legend, pleaded the pressure of his duties as
college physician and withdrew. His withdrawal was promptly
followed by that of Professor Mitchell, who rejoiced at the
prospect of the majority of the votes going to Sills, whose peculiar ability to deal with people without giving offense and whose
loyalty to "the Bowdoin way" were strongly in his favor. On
the third ballot, the faculty cast a plurality of votes for the
adjunct professor of Latin.

Allen Johnson, with whom the new secretary walked down
Federal Street after the meeting, was pleased at the outcome, but
Kenneth Sills showed no elation. He had heard too many stories

at Columbia about promising scholars lost in administrative quicksands. He feared that the imminent publication of Toynbee's book on Dante's influence on English poetry would mean scurrying about for a new topic for his dissertation. To be sure, Fletcher's suggestion that he write upon the concept of the goddess Fortuna was a promising one. That fickle lady, he reflected grimly, had certainly given a surprising turn to her fateful wheel at the faculty meeting. Later in the evening, when Charles Burnett called to offer his congratulations, he was brimming with encouragement. Had not Prex taken heavy administrative duties in full stride and found plenty of time for no end of books and articles? At Harvard, Burnett said cheerfully, Dean Briggs had made every undergraduate his friend without sacrificing either his teaching or his scholarship. Surely the new duties would not be onerous in a small college, and the Bowdoin of President Hyde deserved nothing less than a man's total commitment. Of this latter truth, Kenneth Sills needed no reminding. It was as a Bowdoin undergraduate that the shy Freshman from Portland first became aware of his genius for friendship. And it was at Bowdoin that he discovered the fierce joys of the intellectual life. Gratitude soon overcame his misgivings. Church and college, he believed, are institutions greater than men, and live long after those who founded them. For such institutions he would gladly efface himself in whatever tasks they imposed upon him. As for the secretaryship, he'd see what he would see. And he'd not have long to wait. His first class was scheduled for 8:30 the next morning.

The opening bell summoned Kenneth Sills to a college which had not grown appreciably since his own Senior year, when the enrollment had been 252. Now, five years later, the number had increased to 288. Small enough, Casey thought, to enable men to feel responsible to each other for the way they conduct their lives. In any event, the secretary of the faculty could see to it that they respected the rules and met their college engagements. He remembered the words of James Emery '05, who had been a member of his first Bowdoin class in English three years before. "You taught me," Emery had remarked at the end of the course, "to work under pressure and to meet deadlines." A respect for deadlines, Casey often thought, was not the least of the virtues of a responsible education.

The *Orient* failed to report the election of the secretary, but weatherwise undergraduates soon felt his presence. An item captioned "New Absence and Excuse rules," tucked away on the last page of the issue for October 12, informed the student body that the new officer was invested with the sole power of granting excuses for absences from chapel exercises and recitations. Unsatisfactory attendance, according to the new rules, might result in probation, ineligibility for all extracurricular activities, loss of aid from scholarship funds, and—if the unexcused absences continued—suspension from college. Campus wiseacres at first were disposed to find amusement in the behavior of the shy Latinist who, when confronted with glib excuses, did extraordinary things with his handkerchief, stirred uncomfortably in his chair, and blushed as though he were the defendant in the case. As one culprit recalled, "Casey put me at my ease by looking even more wretched than I felt. He acted as if I had summoned *him* instead of vice versa." The word soon got around the "Ends" and chapter houses that the secretary meant business. By October 10, at the end of his first fortnight in office, he had rounded up enough delinquents to assemble what the *Bugle* described as "a reception in the Faculty Room at which all classes were well represented." Congenital overcutters were surprised to learn that he could even anticipate at least one of their most serviceable excuses. A prominently displayed box in the *Orient* for November 23 not only warned absentees before and after the Thanksgiving recess that they would be placed on probation, but concluded with the knowledgeable admonition: "Students are particularly warned *not* to miss trains." Any lingering doubts about the secretary's efficiency were dispelled by the end of the fall term, when twenty-five men were put on probation. "Professor Sills gets out a black list," the *Orient* lamented on February 2, while the *Bugle* nominated the headline "Casey Gets On to His Job" as the understatement of the year.

Although he kept daily office hours in Massachusetts Hall with his usual conscientiousness, Kenneth Sills merely minored in administration. His major energies went into his three classes in Latin 1. He welcomed meeting each section four times a week, a schedule of twelve hours which allowed him two days for study and reading. The opportunity of teaching Freshmen had its special charm and challenge, and he occasionally interrupted a recitation to beg them to keep their youthful enthusiasm by disregarding the advice of Sophomore Sir Oracles who counseled that it was "bad form" to show a lively interest in one's studies. Perhaps it was a rankling memory of Behrens and Schwan which prompted him to tell his first class that every great language possesses a soul as well as an anatomy. Later in the year, when he detected signs of restiveness at too close attention to grammatical details, he delighted his students by quoting from memory Sir Hugh Evans' farcical efforts to pound Latin grammar into the head of Will Page in *The Merry Wives of Windsor*. Thomas Otis '10 remembered the surprise of the class when Casey suddenly threw professorial dignity to the winds by pacing the platform and intoning, "Nominativo, hig, hag, hog . . . Genitive—horum, harum, horum," and then, just as abruptly, returned to the day's lesson. On other occasions, especially during the soporific class hour directly after lunch, he enjoyed pummeling the Freshmen with questions about current politics or asking them to identify allusions to English and American literature. Always he encouraged questions from the floor, citing with a chortling approval the protest of an uncouth but right-minded lad in a backwoods academy who startled his teacher by asking, "If we ain't to ask questions, and ain't to say what we think, what are we goin' to do?"

A classmate in 1901, impressed by Casey's solid scholarship, noted in the *Bugle*, "He always puts the text before the horse." Now, as a teacher, Professor Sills carried his passion for textual accuracy into every classroom. Students whose temperamental knowledge of Latin syntax was exceeded only by the volubility of their attempts to translate were invariably given a come-uppance, but no member of Latin 1 was allowed to forget the influence of Latin authors on English letters. The faded pages of Kenneth Sills's grade books, which he kept for all his forty-six years of teaching, are filled with notes of assignments on such topics as "Horace and Herrick," "Horace and Milton's Lyrics," and "Horace and Longfellow." One astonished Freshman was asked to write a theme on Horace and Eugene Field; another, on Horace and Austin Dobson. When a perplexed student inquired respectfully, "Who, Sir, *is* Austin Dobson?" his teacher gravely pointed to the library, and then congratulated the youngster upon the enviable discovery he was on the verge of making.

Outside the classroom, the new secretary was also making discoveries of his own. One's alma mater, he soon learned, especially if it happens to be a small college, can be a jealous mistress. At Harvard and Columbia he had rarely encountered any of his students after class, but at Bowdoin they seemed to be, like campus acorns, forever underfoot, and their personal welfare became a responsibility. Although all but twenty-five belonged to the eight fraternities, he fretted about the small minority without a club house of their own, and promised to do something about it. Noting, with the solicitude of a former editor, that the *Quill* needed support, he promptly wrote a letter to the *Orient*, declaring that "The true interests of the College would suffer as much if the *Quill* were not kept up to a proper standard as it would if no one should take any interest in the football team." He enlisted the aid of Professor Woodruff in an effort to revive the classical club, which had grown moribund since his undergraduate days. The members of the faculty also had clubs in need of support. Early in October, Professor Frenchy Johnson organized a faculty club, with Kenneth Sills as its first secretary. Frenchy, indeed, was an ardent begetter of clubs of all sorts and sizes, and he counted upon his favorite student to join and present papers to all of them:

a club to read current biographies, a club to study Browning, a club to explore the lesser-known plays of Shakespeare. Most cherished of all associations were the informal evenings spent with Johnson reading Dante. "When you and I are together we can *see things*," the older man said. "The thoughts that return to invade us are all one, that infinity glowing in the midst of life." On such nights in the book-lined study of his teacher, Casey forgot the inevitable summons of the morrow's eight o'clock bell. Even the threat of Toynbee's book seemed but a horn from elfland faintly blowing.

The duties of the secretary of the faculty were modest enough at the beginning of the term, but as the weeks wore on he found that cuts accumulated as good resolutions decayed. A campus columnist depicted the chores of office with gay accuracy:

> When the irreligious shirk
>   Worship at the morning kirk,
> Casey does the dirty work—
>   Dogmatic Casey.

> When your second cousin's sick,
>   And you want to see her quick,
> (There's sure to be a kick)—
>   But go to Casey.

And to Casey they trooped, in such throngs that he was forced to extend his office hours in Massachusetts Hall. His colleagues were not long in discovering the convenience of being able to refer their "problem cases" to the new faculty officer. In March they asked him to consider "the question of what shall be done with students that are unable to continue in a required course," a tough nut which neither he nor his successors have ever been able to crack. It soon became evident that the secretary—a dean in all but name—was dealing with matters more complex than absences and excuses. His counsel was so often sought by Prex in delicate disciplinary cases that later in the winter, when he spoke to the alumni in Boston on "College Discipline and Disciplinarians," he talked like a veteran administrator. Meanwhile, into his lap were tumbled all the vexatious "incidents" resulting from hazing. A special committee named to study this problem, after endless discussions which got nowhere, unheroically recommended that "the Secretary be instructed to interview the Sophomore Class to the end of discontinuing hazing." Cases of academic delinquency ultimately also found their way to the secretary's office, where the only assistant was a part-time student clerk. The faculty enjoyed the luxury of voting austerely to drop delinquents from college with the comfortable proviso, "unless they can show to the Secretary satisfactory reasons why they should be retained." The wonder grew just how the faculty had managed to get along without so useful an officer.

Calls from the larger world outside the college gates added to the secretary's burdens. At Columbia, Kenneth Sills had admired President Butler's efforts to enlist the university in the service of New York City. He often quoted Joseph McKeen, Bowdoin's first president, who had declared in 1802 that "literary institutions are founded and endowed for the common good, and not for the private advantage of those who resort to them." In Maine the public good seemed to stand cap-in-hand at Kenneth Sills's front door every morning. Whether it was an invitation to address the Bath Men's Club on "The Beauties of the Bible," to read a paper on Dante to the Fraternity Club in Portland, to plead for the classics at the convention of the Maine Teachers Association, or to testify at a legislative hearing in Augusta on Maine's shameful neglect of the common schools, the secretary felt it his duty to accept. In February it appeared as though every Maine village wanted Professor Sills to offer appropriate remarks upon the centennial of the birth of Longfellow. Exhausted after two such addresses on the same day, he returned to 31 Federal Street only to find a letter from Fletcher cheerfully inquiring about the "famous progress" he had promised to make on his doctoral dissertation. Casey winced at the thought of replying. Just a month before, he felt the same sinking of heart when Dr.

John Cunliffe wrote to ask whether his Columbia thesis was ready for listing in the bibliography of the new *Cambridge History of English Literature*. The plausible explanation of being too busy with administrative details may have satisfied his friends, but it ceased to satisfy him.

There were, of course, compensations which could not be translated into bibliographical terms. His Latin courses were going well, and the college was moving smoothly. Even the strain of an indifferent football season, which included a humiliating defeat by Exeter Academy and a 72–0 slaughter by Cornell, had failed to mar the era of good feeling. The editors of the *Orient*, who were rarely averse to reminding the administration of its sins, went so far as to point with pride, in the January 18 issue, to "the harmony of interests between the students and the faculty." As Charles Burnett observed, the secretary had achieved a minor miracle: the students confessed that he was not "too hard," and the faculty agreed that he was not "too soft." Professional colleagues are rarely in the habit of praising each other's work—in or out of faculty meetings—yet a week before Commencement Kenneth Sills's colleagues, by a unanimous resolution, expressed "their confidence in the Secretary of the Faculty for the way in which he has carried on the duties of his office." Most heartening of all were the words of praise from Prex. "After trying, with the usual imperfect success," he wrote in the *President's Report* for 1906–7, "all the mechanical devices for securing attendance at recitations, this year the whole matter was placed in the hands of Professor Sills as Secretary of the Faculty. He has conducted this difficult and delicate task with such firmness and good nature as to give entire satisfaction to both Faculty and students."

Despite the president's commendation, Kenneth Sills looked ahead to the next year with mixed feelings. In June, with Professor Houghton's retirement, he would succeed to the Winkley professorship, but the chair entailed the responsibility of teaching all the advanced work as well as the Freshman course. The

Governing Boards were sympathetic, but pleaded poverty when he asked for an instructor. The joys of being both head and tail of a department were not unlimited. At least part of his summer in St. Andrews would have to be spent in planning a comprehensive program. He would salvage what was left of the precious weeks to plug along on his dissertation. As he packed his notes on medieval tragic stories, he reflected that a conscientious teacher might well devote all his time to his subject and justify his career without publishing a single monograph. In any event, Commencement would bring a temporary release. Perhaps in the bracing air of the Bay of Fundy he could summon up enough courage to resign the secretaryship. Even in a small college there were those who seemed to enjoy the power of making and enforcing rules. Why not let them have their fun? What gave him pause was a conviction that such persons belonged elsewhere. At Prex's Bowdoin the goals of education must never be confused with the machinery of administration.

The tumult and shouting of Commencement had barely ended before K. C. M. S. set out for New Brunswick. Back in St. Andrews, in his familiar haunts of sea and shore, he worried about the health of President Hyde, whose nervous exhaustion had prevented his giving the baccalaureate sermon and presiding at the graduation exercises. Professor Chapman, who conferred the degrees and substituted for the president at the alumni dinner, had reported that the Boards voted Prex a leave of absence to recover his health. Bowdoin's dynamic chief, Kenneth Sills noted sadly, did not always follow his own warning about the danger of making excessive demands on the nervous system. Whatever the demands of courses and thesis, Casey promised himself to get in as much golf and tennis as he possibly could.

He pitched into course-planning at once. On July 13 he reported to Henry Johnson, "I gathered the catalogues from ten or twelve of our leading institutions of light and have been studying the Latin situation from Dalhousie to Columbia." Since he saw no need of changing the format of the Freshman course, he followed Johnson's advice to concentrate on the second-year work. If he was to have any students in his advanced courses, he knew he would have to interest them first in their Sophomore year. "I have adopted your suggestion in part for a general outline of Latin literature," he wrote to his old teacher, "but I made the division by types and not chronologically." In the second term he promised to give them "a good clean taste of Tacitus, the greatest prose writer of them all." Half the summer had passed before he felt satisfied with the syllabus of his more advanced offerings in Latin tragedy and Lucretius. His projected course in Virgil pleased him most. "It is new," he told Johnson, "and not offered anywhere except at Harvard in alternate years."

The first tang of autumn was in the air by the time he had outlined his lectures on Virgil as an epic poet. On this subject he gratified his delight in comparative literature by discussing Virgil's influence on English poetry. "I have no idea how many will elect the advanced courses," he wrote Johnson. "Perhaps no one will, but my outline covers things pretty well for a beginner." He next turned to his dissertation notes, which needed, he was dismayed to discover, a good deal of "warming up" before he could feel sufficiently saturated in the material to make much progress. It was just when he was deep in a survey of the predecessors of the *Mirror for Magistrates* that the calendar summoned him to Brunswick. The threat of Toynbee seemed less menacing, however, now that he saw a promising subject in the influence of medieval tragic stories on the English chronicle plays. He was too candid, however, to count upon making much headway with the project during the college year. The secretaryship loomed up as a bigger bugaboo than Toynbee. Casey wrestled with the temptation to resign his office on the tiresome trip to Maine on the day coach of the Maine Central. He remembered Prex's favorite advice: "Murder your alternatives and no postmortems." He was still undecided when he reached Brunswick, but as he unpacked his notes he hesitated no longer. This year, he vowed, they would not gather dust on the shelf. At the first faculty meeting on September 25, he announced his resignation.

In the next few days, however, Kenneth Sills learned that at
Bowdoin even the simplest decisions are rarely simple. Complications set in at once when his colleagues named him to serve on a
special committee "to consider the question of the secretaryship."
By this time Casey should have known that the only sure way to
avoid a burdensome assignment is to fail to discharge it satisfactorily. Professors Woodruff and Burnett, who were also appointed to the committee, told him that he was "indispensable."
If he needed more assistance, they promised to find ways to get
it. Would an interoffice telephone be convenient? The annual
cost of $6 could be taken from the Contingent Fund. Had he
any need of a card-index file? A new one would be purchased
for $5 and the amount defrayed from the same source. Prex's
illness was also cited as a compelling reason to remain in office.
Professor Chapman, who was acting president during Hyde's
leave of absence, added his own pleas. The secretary, he said, was
needed desperately not only as the staff, but as the rod of the
administration. It was also intimated that Prex's recovery would
be speeded by the news that the secretaryship was to remain in
experienced hands. Commitment to an institution, Casey was fast
learning, is nothing less than total. Two days later, on September
30, when the faculty reconvened to hear the committee report,
Professor Chapman announced that "Professor Sills would be
willing to remain in office provided a second student assistant,
obtainable at a cost of $40, be furnished." Such a provision, the
faculty cheerfully consented to make, and it was duly voted to
draw upon "the Contingent Fund for the amount needed." Although the vote was not punctuated by a blare of bugles or a
roll of drums, Bowdoin never made a happier bargain.

The faculty adjourned under the impression it had retained
its secretary, but the significance of the action was not lost on
the sagacious William DeWitt Hyde, who heard the news while
convalescing in Switzerland. He foresaw that by spending $40
Bowdoin had gained a prospective dean and, perhaps, his suc-

cessor as president. Writing in elation from Oberhofen, Prex actually referred to the secretary as his "Dean," and promised to get him an assistant in classics. "I was most happy to know that everything is going so well with you and the College," he wrote on November 6. "I can see that with one hundred freshmen and the office of 'Dean' you have too much to do."

Formal appointment to the deanship was not to come until 1910, but the secretary's duties were sufficiently decanal to make the eventual title only a matter of time. As Professor Wilmot Mitchell remarked, "Bowdoin has always been reluctant to paste new labels on old bottles." The secretary himself preferred the older and more modest title, and when he was occasionally addressed as Dean Sills he blushed as though he were caught wearing borrowed finery. To many members of the college community he was to remain Mr. Sills or Professor Sills long after he was made dean of the faculty. To the undergraduates and alumni he was Casey everywhere except to his face. So universal was his nickname that at least one hapless Freshman, mistaking it for a surname, addressed him on the campus as Professor Casey—an incident to which the *Bugle* did full justice.

To those unaccustomed to reading between the lines of college calendars, one academic year may look pretty much like another. There was a hard core of truth in the lines attributed to Kenneth Sills in a burlesque, *The Servant Not in the House*, produced by the Brunswick Dramatic Society: "A faculty meeting is just like fishing. You sit for a long time with your rod out like a bump on a log. Very patiently, and once a year you get a great big bite." There were times when he was disposed to agree with a colleague's disparagement of administrative duties as nothing more than suckling fools and chronicling small beer. Being an academic man-of-all-work was not without its occupational hazards. When, as on April 12, 1908, a prankster rang the "rising bell" an hour ahead of schedule, and got most of the college—including the secretary—to morning prayers at the unseemly hour of 6:30 A.M., it was Casey's duty to identify the culprit.

And, when the faculty's sense of decorum was outraged by the hawking of an old-clothes man during religious services, it was the secretary who was requested to notify one Daniel Rosen, tailor, "that he must not use the chapel steps as a receiving and distributing point." Occasionally, of course, the chores were lightened by Gilbertian touches. When the clock on Searles struck the hour at unpredictable intervals, it is not difficult to imagine the relish with which the Latinist, who had never been inside the Science Building, warned the bell-ringer to observe Eastern Standard Time, "no matter what the *Science* Building clock *says*."

Kenneth Sills found his second year in office less burdensome than the first. The additional clerical help enabled him to reduce the unexcused absences to such a point that the *Orient*, affecting dismay, feared the secretary might utilize the new whistle on the steam plant, "an awful screecher," to rout the student body out of bed at 7:00 A.M. Doubtless President Hyde had been overly optimistic in boasting that disciplinary cases had virtually disappeared, but student conduct was improving. In 1908 the secretary encouraged the beginnings of student self-government with authority vested in a senior council, while he instituted a new system of fraternity advisers which, with the Board of Proctors, combined to make for a more responsible administration of student affairs.

With his office duties falling into a familiar pattern, he was able to devote more time to teaching. Although the appointment of John Bridgham as instructor in classics relieved K. C. M. S. of the burden of the Freshman course, he found that his advanced classes were requiring more and more of his energy. It seemed to make little difference, Kenneth Sills decided, whether one taught three courses or five courses: a teacher always finds the day too short. He was also pouring his energies into a struggle to maintain Bowdoin's traditional requirement of an advanced knowledge of Latin for the degree. Faced with an increasing number of applications from prospective students whose preparation in Latin was inadequate, the faculty voted in January, 1909, to make advanced Latin optional for admission, while retaining it as a prerequisite for the degree. It was clearly up to Casey to devise some way to cut one's Latin cake and have it, too.

Foreseeing the faculty's action as inevitable, the Winkley professor had instituted in the fall term of 1908 what the *Orient* described as "free tutoring to students deficient in Advanced Latin." This expedient was followed by requiring all Freshman without four years of Latin in high school to study advanced Latin in college, but without the privilege of counting it as a regular course for college credit. The *Orient* joined the *Quill* in an editorial endorsement of this compromise to save the requirement in Latin, asserting: "There are few who regret that Bowdoin still stands for the Classics." Strong support also came from outside the college, even though the added burden to the Freshman program had resulted in a smaller Freshman class in the fall of 1909. Noting that Bowdoin, alone among the leading small colleges, showed a decrease in the number of Freshmen, the *New York Herald* hailed Bowdoin's courage. "The action is consistent with a century's adherence to high standards," the *Herald* declared. "It has no reason to be ashamed of honorable shrinkage."

Meanwhile, Prex had not forgotten his promise to provide Kenneth Sills with a colleague to help maintain Bowdoin's classical scholarship. Acting upon his almost infallible discernment in the selection of young men for teaching positions, the president appointed as assistant professor of Latin a brilliant Rhodes Scholar, Paul Nixon, whose vigorous teaching at Princeton and Dartmouth had attracted his notice. "Paul Nixon is all right—a man of very abundant ability and attainment—with ideas about the teaching of Latin that will chime in perfectly with yours," Professor Elmer Merrill of the University of Chicago assured Casey in March, 1909. "He'll try to make the thing come alive. If you get him I shall congratulate both you and him." From the fall of 1909, when Professor Nixon, at the age of twenty-seven, began his duties, he fulfilled his early promise. With Casey and Nick sharing the instruction in Latin, the term "dead language" disappeared from the Bowdoin vocabulary; lively teaching of the classics became a Bowdoin tradition.

Despite his efforts to reserve an hour or two each day for work on his dissertation, Kenneth Sills found it difficult to find time for uninterrupted study. His friends at Columbia watched his growing responsibilities with pride and alarm. William Lawrence wrote to warn "the Head and Forepaw of the Dept. of Latin" that devotion, even to Bowdoin, had sensible limits: "I would call you a *fidus Achates* but fear you might think it bookish." Jefferson Fletcher, also writing from Morningside Heights, put his fears more bluntly. "It is first-rate to watch you moving upward and onward so rapidly," he wrote in February, 1909, "but partly for that reason I am getting anxious. In other words, how comes the thesis? I hope for our sakes here—and somewhat for your own sake—that you are not letting it go by default. That would be altogether too bad."

There were other reminders from the world of scholarship. Paul Elmer More, editor of *The Nation*, asked when he might expect to receive the Bowdoin professor's review of Toynbee, now that the two-volume *Dante in English Literature* was definitely scheduled for spring publication. Although Casey had given up the subject after it had been preempted by the English scholar, he was not unmindful of the irony of reviewing a book he had once eagerly looked forward to writing himself. It was just possible, of course, that the limitations of Toynbee's treatment might leave room for another volume on the same topic.

If he cherished such a hope, it was dashed by the scope and thoroughness of Toynbee's work—qualities which Kenneth Sills was quick to recognize. Although he wasted no time on futile regrets, he was touched by the sympathy of those who knew of his original ambition. "It is no comfort for you to know that it often happens," Professor Hutchins told him, "and I suppose there is no way of preventing it yet invented. Meantime you have your place and can try again." As always, Henry Johnson was at hand with encouragement. He was enthusiastic about the alternative topic suggested by Fletcher: a development of the ideas of *virtu* and *fortuna* in the Middle Ages and the Renaissance. Fletcher himself wrote to remind his former student that he had already collected considerable material on the subject in his researches on Dante and the *De casibus*. With so much spadework behind him, Fletcher continued cheerfully, the dissertation must be well under way. The letter had its intended effect, and K. C. M. S. promised to get to work with good heart as soon as he finished the review. The Columbia scholar, fearing his Bowdoin friend's discouragement, responded at once: "I was glad to hear that you have recovered your fortitude with respect to the thesis. Do!"

A scholar of Casey's temperament would have found it impossible to annihilate his rival in a slashing review even if the book had deserved it. Toynbee had disarmed his critics by soliciting their aid in supplying additions and corrections. To this invitation, Kenneth Sills complied with his usual modesty. His studies enabled him to add interesting references to Dante in Milton and Thomas Fuller; he noted the shortcomings in Toynbee's disappointing treatment of Dante's influence on the Scottish Chaucerians; and he answered, with a show of pride, the imputation of American ignorance of Italian litreature by citing, among other evidence, Longfellow's inaugural address at Bowdoin in 1830, and the translations of Thomas Parsons. These and other lapses, especially failures in critical insight, were gently mentioned, but always subordinated to a generous appreciation of Toynbee's "Herculean task," and tributes to his sane and thorough scholarship. The closely packed, four-column review was printed in *The Nation* for August 19, 1909. As he scanned the galley proof during his vacation in St. Andrews, Kenneth Sills felt as though he had reached the end of a chapter in his career.

Back at Bowdoin, however, a new chapter was beginning. After four years as secretary it had become apparent to all his colleagues that Casey had established himself as the good right arm of Hyde's administration. Although Prex had apparently recovered from his breakdown suffered in 1907, he gladly delegated many of his activities to his "dean." Certainly the lack of a dean's title had not prevented him from shouldering the responsibilities of this office. Since the inception of their organization in 1907, Casey had attended regularly the meetings of his fellow administrative officers of the New England colleges for the exchange of information on matters of common interest. In these sessions, as well as at those of the older Association of New England Colleges, he was frequently addressed as Dean Sills, an anomaly which Hyde resolved to correct, even at the expense of the secretary's aversion to academic titles. The president felt less compunction about asking the Winkley professor of Latin to devote more time to administration now that Professor Paul Nixon had shown his ability to maintain the high standards set in the department. The time had come, Prex believed, to consolidate the old offices of secretary and registrar in a single position. "Fortunately," Hyde told the Governing Boards in the spring of 1910, "Professor Sills has consented to undertake the entire work of this office with the title of Dean; and I recommend that at the coming Commencement this office be created, and that he be elected to it."

Several of the more conservative trustees and overseers demurred at the expense of setting apart a large portion of the time of a full professor for nonteaching duties, but the president cited the experience of other colleges, and emphasized the secretary's "exceptional tact and executive ability in the most delicate side of administrative work—that of keeping the students up to attendance on exercises and reasonable standards of attainment." The most persuasive argument of all, Prex reserved for the end, submitting "that the officer who comes into intimate contact with the students in their choice of studies and in the discussion of the success or failure of their work, must be a man who, in his own person, represents the highest attainments and ideals of scholarship and character." Upon this point there were no dissenting votes.

# 5

## DEAN OF BOWDOIN

### 1910-1917

Thus—to the surprise of virtually no one—it was to be Dean Sills. The Behrens-Schwan pillow-kicking associates sent their congratulations with a whoop of joy. Professor George Chase of Harvard, who was later to become a dean himself, scribbled a cryptic note from Cambridge: "Unser lieber Schwan has kicked another goal through the center of the transom!" William Lawrence took advantage of the occasion to warn against making the dean's reports too "bookish." And Prex, who was receiving felicitations on the twenty-fifth anniversary of his own election to office, warmed Casey's heart by saying gratefully, "May something equally welcome come to you after twenty-five years as Dean in 1935." The dean himself realized that his new title would mean few changes in his old duties, although he soon learned there were to be more of them both from within and without the college. As a mark of his new dignity, he was invited to share the president's office, a rectangular room with two doors on the ground floor of Massachusetts Hall, where he occupied one end of a long table. "It was like our barn at home," said a Freshman from rural Maine. "It had two holes, one for the cat and one for the kitten." Such an arrangement was not without inconveniences. When either the president or the dean had a private conference, it became necessary for the other to wait outside on a bench between the two doors. This regular bobbing in and out reminded one alumnus of a "weather cottage," with mechanical images emerging and retiring alternately through their respective doors to indicate changes in the barometric pressure. Generations of students remember the Bowdoin administration affectionately as Prex at one end of a table and Casey at the other.

Kenneth Sills filled his first dean's report with the requisite number of statistical charts, but he considered such compilations to be mere academic bookkeeping. "I feel very strongly," he told President Hyde, "that the most important part of the Dean's work consists of informal interviews with the undergraduates." In 1910–11 he had a twenty-minute conference with every student in college. Beginning with the Freshmen, he urged a selection of courses to connect the work of the first year with what follows. Sophomores and upperclassmen were advised to see their college course as a whole, rather than as a haphazard patchwork of subjects without unity or direction. There were occasions when the dean regretted the lack of regulations to compel students to choose an integrated program, but he preferred to have the compulsion come from within, motivated by the students' own intellectual objectives.

From his vantage point in the Dean's office, he saw clearly how these objectives were often thwarted by the blandishments of college life. In this war between campus and classroom, between college life and college work, the dean was firmly on the side of the classroom. Since the eight fraternities, comprising 290 of the 339 members of the student body, formed the basic social units, he resolved from the outset to regard them not as enemies but as allies. Noting that the scholastic average of their members was higher than that of nonfraternity men, he sought to strengthen rather than weaken the fraternities. He encouraged the feverish but short "fishing season" during the opening days of the fall term as a happy means whereby each chapter attained a Freshman delegation of varied talents and interests. In a series of fireside talks to each group, he urged the fraternities to take greater advantage of their opportunities for mutual stimulation and the reenforcement of their ideals. It was the nonfraternity men's lack of such opportunities to live and dine together, the dean believed, which was partly responsible for their comparatively unsatisfactory scholarship. His first year in office convinced him of the unfairness of depriving those without fraternity affiliations of the social amenities that a small residential college was so well suited to provide. Accordingly, he recommended in 1911 that the college buy and furnish "some sort of home for them until a nonfraternity organization can be set up." The wisdom of his proposal was realized a year later, with the opening of the new Bowdoin Club in a commodious house at 264 Maine Street, where the nonfraternity men enjoyed living quarters which rivaled those owned by Greek-letter societies. Their improved scholarship after having a house of their own deepened Casey's belief that whatever evils lurked in the fraternity system, the remedy was not in weakening the chapters, but in intensifying their influence for the common good.

Such influence, along with those of other campus activities, Dean Sills strove to direct toward the intellectual side of the college. He never wearied telling undergraduates who wished "to do something for the College" that they extend their ambition to include distinguished work in the classroom. In chapel talks and informal meetings, he constantly reminded them that the success of their alma mater rested on intellectual achievement, and that they, as well as their teachers, had a responsibility to contribute to her reputation. "If this is done," he remarked in his first dean's report, "the College cheerfully acquiesces in football games, dramatics, dances, and all the other multifarious activities of the undergraduate world. If it is not done, the College is sending out graduates without a sense of responsibility and without knowledge of doing a task honestly and on time." Dean Sills's concept of his office is nowhere better illustrated than in this first report. More than half of that twenty-four-page document was devoted to a list of "the first scholars" of every Bowdoin class from 1806. Such an emphasis upon scholarly achievement, he declared, was nothing more than a reassertion of the central purpose of the college.

His early years in the dean's office sometimes reminded Casey of students' excuses: one bore an astonishing resemblance to another. It came as a surprise to be told by Prex that his length of service as professor and administrator entitled him to a sabbatical in the spring term of 1913. The invitation came at a propitious time. The growing demands upon his energy were beginning to sap his strength. In addition to office and classroom duties, he had continued his studies of *virtu* and *fortuna*, written several monographs, and published *The First American and Other Poems*. The number and variety of his speaking engagements drew a taunt from William Lawrence, who feared that the long-awaited dissertation would evaporate in talk. "If you finally run out of topics," Lawrence wrote after marveling at the dean's schedule of public addresses, "why not speak on 'Virgil in Topsham,' or 'Virgil in South Dakota,' or 'Virgil in Hell—Personally Conducted?'" But the dean was reluctant to refuse invitations from the Maine schools where Latin was having a rough time.

He also found it impossible to decline Bishop Codman's pleas to serve his church. As an active vestryman at St. Paul's in Brunswick since 1907, he regularly represented his parish at diocesan meetings in Maine, and was elected a deputy to the general convention of the Protestant Episcopal Church in 1910, a position to which he was elected every three years for the remainder of his life. Local and state politics also claimed his attention. The Democratic Town Committee promptly named him to its membership in 1906, and made him a delegate to the biennial party conventions, as well as chairman of the local election committee in the presidential campaign of 1908. Four years later he was the moving spirit behind the Woodrow Wilson Club of Brunswick, which did yeoman service in getting out a record vote when the Democratic candidate carried the state. The *Orient*, recalling the usual fate of Democrats in Maine, observed with surprise: "This year the Dean apparently has more company." Citizens of Brunswick also turned to the dean for community service. In 1909 he began a decade of leadership of the local chapter of the American Red Cross, and in 1912 he promised to run for the school committee when he returned from his sabbatical leave. If there were times when he envied the scholarly seclusion enjoyed at Columbia by his friends Lawrence and Fletcher, such moments became less frequent. Although Fletcher continued to ask, "Aren't we *ever* to have that dissertation?" the dean could not promise in good faith to devote his entire leave of absence to grubbing in foreign libraries, just as later he would never insist upon his own faculty "justifying" their sabbaticals. Kenneth Sills was content to wait patiently for the kind of scholarly work not done under duress. The learned journals contained enough soggy evidence to convince him that "the other kind" was hardly worth the doing. Bowdoin teachers, he believed, had earned their sabbaticals, and could be trusted to spend their time wisely.

Added strains of an unexpected sort made the prospect of a restful change doubly welcome. Early in the winter of 1912, Kenneth Sills was compelled to consider the possibility of leaving Bowdoin for the presidency of Hobart College in Geneva, New York, where his father was the rector of Trinity Church. While visiting his parents, he had often discussed college problems with his father's Hobart friends, some of whom were members of the corporation. And now, during the Christmas recess, they sought his advice about selecting a successor to President Langdon Stewardson, who was to retire at the end of the academic year. It soon became apparent, however, that the dean himself was being favorably considered as a likely prospect. The possibility alarmed his Brunswick friends, to whom he had intimated the surprising turn of events. "You don't mean you are seriously considering Hobart, do you?" asked Professor Frederic Brown in a worried note sent hastily to Geneva on December 28. "The mere thought of Brunswick without you is a little too much. . . . Come back and tell us what you really mean." President Hyde answered his dean's plea for advice with characteristic forthrightness. "You would be just the man for them," he replied at once. "And though it would be the greatest loss that could come to Bowdoin, it would give you a great chance: you know just what to do and how to do it."

During the next ten days Casey wavered, hesitating to tell the Hobart corporation that he would accept the offer were it made to him formally. There is no doubt that he was strongly attracted by the presidency of a college situated near the home of his parents and bound by close ties to his Church. On their side, Hobart's trustees were impressed by the dean's career as scholar-administrator and influential Episcopalian layman. Prex wrote wistfully in his New Year's greeting: "I hope they will not be wise enough to call you, for you are *magna pars* of that superb condition in which Bowdoin is just now, and would be in danger of losing if she were to lose you. But as President Eliot says, 'the Colonel is for the regiment *not* the company,' and I might live long enough to find another Dean." Casey's fellow bachelors in The Octopus pretended to find comfort in the hope that their friend's seemingly inveterate celibacy would make him unavailable. One of them predicted, "They probably won't wait for *you* to qualify." Other Brunswick friends tried to conceal their fears by asking ironically, "For Heaven's sake, don't we kow-tow to you enough here, and tremblingly heed all your typewritten mandates? Are you still insatiate in your lust for power?" As always, Kenneth Sills maintained his sphinx-like inscrutability, but he assured Prex early in January that the Hobart corporation would undoubtedly choose a married man and a cleric. There was a collective sigh of relief when this prophecy was fulfilled by the election of the Reverend Lyman Powell. In the following autumn Dean Sills represented Bowdoin at President Powell's inauguration, but if the felicitations he carried with him to Geneva were tinged with the slightest trace of regret, Kenneth Sills's most intimate friends were never made aware of it.

Bowdoin cares and responsibilities faded with the New York skyline as the dean embarked on January 30, 1913, for his first sabbatical. Although he had crossed and recrossed the frontiers of the United States any number of times on his way to and from New Brunswick, this was to be Casey's first trip abroad. That he should have chosen to visit the Mediterranean countries was inevitable. His mind was crowded with images of the ancient world powers of Egypt, Syria, and Mesopotamia. His studies had taught him to regard the Mediterranean area as the cradle of art, architecture, and literature. Much Greek mythology, he knew, had its beginnings in the region which saw the commingling of the cultures of East and West. He was also drawn to the land of the ancient Semites, whose Koran and Bible had transformed the medieval and modern worlds. He looked forward to spending Holy Week in Jerusalem, and then traveling to Greece and Italy. As his boat entered the Mediterranean on February 8, he recalled the words Longfellow had jotted in his Journal in 1826: "My heart swelled with the deep emotion of the pilgrim, when he sees afar the spire which rises above the shrine of his devotion."

The scanty record of Kenneth Sills's *Wanderjahr* is to be found in a few hastily scrawled postcards to his parents and friends. Although he started to keep a conscientious diary, he was too busy soaking up lively impressions to spend precious time recording many of them. The entries in his daybook, begun on the floodtide of sensations evoked by his first glimpse of Gibraltar on February 8, soon dwindled to a trickle of picturesque details, and, by the end of the month, petered out altogether. It was enough merely to list the magic names of places: Algiers, Naples, Alexandria, Cairo, Luxor, Jaffa, Jerusalem, Athens, Rome, Florence.

As a youngster in Portland, Kenneth Sills had spent long afternoons at his father's desk in the house on State Street pasting colored pictures of faraway places in a scrapbook. Now they were before him in all their poignant reality. Gibraltar was made memorable by the sight of a small boy driving a flock of turkeys through a waterfront street at high noon, while a band in scarlet coats played military airs on the square. At Algiers, a tall sheik, "very dark and very proud in his desert dress," caught his eye. He ventured into the gambling rooms at Monaco where he noted "the harpy look of some old women" when a gamester "lost two 1000 franc notes in two minutes." Surprisingly cold weather and the choppy Bay of Naples did not deter him from visiting Capri and marveling at Vesuvius and Stromboli at sunset. He was fascinated by the Arabs unloading baggage from his ship in Alexandria, where he spent an afternoon admiring the Tanagra figurines in the Graeco-Roman Museum. During his three days in Cairo, he thought he could never tire of looking at the richness and grace of the slender minarets. The camel he engaged for a trip to the pyramids seemed, he thought, to regard foreigners too haughtily, but he rejoiced when a Mohammedan sipping Turkish coffee in an Arab cafe praised British rule because it ensured justice for the poor man. Anticipating his father's delight in the story, he reported the Egyptians' reverence for Kitchener, whose picture was salaamed when it appeared in a shop window. A morning in the Museum of Egyptian Antiquities led him to wonder "why the Egyptians are so far along when people in the Caribbean are still savages." Often, in the midst of his exciting pilgrimage, he missed the companionship of Henry Johnson. "What fun it will be to talk in your study next fall," he wrote to his old teacher. "I have so much to communicate to you bye and bye that I intend now to outline one or two impressions. Discussion will follow."

In the meantime, he would concentrate on impressions. Close reading could be postponed until he reached Rome and Florence. Had not Emerson said that books are for a scholar's idle times? After sixteen years of studying and teaching, Casey thought he might be permitted a holiday. Aboard the *Victoria*, which bore him up the muddy Nile, he tried to read for several hours daily in a pocket history of Egypt. He preferred, however, leaning on the ship's rail as it glided by the pyramids and ruined temples, whose silent commentary on the striving for superhuman greatness reminded him of Shelley's "Ozymandias" and Emerson's "The Sphinx." Perhaps he recalled the protests at his own sphinx-like behavior. Any dean, he may have thought, needs the inscrutable wisdom that refuses to reveal the answers, even in the unlikely event that he knows what they are.

Later he was to remember his trip up the Nile as a series of pictures rather than the names of pharaohs or the dates of dynasties. Now he felt humbled by his inability to read the histories carved on the temple walls and obelisks. At Abydos, which he reached in the late afternoon, he chatted with excavators about the colored reliefs in the chapels of the Sethos temple. Returning from an excursion to Sakkara under an impressive escort of mounted police, he was unable to determine whether the Step Pyramid, the oldest in Egypt, or an ancient dragoman asleep in the tomb of Ti was the more memorable. The dragoman, Casey noted in his journal, "looked like the mummy of Rameses."

Five days at Luxor and Aswan in the environs of ancient Thebes brought his Nile voyage to a climax. His first impression as he went ashore was of the sound of a muezzin calling to prayer from a minaret in the temple of Luxor "in a sad key but rather sweet." At Philae he was awed by the loveliness of the temple of Isis, where "the capital appeared to float in the water." Armed with his Baedeker, he tried to discern some order amidst the crushing heaviness of the gigantic stone columns, but he soon discarded the guidebook labels for his own impressions. The temple of Ammun appeared too overpowering to be considered beautiful at first. He was confused but awed by the labyrinth of ruined halls in the principal temple of Amon-Re in Karnak, preferring the avenues of smooth columns built by Amenophis III in Luxor. In the very heart of Egyptian antiquity, Casey reflected on the way the temples of ancient deities had been adapted by Romans, Christians, and Mohammedans. Before leaving Aswan, he attempted to impose a pattern on the profusion of images thronging his mind by writing a poem on the temple of Luxor. The penciled lines, smudged by erasures and the marks of indecision between alternative words and phrases, remain unfinished:

> O'er pillars vast the sparrows endless fly
>   And Arab children in the ruins play;
>   The blue Egyptian sky looks down each day
> Serene, untroubled by the men that ply
>   Their tiny, idle trade on columns high
>   On statues still
>
> No great processions wind their stately course
>   No priests to Annuch great libations pour;
>   On Rameses the Great the people gaze—
> Still is their grandeur in the columns—
>   Still is their beauty
>   And still the temple worships and still prays.

There were stops at Dendera, Abydos, and Assuit on the return downstream. Casey struck up an acquaintance on the *Victoria* with Abel Chapman, the English naturalist, who was on his way back from Uganda, full of stories about the cannibalism of the native workers on the new English railway. With his new friend he went ashore for a farewell view of the chapels at Abydos, admiring the blueness of the sky seen through the roof, and pausing to watch several Nubian policemen mounted on Arabian horses. At Beni Hassa, the dean arose before 7:00 A.M. to get an early morning view of the rock tombs with their square chambers, but found more interest in a band of little girls clad in pink robes, "one with a Medusa-like hairdress," who stood on the bank near the steamer. Chapman proved to be a lively conversationalist, and Casey was surprised at how quickly the boat reached Cairo, where he set out the next day for Palestine by way of Port Said and Jaffa.

His arrival at Jaffa on Tuesday, March 17, enabled him to achieve one of the goals of his sabbatical, to spend Easter in Jerusalem. As he landed at the ancient port of Jaffa, which would take him to Jerusalem by the nearest way, he felt as though he had been there before. Unlike so many modern pilgrims who have reported their disappointment upon first seeing the places so full of hallowed associations, Kenneth Sills suffered no depression of spirit. The son and grandson of clergymen, he had from earliest childhood heard the sacred names so often from beloved lips that they had become part of his consciousness. He came upon the Holy Land as one encounters a familiar book remembered for its pictures. For him there was no surprise that the "black tents of Kedar" are still pitched upon the northern slope of Mount Carmel. There is nothing more characteristic of the mind and heart of Kenneth Sills than his refusal to confide to his notebook any intimate impressions of the places once trod by the Saviour. There is no record of what he thought as he reached the hill town of Nazareth after climbing up from Haifa and crossing the river Kishon. Only a few hurriedly written dates and place names in his pocket calendar indicate that he saw the Mount of Beatitudes or the Lake of Galilee, visited the site of Capernaum, crossed the plain of Sharon, entered the walled city of Bethlehem, journeyed through the Jordan valley, and worshipped on Easter Day in Jerusalem. He needed no physical witnesses of the glory of the Lord, just as he apparently never had to wrestle with the stubborn doubts which often assailed many of his friends. Serene in his personal faith, he walked the soft, sandy soil of Palestine as he was later to move through life, without seeking proof that his Lord and Master once lived upon the earth.

Back in Alexandria on March 26, he sailed the same day for Athens, noting ruefully that two months of his half-year leave of absence had passed all too quickly, but his heart was lifted when he thought of Greece and Italy. There he knew the past centuries would whisper their enchantments in languages he could understand. His ship reached Athens at noon on the 28th, and he settled immediately at the Hotel Minerva for a two-week stay. The Minerva, he wrote Henry Johnson several days later, was comfortable, the prices moderate, and the food excellent. Although he found modern Athens attractive and its people friendly to Americans, he plunged at once into a study of the monuments and museums. "Time here goes by like the wind," he reported to Johnson, "and I am having my eyes opened every day." The figure of the Nike stooping to tie her sandal at the Acropolis Museum and the Tomb of Hegeso in the old cemetery compelled him to return again and again. "I have been to the National Museum three times," he told Johnson on April 2, "and have spent the time in three rooms. I know so little about art that I have to go very slowly, but there may be worse ways to begin." Feeling the pull of the treasures of the past, he lamented his lack of time for systematic study, and vowed to do more work with the neglected classical collections in the Walker Art Building when he got back to Brunswick. In Athens nothing seemed important but humane scholarship in antiquity. Yet the thought of his unfinished doctoral thesis reminded him how the routine of the dean's office had steadily encroached on his leisure hours. He may have reflected how the cumulative pressure of petty details can impose a tyranny more absolute than that of Babylon or Rome.

The traveler had predicted to Henry Johnson early in April that it would be hard to leave Athens, a reluctance he confirmed by stretching his planned two weeks into three. He felt himself being drawn almost equally to the mythical and historical past. The Greeks, he knew, had not only given the world its most enduring myths but had become mythical themselves. Homer and Herodotus now filled his reading hours, and he abandoned for a time his daily custom of doing a canto of the *Divina Commedia*. Never entirely happy when separated from his books, he could now understand what had prompted Emerson to write home impatiently for his history and his Plutarch, his maps and gazetteers. As the dean moved about the monuments of the ancient city, he tried to imagine the daily life of the Athenians in the middle of the fourth century, before decadence set in after the triumph of Macedon. Impressed by many evidences of the astonishing development of competitive athletics in Greece, he may have wondered whether it brought the same kind of problems which followed a disastrous football season in Brunswick.

When Kenneth Sills finally sailed for Naples he was in despair at leaving behind so much undone, unseen, and unrealized. To know what the Greeks really were after centuries of worship had transfigured their achievements was the enterprise of a lifetime rather than the quest of a scholar's holiday. His studies in the Italian Renaissance had taught him how much the glory of Rome was indebted to Hellenism, and he was teased out of thought by speculating on those unique qualities of the Hellenic spirit which had left the entire world as its beneficiary.

Although Casey's thoughts were of hurrying on to Rome when his vessel entered the Bay of Naples, he lingered over the antique sculpture in the Museo Nazionale, and returned the next day to see the rich collections of the art of southern Italy. Excursions to Pompeii and Herculaneum, where he contrasted the impressive silence with the brash gaiety of the Neapolitan streets, kept him for another two days before he took the *rapido* for Rome. His brief stay, however, was not without an incident which set Brunswick tongues wagging. In a facetious postcard message to Professor Frederic Brown, he described his purchase of a lottery ticket from "a young countess" at a street bazaar. "How could I refuse a request made so charmingly?" the dean asked. "She took my money and my heart. Even the lovely Venetian ladies will not make me unfaithful to my unknown Neapolitan." Brown was mischievous enough to report "the romance" at a faculty tea party and to enjoy the subsequent fluttering in Brunswick's dovecotes.

Of all the cities on Kenneth Sills's itinerary, Rome was destined to make the most abiding impression. Even the Florence of his beloved Dante could not match Rome's appeal to his senses and his soul. "Florence has never been the center of the world," he wrote Brown. "There is no Forum, no Saint Peter's, no Coliseum, no garden like the Pincio, no catacombs." From his *pensione* near the Spanish Steps, he set out each morning to walk through the city of the centuries where, during the course of a short stroll, he was delighted to observe classical antiquity rubbing elbows with modernity, and the Middle Ages jostling the Renaissance in exquisite harmony. He climbed Monte Gianicolo to gain an impression of the ancient city's topography and almost stumbled upon Tasso's tomb in the church of Sant' Onofrio. Haunted by his memory of Gibbon's account of the conception of his great history as the author sat musing amid the ruins of the Capitol while barefooted friars sang vespers in the Temple of Jupiter, the dean found what he believed to be the very place.

Each day the splendors of the city seemed to happen to him all over again. With a strong feeling of association, he savored the sensation of being where great men had lived. Much to his surprise, *The Marble Faun* proved to be a charming guidebook, and the traveler added Hawthorne to Browning and Ruskin as his favorite literary interpreters of the Roman scene. Like Hawthorne, Kenneth Sills was too ardent a Protestant to succumb unreservedly to the religious pomp of Saint Peter's, but he fell in love with many of the smaller churches, and was profoundly moved by the beauty of their religious services. Apparently believing that when in Rome one should behave as the Romans do, he joined other pilgrims to the Chapel of Saint Lawrence, ascending the Scala Santa on his knees. After seeing so many sublime religious spectacles, he found spiritual refreshment by wandering alone in the quiet of the Protestant cemetery near the Porto San Paolo, paying homage at Keats's tomb and Shelley's urn. Where one might read the past in columns, towers, and temples, books seemed to be almost an impertinence, but he adhered to his plan of working for two weeks in the Vatican library, adding to his bibliography of references to *virtu* and *fortuna*, and gathering notes for his projected article on universal peace in Virgil and Dante. He told Henry Johnson of returning again and again to contemplate the original manuscript of Petrarch's sonnets and the copy of the *Divina Commedia* in the handwriting of Boccaccio.

There were times when the dean wished he might have devoted

his entire sabbatical to Rome. He alternated excursions to the Campagna, Ostia Antica, Tivoli, and Hadrian's Villa with return visits to favorite places in the city, especially the Pantheon and Castel Sant' Angelo, whose winding ramps never failed, for some reason, to evoke memories of Scott's fiction. Warned of the exigencies of the calendar by the coming of warm weather, he resolved to tear himself away. Not, however, without walking, on his last evening in the city, to the terrace of the Piazzale del Pincio for a lingering look. As he descended the Scalinata di Trinità dei Monti he was almost ready to believe that one might live contentedly in Rome for life.

Florence lay ahead. "For many years," he wrote Henry Johnson, "I have had the strongest desire to visit Florence." As soon as he was settled at Hotel Paoli, he hastened to describe his impressions to the man to whom he owed his love of Dante. "It is a lovely and fascinating city," he wrote on June 17, "inspiring art, poetry, and romanticism. Every part recalls Dante to me." He set out promptly to visit each of the homes and palaces that have historical connections with the *Divina Commedia*, noting that Florentines "are very proud of their city's great past though uneasy about the future." To a greater degree than in Rome, the traveler became engrossed with the present life of the inhabitants. "I don't believe," he wrote, "that humanity is much changed since Dante's time. Perhaps today in the streets of Florence a young Dante walks and dreams. Who can say? Perhaps another Beatrice 'dressed in the color of bright flame' inspires another poet to say of her 'what has never been said before of woman.' And perhaps there are girls who are beautiful and bold and tear the heart from peace and kindness. The years pass, the cities change, but men and women always remain men and women."

In his daily excursions to all parts of the city, he was occasionally depressed by commercialism and vulgarity. He bridled at signs in the churches imploring worshippers "Out of respect for the House of God, please don't spit on the floor," and he was irked by the copyists in the Pitti and Uffizi galleries. "If all the men and women copying paintings could be decapitated and all the guides clapped in jail for life," he wrote Frederic Brown, "there would perhaps be more peace and joy for the poor visitors." Although he was shocked by the sordidness of the crimes reported in gory detail by the *Corriere della Sera,* he rejoiced in the friendliness and decency of the people. He was especially impressed, he wrote Henry Johnson, by the gentlemanliness of "the waiters, coachmen, and the little people. . . . Italians of this class could give many lessons in courtesy and joy and other homely virtues. Good men of every country are good." What is needed, he told Johnson, "is a poet who will interpret today's vibrant and full life, but a life so similar to the life of all past times." On the whole, contemporary Italian literature disappointed him, and he could allow D'Annunzio only "a considerable talent." After seeing a production of *Pisanella,* he concluded that "A writer who ends a tragedy with the death of the heroine suffocated by roses shows not a rebirth of poetry but decadence." The goodness of "the little people," however, continued to buoy his spirits. "I don't believe for a minute," he wrote, "that all is commercial and materialistic."

He regretted leaving Italy just as he was beginning to speak the language confidently and to feel thoroughly at home. To Frederic Brown, who was planning to come to Florence for his sabbatical the following year, Casey confessed his envy. "I would give so much to be staying here in Florence next winter," he wrote. "When you stroll along the Arno and talk with the pleasant Florentines and drink Chianti, I shall be locked in my office talking with lazy American students and drinking plain water." As the weeks passed with pleasant trips to Fiesole, San Miniato, Lucca, and Pisa, he sensed that Rome and Florence would remain the spiritual climax of his sabbatical. Like so many travelers, he was dazzled by Venice, finding it perhaps the only city in the world which fully lived up to the pictures of it. Neither Venice, nor the chateaux country in France, nor even his week in London before sailing for home gave him the profound sense of having his whole being transformed by what he saw there. His mind was still filled with images of Roman fountains, the Coliseum, and the Arch of Constantine when he reached New York late in August. He vowed that if ever he were to have the authority to do so he would make sabbaticals mandatory for all members of the Bowdoin faculty.

Although Professor James McConaughy had served as acting dean to everybody's satisfaction during the spring semester of 1913, the warmth of President Hyde's greeting left Casey with no doubts that Prex was happy to have him back. After a few days he was surprised how easily he slipped into the familiar routine at the other end of the long table in Massachusetts Hall. McConaughy had left no backlog of correspondence to be answered, and had apparently conducted the office with admirable smoothness. Deans, K. C. M. S. decided, whatever else might be said about them, are entirely expendable. In any event, he later enjoyed reminding colleagues absent on leave that "on the whole and in the main" Bowdoin seemed to be getting on very well without them.

A glance at the yearbook of the preceding spring reminded the dean of an evil of undergraduate life needing immediate attention. He noted that a gifted Junior, a member of Phi Beta Kappa, had edited the *Orient*, managed the football team, presided over the Student Council and Dramatic Society, and participated in several intercollegiate debates. As a means of discouraging such overloading, he volunteered to head a committee of faculty and student leaders to advise undergraduates about the folly of "majoring" in extracurricular activities. Casey insisted that the committee's powers be purely advisory, but he warned in a chapel talk that it was only a misguided sense of loyalty to class or fraternity which enjoined a service to activities that interfered with Bowdoin's main business as an institution of learning. In his report for 1913–14, he wrote, "Bowdoin is apparently solving this difficulty along lines that have not been followed by other colleges." He knew the solution could be only a partial one, but friendly counsel was to be preferred to hard-and-fast rules.

Sweet reasonableness continued to be the dean's favorite policy in handling the many problems which found their way to his office. "We don't know how he managed to do it," a campus wit recalled, "but the angry young men who entered *rampant,* always emerged *couchant.*" When in November, 1913, the *Orient* criticized the faculty for ruining an athletic rally by perversely scheduling a lecture by Alfred Noyes on the eve of the "big game" with the University of Maine, the dean disarmed a disgruntled delegation by talking about Longfellow and Hawthorne. "Some happy, far-off day, when the literary interests of the College will seem of real importance to the undergraduate body," he said hopefully, "and when students recall their literary heritage, they will not feel aggrieved if by some accident a reading by a distinguished foreign poet is scheduled before a football game." Since there was no ready answer to so gentle a remonstrance, Casey dismissed his subdued critics by urging greater support for the *Quill,* which was then languishing for contributors.

Indeed it proved difficult for undergraduates to remain indignant in the dean's benign presence. For one thing, he invariably permitted them to present the full force of their complaints while he remained imperturbably silent. More often than not, the longer they talked, the more absurd their grievances began to appear, especially to those who voiced them. In an exceedingly wet December in 1915, Casey listened patiently to those who complained that "merely because George Rogers Clark and his backwoodsmen waded through icy waters up to their middles is no proof that wet leather is conducive to regular attendance at chapel." Such a view, the Dean replied, was "interesting," but there was "much to be said on the other side," and he pointed to the rubber boots he was wearing. Perhaps, he conceded, something might be done about boardwalks on the campus, but was it not a shame to witness the decline of the pioneer spirit?

After a long morning in his office followed by an afternoon faculty meeting, Casey might have been justified in thinking that the time not spent in defending the faculty to the students was used in defending the students to the faculty. There were, of

course, more challenging duties. In the days before the advent of
guidance and placement officers, the dean shouldered many of
their responsibilities. "In talking over the plans of students," he
wrote in 1914, "it is surprising to find how very few of them have
any idea of what their life work will be." Although this was to be
expected in a college of liberal arts devoted to general rather than
technical training, Dean Sills regretted that so little was being
done to advise students about the choice of their future careers.
In 1915 he began the practice of arranging interviews between
Seniors and prospective employers, and several years later he invited successful alumni to return to the campus to discuss the
opportunities in the various professions and business enterprises.
Useful as these services proved to be, Casey saw a possibility of
the college "doing too much" in this direction, maintaining
stoutly that undergraduate initiative and old-fashioned New England "gumption" were more valuable than a director of placement—a conviction which he was compelled to abandon thirty
years later amid the dislocations of the Second World War in
1944.

The dean's bulging portfolio seemed to expand each year with
the addition of new responsibilities. There was always the tortuous problem of selecting a Freshman class from the candidates
applying for admission, and, since a college dies first at its roots,
the no less vital task of encouraging the most likely lads to consider Bowdoin's advantages. K. C. M. S. soon became a familiar
figure to conductors on the Maine Central as he traveled up and
down the state in quest of promising boys. Almost always he was
able to combine his visits to the schools with talks to the student
body on the values of a liberal education. On such occasions, he
rarely failed to plead for the study of Greek and Latin in secondary school. His efforts were rewarded by the steady improvement
in the quality of candidates for admission. Professor Roscoe Ham
spoke for all his colleagues in 1916 after a bumper crop of 142
new men had done especially well in the fall term. "I have no

doubt," he wrote, "that the large freshman class of good quality was due in large part to your active canvass."

Early in his career the dean saw the importance of enlisting the cooperation of Bowdoin alumni in attracting able Freshmen. In 1913 he had served as secretary of a committee to consider the desirability of forming an alumni council, and, two years later, following the creation of such a council, became an active member. Alarmed at the steady rise in the percentage of students from outside Maine, he told the Portland alumni in February, 1914, "the fact that nearly half of the students at Bowdoin come from outside Maine reflects to a certain extent on the alumni of the State." Observing that the number of Maine schools represented at Bowdoin had dropped from thirty-eight in 1913–14 to thirty-four in the following year, he submitted in his annual report for 1915 that "In many of the small high schools of the State there are many boys of promise; it is a pity that Bowdoin does not draw more successfully from this constituency." He urged his fellow members of the alumni council not to neglect the source of so much of Bowdoin's strength.

In face of increasing competition for the most desirable candidates for admission, Kenneth Sills insisted upon high standards of mind and character. After reading hundreds of recommendations in 1915, he deplored both the wide charity of schoolmasters in testifying to the character of candidates as well as the eager carelessness of colleges in accepting them. "Both school and college to a certain extent neglect character," he reported. "It would be perfectly feasible to require a more definite statement in regard to the attainments and moral stamina of students entering." The toughness of moral fiber which he sometimes thought of as the peculiar heritage of boys from rural Maine seemed to him to be threatened by the growing practice of colleges to award prematriculation scholarships. Bowdoin's policy of promising no financial aid in advance to any individual was dictated in part by a lack of sufficient funds. It also reflected what the dean felt was an old-fashioned virtue. He believed that students should be made to realize they must earn the aid they receive by success in their first term of college work. Such a reward for work done would be, he was convinced, a wholesome tonic to those who deserve it. "It is not well for recipients of any form of beneficiary aid," he declared, "to be without such a tonic." He foresaw accurately, as early as 1913, the dangers inherent in dangling fat scholarships before the eyes of immature youngsters of high school age. "Furthermore," he wrote in his annual report, "if we were to promise aid in advance to some, then others who had not exacted such a promise in advance would be shut out of aid which they might deserve much more than the ones to whom it had been promised in advance."

Each year Casey knew that many Freshmen came to Brunswick with only their summer savings in their pockets, yet were able, with the help of scholarships granted after a successful first term, to complete their college course. So firm was his conviction of the need for students to prove their right to grants-in-aid by the quality of their performance after they reached college that he never became fully reconciled to prematriculation scholarships even long after they had become a common practice. If continuing the Bowdoin policy would mean fewer students, the dean was ready to take the risk. "If we were to drop both our educational standard and our requirement of proved proficiency for pecuniary aid," he said in June, 1913, "in four years our numbers would rise to at least five hundred." It was only in the grim days of the Great Depression in the early 1930s that he was persuaded, and then with grave misgivings, to consent to a change in Bowdoin's policy.

Although his undergraduate days were spent in Appleton Hall, a dormitory built in 1843, which encouraged plain living if not high thinking, Casey saw no special virtue in what one alumnus recalled as "open plumbing openly arrived at." As an admissions officer without benefit of title, the dean began to hear more than occasional complaints from parents of prospective students about the lack of modern living quarters. "Our present halls are clean and decent," he told President Hyde, "but we have no modern dormitory." In his dean's report for 1915–16, he urged that such a building be erected, not only to keep pace with the increasing amenities of college life, but as a means of enabling more students to live on the campus. He was also disturbed by the mounting number of Freshmen living in fraternity houses. In 1915 he called attention to the fact "that twenty-one freshmen who are now in fraternity houses ought to be in dormitories where they can get a proper introduction to college life as a whole." In the following autumn he persuaded the faculty to take steps to withdraw all first-year men from the chapter houses, except for their meals. He also recommended that more Seniors be urged to return to the dormitories for their last year. "At present fifty-one seniors live in chapter houses, and seventeen in dormitories," he wrote in the alumni issue of the *Orient* for January, 1916. Asserting that these figures should be reversed, the dean went on to say, "If a man rooms on the campus his first and last years, and spends his sophomore and junior years in a chapter house, he will get all the luxury he should have."

Now that the size of the student body had reached 400, with 80 men compelled to seek rooms in private homes, Casey feared the loss of the unique advantages of a residential college. To preserve these values, he envisioned a new hall next to Appleton, an addition which would not only complete the symmetry of the quadrangle, but—of far more importance—would unify the scattered student body. "I should not wish to see the new dormitory a senior house or a freshman house," he concluded, "but many freshmen and some seniors should live there." When a year later, in 1917, alumni and friends presented the college with Hyde Hall, the hopes of the dean were realized. By assigning a few rooms on each floor to Seniors, he enabled them to make a more effective contribution to student life by bringing them into closer contact with Freshmen to whom they might pass on Bowdoin's traditions and ideals. Casey rejoiced at the gift but restrained his enthusiasm, a lesson he had learned in 1906 when he heard Prex tell the Portland alumni, "At last Bowdoin has all it wants financially." The dean knew all too well that the next need was for a student union, where the democratic social life of the whole college could be centered.

Perhaps the peskiest of all the problems with which he had to contend were those arising from intercollegiate athletics. As an undergraduate he remembered Professor Hutchins' ominous prediction the first time admission was charged for a game on the Delta. While the hat was being passed, Hutch shrugged his shoulders and remarked, "Humph! This is the beginning of trouble." For a decade after the advent of professional coaching in 1892, a succession of outsiders from other colleges and athletic clubs handled Bowdoin's teams. The turnover was so rapid that no one system of play had time to establish itself. Following a languid season in 1901 when Bowdoin was beaten by every Maine rival, the *Orient* protested, "One poor coach is better than ten good ones at different times. What would we think of a course in language in which the instructors were changed three or four times?" For a year the college tried alumni coaches, but shortly after Casey's return to the faculty in 1906 and throughout his deanship there was a return to professionals from outside the state. When a steady parade of these visitors produced little improvement, a popular coach from a Maine high school was appointed, but with disappointing results. There was another "crisis" in 1914, after the Bowdoin eleven failed to score against Bates, Colby, and Maine while the opponents piled up more than 100 points. In November, thirty Bowdoin alumni in Philadelphia sent a joint letter to the *Orient* deploring what they described as "the most disastrous season in the athletic history of the College." Their suggested remedy was more money for better coaches.

As criticism continued to mount, the dean was compelled to use all of his not inconsiderable powers of appeasement. In June, 1915, however, he took to the offensive against unreasonable criticism of the administration by remarking in his annual report:

"The College has reason to be grateful to those who have been here as coaches during the past three or four years. I have never been asked by a coach to favor an athlete who is down in his studies." He reminded the most vociferous of the critics that "Those of the alumni who are most interested in athletics could learn much about the proper attitude toward athletics from those who have been here as professional coaches." Casey had braved fire from the front lines during his circuit of alumni dinners, where he discovered that no topic could arouse the emotions more quickly than that of athletics. He read a lecture on a proper sense of values to the Boston alumni in April, just after they had appointed "A Committee of Twelve to consider the athletic situation." Manfully facing a critical audience, he declared flatly, "The great trouble with athletics is not that they require too much time from the students. . . . Such troubles can be easily regulated. But athletics so fill the horizon of the typical under-graduate and often of the young graduate that other things are neglected, or not regarded as of much importance." The dean went on to remind his listeners of their own responsibilities. "In the last eighteen months," he continued, "many a student has read the athletic columns of our newspapers with more attention and zeal than he has read about the war. He is, to be sure, no worse than many of his elders. But we have a right to expect an intelligent interest on the part of undergraduates in state, na-tional, and international affairs. One reason why we do not al-ways get such an interest is organized athletics. Oxford used to be called the home of lost causes. Our campus is too often merely the home of lost games."

Kenneth Sills was plainly hurt by the furor caused by football defeats when the fate of European civilization seemed to hang in precarious balance. He regarded athletics, even in the best of times, as a college sideshow. It seemed unthinkable that now there were those who wanted to make it the main performance. On January 15, 1915, he was troubled when, on a petition by the Athletic Council, the faculty voted to approve alumni contributions to the financial support of coaches. Yet there seemed to be no other solution. In his report for 1914–15, he assured the graduates that so long as Bowdoin had organized athletics, nobody wished to have them conducted stupidly or to fail to have them inculcate the best sportsmanship. He reminded them, however, that "The Faculty realizes athletic success or failure has very little to do permanently with the life of the College." He also insisted that "studies must come first . . . that the football team must play half its games at home . . . and no upperclassman may compete if he is below standing in two studies, and no freshman if he is below in one subject." The dean returned to the attack a year later in his annual report. In praising the successful careers of the Bowdoin members of Phi Beta Kappa, he added the barbed suggestion that their records "should at least give food for thought to those gallant souls who believe it is right for all college men to have red blood in their veins but who do not seem to care whether it is in the legs or in the head." In another year America's entrance into the war postponed but hardly solved the athletic problem. The dean, however, breathed more easily when Bowdoin agreed with its Maine football rivals not to employ a regular coach for the duration.

With his mind resting on the state of Europe, the dean foresaw that the United States could not long remain a spectator of the conflict. "Outwardly every thing seems to be the same here," he wrote Henry Johnson from St. Andrews in July, 1915. "But in reality the war is leaving its marks. A number of lads who used to make the summer merry are at the front, and nearly forty boys have gone from the village. We seem in Brunswick to be far removed from the horror of it all." He told Johnson he had looked forward to a leisurely summer at Ifield Cottage where "Theocritus is to be my companion in the Greek and Lucretius in the Latin." These friends, however, were often pushed aside by the news from the Front and the American attitude to Germany. "Was there ever a sillier, a more puerile state document than the latest note from Germany?" he asked Henry Johnson. "Power to Wilson's elbow when he replies, say I."

Upon his return for the opening of the college, he was dismayed by the undergraduates' apathy to current events. His class in Latin I was surprised when he subjected them to a quiz testing their knowledge of names and places prominent in the war news. The sorry results—an average of 55 percent—were promptly printed in the *Orient*, picked up by the Associated Press, and widely commented upon. "More notoriety for Bowdoin," sighed the *Orient*, but its editor asked, "Where there is so much ignorance is not there something the matter somewhere?" When the undergraduate protests took the usual form of a demand for a course in current events, the dean replied that college men might be reasonably expected to read for themselves.

Meanwhile, on a motion by the dean, the faculty considered the question of academic credit for attendance at summer camp at Plattsburg. Although Casey assured the alumni "there is no thought of militarism or of compulsory service at Bowdoin," he ventured the hope that "students who have the time and means will perform a patriotic service by attending military camps at Plattsburg and elsewhere, and that they should be given credit for their degree for such work." During the spring, Kenneth Sills took to the road to explain the obligation of the college. "One thing is clear," he told the Boston alumni on April 25, 1916, "our students must be trained in patriotism and in good citizenship, as in other things; and they must be taught that they are not to look forward so much to being cared for by the State as to doing something for the State." Elsewhere, in addresses in Lewiston, Portland, New York, and Philadelphia, he voiced his belief that this idea might be realized by volunteer military service. In recommending an elective course in military tactics, he warned the undergraduates not to lose sight of the fact that the rising sentiment looking toward the betterment of international relations was at least of equal importance.

During these difficult months, Kenneth Sills took his meals with a dozen of his colleagues and their families at Mrs. Mosher's boarding house on Cleaveland Street, where the atmosphere was increasingly colored by discussions of the war, particularly of the role which the United States should play. Here the dean's intellectual poise and consummate tact proved to be a blessing when differences of opinion, often sharply expressed, made for inevitable tensions. To President Hyde, an unflagging champion of the "good will" philosophy of Immanuel Kant, the war was a sad disillusionment. Professor Herbert Bell, senior member of the department of history, was at that time bitterly critical of the policy of "watchful waiting," although he later made amends in a sympathetic biography of Wilson. Bell's views were shared in large measure by his colleague in history, Thomas Curtis Van Cleve, who had recently arrived from the University of Wisconsin, where he had been made uncomfortable by the pacifism and pro-German spirit of that state. Professor Charles Hutchins, trained in Leipzig and deeply committed to the generous culture of the old Germany, often sat in moody silence, grieving at the necessity of slaughter. The pastor of the First Parish Church, formerly minister in the American Church in Paris and later to be recalled there by his old congregation after America entered the war, was ardently pro-French in his sympathies. Casey, like Herbert Bell, was of Canadian birth and firmly pro-British, but he was also a stanch Democrat and disposed to defend Wilson's policies.

Explosions were almost inevitable in so combustible an atmosphere, but they were prevented by the tact of the dean. Professor Van Cleve, who had joined the faculty in 1915, was especially impressed by the skill with which Casey steered a middle course in the tense conversations, at no time offending any of his dining companions. "I am quite sure," Dr. Van Cleve recalled more than forty years afterward, that "he felt as deeply as Bell with respect to the British, but I do not remember a single instance in which he made a statement which he would later regret." Perhaps no one in that intimate faculty company observed Kenneth Sills's innate courtesy and tolerance with more thankfulness than President Hyde. Never in robust health since his nervous breakdown in 1907, he was finding it difficult to rest at night, and was compelled to decline making all but a few public appearances. "I shall have to be judged," he told Samuel Valentine Cole, of the Trustees, "by what I have done rather than by anything more I can do." Sensing, perhaps, that he would never regain his old vigor, he delegated more and more responsibilities to his dean. None of Kenneth Sills's colleagues, whatever their differences of opinion about the war, had any doubt that of all their company it was Dean Sills who understood best what Hyde's achievement had been.

By the spring of 1916, Casey gave his blessing to Carleton Pike of the Junior class, the first of a gallant band to enlist in the American Ambulance Corps for service in France. There were other signs that the seemingly carefree behavior of the under-graduates belied their serious concern for the international situation. When on April 19, just after Wilson read his message to Congress, a member of the faculty asked a student, "Hasn't this been an exciting day?" the boy replied, "Yes, Bates beat us." The disturbed professor reported the episode to the dean. Kenneth Sills, however, happened to know that the youngster had read the President's message. "After all," he reassured his friend, "such an attitude is only that of youth." The dean understood the quality of Bowdoin youth well enough to be confident of its readiness, in case of need, to maintain Bowdoin's proud traditions of the 1860s. Until that need became acute, Kenneth Sills insisted that the college must stay by the stuff and go about its usual task of training men to think clearly and keep their heads in emergencies. The dean recalled David's words in I Samuel: "For as his share is who goes down into battle, so shall his share be who stays by the stuff." This, too, was not without its element of heroism.

# 6

## SCHOLAR IN POLITICS
## CASEY RUNS FOR THE SENATE, 1916

There was the usual flurry of pre-Commencement activities in Massachusetts Hall in June, 1916. Senior standings had to be compiled, prizes awarded, program proof corrected, diplomas inscribed. Inevitable, too, were the borderline cases to be resolved at last-minute meetings of the recording committee. Six years in the dean's office had taught Kenneth Sills how to take such details in his unperturbed stride. Commencement in 1916, however, was not to be all routine. On June 14 he traveled to Orono to receive his first honorary degree, an LL.D. from the University of Maine, where he heard President Robert Aley salute him as a friend of youth and an upbuilder of the state.

The future of the state was in his thoughts as he hurried back to Brunswick after the ceremony. Newspapers carrying the story of his honor at the university had also noted the critical illness of Maine's senior U.S. senator, Edwin Chick Burleigh of Augusta. Two days later on June 16, when the seventy-three-year-old senator died, there was lively speculation about candidates to fill the unexpired term in a special July primary.

The demands of practical politics were temporarily forgotten in the gay round of Bowdoin Commencement festivities. The dean's own classmates, gathered for their fifteenth reunion, enjoyed twitting K. C. M. S. about his new alma mater. At their class dinner they clamored for Dr. Sills until he responded blushingly to acknowledge his recent glory as a Maine alumnus, but to protest that his heart still belonged to Bowdoin. Although the shadows of war had not yet darkened the campus, the merriment was clouded with sober references to the world outside the college gates. Donald Edwards, in his Class Day oration under the Thorndike Oak, discussed the government's strained relations with Mexico. In his baccalaureate on June 18, President Hyde warned that the great war in Europe had ended forever the isolation of the United States. "Henceforth," he declared, "we must assume world-wide responsibilities." Within less than a fortnight, Dean Sills himself was faced with a responsibility not of his own choosing.

The hurly-burly of Commencement was hardly over when prominent Democrats met with the State Committee in Augusta on June 27 to select the party's candidate for the primary election made necessary by Senator Burleigh's unexpected death. Their first choice was Bertrand G. McIntire, of East Waterford, and nomination papers were placed in the hands of the committee, contingent upon his consent to run. Mr. McIntire, however, who was chairman of the State Board of Assessors, refused to consider the nomination. "The Democrats are all at sea as to whom their senatorial candidate will be," reported the *Portland Evening Express* for June 28, "and there is no time to lose."

Meanwhile, with time fast running out before the deadline for the announcement of candidates, the name of Kenneth Sills occurred to Attorney General William R. Pattangall, the Democratic campaign manager. Governor Oakley C. Curtis, himself a candidate for reelection and eager to enlist a strong statewide ticket, endorsed the idea with enthusiasm. In recommending Dean Sills to the State Committee, his sponsors hoped that the thirty-seven-year-old Bowdoin classicist would not be entirely unknown in the state. As the *Boston Transcript* was to note on June 29, "He stands high as an educator, and has been mentioned favorably as successor to Payson Smith, State Superintendent of Public Schools, who becomes Commissioner of Education in Massachusetts on July 1." Some members of the committee recalled that the Maine Democratic party had looked to Bowdoin for leadership in somewhat similar circumstances in 1911, before the advent of the direct primary, when Governor Harris Plaisted

had offered President Hyde an *ad interim* appointment to the
U. S. Senate upon the death of Senator William P. Frye.

The committee also knew that Dean Sills shared Hyde's ardent
admiration of the policies of Woodrow Wilson, and they had
heard of the young professor's political activity in 1912 as head
of the Wilson Club of Brunswick, where he had helped to get
out the largest vote ever cast by the town for a presidential candidate. President Wilson's own career as a scholar in politics may
have had its influence. As Thomas D. Austin of Farmington
reminded the committee: "Woodrow Wilson himself was a
college professor." With these considerations prevailing, the vote
was unanimous. The committee could assure the dean, as an
added inducement, that he would have no opposition in the
special primary on July 24. The all-important questions remained. Would Sills be persuaded to run? Would he yield to a
draft by his party?

At this juncture, Governor Curtis and Mr. Pattangall appealed
to Kenneth Sills's Bowdoin friend Leonard Pierce '05, of Houlton, candidate for Congress from the Fourth District, who
happened to be at the State House on legal and political matters.
Mr. Pierce telephoned the dean from Augusta. Would he consent, Pierce asked, to see the governor and the attorney general
that very evening on a subject of considerable importance?

As Pierce drove his associates to Brunswick, he may have had
some misgivings. He, too, had thought of Dean Sills as a promising candidate, but wondered whether a decision to run on the
Democratic ticket might hurt his friend's chances of becoming
president of Bowdoin in the event a vacancy occurred. With so
many influential Republicans on the Governing Boards, one
could not be sure. Had not Hyde's Democratic sympathies
caused grumbling which still persisted among certain Trustees
and Overseers? His vigorous championing of Grover Cleveland
had certainly been resented in Brunswick, where outraged partisans had retaliated by surrounding the president's house at 85
Federal Street and making the night hideous with horns and jeers.

Would Prex now be willing to sacrifice his indispensable dean to the uncertainties of Maine politics? And what would the dean himself have to say?

Kenneth Sills could not have been without some idea of the motive prompting the visit of so formidable a deputation of Democrats, but there was little time for unhurried reflection or the advice of his colleagues. Most of his associates on the faculty were stalwart Republicans with the scholar's conventional distrust of politics. The dean could anticipate wryly what his friend Marshall Cram would say. To him politicians were the lowest form of life. To be sure, Roscoe Ham was an ardent Democrat, but he had left town the day before Commencement and was now on his way to Petrograd to become a special assistant to the American ambassador. Charles Burnett was a confirmed Wilsonian, but he was torn between a conviction of the teacher's duty as a citizen, and a distaste for the steaming jungle of practical politics. The dean's most intimate friend, Henry Johnson, always sympathetic, was now gently quizzical. No one could really make up the dean's mind for him except, perhaps, President Hyde. Prex's counsel would at least have the merit of decisiveness. Prex might be relied upon to season his advice with the precepts so many Bowdoin men knew by heart: "Accept the necessary evils and call them good; murder your alternatives, and allow no post-mortems."

The dean's professional specialty of keeping his options open without committing himself again stood him in good stead. First of all, he would take his surprising visitors to see Prex. There would be no fuzziness from that quarter, and the president ran true to form during the interview. No, Prex said, he did not see how the candidacy could interfere with the dean's academic duties in as much as the election was to come early in September. It would be another matter, he added smiling, if the dean were to be elected, but there was no use crossing bridges before coming to them. It would, he told his visitors, neither be improper for a professor, nor embarrassing to his college, to have him seek political office. Members of a college faculty, he remarked, could not expect to be free from the burdens of citizenship. It was up to the dean to decide. And then, mind you, no post-mortems!

Back in the security of his study, Kenneth Sills manfully confronted the question: to run or not to run. The action of the State Committee had been entirely unexpected. He had looked forward to a leisurely summer with his parents in St. Andrews, to long days of golf, tennis, sailing, and reading. Modest to a point of diffidence, he winced at the prospect of a feverish succession of clambakes, field days, rallies, and smokers, all the way from Kittery to Calais. More at home at vestry meetings than at party caucuses, he had only a meager store of small talk. He was always ill at ease amid the superficial geniality of men of measured merriment and he was never entirely comfortable in the rough jocularity of smoking-car and hotel-lobby companionship. To murder the alternatives was sound enough advice, but the alternatives had never seemed more inviting. In St. Andrews there was the likelihood of long rambles and animated book talk with Jeff Fletcher from Columbia. Harvard's crotchety but delightful Copey was always ready to leave his summer retreat at Kennedy's Hotel in Calais for evenings of whist and university gossip. The thought of returning to Bowdoin in the autumn evoked even more compelling delights: the pleasant routine of the office to which he had grown accustomed, the joys of his Latin professorship, and—most precious of all—the magic hours in Henry Johnson's study poring over Dante with his beloved master and friend.

Yet had he not always urged his students to accept cheerfully the responsibilities of citizenship? Democracy, he was never tired of reminding them, was not a one-way street. Were the cynics justified in saying that *noblesse oblige* is a maxim fit only for chapel talks and baccalaureate addresses? Kenneth Sills envied the British for their tradition of hospitality to scholars in public life. Perhaps Woodrow Wilson's career as governor and president was a hopeful sign that the United States might also be ready to heed the voice of a scholar. Weighed against the common good, private objections seemed trivial. Dean Sills was not the man to refuse doing himself what he had often urged upon others. Now he would practice what he preached and murder the alternatives by announcing his candidacy. When his decision was reported in the press on June 29, he assured some of his surprised friends, "I have not the dread of politics that so often is felt by members of my profession and others too." His nomination papers reached the State House on July 6, with the name of William DeWitt Hyde heading the list of signatures. When the news reached Warren, Maine, General Ellis Spear, a doughty Bowdoin Overseer, brandished his cane menacingly. "The young Dean," he snorted, "would do better to stay out of politics."

The announcement drew scattered sniping from Republican newspapers. On July 3 the *Lewiston Evening Journal* charged the State Committee with arbitrarily hand-picking its candidate, and returned to the attack on July 15 by observing: "The Democrats have paid scant attention to the primary law. Their State Committee has picked the candidate and practically said to the others, 'Hands off.'" The editor of the *Bridgton News*, after complaining that the Democrats had nullified the popular will "by permitting party committees and ward-heelers to 'set up the pins,'" took comfort in the reflection that "no one seriously thinks of sending the young Prof. to the Senate. 'Patt' put him in just to fill a gap in the ticket." The *Brunswick Record* sought to explain the unwonted presence of a distinguished fellow townsman on the Democratic ticket by remarking, "There is but one aspirant for the Democratic nomination and he is not exactly an aspirant, having been pressed into the contest by an appeal of patriotism and party loyalty. . . . The vote for him will be but perfunctory." Politely condescending to the dean as "a charming young gentleman," the *Lewiston Evening Journal* repeated a rumor that following McIntire's refusal to run the desperate State Committee had offered the nomination to President Hyde who "gracefully turned it over to Dean Sills." Thus, said the *Journal* ironically, "Some have greatness thrust upon them." Conceding that the youthful Dean was "modest and retiring," Major Shorey exclaimed in the *Bridgton News:* "May he be equally *modest and retiring* in the campaign. . . . Like President Hyde, he is better adapted to educational work than state-craft."

Other papers, like the *Republican Journal* of Belfast, chose to regard the dean as "a political tenderfoot" sufficiently naïve to have fallen victim to the cynical machinations of an old pro like Pattangall who, as the *Bath Daily Times* warned its readers, was "the Mephistophiles of Maine politics." "Perhaps Mr. Sills will appreciate later, when he emerges from the campaign," the *Lewiston Evening Journal* predicted, that "Patt's tactics never made votes." There could, of course, be no question about the dean's character or ability. The *Courier-Gazette* of Rockland went so far as to admit that "the young man" from Bowdoin is "evidently in earnest about the whole business"—but probity and sincerity were not enough. The editor of the *Kennebec Journal* quoted with relish a comment by the *Manchester* (Vermont) *Union:* "We know Kenneth Sills . . . and we like him; but we feel constrained to remark that this year is no time to send a Democrat to the United States Senate." Even tender college loyalties must yield to political principles. "One of the saddest things for Bowdoin men in the coming campaign," lamented Arthur G. Staples '82 in the *Lewiston Evening Journal*, "is the necessity of defeating 'Casey.' "

Another Bowdoin editor, Henry A. Shorey, Jr. of the *Bridgton News*, wrote in a less elegiac vein of the young "tutor" possessing no qualifications for public office, "who has so unexpectedly been thrust upon the public by the Democratic politicians as the party's candidate for United States Senator. Just why, 'deponent saith not.' " To taunts such as these, Kenneth Sills had long been inured. "Being brought up in Maine," he recalled in 1952, "almost all my contemporaries were Republicans. In the Park Street Primary School I felt sure I was the only Democrat in the room, and in the Butler Grammar School I met the same fate." There were, of course, some grateful exceptions. His beloved Bishop Neely of the Episcopal Diocese of Maine was a firm Democrat, and so were a few of the influential friends of the elder Sills, like Judge William LeBaron Putnam and John F. A. Merrill. It was for the latter that Kenneth Sills cast his first vote in the Portland mayoralty campaign in December, 1900, shortly after he had become naturalized. The prevailing tone, however, was overwhelmingly Republican. Even Bishop Neely, for all his saintliness and eloquence, had never succeeded in converting Mrs. Neely and their son Albert to the Democratic faith which seemed little short of heretical on State Street.

Later, during his undergraduate years at Bowdoin, Kenneth Sills's political sympathies were generously tolerated by his class and fraternity mates as the harmless whims of a scholar who was also sufficiently quixotic to be excited about Latin and Greek. Perhaps his brothers in D. K. E., secure in their comfortable majority opinion, enjoyed the novelty of dining with an avowed Democrat. It was, after all, an added proof of their broadmindedness. Then, and for the rest of his long life, Kenneth Sills often marveled at the calm way in which many of his Republican friends acted as if every rational person must agree with them, even when they knew the assumption must have been insulting. In any event, if the Democratic candidate for the U. S. Senate had chanced upon the editorial page of the *Portland Evening Express* a few days before the primary election, he could have been neither discouraged nor surprised to read that no "man of sound common sense" could possibly be a Democrat. Thirty-five years of breathing the unsullied Republican ether in Portland and Brunswick had immunized him to the shock of such pontifical pronouncements. They had become something more than twice-told tales.

The Maine election in September in which the dean was to play his part had more than its usual popular but adventitious interest as a straw to show the nation which way the presidential wind was blowing. As the Washington correspondent of the *Bangor Daily Commercial* reported on June 24: "Maine politics has been much discussed here since the death of Senator Burleigh. . . . Maine will elect two United States Senators this autumn, and that has an important bearing upon the contest for the control of the Senate in the next four years." This national significance led the *Boston Globe* to predict that the influx of "Campaigning Congressmen will be as thick as kitchen bar-rooms," while the Rockland *Courier-Gazette* warned that "From end to end the State will be harrowed by spell-binders and sown with campaign literature." The anticipated appearance of Charles Evans Hughes and Charles W. Fairbanks on the campus of Maine Central Institute, boasted the *Pittsfield Advertiser*, will mark "the first time in the history of the State that a candidate for president and vice-president will speak from the same platform." In the final week of the campaign, the *Portland Evening Express* could remark accurately, "It is a pretty small town that has not had a big political rally this year."

Other factors also contributed to the unusual interest in the election in 1916. The amendment to the national constitution providing for the direct election of U. S. senators was now in force for the first time in the state, and on June 24 the Republicans had nominated Frederick Hale of Portland to oppose Senator Charles Johnson, the Democratic nominee who was seeking a second term. Johnson had owed his election in 1910 to a serious split between "regular" and "progressive" Republicans, receiving substantial support from those dissidents who were to bolt their party to vote for Theodore Roosevelt in 1912. In that presidential year, Maine was the only New England state to give a larger vote to Colonel Roosevelt than to Mr. Taft, enabling Woodrow Wilson to carry the state. This breach remained unhealed two years later in the gubernatorial contest of 1914, when the Republican vote was again divided between a "regular" and a "progressive" candidate, with the result that Oakley C. Curtis, a Democrat, was elected. Although the Progressive vote of 48,495 for Roosevelt in 1912 had dwindled to 18,226 for Halbert Gardiner, the Progressive candidate for governor in 1914, the combined Republican and Progressive vote exceeded the Democratic total by more than 15,000. Just where, the party managers were asking, would the old Progressive vote go in 1916?

The Republicans sought to woo their disgruntled members back to the fold by nominating former Progressives for all three major offices. In choosing Hale as their nominee for the long term in the Senate, they selected one who had deserted Taft for Roosevelt in 1912. Former Governor Bert Fernald, of Poland, their choice to oppose Sills for the short term, was also a former Progressive leader, as was Carl Milliken, their gubernatorial candidate. All three enjoyed the blessing of the *Lewiston Evening Journal*, the most articulate of the Maine papers which had supported the Bull Moose ticket in 1912. Although the *Journal* as recently as 1914 continued to brand such Republican "regulars" as Senator Burleigh and Congressman John A. Peters "Bourbons and reactionaries," whose ideas were violently antagonistic "to the fundamental principles of the Republicans of the days of Abraham Lincoln," it was now ready in 1916 to dismiss the Maine Progressive party as "superfluous political machinery" whose only effect would be "to litter the pathway to good government."

Kenneth Sills was fully aware of his party's precarious position. An avid reader of political news from his high school days, he knew that the Democrats had controlled only four of the thirty-six state administrations up to 1916. He also realized that the moribund Progressive party in Maine had virtually gone out of business on July 6 when its State Committee discouraged its members from seeking office under the Progressive label. It was clear that Republicans and Progressives were preparing to act together to prevent a recurrence of the disastrous splits of 1912 and 1914. There were also signs that the strategy was to get out a heavy vote in the rural areas—and Maine farmers were unswervingly Republican.

It was in the face of such odds that the candidate whose only previous elective office had been an uncontested seat on the Brunswick school committee entered the campaign. Encouragement came from unexpected, if distant, sources. The Republican *Boston Herald* declared, "Professor Sills . . . is exactly the type of man who should take interest and part in public life—a scholar in politics—and there are none too many." In an editorial lamenting the lack of fitness in the 1916 crop of senatorial candidates, the *New York Evening Post* made a notable exception of Dean Sills. "It would be a pleasant bit of news," the *Post* concluded, "to find Maine voters sufficiently discriminating to send him to the Senate, whatever they may do about the governorship." The *New York World* added its endorsement by remarking, "There is not an intelligent Republican in Maine who would pretend that Fernald can be compared with Dean Sills." Although the Maine small-town weeklies either ignored or belittled his candidacy, support came from some of the city dailies like the *Portland Eastern Argus*, the *Waterville Sentinel*, and the *Bangor Commercial*. Kenneth Sills's old Portland friend Judge Putnam was elated. "Your picture in the Sunday paper," he wrote upon learning of the nomination, "was good enough to carry you through the primaries, and also the election." From Petrograd, Roscoe Ham exulted, "The State hasn't had such an opportunity since 1900. . . . The Republican party in Maine must be well-nigh bankrupt if against such stalwarts as you and Johnson they had only Fred Hale and Fernald to offer. In any other state there could be no doubt of the outcome."

The fight was on. Candidate Sills would fire his opening gun at the Democratic rally in Augusta on July 12. Disarming candor and complete intellectual honesty had been effective in faculty meetings. These qualities would at least have the merit of novelty before a wider audience. Whether or not they would be successful was another and quite an irrelevant matter. He might lose an election, but he would keep his self-respect. Had not Patt, his campaign manager, welcomed him to the ticket on the candidate's own terms? At any rate, he would say nothing on the platform which he did not believe in the privacy of his own heart. He made the promise then that he was destined to repeat at a more momentous turning point in his career in 1918: "I will give my best."

Dean Sills's maiden speech set the tone of high seriousness from which he was never to deviate in his public utterances whether he was talking to the Brunswick Fire Department, a convocation of Phi Beta Kappa, or a political rally at Bryant Pond. To the jibe that he was an academic fish out of water, he agreed cheerfully that the call to represent his party surprised him fully as much as anybody else. "I need hardly say that I accepted only with hesitation," he told a gathering at Augusta, "realizing that to many questions I shall be obliged to answer, 'I don't know,' but that phrase can nearly always be followed by, 'I will find out.' " He urged his critics to note his remarks throughout the campaign so that he might be held accountable for any incorrect statements or intemperate expressions. "His earnestness and sincerity," the *Bangor Daily Commercial* reported on July 13, "and the fact that he is a different type of man from any that has appeared in the Maine political arena for a generation, made a big hit with the crowd." But the "crowd," as the *Portland Evening Express* was quick to retort, "consisted of only 124," and "this included the travelling orchestra, the ladies, boys and speakers . . . the larger part of the men present were either office holders at the State House or candidates." If the dean's frankness was not the usual fare served at party jamborees, neither was his conception of the senatorial function. "A senator represents primarily his party and his state," the candidate declared. "But he also represents all the citizens of the state and he is an officer of the nation . . . prepared on occasion to set party and local issues aside and vote and act as his conscience alone dictates." Such an opinion was rank heresy to the *Bridgton News*. "That isn't exactly the way Daniel Webster put it in his great speech in the Senate in reply to Hayne," the editor commented acidly. "But possibly they don't peruse Webster at Bowdoin now-a-days."

The editorial response to his first major political speech followed a pattern to be repeated with wearisome monotony whenever the local press deigned to notice his remarks. More often than not, the newspapers ignored him completely, or, instead of summarizing his remarks, found it simpler to say—as did the South Paris reporter after a rally on August 1—"The other speaker of the afternoon was Professor Kenneth C. M. Sills." The dean's patient analysis of public affairs frequently seemed too irrelevant to deserve notice. "The candidate," wrote a newsman covering a rally at Parker Head on August 26, "confined himself wholly to national issues and a defense of the Wilson administration." The dean's youthfulness, however, was invariably noted. "Never send a boy to do a man's work," quipped the *Bridgton News* on August 18. The *Fort Fairfield Review* estimated, "He could serve seven full terms in the Senate without being as old as Uncle 'Joe' Cannon now in active service." The candidate's age, incorrectly and variously cited as thirty-six, thirty-seven, or thirty-eight, was always "youthful." His name and family were treated temperamentally. As late as August 1, the Rockland correspondent of the *Portland Eastern Daily Argus* referred to him as "James B. Sills," while the *Bath Daily Times* erroneously stated that he was born in Portland, had taught at Dartmouth, and was a son of "the late Rev. Sills." The *Bangor Daily Commercial*, after spelling his name Sillial, hardly atoned for the error by praising his "war-sighted views," presumably a misprint for "far-sighted." At the Rockland rally, according to the *Courier-Gazette*, the candidate was so little known that Tyler Coombs, chairman of the Knox County Committee, knew nothing about him and was compelled to ask a Bowdoin undergraduate, E. Carl Moran, Jr., to introduce him. In Aroostook he was gratuitously described as "a son of the late Bishop." The dean fared no better at the hands of the cartoonists. In a three-column caricature in the *Kennebec Journal*, the candidate was depicted as a professorial dummy clinging to Attorney General Pattangall, while that "famous ventriloquist" boasted, "They say just what I tell them to say."

So odd a mixture of condescension or distortion was perhaps more palatable than the attitude of Dean Sills's opponents, who ignored him almost completely. In reviewing the senatorial contest after the election, the *Portland Daily Press* reported quite accurately, "Sills has been subjected to no criticism by the Republican campaigners." They may have shared the view of the Belfast *Republican Journal* that "Dean Sills was only put up to be knocked down," and that the Democrats themselves were ready to sacrifice his candidacy by concentrating wholly on an effort to reelect Senator Johnson and Congressman McGillicuddy. Perhaps they found his scholarly appraisal of the accomplishments of the Wilson administration awkward to attack and preferred a silent treatment of his campaign speeches as more effective than rebuttal. President Wilson was, after all, a more conspicuous target. Since he also had been a professor, they could kill two birds of the same academic plumage with one stone. "A vote for Sills," the *Eastport Sentinel* admonished its readers on September 6, "is a vote for Wilson."

The dean's opening address in Augusta revealed not only the qualities of mind and the political stance which were to characterize him throughout the campaign, but also indicated his conviction that the leadership of the President was the one issue upon which all others would turn. "Do the administration and policies of the Democratic Party as set forth by Woodrow Wilson deserve the endorsement of the people of Maine? Do we voters of Maine believe that the President has maintained peace with honor? Shall we be content to follow his leadership for four years more?" To these questions he addressed himself almost exclusively as he traveled up and down the state. His answer was a reasoned conclusion that "in the most difficult situations that have confronted any one of our chief executives since the Civil War, the President has acted with dignity, courage, and patriotism." "His policies," the candidate predicted, "will receive the approval of fair-minded men and the favorable verdict of history."

Such views, however, received scant support in rural Maine, where the small-town weeklies belittled Wilson as a maker of puzzling phrases and a sender of ineffectual notes. The phenomenon of a professor of Latin defending the record of a President who had also been trained as a scholar and teacher only served to confirm the traditional prejudices against intellectuals in politics. The *Republican Journal* of Belfast shuddered at "the schoolmaster's ferule" as a more dangerous weapon than "the big stick." "Is it not becoming increasingly evident," asked the editor, "that the traits and tricks of a politician which had been dormant in the college professor may be turned to personal and selfish ends?" "College professors are not always good judges," observed the *Kennebec Journal,* "but boards of trustees of colleges are generally composed of business men who can see the trend of events." The *Courier-Gazette* of Rockland, scoffing at Dean Sills as "the rah-rah candidate" who had been "some pumpkins as a collegian," preferred Bert Fernald's practical experience as a salesman and farmer to that of one "whose life has been spent in the chair of a college professor." In supporting Fernald as "genial" and "safe," the *Bath Independent,* a weekly serving rural Sagadahoc County, rejoiced on August 6 that "Maine has nothing to fear in sending the former trudging commercial traveller to the Senate." The same preference for a sound businessman candidate was felt by all the farmers along the Kennebec River who were reported by the *Richmond Bee* as "well-satisfied that Mr. Fernald possesses all the qualifications to fill the vacancy in the United States Senate."

In Lincoln County, where Dean Sills urged a consideration of problems arising from the European war, he felt as though he were teaching an apathetic class whose real interests were elsewhere. After his visits to Wiscasset and Boothbay Harbor, the *Sheepscot Echo* asserted, "The question of greatest moment is not whether President Wilson will be reëlected . . . but whether this country of ours will longer submit to the domination of the Beer Trust and the Whiskey Trust." The professor in politics had corrected too many irrelevant answers on examination papers to be discouraged. If undergraduates "grew up," voters might also mature. The remedy was more education, more lecturing from the stump. When the *Eastport Sentinel* charged his party with catering to the "booze vote of the cities" rather than "to the vote of the farmer . . . and the respectable better element of our people," he told the voters of Washington County that "prohibition should not be a partisan question." When the *Machias Republican* derided Wilson for "delivering academic speeches with a lot of high-flown English which didn't mean anything," he would explain patiently what the President meant by such phrases as "watchful waiting" and "too proud to fight."

The going was tough, however. His defense of Wilson's notes, as the *Sanford Tribune* remarked on July 28, was merely an example of "One professor being loyal to another!" So slippery is the language used by the President, declared the *Lubec Herald* for July 12, that to "stand by" his utterances "is a feat that should be attempted in most cases only by a contortionist." "Again words, always words, empty words," complained the *Kennebec Journal*, which on July 31 carried a cartoon of the President in cap and gown flanked by copies of the Oxford dictionary and a mammoth thesaurus. Dean Sills's own words were described by the *Courier-Gazette* following his speech at Rockland as "sugar-coated, wind-filled bullets." Yet this was a game at which two might play. He struck back in Bangor on July 25 by retorting that even Germany's vaunted submarines "have been caught in a web of Wilson's notes." "These notes," he asserted, "will yet be highly regarded in the annals of our country." And in South Paris, on August 1, he insisted that Governor Hughes's language would hardly stand up under close scrutiny. Ironically praising the "rhetorical style" of the Republican nominee's acceptance speech, the dean likened it to a beautiful stream in which a man might fish for weeks without catching a single live issue. "The most beautiful thing about that speech," he continued in Saco, on August 2, "was what Mr. Hughes omitted. There is no mention of the Income Tax, the Federal Reserve Act, the Federal Trade Commission, the Rural Credits Bill, and the proposed Child Labor Bill." As for Hughes's belief that we should have 'firm, consistent, and friendly dealing with Mexico,' what do these words mean?" the Democratic candidate asked. "Would the Republican nominee withdraw our troops? Would he send in more troops? How could he be more friendly to Mexico than Woodrow Wilson is now?"

Dean Sills continued his running attack on Hughes's campaign in speech after speech. If the *Brunswick Record* was correct in asserting that local issues were less important than the test of character between Hughes and Wilson, he would welcome such a test. How, he asked, could the Republicans indict the President for being lukewarm to the Allies and—with a shameless bid for the German-American vote—at the same time be blamed for an unfriendly attitude to Germany? Would the Republican candidate "have broken off diplomatic relations as a result of the sinking of the *Lusitania* and thrown the country into a state of war?" He noted, too, that Hughes had consistently ignored, in his criticism of Wilson's Mexican policy, the President's concern for the larger question of the relations of the United States with the other republics of South America. In Greenville, on August 18, he objected to Hughes's advocacy of the "old-fashioned high protective tariff" and isolation after the war: "We listen respectfully to his criticism and ask, 'Well—and then?'"

Although Kenneth Sills kept insisting that more imagination is required to see the importance of foreign affairs, he did not neglect domestic policies. In a score of addresses he hailed the creation of the Federal Reserve Act as a permanent reform of banking and currency systems which made banks the servants rather than the masters of business enterprise. He cited the provisions of the Federal Trade Commission Act as effective checks on monopoly and unfair competition. He praised the federal income tax not only as a fair means of producing revenue, but as a source of valuable information about the distribution of our national wealth. He found in the Underwood Tariff Bill a measure based "not on the principle of protection and bounties, but on the principle of necessary revenue." He was always ready to concede that "some errors took place," but with such shining accomplishments to its credit, the Democratic nominee submitted that his party had, on the whole and in the main, proved "that it could be trusted with power."

If he had looked forward to rebuttals from his senatorial opponent, he must have been disappointed. Except for the tariff issue, he failed to draw the enemy's fire. Upon this point, however, he was showered with God's plenty. Even the "genial" Bert Fernald, whose speeches give no clue that he was aware of Dean Sills being in the same state, made much of the relationship between a high tariff and a full dinner pail. The format of his speeches was accurately reported by the *Norway Advertiser* after a Republican rally in Oxford County on August 7. "He extolled the virtues of Oxford County," said the *Advertiser*, "and spent much of his speech on the tariff question." County virtues doubtless remained the same. In York County textiles were the victim; in Washington, fish; in Penobscot, lumber; in Aroostook, potatoes. Although the Underwood tariff was far from a free-trade measure, Senator Johnson was branded as an arrant free-trader, and his running mate was presumed to be cut from the same shabby cloth. "To all intents and purposes, the Senator voted as if he were representing New Brunswick, rather than Maine," the *Eastport Sentinel* complained. "He cannot expect Maine farmers, fishermen, and lumbermen to endorse him."

In Aroostook, where Dean Sills had counted upon the proximity to Canada and Wilson's sympathy for the Allies to win friends for the administration, he found the voters could be stirred only by the tariff on potatoes. "Maine is a protective state," asserted the *Presque Isle Star-Herald* for September 7. "The Democratic boasting about blood-stained prosperity did not over-balance the cool thinking of the Aroostook farmer. . . . stripped of every vestige of protection on his great staple product." In neighboring Washington County, Calais farmers along the border of Canada were equally sensitive to threats of foreign competition. "The present Democratic tariff . . . is both a calamity and a farce," charged the Calais *Advertiser*. "Potatoes and Prohibition" became a Republican battle cry.

A hardened campaigner by this time, the Democratic nominee met the issue squarely. In a dozen Aroostook towns where he occasionally surprised his audiences by addressing them in French, he assured the farmers that his party had set up a tariff commission to recommend revisions of the duties whenever economic conditions or the public interest warranted changes. He stuck to his guns by praising the Democrats for an honest and scientific revision of the tariff, "a problem that the Roosevelt administration had not dared to tackle and which had wrecked the Taft administration." Bernard Archibald, an influential citizen of Houlton, voiced what was perhaps a typical attitude toward the dean's candidacy in Aroostook. Mr. Archibald, whose son and grandson were Bowdoin graduates, listened dutifully to the earnest young professor. "How fortunate the Democrats are to have so high-minded a candidate!" he exclaimed. "But what a pity he's not a Republican!" If the *Sanford Tribune* was justified in believing that newspapers, not stump speeches and torchlight processions, "are the real political educators," the voters of Aroostook had ample instruction. The *Mars Hill Review*, the Caribou *Aroostook Republican*, the *Fort Fairfield Record*, the Houlton *Aroostook Pioneer*, the *Ashland Gazette*, and the *Presque Isle Star-Herald* all taught the same lesson: "If cheap German potatoes are permitted to find a market in America, they will absolutely displace Aroostook." Fred Putnam '04, a Bowdoin friend and contemporary of the Democratic candidate, has said the last word on the dean's Aroostook campaign. "Kenneth Sills made no enemies anywhere in the County," he recalled, "but when Don

Powers shouted, 'A Democratic low-tariff victory would cost every Aroostook farmer fifty cents on each barrel of potatoes,' sweet reasonableness did not stand much of a chance."

Sweet reasonableness hardly characterized the speech of former President Theodore Roosevelt, in Lewiston, on September 1, when he urged all his former Progressives to vote a straight Republican ticket in the Maine election. Only by returning to their old party, he declared, could they "remove the moral stain" and "the bitter national disgrace" of the Democratic administration. Woodrow Wilson's neutrality, he said, was like the conduct of Pontius Pilate. Roosevelt's speech was acclaimed by the *Brunswick Record* as the turning point of the campaign. "Practically all of the Progressives are back in the fold," exulted the *Calais Advertiser*. "There are not enough left for a coroner's jury." The appearance of the old Rough Rider was the emotional boiling point of the contest, although Charles Evans Hughes's whirlwind tour a week later provided a formal climax. Dean Sills was an inconspicuous but interested listener when the Republican nominee spoke briefly at a noon meeting in the Brunswick Town Hall on September 9, urging the election of Hale and Fernald. It was from the same stage that evening that the dean closed his own campaign. He told his fellow townsmen that he had fought the battle largely on national issues, with due attention to the businesslike administration of Governor Curtis. He still hoped that a large share of the "silent," independent vote would fall to the Democrats. He spoke movingly of his profound sense of the honor and responsibility which his nomination entailed. He repeated President Wilson's statement that "no party can retain the confidence of the American people unless it deserves it." In the campaign, he said, he had given his best.

That was all, except for Monday's voting. As he walked back to "the hill," he reflected upon the contrast between the quiet campus and the torchlight processions and blare of bands to which he had almost become accustomed. On the whole, the contest had been fun. Now that it was over, he was surprised at his facility in remembering the names of strangers while his experienced running mate, Governor Curtis, often fumbled helplessly without his prompting. He marveled at his readiness to exchange taunt for taunt. Even Pattangall had admired his jab at those who sneered at schoolteachers in politics: "Democrats don't have to be taught, and it is hard to teach Republicans anything." There was also that reply to Hale's ridicule of the Democratic candidates as "a mutual admiration society," traveling around the state throwing bouquets at each other. Although he was the least partisan and most charitable of men, the dean found himself able to repay the compliment in kind at Rockland: "The Republicans will not throw bouquets at each other for they are too well acquainted, and such is their mutual suspicion that they certainly could not form a mutual admiration society." In retrospect, it was difficult to believe that such things had been said or that he had said such things. Spontaneity of this sort must be disciplined. It would never do in the dean's office or at meetings of the faculty. Yet there were arguments one could not answer temperately. How reply to the *Bath Independent* when it pointed to the luxuriant whiskers of the Honorable William Widgery Thomas and Hiram Ricker as evidence of the greatness of the similarly adorned Charles Evans Hughes? Or how deny the *Lewiston Journal*'s claim to the manifest superiority of the Republican candidate because, unlike Wilson, he had climbed not only Mount Kineo but also Katahdin? How be entirely calm when the *Brunswick Record* quoted as "a gem of thought," Roosevelt's statement at Lewiston that "President Wilson did not merely kiss the hand that slapped his face. He kissed that hand when it was red with the blood of American men, women, and children?" Statements like these almost deserved to be ranked with the *Presque Isle Star-Herald*'s editorial which cited "As further evidence that he is warm-hearted and human," the artifact that "Mr. Hughes likes apple pie." Could not fair-minded men be trusted, Kenneth Sills asked, to weigh the evidence before they cast their votes?

He had not long to wait for an answer. Quite early on the evening of Monday, September 11, the returns showed clearly that the Republicans had swept the state, sending Hale and Fernald to the Senate, all four Republican congressional candidates to the House, and Milliken to Augusta as governor. Fernald led the senatorial vote with 81,369 to Sills's 68,201, a plurality of more than 13,000. "I had expected an election, not a resurrection," Pattangall observed ruefully as the news trickled into Augusta. "The clean sweep," rejoiced the *Star-Herald*, "was the beauty of the thing, and the handsomest thing Maine did was to elect *two* Republican senators." Some solace may have been salvaged from the details of the voting. Dean Sills ran remarkably well in Portland; he carried decisively the cities of Bangor, Lewiston, and Waterville; he also received a larger vote than that of Fernald in the fair-sized communities of Bath, Belfast, Biddeford, Brunswick, Camden, Hallowell, and Rockland. The rural and small-town vote, however, was overwhelmingly against him. As the *Bangor Daily Commercial* and the *New York Times* agreed: "The country vote as usual controlled the election."

There would be no post-mortems. Before he retired on Monday night, the defeated Democratic candidate penned generous congratulatory letters to Senators-Elect Fernald and Hale, and to the newly elected Governor Milliken. No post-mortems, certainly, but it was altogether human to wonder wherein he had failed to persuade the "silent," independent voters to whom he had appealed so often and so earnestly during the last two months. "If we can hold a third of the Progressives, we may pull through," Governor Curtis had told him as recently as September 5. Patt had been sanguine up to the very end. Even the *Brunswick Record* feared, in the midst of the campaign, that many of Kenneth Sills's "friends outside the Democratic ranks" were in grave "danger of losing sight of party principles and casting a vote for this man whose entire fitness for office is unquestioned." Such fears proved groundless; there were few split tickets. "Silent" voters apparently shared the view of the *Portland Evening Express* that "This is the year when personal interests, likes and dislikes should be eliminated." Other papers, like the *Bath Daily Times,* urged voting the straight ticket as a stern moral obligation. As the Bath editor put it, "Really it is party policies that should command the vote rather than the candidate." Despite his recent experience, Kenneth Sills could not quite bring himself to agree with the opinion of Samuel Untermeyer in the September 6 issue of the *New York Herald:* "There is no earthly use in a political campaign on complex national issues in the rural sections of Maine. . . . They appear to know little about our foreign policy and care less just now." In light of the returns, this was an interesting but a debatable view. Yet Roscoe Ham, who had received the returns at the American embassy in Petrograd, held pretty much the same opinion. "It was gratifying to notice," he told his friend, "that you had a clear majority in the cities—for in a state like Maine the cities are the real centers of civilization and probably cast the most intelligent votes."

However that might be, the dean had no intention of resigning, even though both the *Lewiston Evening Journal* and the *Boston Commercial Bulletin* had asserted on August 23 that were he to sever his Bowdoin connections the trustees "would be as much relieved as were the trustees of Princeton when they accepted the resignation of another college official whose political activities have belied much of his teaching when he was in their employ." The same two Republican papers had also intimated cheerfully that Dean Sills could have done less mischief in the Senate than "in an institution of learning which professes to instill the truth into the minds of the young . . . where the minds upon which he works are as wax to receive but as marble to retain."

The dean's morning mail a few days after the election brought an invitation which seemed to imply that the Bowdoin students at least were ready to take the calculated risk. The officers of the College Y. M. C. A. wanted him to welcome the Freshmen on the eve of the new academic year. And would he speak, please, on "The Mind of the Student?" Perhaps his sponsors had not read in the *Boston Commercial Bulletin* that "It is such men as Sills, Nearing, and Taussig who furnish the ammunition to those who belittle the value of a college education." In any event, he would accept the invitation in good cheer. He had learned a good deal, in one way or another, about minds of wax and marble. The kind he had been addressing recently seemed neither to receive nor to retain very readily. Now he could surely be trusted to speak to the Freshmen without doing any mischief, even on minds of wax. Apparently his talk went off very well indeed. "Dean Sills received a great ovation," reported the *Orient* on September 26. The same issue of the college newspaper also printed an account of those Bowdoin students who had spent their vacation driving ambulances in France, serving on the Mexican border, and training at Plattsburg. It was entitled, "Bowdoin's Summer Warriors." To this roster of summer soldiers might have been added the name of their dean. On a different battle line, he had also done his patriotic duty. Like his fellow Bowdoin men, Kenneth Sills had given his best.

# 7

## *DEAN, ACTING PRESIDENT, AND THE FIRST WORLD WAR*

During the hurried days between the Maine election on September 11 and the opening of the fall term, Kenneth Sills had little time to nurse his political wounds or to reflect upon his recent campaign. Faced with a class of 157 Freshmen, the largest in Bowdoin's history, he was too busy to engage in post-mortems. "This has been my hardest week," he noted in his journal. To Portland friends who despaired of ever getting him to the city for dinner, he pleaded for time. "Some day or other I may have some leisure," he wrote. "After the election I found myself in the midst of parents and freshmen who have all got to be straightened out and sent their respective ways rejoicing." On September 22 Governor-Elect Carl Milliken was solicitous about the dean's lack of rest. "Perhaps the work of the summer, though strenuous and exacting," he wrote cheerfully, "was enough different from your regular work to serve in some degree as a vacation in itself."

On this point the dean had some doubts. The campaign was not such a strange interlude after all. Indifference to national and world affairs was an enemy who rarely went on vacations. The dean knew that any college professor worthy of his hire must fight apathy in and out of the classroom. When his Republican opponents had accused him of poisoning the minds of the young, he was tempted to reply that the compliment was undeserved. In any event, the dean had not been conspicuously successful in persuading his own students to keep abreast of the news, even in the critical years of a European war. He recalled the perplexity of a Freshman in 1915 who had written on an examination paper, "King Albert rules Greece," and then asked his instructor

Kenneth Sills as a boy of six, seated (bottom row) with his mother, Mrs. Charles M. Sills (Elizabeth Ketchum), his maternal grandfather, Canon William Q. Ketchum, and his sister, Mary Neely Sills.

The Portland High School tennis player, 1896. With his classmate Ripley Dana, Kenneth Sills helped to organize interscholastic competition.

Sergeant major K. C. M. Sills of the Portland High School Cadet Battalion, 1897.

The Portland High School Senior with his dog Boxer, 1897.

The Bowdoin Freshman: Casey Sills studying in 10 Appleton Hall. After the graduation of his roommate, Percival Baxter '98, Kenneth Sills shared 10 Appleton with Ripley Dana '01.

The Bowdoin Senior, 1901. As the ranking scholar of his class, he gave one of the four Commencement orations, "The Shortcomings of Stoicism," which was awarded the Goodwin prize. In his Class Day address, he said, "Today we are the lords of the campus; tomorrow ...these very halls will look down on us with gentle indifference."

As Democratic candidate for the U.S. Senate in 1916, Dean Sills campaigned vigorously for the domestic and foreign policies of Woodrow Wilson. (From the New York *Evening Post*.)

The Dean of Bowdoin at the time of his election as acting president, 1917.

The president's house at 85 Federal Street was built in 1860 by Captain Francis Jordan, a Brunswick shipmaster. The addition in 1926 of a spacious reception room and ballroom resulted in a charming combination of official residence and family home.

Ifield Cottage in St. Andrews, New Brunswick, Canada, the summer home of President and Mrs. Sills. Kenneth Sills was unable to remember a time when he did not spend at least part of his vacations near the rectory of his grandfather in St. Andrews.

The president as teacher. Throughout his 34-year administration, Kenneth Sills taught a course in comparative literature known popularly as "Casey's Lit." Except for the period of swollen enrollment after the Second World War, he corrected all papers and examinations himself.

The Bowdoin faculty in 1930. "The strength of the College," President Sills often remarked, "is its teaching staff."

Afternoon tea at 85 Federal Street. On at least one afternoon each week in term time, the Sillses were at home to undergraduates. In conferring the honorary degree of L.H.D. on his wife in 1952, President Sills cited her as a "Doctor of ease and graciousness."

The president as administrator, seated at one end of a long table in Mass-achusetts Hall. Dean Paul Nixon sat at the other end. "For the past thirteen years," Kenneth Sills noted in 1933, "the President and the Dean have been playing Cox and Box, and while their relations are still amicable, the strain on the Dean has been quite heavy." Separate offices were not provided until 1936.

President and Mrs. Sills with a group of members of the class of 1940 in the garden at 85 Federal Street. Each spring the Sillses entertained the entire Senior class at a series of dinners. "I use our best china and silver... that I would have for the most distinguished visitor," Mrs. Sills said, "because there is no one we would wish to honor more than our Bowdoin Seniors."

President Sills (left) and Dean Paul Nixon. To several thousand alumni, the Bowdoin administration consisted of "Casey" and "Nick." For almost 30 of his 43 years of service to Bowdoin, Paul Nixon was dean of the college, succeeding Kenneth Sills in that office in 1918. In 1943, on the 25th anniversary of his appointment, Paul Nixon was made an honorary L.H.D. by his grateful president, who cited him as "Dean of Deans... witty, incomparable, and understanding."

Kenneth Sills was always at his best as a speaker presiding over Commencement dinners, introducing the recipients of honorary degrees, and reporting on "the state of the college" to the entire Bowdoin constituency of alumni and friends.

Kenneth Sills aboard the *Millicette* to inspect the Bowdoin Scientific Station on Kent Island in the Bay of Fundy, New Brunswick, Canada.

The presidents of the "pentagonal colleges": John S. Dickey (Dartmouth), Kenneth Sills (Bowdoin), Charles W. Cole (Amherst), James P. Baxter (Williams), and Victor L. Butterfield (Wesleyan). At the time of his retirement in 1952, Kenneth Sills was the senior college president in New England.

"Casey at the throttle." The president was persuaded to take over the bulldozer at the ground-breaking ceremonies for the new classroom building in the spring of 1949. Later, in 1952, on the occasion of his retirement, the Governing Boards named the building Kenneth Charles Morton Sills Hall.

When President Sills saw the plaque for the new classroom building named in his honor in 1952, he remarked, "That's too long a name to spell out twice on one tablet."

Kenneth Sills paused for a photograph as he left the campus for the last time as president of the college, 1952.

On October 15, 1952, two days after Kenneth Sills attended the inauguration of his successor, Dr. James Stacy Coles, the Sillses sailed for an extended trip to India, the Far East, and Europe. The flood of bon voyage messages was so great that the *Queen Elizabeth* docked at Southampton before half of them could be acknowledged.

to explain his red-penciled exclamation, "Would that he did!"

The contrast between the rigors of political barnstorming and his outwardly placid duties as a teacher impressed the dean as less striking than the difference between the self-contained campus life and a situation which threatened to involve the United States in a world war. To be sure, an enterprising newsboy carried a stock of morning papers to the chapel steps every day, but Professor Marshall Cram observed that those who bought them "turned to the sports page rather than to the news from Europe or Washington." The prevailing apathy was deplored by Austin MacCormick in a letter to the *Orient*. "We go on in our little circle of thought," he protested on October 10, 1916, "getting tremendously stirred up about 'Proc Night' and our hectic rushing season, yet most of us do not care whether Verdun falls or not as long as the Red Sox win the first game." It was not until early in 1917 when Germany's resumption of unrestricted submarine warfare jeopardized American rights that most undergraduates were aroused by the gravity of the situation. Then, when the pendulum swung to the other extreme of war fever, Dean Sills was compelled to advise students that they could perform their highest patriotic service not by enlisting impetuously but by remaining at their studies until they were called to the colors. In the meantime, he urged all college men to recognize their moral obligation to be intelligently informed about the issues of the war.

Some of these issues were being discussed daily by President Wilson and Charles Evans Hughes in the closing weeks of the presidential campaign in the autumn of 1916. On these matters the dean could now talk like a veteran, but there was no trace of partisanship in his repeated pleas to eligible undergraduates to cast their ballots in the November election. He was encouraged by the large enrollment and lively interest in Professor Orren Hormell's new course in American government, which had been opened to Freshmen for the first time. "Seldom in recent years," the *Orient* remarked on October 3, "has a course been introduced at Bowdoin which has been so popular with the students." Noting that at least 160 undergraduates were of voting age, Dean Sills announced on October 24 that "the College would be glad to excuse students from their regular exercises on election day and give them time enough to reach their homes for the election." The editor of the *Orient*, who had commended the dean for spending "an active summer in big politics," believed that the campus was "at last waking up a little," although only forty of the eligible undergraduates availed themselves of their privilege of voting. Undeterred by his apathy, Kenneth Sills did what he could to offset it by precept and example.

On October 30 he spoke to the Woodrow Wilson Club at Colby College on "Why College Men Should Be Interested in Politics," and three weeks later he traveled to Geneva, New York, to lecture at Hobart on "Politics in Theory and Practice." Back home in Brunswick, he addressed the Adults' Night School on "The Working of Political Parties in the State" on November 21, helped to organize Wilson Clubs in town and at the college, and assisted the Brunswick Democratic Town Committee in getting out a record vote. If the defeated candidate for the U. S. Senate carried his enthusiasm for President Wilson into his Latin classroom, such influence was not discernible. Hughes remained a 3–1 favorite in the student body. Wilson, however, fared better in a faculty straw vote, which was almost evenly divided between the two candidates. Doubtless the dean was elated at the decisive majority given the president by Brunswick voters who cast 716 ballots for Wilson to 535 for Hughes. When the President came within 5,000 votes of carrying Maine in November, Kenneth Sills may have felt that his own stout defense of Wilsonian policies in the Senate campaign had not fallen entirely on deaf ears.

Interest in the results of the election were soon overshadowed by the growing concern over Europe. On October 10 it had been possible for a writer in the *Orient* to attribute the students' complacence to the remoteness of the theater of war, but by January, 1917, the conflict was brought home by the return to the campus of Bowdoin men who had seen service in France. On January 9, John Sullivan, who enrolled at Bowdoin after being invalided out of the British Army, addressed a student rally on his experiences at the Front. A week later, Carleton Pike and Loyall Sewall, members of the class of 1917 who had driven ambulances in France, pleaded for support of the American Field Service. Dean Sills presided at a series of mass meetings at the student union and was made treasurer of a committee to purchase an ambulance. By February 20 he reported the collection of enough money to start a new fund for a second one. Amid the mounting enthusiasm, the *Orient* predicted that "Bowdoin would send seven or eight more ambulance drivers to France during the next two months." Meanwhile, about 100 students, chafing at the War Department's delay in detailing an officer to give instruction in military tactics, began drilling early in February under the direction of Philip Johnson and Richard Schlosberg, Juniors who had won distinction at Plattsburg during the previous summer. Dr. Whittier promised his impatient gymnasium classes that he would soon be able to provide them with rifles instead of dumbbells. Although the drill corps was without uniforms, the dean urged them to take part in the Preparedness Parade in Portland on March 16 and, as a symbol that faculty as well as students were ready for duty, he marched with Professors Ham and Nixon at the head of the Bowdoin contingent.

Before the national emergency made college problems seem comparatively trivial, Kenneth Sills had looked forward to having the faculty consider several matters which were causing him concern. One of these was the steady decline in the percentage of students from Maine. From the time of his senior year in 1901, when Maine boys constituted more than 90 percent of the student body, he had witnessed an annual increase in the out-of-state registration. Now, fifteen years later, only 68 percent of the undergraduates came from Maine. This shrinkage was accompanied by an increasing number of candidates for the B.S. degree. In 1915–16, fully one-quarter of the entering class lacked sufficient Latin or Greek to be eligible for the A.B. without further study of ancient languages in college. And in the autumn of 1916 more than one-third of the Freshmen preferred to become candidates for the B.S. rather than begin or continue their Latin or Greek. Convinced of the value of classical studies, and sharing President Hyde's belief in the superior stamina of Maine boys, the dean could only deplore the current trends. He reminded the faculty that of the fifty students elected to Phi Beta Kappa in the last five years forty-five had either studied Latin or Greek in college or had entered with full preparation in the classics. He also reported that twenty-nine of the thirty-three ranking Seniors were candidates for the A.B. Such evidence, he told his colleagues, was proof "that students with classical training are found in much more than the expected proportion in the highest group of the class intellectually."

These and other matters affecting the quality of college work were, however, brushed aside by more pressing problems. "Academic concerns must take a seat in the rear," he remarked early in March, 1917, "until nationally and internationally we have our house in order." The first of the dean's special duties came with his appointment to the Board of Visitors of the U. S. Naval Academy in Annapolis. Secretary Josephus Daniels had spoken to President Wilson about Sills's qualifications for the post following the senatorial campaign. In Oakland, Maine, where the secretary shared the platform with the dean at a Democratic rally in July, Daniels was impressed by the candidate's refreshing political candor as well as his vigorous support of social legislation such as the Child Labor Law. He knew that Wilson was eager to strengthen the academy board by naming a persuasive advocate of liberal education. The appointment was confirmed on January 30, 1917.

At Daniels' invitation, Kenneth Sills went to Washington early in February to meet the President and to discuss academy affairs. Although Mr. Wilson had canceled all his other social engagements, he attended a small dinner party given by the secretary on February 5 at which the dean sat on the right of the President. "I had a fine chance to talk with him," Sills recalled later. "He strikes me as an *intellectual*. He has a real gift of humor and tells a story very well indeed. He seemed excellently well and in good spirits. He is a strong man—no doubt about that." Mrs. Wilson pleased the dean by inquiring about mutual friends in Geneva, and the President spoke of the need of preserving humane studies, especially when the national emergency made technology seem all-important.

The next day the dean conferred with Secretary Daniels at the Navy Office and later was accompanied by Senator Charles Johnson '78, a Bowdoin trustee, to the Treasury to meet Secretary McAdoo, and then to the heavily guarded War Office. There he discussed plans for military training with William Ingraham '95, assistant secretary of war, who suggested that Bowdoin students form a battalion similar to the Harvard Regiment recently organized in Cambridge, and promised to detail an army officer to the college as soon as possible. That evening at the annual dinner of Bowdoin alumni in the capital, Senator Johnson and Admiral Robert E. Peary '77 urged greater national preparedness, and in his own remarks the dean assured the graduates that the students were ready to enlist in their country's service whenever the need arose. The immediate possibility of war loomed large at the dinner. No one present felt America could stay out of the conflict if Germany persisted in her ruthless policy of submarine warfare. On February 7 when Kenneth Sills left Washington, the huge Union Station was filled with men in uniform and flags were flying everywhere. It was all very exciting. Yet the next day, at his desk in Massachusetts Hall, he had the curious impression that the events of the last few days were pure fantasy and that "nothing had really happened."

Such a mood, however, did not survive his first twenty-four hours in Brunswick. At his customary "at home" to students on Sunday evening, a dozen undergraduates called to volunteer for any duty the government might ask of them. The present uncertainty, the dean told them, was hard to endure patiently. He reminded his callers that an important duty of the college in the line of national service is to go about its usual tasks by continuing to train as many men as possible in their regular work. He hoped that many students, if the age of men subject to the selective draft were set at twenty-one, would be able to qualify for their degrees before being called for military duty.

Amid rumors of war the dean found it a relief to busy himself with details of a less exciting kind. As head of the General Alumni Association, he wrote to all graduates of the college, soliciting contributions for the $80,000 needed for the new dormitory to be built next to Appleton Hall, suggesting that it be named William DeWitt Hyde Hall in honor of Hyde's more than thirty years of service. Kenneth Sills could no longer ignore evidence that this long service was beginning to exact its toll on the president's health. He noticed the painful attempts Hyde made to stride across the campus with his usual vigor, and he knew that the effort often left him exhausted. Although Prex continued to teach Philosophy 2, the flashes of his old fire were becoming less frequent, and he was often compelled to ask colleagues to take his place in the lecture room. Hyde's public appearances were also becoming rarer, and the dean was called upon to assume a larger share of administrative duties. Despite his added burdens, he found time to write a paper for the meeting of the New England Classical Association at Amherst late in March, and looked forward to a New York visit during the spring recess. "But all plans are uncertain nowadays," he wrote his parents in Geneva on March 26. "This week is our Spring—God save the mark—vacation. I had planned to go to Geneva when suddenly I was asked by the Governor to serve on a State Committee of Public Safety. So here I am at Brunswick ready to do my bit—and no holiday."

When the students returned from their vacation on Tuesday, April 3, they came back to a different academic world. On Monday, the day before the opening of the spring term, President Wilson had asked Congress for a declaration of war, and classes had barely been resumed before war resolutions were adopted by the Senate and House of Representatives. Within a few hours after the news reached Brunswick, students began preparing to leave the campus and every chapter house tried to organize a Coast Patrol Unit. At morning chapel on April 4, President Hyde told the student body that the college would encourage the enlistment of not more than three units. Further recruitments, he warned, would withdraw too many men who otherwise would be available for the officers' training corps soon to be formed. Meanwhile, the dean strove to persuade as many men as possible to remain in college. Leaves of absence would be granted, he said, only to those called up by the government. On April 10 he received a petition from virtually all members of the three lower classes begging the faculty to subordinate academic to military courses, and to institute at once intensive training in military tactics.

The dean replied in an open letter to the *Orient* on April 10, promising that the college authorities would keep in close touch with the War and Navy Offices. For the present, he advised, "it is very much wiser for students to remain in college, to do their regular work, and then to receive such instruction in military matters as will shortly be provided." This instruction, he pointed out, would increase their chances of being accepted at Plattsburg. By April 23 the student battalion was organized and intensive instruction was begun under the command of Captain Sherman White, U. S. Army, who was ordered to Bowdoin through the influence of the assistant secretary of war. Mr. Ingraham had not forgotten his promise to the dean in Washington. With a military program of ten hours a day in full swing, the *Orient* predicted hopefully on May 8, "Probably before the week is over a quarter of the student body will leave for Plattsburg to train for army commissions." The prediction proved to be too optimistic. Only twenty-five men were chosen in the first selection of candidates, but the morale remained high.

On May 3 the colors voted by the Maine legislature were presented to the Bowdoin battalion by the dean's former roommate, Percival Baxter '98, and were accepted by President Hyde in a ceremony on Whittier Field. Prex spoke eloquently, but Kenneth Sills was apprehensive when gusts of cold wind swept across the field where the ailing president stood bareheaded under threatening skies. It was Hyde's last public appearance, and his last speech. A few days later, Professor William Moody was distressed to observe that the president was suffering from strange lapses of memory and seemed on the verge of a nervous breakdown. Less than a fortnight later, on May 15, the dean announced in chapel that Dr. Hyde had been obliged to give up all college work for the remainder of the term. Although the *Orient* spoke of the benefits of a complete rest, the college community sensed the gravity of the illness. Dean Sills confided to friends that he had been given the president's power of attorney, and that Hyde himself was discouraged about his chances of recovery. "Faculty meeting with President Hyde absent," Marshall Cram noted sadly in his diary, "is like running the engine without being able to throw in the clutch."

Men were now leaving every week. When they called at Massachusetts Hall to receive the dean's blessing, Kenneth Sills invariably reminded them of the words of President Hyde. "The College was sorry to see them go," Prex had said, "but the College would have been more sorry if they were not willing and eager to go." Members of the faculty were also responding to the call. The first to leave was Dr. Whittier, who was commissioned in the Medical Corps on March 24, to be followed by Professors Herbert Bell and Thomas Van Cleve, who received appointments to Plattsburg before the end of the spring term. Marshall Cram, with a genius for imagining the worst, told his neighbor Professor Philip Meserve on May 9 that "Dean Sills had a nightmare last night, dreaming that all the rest of the faculty had been called out by the government, and that the Governing Boards had elected women to their places. Everything is in complete

chaos." By the middle of May the dean had said his good-byes
to eighty-four men who went directly to Plattsburg, the Coast
Patrol, the Ambulance Corps, and the National Guard. Of the
424 students remaining on campus, all but eighty were enrolled
in the military-training program. To those ineligible for the
armed forces, Sills advised summer jobs on farms or in the ship-
yards in Bath and South Portland.

Dean Sills often envied the men wearing their country's uniform. For them at least there could be no unspoken question
about failing to do one's duty. Khaki carried its own credentials.
There were times when he winced at recalling the rebuke of
Henry IV of France to a tardy soldier after the battle of Arques:
"Go hang yourself . . . we fought at Arques and you were not
there." Enthusiastic letters from his friends Robert Hale and
Rip Dana at Plattsburg only added to his restiveness. "Very
many things about serving in the Army appeal to me immensely,"
he told Dana who was now a second lieutenant, "but apparently
I could not get in on account of my near-sightedness, and just
at present my job is here. What a lot I shall have to do if the
war lasts." His immediate task, complicated by President Hyde's
illness, was to try to hold the college together. Although many
of the usual student activities were curtailed, the dean hoped to
salvage at least some remnant of normal intellectual and social
life for those who were too young or physically unfit for service
in the army and navy. On this slender minority, he believed,
would depend the continuity of the college. He insisted upon
retaining compulsory morning worship for all members of the
college, military and civilian. He surprised a few incredulous
trainees by putting them on probation for unexcused absences
from morning chapel. "I am firmly convinced," he wrote after
the armistice, "that holding to the college chapel service did
much for the morale of the student body in days when it was
none too easy to hold to the integrity of tradition."

With reveille sounding at daybreak followed by setting-up
exercises on the Delta before breakfast, the wartime campus

presented some strange sights. The dean soon accustomed himself to Bowdoin as an armed camp, hoping against hope that the
next summer might see the end of the fighting. "Won't it seem
strange when the peace comes?" he asked a colleague. "How
abnormal it will seem not to reach for the paper. I live in a newspaper world—and almost all my thoughts are on the war." His
hopes for an early peace, however, were dimmed by what he
saw and heard in Washington and Annapolis during the last week
in April, 1917. There, on his first official inspection of the Naval
Academy as a member of the Board of Visitors, he reviewed
plans for an accelerated program to fill the need for more officers.
While in the capital, the Board was received by President Wilson
at the White House. The dean was thrilled to catch a glimpse
of Balfour on his way to call on Secretary Lansing, but was
disappointed at not seeing Marshal Joffre, whom he revered as a
hero.

Back in Brunswick by the end of April, he found his duties less
glamorous but more exacting. The Maine Committee of Public
Safety, beset with unexpected difficulties, was now meeting almost every week. "Meserve says that Sills is having his troubles as
conciliator of the Public Safety Committee," Marshall Cram
reported on May 5. "The Red Cross in Portland and the Commission there are in a row, and the Maine Central Railroad has
put its men sent to guard bridges in sheds without toilets." In
these and other matters, the dean brought his powers of sweet
reasonableness to bear with his usual success. At a time when so
many men were making sacrifices, he could not in good conscience refuse further demands upon his energy. In the spring he
cheerfully accepted reelection as chairman of the Brunswick
Red Cross for his eighth term, and he yielded when the town
Democrats and Republicans nominated him for another term on
the school committee. "I have more or less to keep me out of
mischief," he wrote his parents in Geneva. "I have worked
harder these past six weeks than ever before in my life—and
given more advice than I like to think of." Meanwhile, the war

came home to him poignantly when a Canadian cousin was killed in action in France early in May: "An only son and I had to go down to Woodstock, New Brunswick, for the memorial service. After one has seen a single home made desolate, he can realize a little what it all means."

As the spring term of 1917 came to its close, Kenneth Sills foresaw a cheerless Commencement. The bleak weather, which had been ungracious even by Brunswick standards, added to the gloom caused by Hyde's illness. To the dean's already heavy tasks was added the burden of preparing the budget for the uncertainties of the next academic year. "Hyde has put everything into the hands of Dean Sills," Marshall Cram noted after a meeting of the senior faculty on May 23. "The future looks very serious financially. How we shall come out no one can say." Five days later at a session of the full faculty it was voted "that all matters pertaining to Commencement, usually attended to by the President, be left to the Dean with power." His first melancholy duty, in view of Prex's continued inability to concern himself with college affairs, was to assign appropriate credit for students enrolled in the president's unfinished course in philosophy.

With the dean's encouragement, the students held their traditional Ivy Day exercises on June 1, attended by forty Juniors. The night before, a small audience saw the dramatic club's production of *Master Pierre Patelin,* and the next forenoon the baseball team, which had got in its only practice at 6:00 A.M. on the morning of the game, defeated Bates. Every member of the Bowdoin squad was a candidate for Plattsburg. Ivy Day itself was overcast and cold. The dean, who presided at the Seniors' last chapel, counted thirty-two members of the class of 1917 as they solemnly marched down the broad aisle singing "Auld Lang Syne." It was all very moving. "This isn't a time for gaiety and after all one could not wish it," he wrote after the ceremony. "It has been splendid to me to see how well college boys have responded, but it takes it out of you, too, to see so many plans and hopes deferred." Only about half of the student body was left on the campus to take their final examinations in June. Upon the dean's recommendation, the faculty had granted full credit for courses left incomplete when men entered the service if, at the time of departure, their grades were "C" or better. By Commencement the *Orient* reported 163 Bowdoin men active in fourteen branches of the armed forces, the greatest number being in officers' training camps.

The dean's prediction of a grim Commencement week proved all too accurate. Rain fell incessantly throughout Baccalaureate Sunday on June 17. Since President Hyde had written his address before he was stricken, Professor Wilmot Mitchell read the sermon in the First Parish Church to slightly more than one-third of the Seniors, who had numbered eighty when war was declared in April. The gloom was accentuated by large drops of rain which fell intermittently from a leak in the roof and spattered each page of the manuscript. The national emergency and the illness of Prex cast their shadows athwart the graduation activities. At the Alexander Prize Speaking Contest the following evening, Dean Sills noted that five of the parts were concerned with war. Although the Seniors and their guests made a brave attempt to achieve the customary merriment on Class Day, the audience was pitifully small. But, as Marshall Cram observed to the dean, "Every audience seems small now." At the president's reception on June 20, Mrs. Hyde was assisted in receiving the parents and alumni by the dean and Professor and Mrs. Henry Johnson. It was apparent to everybody that Kenneth Sills was taking the president's place in all public functions. On the next morning at the graduation exercises, before conferring the baccalaureate degrees, he read the names of those members of the class who were on active duty. Their unseen presence, he said, gave a special distinction to the ceremony. Only those who knew the dean intimately could have sensed his feelings when he conferred an honorary Litt.D. upon his Portland friend, William Witherle Lawrence, now a distinguished medievalist at Columbia. But the most poignant moment in the drama of the 1917 Commencement was reserved for the end of the program. Kenneth Sills's face shone with gratitude and affection when, by the authority of the Governing Boards, he made his absent chief, William DeWitt Hyde, a Doctor of Laws, *honoris causa*.

At their meeting the previous evening, the Trustees and Overseers voted the president a year's leave of absence, and named Dean Sills as acting president for the interim. His first official act was to summon the faculty for a special session on June 27 to consider the various Board actions and to plan for the next academic year. Although he had been presiding over the deliberations of the faculty since the first week in May, the meeting after Commencement marked the first time he occupied the chair as acting president. As a token of their confidence, his colleagues had before the meeting placed a vase of red roses at the head of the table. Perceiving at once the inappropriateness of the symbol, and anticipating Sills's embarrassment, Professor Roy Elliott of the department of English remarked prophetically, "Instead of roses there should have been a seedling oak."

The usual post-Commencement lull was broken by heartening news of an improvement in the president's health. On June 27 Mrs. Hyde told callers at 85 Federal Street that her husband seemed better than he had been for some time. Kenneth Sills was also reassured when he called to offer his congratulations and to report the enthusiastic approval which had greeted the award of the LL.D. at Commencement. Even Marshall Cram, Hyde's next-door neighbor whose predilection for panics was a campus legend, thought the president had safely turned a corner on the road to recovery. Under the circumstances, the acting president felt justified in leaving town for a brief vacation. He was packing his bags for a few weeks of needed rest at St. Andrews when the news came. President Hyde had suffered a shock shortly after midnight on June 29, followed by a second seizure eight hours later, and then a lapse into unconsciousness. At noon he was dead.

"He was not only a great man," Kenneth Sills wrote, "he was one of my best and most helpful friends. He was always fatherly to me. It seems as if the bottom had dropped out of things, and I don't know what we shall do without him. He was the greatest president Bowdoin ever had or is ever likely to have." As the mourners walked back from the Pine Grove Cemetery on the eastern edge of the campus, the masons had resumed work on the walls of the dormitory which was to bear Hyde's name. Later the same afternoon, the acting president walked across the campus and stood silently in front of the rising building. In his pocket he carried the watch that President Hyde had worn. It had been given to him earlier that day by Mrs. Hyde who said, "It has not stopped. Will you wear it and keep it going?"

The next morning a bereft faculty gathered in Massachusetts Hall to adopt its formal tribute to the late president. All but two of their number had been brought to Bowdoin in Hyde's long term of thirty-two years. His passing, the faculty said, "comes near to being an alteration in the very course of nature, an alteration whose full meaning can but slowly come to light." They recalled the leadership and departmental freedom he had accorded the faculty, the personal interest he had shown in their private welfare, and the wisdom with which, in administrative matters, he gave them consultative powers that were in spirit faculty control without its constitutional machinery. Such policies had won for Bowdoin an allegiance of teachers which was the envy of many colleges. Kenneth Sills's appointment as acting president was the best guarantee to his colleagues that Hyde's spirit would continue to inform the administration. Their first act was a standing vote of gratitude "to Dean Sills for his performance of the arduous work of President and Dean for the last few weeks," and an expression of confidence at the prospect of his leadership "until the Boards shall decide the matter." The "until," of course, embodied considerable suspense—and risk. The concern of all his colleagues was voiced by Professor Roy Elliott, who wondered whether any Board of Trustees and Overseers could be expected to have the wisdom to appoint two excellent presidents in succession.

If such fears troubled the acting president, no trace of them is to be found in his few letters from Ifield Cottage in July. St. Andrews had never looked more inviting than when he arrived for his postponed holiday. "For the first time in my life I have not brought down here any professional or improving books," he wrote on July 20. "I am just loafing to my heart's content and letting E. Phillips Oppenheim supply intellectual refreshment. There is also good golf, good tennis, good swimming." Before the United States entered the war, Kenneth Sills had been conscious of a sense of guilt during his summer vacations in St. Andrews. "It is intolerable," he remarked to a New Brunswick friend, "to think we are letting other and more sacrificing nations do our fighting for us." Although he still envied the Canadians in uniform, he now rejoiced that his own fellow countrymen were their allies. Ordinarily he tore himself away from St. Andrews with regret, but by the end of July, 1917, he was eager to return to the task of promoting whatever contribution the college could make to the war effort.

His new duties made it desirable that he find lodgings somewhat nearer the campus than the apartment at 31 Federal Street which he had occupied since 1906. He also needed quarters large enough to enable him to entertain college guests. Happily a comfortable house at 265 Maine Street was available in September, and he welcomed the offer of Violetta Berry, wife of his classmate Harold Lee Berry, to help him arrange his furniture. An added attraction of his new address was its nearness to the home of Professor Henry Johnson. So congenial a situation clearly called for an informal party of friends to celebrate the occasion. "I haven't had a merrier party or more welcome guests than those who descended upon me that evening in September," he wrote gratefully to one who was certainly not the least welcome member of his house-warming party. She was Miss Edith Lansing Koon, a teacher of Latin at Miss Finch's School in New York

City. The acting president begged her to think of him as *semper amicus fidelis*.

Classes began on September 20 in an atmosphere which seemed calm after the excitement of the spring term. The editor of the *Orient* questioned whether there was any "valid justification for keeping three hundred healthy young men of military age sequestered in a peaceful atmosphere when the country is making such great exertions." Anticipating such queries, Kenneth Sills declared in his opening address that "students at the present time can perform their highest patriotic service by remaining at their studies" until they are called to the colors. "Not only in the days of reconstruction that must come before many years," he said, "but now at the darkest moments of the war, the country needs men well trained intellectually as well as physically." To the undergraduates, the new leader of the college continued to be known as the dean. His colleagues also preferred the title they had been accustomed to use even while he was performing many of the president's duties. These responsibilities, however, were now too heavy to be borne alone. The *Orient* announced, "Beginning Monday, October first, Professor Paul Nixon will assist the Dean in the office, and will have charge of the chapel and classroom absences, and the studies of the freshman class."

As the new term got underway, Kenneth Sills was surprised to encounter less restlessness than he had expected. Two hundred and twenty undergraduates enrolled in the military training unit to become eligible for the new officers' training camps authorized by Congress. Captain Sherman White, who had been ordered to France, was succeeded in September by Major John Duval, a retired army officer, and the cooperation between military and college authorities continued to be excellent. Meanwhile, when three more faculty members, Professors MacCormick, Meserve, and Miles Langley, received their commissions, the acting president himself became restive. "It's not so easy," he told a colleague in November, "and I envy them, but the only thing to do is the best you can with the immediate task." The burdens of office, however, were not without their cheerful interludes. "My job also includes some cakes and ale. I have the pleasant opportunity of entertaining a good many interesting people," he wrote on November 12. "Ian Hay, a former schoolmaster and veteran of Kitchner's army, comes Wednesday and is to stay with me while he is here." On this as on countless similar occasions, the host invited a group of faculty and students to his house for an informal party after the lecture.

Even the pleasantest duties, he soon discovered, took a great deal of time. The acting president was expected to welcome college guests, introduce visiting lecturers, conduct chapel exercises several times each week, teach two courses in Latin literature, make himself available for conferences with his faculty, keep an eye on the routine of the dean's office, and perform the functions of president. He was surprised to learn how many occasions in Maine seemed to require the appearance, if not a speech, of even an acting president. The world, he thought, was in danger of being talked to death. At times he wondered how President Hyde had managed to be alone long enough to read, much less write, a book. "I can't settle down to much *real* reading," he told Professor Johnson who had hoped to continue their evenings over their pipes and Dante. "The newspapers, the journals, some poetry and fiction now and then, lots to do each day, and so the world wags on."

As far as he could foresee, the small but busy world of Bowdoin and Brunswick would keep him fully occupied. Yet a much larger world of affairs was about to make its demands upon Kenneth Sills almost at the outset of his new career as acting head of the college. When the United States entered the war, Mr. Henry P. Davison had relinquished his responsibilities as a senior partner in J. P. Morgan and Company to head the Council of the American Red Cross. Before 1917 the Red Cross had depended almost wholly upon the services of volunteers. As a move to put the organization on a wartime basis, Davison sought the advice

of Dwight Morrow about filling a key position in the fast-grow-
ing national headquarters in Washington. Morrow, who had
often heard his Amherst classmate and friend Professor Charles
Burnett speak glowingly of the judgment of Dean Sills, suggested
his name to Davison as a likely prospect. Morrow knew that
Davison had already turned for help to another Bowdoin graduate, Harvey Dow Gibson '02, and had made him general manager
of the Red Cross for the whole United States. Late in August,
1917, Davison sounded out Mr. Gibson about Sills's availability.

Gibson's response was characteristically forthright. There was
no question, he said, about Sills's fitness for the job, or his eagerness to serve his country in the national emergency. But Gibson
had been elected an overseer of Bowdoin in the previous June,
and had concurred enthusiastically in the Boards' decision to
name the dean as acting president. He knew that Sills was the
inevitable choice to guide the fortunes of the college during
Hyde's illness. When the President died nine days after Commencement, Gibson realized that the acting president had become virtually indispensable to Bowdoin. Since Mr. Gibson was
in the habit of moving decisively as a New York bank executive,
he may have been surprised at the Governing Boards' failure to
meet in special session to name Sills to the presidency before the
opening of the college in September.

Gibson was in a difficult position—torn, on the one hand,
between his responsibility as an overseer convinced that Sills was
desperately needed in Brunswick, and, on the other, by his
desire to enlist Sills for an important national service to the Red
Cross. In the meantime, at Davison's request, Dwight Morrow
asked Professor Burnett to use his strong personal influence on
Sills in Brunswick. "I cannot help feeling," Morrow wrote, "that
Sills—if he is to be President of Bowdoin—would be a better
president if he spent even as much as one year in important Red
Cross work. He would still have, in all probability, a long life at
Bowdoin and would start with widened experience. It might be
work in this country; it might be work abroad; and, of course, it

would be work of sufficient importance to attract any man's interest."

At this juncture Gibson saw an opportunity to jog the Boards into immediate action. Believing that they would eventually elect Sills to succeed Hyde, he sought by a single stroke to ensure that office for him at once, and at the same time to recruit a leader for the Red Cross. Accordingly, he took into his confidence Mr. William J. Curtis '75, a senior partner in the law firm of Sullivan and Cromwell, a Bowdoin benefactor and trustee whose voice was especially influential in the councils of the College.

The problem, he told Mr. Curtis, was of considerable importance because of its implications not only for the Red Cross but for the leadership of Bowdoin and the career of Kenneth Sills. "Mr. H. P. Davison has a very high opinion of Mr. Sills," Gibson wrote. "He has heard of his ability and judgment from various sources." Despite this enthusiastic endorsement, Gibson intimated that Sills's temporary status made the situation exceedingly awkward both for the college and its acting president. "I told Mr. Davison," he continued, "that as an Overseer of the College, and as a friend of Kenneth's, that I was not in favor of the appointment *unless* he could come to the Red Cross as President of the College. It did not seem fair to the College to have *another* Acting President to take the place of an Acting President, and it certainly was not fair to Kenneth, who has been doing such wonderful work at the College, to have someone else come in while his position was still in an unsettled state."

Gibson was aware of the conservatism of the Governing Boards, most of whose members had been graduated from Bowdoin before he was born, and he knew of their profound veneration of the late president. For them Bowdoin *was* President Hyde. As the youngest overseer, he feared injuring Kenneth Sills's chances by seeming to be overhasty or brash in urging the advantages of electing him to the presidency at once. At the time of his appeal to Mr. Curtis early in September, 1917, Gibson was only thirty-five years old, and the acting president less than three years older. Yet the risk appeared to be worth taking because Gibson knew that the Red Cross position had to be filled by the end of the month. "It would be a great thing for Bowdoin College," he wrote, "for the President of that institution to be made Secretary of the American National Red Cross. There are only five elective officers: President Woodrow Wilson is the president; Robert W. DeForest in New York is the vice-president; John Skelton Williams, controller of the currency, is the treasurer, and John W. Davis, solicitor general, is the counselor. We desire to elect Mr. Sills as Secretary; the job is a big one, and one which will bring credit to Bowdoin and to Sills, and it will be doing a greater service to the Red Cross." Under these circumstances, Mr. Gibson concluded, "I am wondering if it is not of sufficient importance to deserve the immediate consideration of the Emergency Committee of the Boards of Trustees and Overseers."

So persuasive a presentation of the case led Mr. Curtis to summon the committee to meet in Brunswick on September 20, the day of the opening of the fall term. The committee had before it on the table urgent pleas by Davison, Morrow, and Gibson for Sills's release from his college duties so that he might accept the secretaryship. At least some members of the committee knew of Mr. Gibson's hope that their action would enable the former dean to go to the Red Cross on a leave of absence as *president* of Bowdoin. The Committee, however, proceeded cautiously. It prefaced its report by stating: "The Emergency Committee recognizes both its own obligation to the Country and the prestige that may come to the College" were Sills to accept the position offered him. It then voted that "the Committee, while wishing to retain such part of the services of Dean Sills to the College as he may still be able to perform, grants him a leave of absence of sufficient duration to enable him to accept the position of Secretary of the American Red Cross, provided a working arrangement can be conserved during his absence." It further voted "that this Committee hereby authorizes Dean Sills, together with members of the Faculty, to effect such practicable arrangements as may be for the interests of all concerned, and that may carry out the spirit and provisions of this vote."

If Kenneth Sills shared Gibson's hope of receiving definite assurance of his election as Hyde's successor, he kept his disappointment to himself when he learned of the vote. Doubtless he would have welcomed a more clear-cut statement from the committee, a directive less hedged with conditions. He may have been mildly puzzled, as were some of his friends, at the omission of his title as acting president. Despite the fact that his official position was duly listed in the current issue of the catalogue, the committee consistently referred to him as "the present Dean" or "the Dean." Maybe he was destined to remain Dean Sills after all. He was, however, more perturbed about matters of immediate practical concern. The phrasing of the vote left him perplexed about the precise extent and nature of his services which the committee wished to retain for the college. Certainly the duties of secretary of the Red Cross would require his full time and energy. Upon this point Mr. Davison and Mr. Gibson had been most clear. He was also troubled about the difficulties of devising "a working arrangement" for conducting the college during his absence. Nevertheless, despite the vexing conditions imposed by the vote, a doorway leading to national service had been at least partially opened. He might have preferred somewhat less equivocal terms, but he was now brought face to face with an important decision.

It was not an easy one to make. Hyde's celebrated dictum about murdering your alternatives offered small comfort where the alternatives were so tortuous. The opportunity to serve his country in a great humanitarian enterprise appealed to him strongly. Charles Burnett, to whom he turned for counsel, shared Dwight Morrow's conviction that wide administrative experience would increase his effectiveness as a college president. Yet his friends on the faculty had recently given him a touching vote of confidence as their new leader. His old teachers Henry Johnson and Wilmot Mitchell begged him to remain for the good of the college. Scholarly presidents, they said, were rarer birds than efficient administrators. They both feared that in his absence a lesser man might win the confidence of the Boards and pop in between the election and their hopes. Characteristically, Kenneth Sills paid scant attention to selfish considerations. He had not even inquired about the salary to be paid the secretary of the Red Cross. "I do not wish to impose any financial burden on the college," he wrote to Davison and Gibson on September 22. "All I ask of the Society is enough to live on in a fitting manner in Washington."

After two days of deliberation, amid all the countless distractions of the opening week of the fall term, he seemed ready to murder his alternatives and accept the position. "When must the Red Cross have my answer? When is the latest date that it would be possible to begin the work? Is the election by the Executive Committee, and will there have to be another election by the whole organization in December?" he wired Gibson on September 22. The reply was reassuring. "Although formal election would have to await the full meeting in December," he answered, "with the backing of the Executive Committee there would be no question about election. In the meantime, the Committee would name you as Acting Secretary. It is of utmost importance that the matter be settled as soon as possible."

The presence on the campus of the Boards' emergency committee had not gone unnoticed by the anxious faculty. "The Red Cross is after Sills to serve as secretary in Washington," Cram wrote in his diary. While Kenneth Sills was making up his mind in Brunswick, Mr. Gibson reexamined the report of the committee, and conferred again with Mr. Davison and Mr. Curtis. Davison had now become disturbed by the prospect of Sills's acceptance at a time when the acting president's relations with the Boards were in so unsettled a state. "I feel more definite on that score than Mr. Davison does," Gibson wrote, "and my interest is twofold, namely from your standpoint, and from the standpoint of Bowdoin College."

On the morning of September 27, the acting president received a special delivery letter which proved to be decisive. "I advise you *not* to accept the position," Gibson wrote. "If you accepted it and it later developed that your being absent from the College directly or indirectly prevented the very thing happening which we all expect, I would never forgive myself for having suggested such a move. On the other hand, should it develop that you were not made President of the College, you might feel that you had lost an opportunity in not accepting this Red Cross position, but I think that I can assure you that in such a contingency as that there would always be as equally an attractive position open to you. If the war continues the Red Cross will continue to be more and more important, and there are other positions in the Red Cross equally as attractive as that of Secretary. . . . Please believe me when I tell you that my suggestions are made only after careful consideration, and perhaps in a selfish spirit both as respects yourself and the College."

The next day Kenneth Sills formally notified the emergency committee of his decision to decline the offer. Some embarrassment was felt by those who thought that the ambiguous phrasing of the report concealed the committee's desire to eat its administrative cake and have it too. "I sincerely regret that so much confusion has arisen about the offer made to you," Mr. Curtis wrote on September 29. "I suppose the incident is closed for the present." Although the acting president wished to avoid postmortems, he was not allowed to escape them entirely. A senior trustee, Mr. Edward Stanwood, confessed to having mixed feelings about the matter. "I am delighted that you are to stay," he said, "but I have serious doubts if you have done the thing that is most to your advantage. It is a good thing for the College. Whether it is a good thing for you the future must determine." Another trustee, Federal Judge Clarence Hale, was disturbed when he heard of the decision. "I am very sorry that the affair has turned out in just this way," he wrote on October 1. "Perhaps, however, it is better for you and for the College as a whole." Samuel Valentine Cole, President of Wheaton College and a close friend of the late President Hyde, hastened to assure Sills that there was no intention "to put obstructions in the way of any real preference you might have had in regard to the Red Cross position." Still others, like Governor William T. Cobb, a trustee, and John A. Morrill, an overseer, ventured to hope that a decision made with the best interests of the college uppermost in the acting president's mind would, in the end, also prove to be in his own best personal interests. Whatever their differences of opinion upon this latter point, all the board members concurred in Judge George Bird's statement to Sills on October 8: "Your absence would have been a very serious matter for the College." Marshall Cram spoke for the whole faculty when he remarked that he could now breathe easily again: "Sills has finally decided not to go."

No one could have confused Massachusetts Hall with the national headquarters of the American Red Cross, but there were moments during the fall term when Kenneth Sills wondered whether he would have been much busier in Washington. College problems, of course, were on a comparatively small scale, but there were enough of them to crowd his days. The town continued to look to Bowdoin for leadership in a wide variety of causes. As a conscientious citizen in a small community, it was difficult not to feel personally responsible for almost everything from the town budget to the town drunk. Brunswick had no impersonal agencies to hide human misery or to enable a decent man to look the other way when confronted with distress. Thus it was natural enough for the local station agent to call the acting president when a Canadian soldier, without a ticket and "somewhat the worse for wear," had been put off the midnight train in Brunswick on October 9. It was an occasion for no surprise a few minutes later when Kenneth Sills was seen at the Hotel Eagle arranging for the man's lodging and making sure the next

morning that he was put on the train for St. John. The secretary
of the American Red Cross might never have been called upon
for such a duty, but it was a duty none the less.

His first six months as acting head of the college passed swiftly.
Indeed the *Orient* seemed guilty of an understatement when it
reported, "more is happening in a week of this year than in an
ordinary month." Later, during the hectic days of the Student
Army Training Corps at Bowdoin, Kenneth Sills would look
back on the present term as comparatively uneventful. Now he
seemed to move from one crisis to another. The mounting deficits incurred by the Medical School not only threatened the
existence of that institution, but were eating away at the endowment of the college. At almost every faculty meeting the policy
of keeping the Medical School alive at the expense of the college
was sharply questioned. Bowdoin was also embarrassed by the
loss of $3,000 in tuition fees from students who were suddenly
called up by the armed forces. The treasurer, Samuel Furbish,
declared flatly on December 6 that he was unable to pay any
November bills, all the available income having been used to meet
payments on the new dormitory. The acting president warned
of further shrinkage in the enrollment in the event Congress
lowered the draft age to eighteen. "Bowdoin will be harder hit
than most institutions," he predicted on December 18, "because
it is not connected with an engineering department, normal
school, or woman's college." His suggestion that Bowdoin join
other independent colleges in an effort to persuade the public of
the value of training in the liberal arts in wartime met with some
opposition. Despite the fear of the faculty that such action might
stir up latent hostility to colleges and appear to be unpatriotic
when all were asked to make sacrifices, he appointed a committee
to explore the problem. In the meantime, the acting president
effected economies by closing the art building and unused portions of the dormitories to save the dwindling coal supply. His
chief energies, however, went into the task of maintaining the
morale of the student body. Foreseeing that unrest would be-

come acute in the weeks preceding December 15, after which
date the government planned to stop all voluntary enlistments,
he urged men to accept willingly whatever they might be called
upon to do under the Compulsory Service Law. In chapel talks
and at after-dinner conversations in the fraternity houses, he
questioned the motives of those who sought by premature enlistments to avoid the draft. Their highest patriotic duty, he declared
again and again, was to remain at their studies until the government needed their services.

As the members of the college gathered on December 22 for
their last chapel service of the year, Kenneth Sills's thoughts
traveled back over the events of the last twelve months. "No
institution in the land—governmental, ecclesiastical, or business—," he remarked, "is more affected by the changing tides
of human experience than is the college." There passed in review
memories of the opening of the spring term a few days after the
declaration of war, of boys armed with dumbbells and Indian
clubs drilling on the Delta, of delegations leaving eagerly for
Plattsburg, of the formation of the Bowdoin battalion and the
R. O. T. C., of reveille and taps sounding in the pines, of de-
pleted classrooms and chapter houses. Perhaps most poignantly
of all, he remembered the Commencement shadowed by war and
the death of the great leader whose passing seemed like the end
of an era. "Truly we have lived through a wonderful year," the
*Orient* noted on December 18, 1917. Yet for Kenneth Sills the
year ahead was also destined to be an *annus mirabilis*.

# 8

## *THE YOUNG PRESIDENT*

### *1918-1919*

The new year opened in subzero weather amid an epidemic of bursting water pipes which flooded the kitchens of six fraternity houses and, with fine impartiality, refused to spare the home of the acting president. At a meeting of the faculty on January 2, he warned that a shipment of coal ordered by the college would probably be commandeered by the government, but he refused to save fuel by giving up the daily chapel exercises. When his colleagues finally decided to reduce the heat in that building, Marshall Cram begged those faculty members who made up their own prayers to temper them to the unshorn lambs on frosty mornings. He startled his students of chemistry by lecturing in a fur cap and overcoat. Unless they had the constitution of a rhinoceros, he said, they would do well to follow his example.

In his first chapel talk, Kenneth Sills reported that five chapter houses were down to their last few bushels of coal, but that he had found a supply to tide them over the cold spell. By closing the art building and unused portions of other halls, he said it might be possible to stretch the college fuel to last through March. In the meantime, he urged everybody to be sparing in the use of light and heat in the dormitories. All able-bodied undergraduates, he continued, could be of very real help by cutting wood on the college lot. When on January 10 he entertained members of the classical club at his house on upper Maine Street, the guests were invited to sit close to his fireplace. He told them that he had cut some of the logs himself.

Kenneth Sills's own heart was warmed a few days later by a cheerful letter from a former student, Charles Boardman Hawes

'11, filled with praise of the acting president's leadership during the last six trying months. "I want to congratulate you with a sincerity that I hope will atone for a certain Fabian quality in your position," Hawes wrote. If there were any Fabian elements in the Boards' delay in choosing Hyde's successor, K. C. M. S. had been too busy to reflect upon them. Certainly his immediate problems were too pressing to be solved by a strategy of delay. He acted swiftly to save coal by persuading the fraternities to combine with each other instead of attempting to operate half-empty houses. He told Professor Wilmot Mitchell that he was learning how to bargain like an Italian huckster with local coal dealers and the State Fuel Board.

The second semester had just begun when the acting president was saddened on February 5 by the death of one of his oldest friends, Judge William LeBaron Putnam, of Portland, the senior trustee of the college. It was Putnam who had encouraged the Reverend Mr. Sills to send his son to Bowdoin. For fifty years Judge Putnam had been an influential member of the Governing Boards. "To him more than to any other single man," K. C. M. S. said, "is due the present financial stability of the College." Although infirmities had prevented the judge from attending the last meeting of the Boards, he rejoiced in the appointment of the acting president, and looked forward to seeing him guide Bowdoin's fortunes. Even more poignant was the loss during the same week of Kenneth Sills's beloved teacher Professor Henry Johnson. The scholarly poet seemed to be recovering from an operation for appendicitis when he suffered a relapse on February 6, and died the next morning. Henry Johnson typified for Kenneth Sills all that was vital in humane learning. To him he owed his love of the humanists of the Italian Renaissance and his lifelong devotion to Dante. From Johnson's teaching he derived an intense admiration of *virtu*, the quality of excellence wherever it manifests itself. Johnson's lectures on Dante had taught him that the end of man should be the attainment of his "potential intellect." The acting president, who was one of the pallbearers on

February 10, felt as though Bowdoin were burying the better part of herself. The toll taken from the college by death since June was a heavy one, but Kenneth Sills reflected that an institution which could command a lifetime of consecrated service of men like President Hyde, Judge Putnam, and Professor Johnson had strong and abiding qualities.

The middle of February brought a break in the cold spell, but there was no easing of the tension in the news from Europe. The collapse of Russian resistance and the imminent threat of a giant German offensive in the west kept the war in the forefront of all college affairs. Every morning when K. C. M. S. plunged into what he called his "newspaper world" of bulletins from the Front, he worried about the discouragingly modest role being played by the college, yet he was convinced that he and the faculty were working on sound principles. "We are giving elementary military instruction to all who can profit by it," he wrote. "We are endeavoring to hold all of our students in college until they are twenty-one, and to give them the rigorous intellectual training for which Bowdoin stands . . . a liberal training is essential as never before." At a rally in Memorial Hall on February 15, he urged high school seniors to regard college study, not as the refuge of slackers, but "as the work of patriots preparing to take their part justly, skillfully, and magnanimously in all the offices of citizens, both of war and of peace."

With Professor Paul Nixon serving admirably as assistant dean, Kenneth Sills was now able to devote more of his time to the tasks of the acting presidency. Although he had no wish to see Bowdoin become "a strictly military institution," he sought to adapt the curriculum to the nation's war needs. He persuaded the commandant of Fort Preble in Portland to permit Dr. Whittier, now a captain in the Medical Corps, to travel to Brunswick for lectures on military hygiene and camp sanitation. Professor Charles Hutchins of the physics department agreed to modify his course in astronomy to meet the demands of the Navy by emphasizing navigation, while his junior colleague, Rhys Evans, taught military topography and organized a course in radio under the aegis of the Federal Board for Vocational Education. The departments of history and mathematics also responded to war conditions by offering instruction in military history and specialized work in trigonometry. Such modifications, however, were not permitted to supplant any of the courses regularly required for the degree. "From colleges such as Bowdoin," Kenneth Sills declared, "the country expects well-trained, broadminded, high-spirited graduates." He had the firm support of his faculty in holding to the usual offerings in ancient and modern languages, the laboratory and social sciences, philosophy, and the fine arts. "The College has fortunately been able to give all the courses promised at the beginning of the year," he wrote in spring, 1918, "and despite fuel difficulties, to adhere to the academic schedule."

Along with his titles of dean and acting president, Sills also retained his chair as Winkley Professor of Latin, and continued to give courses in Virgil and Lucretius. This variety of offices often made him feel like an academic Pooh-Bah, but he could not bring himself to refuse additional demands made by the community, state, and nation. The war had increased his responsibilities as chairman of the Brunswick Red Cross and school committee. To these assignments were now added activities as a member of the Maine committees on war saving stamps and public safety. His frequent engagements as a four-minute speaker reminded him of his senatorial campaign of 1916, when he left few grange halls unvisited. Nor did he forget his former advocacy of the League of Nations. As a member of the State Executive Committee of the League to Enforce Peace, he accepted every opportunity to gain popular support for an association of nations, and appealed to the State Democratic Convention on April 3 to include such a plank in his party's platform. Two weeks later, President Woodrow Wilson reappointed him for another term on the Board of Visitors at Annapolis. "I count you as an officer of the Navy," Josephus Daniels wrote in urging acceptance of the post. Kenneth Sills was more deeply moved when Secretary Daniels told him that the teachers at the Academy were eager to have him remain on the Board. To K. C. M. S. this was the highest compliment of all. A college administrator who loses the confidence of his faculty, he said, also loses his usefulness.

To colleagues and undergraduates alike, Kenneth Sills seemed to perform his multiple duties without visible strain. Whether they encountered him in his office or in his classroom he appeared equally imperturbable. Paul Nixon, who shared his office in Massachusetts Hall, marveled at the unruffled ease with which the acting president could resume dictating a letter at the very break in the sentence at which he had been interrupted. Yet 1918 was the winter of his discontent. "I never faced so many complicated tangles and problems to be straightened out, or so much to worry over," he confided to an intimate friend. "A college very short of coal, with faculty and students going off every other day, with serious financial difficulties ahead—mine is no easy job. I don't see how any one could envy or covet such a position. It was *only* twenty below zero yesterday morning. I must get out the snow-shoes to get over this grouch."

Nothing could alleviate his sense of loneliness. On his way to and from the campus, he dreaded walking past the darkened study of Henry Johnson. "I feel we are in a transition here," he wrote, "with all the giants on the faculty gone. It has been a terrible year. I wonder sometimes if the happier part of life lies behind." In less gloomy moments, he attributed these moods to the approach of middle age, and lack of time for study and reflection. He realized that the present faculty still had its giants, even though Henry Johnson was the most wonderful man he had ever known. He found himself being drawn more and more to the cheerful living room of Professor and Mrs. Charles Hutchins on lower Federal Street. Although Hutchins' processes of thought were poles apart from those of Henry Johnson and his own, he admired the scientist as a veritable Renaissance man, one who learned Italian in order to read Leonardo da Vinci in his native tongue. Hutchins' impatience with all forms of cant, but above all, his passion for excellence, were welcome signs that *virtu* was still alive in Brunswick.

As the second semester dragged through March and the spring thaws made a lake of the front campus, the faculty grew increasingly apprehensive about the seeming reluctance of the Governing Boards to fill the presidency. "I remember vividly the period of suspense," Professor Roy Elliott recalled thirty years later. "Would the Bowdoin Trustees have the insight—and the guts— to appoint the only one who could be a worthy successor to President Hyde? The Faculty was overwhelmingly for Casey." Allen Johnson, who had left Bowdoin for a Yale professorship in 1910, was puzzled by the situation. "All these months," he wrote from New Haven, "I have wished to say to the Trustees, 'eventually—why not now?' Such an appointment would go far to restore our confidence in Boards of Trustees." A college contemporary of the acting president, Ellis Spear, Jr. '98, remarked that his own exasperation at the Boards' glacial slowness was shared by many alumni. "There has been murmuring in the ranks of late," he complained in May, "if only somebody would get busy it would relieve our minds." Kenneth Sills's old friends were more outspoken. The Reverend Herbert Jump, who had been one of Casey's fellow bachelors in The Octopus during his pastorate in the First Parish Church, was indignant at the protracted delay. "I don't see for the life of me why the trustees are such numbskulls as to wait all these months," he wrote from Manchester, New Hampshire. "Their duty is as plain before them as the noses on their cautious old faces." Meanwhile the Boards proceeded warily by sending emissaries to canvass in thorough but leisurely fashion the opinions of the faculty. Anything less than circumspection and thoroughness, they believed, would have been unthinkable in choosing the successor of William DeWitt Hyde.

Kenneth Sills was too modest and too patient to be unduly

concerned. He was also too busy. Among the uncertainties in the next academic year, he feared for the future of Bowdoin's fraternity system. In many colleges, he told the faculty early in May, fraternities were compelled to suspend their operations altogether. Foreseeing the inability of the fraternities to maintain their houses during the emergency, he proposed that the college compensate the chapter corporations for the loss in room rent by paying insurance premiums and interest on existing mortgages. At Bowdoin, he said, where the chapters are built into the college fabric, it is important that they should be able to resume their activities after the war. Men returning from the service would thus have friendly groups to welcome them and help their readjustment to college life. He assured the alumni that "on the whole and in the main," he was convinced that "the division of the College into fraternities, both from the standpoint of the administration and from the social benefits to the students, is of great benefit."

At the moment, however, his chief concern was with the consequences of the departure of men rather than with their return. At the annual Town Meeting in March, he presented a resolution assuring all Brunswick boys in the service of the town's support and care of their dependents. The *Brunswick Record* reported, "Dean Sills's proposal was enthusiastically received." As a further aid to the morale of the drafted men, he helped organize a parade and rally on April 29 in honor of the first contingent of those inducted from Brunswick. "The Red Cross with whom Dean Sills and I marched," Marshall Cram noted in his diary, "came right behind the college battalion, and on Mill Street the boys put up such a fast pace that we lost them completely, but by cutting corners we caught up." Catching up with his work in Massachusetts Hall, however, was more difficult. There K. C. M. S. refused to cut corners, even when each morning's mail seemed to bring new demands upon his time. The acting president had become so prominently identified with efforts for the public welfare that his influential help was sought from all corners of

the state. Acting promptly upon appeals from many families of
men drafted under the Selective Service Law, he urged President
Wilson and Adjutant General John Johnson to assign an appreci-
able number of Maine draftees to the same army division. "I do
think that it will help that unity of action which we are all aim-
ing at," he wrote Wilson, "if some such solution of this problem
could be worked out." The favorable response of the adjutant
general caused statewide satisfaction. He was also assured,
following a plea to the Departments of the Army and Navy, that
families of the men who lost their lives in the service would be
informed of their loss prior to the publication of casualty lists.

The sad duty of announcing the death of Ensign Michael Dele-
hanty, Jr. '20, Bowdoin's first war casualty, fell to the lot of
Kenneth Sills on April 2. In a brief but moving chapel service,
he spoke of the boy's student days and of his service record,
followed by the congregation's singing "The Son of God Goes
Forth to War," and a concluding prayer. The format of this
memorial service was destined to be repeated twenty-eight times
before the signing of the armistice in November, and always by
the same compassionate leader who was to perform a similar
solemn office twenty-five years later. As they heard their president speak the familiar words "another son of the College," many
undergraduates realized for the first time that they, too, were
Bowdoin's sons, and that Kenneth Sills's affection for them was
no less sincere because there were so many of them. In the quiet
of the chapel, they sensed intuitively that whatever the future
had in store, or wherever their paths might lead, Kenneth Sills
would somehow be there to help them.

May, 1918, was to be a memorable month. At home on the
campus the acting president faced the problem of preparing a
budget for the uncertainties of the next academic year. In the
current session, expenditures had exceeded income by $1,869.
He knew that this was not the only deficit confronting the visiting committee of the Boards. Although the Medical School employed a separate method of accounting, it was a department of

Bowdoin College for which the president and trustees were financially responsible, and during 1917–18 the school had incurred a deficit of $7,805, making a total of $9,674 to be borne by the college. In Portland, where he attended the monthly meetings of the medical faculty, Kenneth Sills sympathized with the efforts being made to continue the century-old school, many of whose staff members were serving without compensation. Yet he shared the opinion of his faculty in Brunswick that the heavy annual drafts on the general funds of the college were unjustifiable. The whole problem had become sufficiently acute to warrant a special meeting of the Governing Boards on May 14 to consider the future of the Medical School. Fearing that a decision to close the school's doors was imminent, Dr. Addison Thayer, the dean of the medical faculty, and a committee of staff members, asked permission to appear before the Trustees and Overseers during the session. As the date approached, the acting president became alarmed at the prospect of a bitter controversy which might alienate friends of the college.

Business at the Naval Academy required the presence of Kenneth Sills in Annapolis from May 6 through May 8. He spent the remainder of the week attending a conference of eastern college administrative officers at Princeton University. There, in the company of his fellow deans, with whom he had been meeting annually since 1910, he felt thoroughly at ease. K. C. M. S. was not allowed to forget that he was the only dean present who was also an acting president. He blushed when his friend Dean James Stevens of the University of Maine remarked that even such handicaps as membership in the D. K. E. fraternity and the Maine Democratic party might not be fatal disqualifications for election to a higher office. Dean Frederick Jones of Yale added owlishly that President Hadley was a Deke. Sills was also reminded that two former members of the conference, Presidents Alexander Meiklejohn of Amherst and Frederick Ferry of Hamilton, had once been respectable deans at Brown and Williams. "We made them honorary members of our little association when they deserted us," Dean Stevens said, "and we're prepared to behave with equal magnanimity when your turn comes."

It came with unexpected suddenness on the day after K. C. M. S. returned to Brunswick on May 13. Many members of the Boards and almost all the faculty thought the special session of the Trustees and Overseers had been called to settle the problem of the Medical School and to discuss plans for the establishment of the Student Army Training Corps in September. This impression was partially confirmed on Tuesday morning, May 14, when Kenneth Sills devoted his chapel talk to outlining a new policy announced by the War Department. With the opening of the college year in autumn, all physically fit students who were eighteen years of age or over were to be enlisted regular members of the U. S. Army. It was the intention of the War Department, he said, to withdraw men from time to time for further training at officers' schools. Bowdoin was soon to become an armed camp.

While the acting president was speaking in chapel, the Governing Boards assembled for their special session on the second floor of Hubbard Hall. They listened sympathetically as Dean Thayer and Dr. Drummond, Dr. Moulton, and Dr. Whittier pleaded for the survival of the Medical School. The doctors submitted that the medical department had been an organic part of the college since 1820, and that it had supplied small towns with family physicians for almost a century. They cited the fact that of the eighteen M.D's. who were graduated in March nearly all were serving their country in the Medical Corps, and that the demand was outrunning the supply. Conceding that the school was not self-supporting, they argued that success or failure should not be measured by money alone, but by the usefulness of its graduates and their value to society. In their opinion, these considerations justified the continuance of the school under the present or even greater financial losses in the future.

Despite the cogency of such pleas, the Trustees were unconvinced. The diminished number of students, the steadily mounting annual deficits, and only the most remote prospects of improvement in the situation led them to recommend to the Overseers that no new medical students be admitted, and that the school close its doors at the end of the academic year 1920– 21. By the terms of the Bowdoin charter, the Trustees initiate all legislation, while the Overseers possess the right to concur or to decline to concur in the decisions. The recommendation of the Trustees met lively opposition when it was presented to the Overseers, many of whom lived in Portland where the advanced work of the school was carried on. Reluctant to lose the distinction which the Medical School brought to their city, they finally declined to concur in the Trustees' vote, thus leaving the status of the school unchanged. Earlier in the month, when Dean Thayer failed to submit his annual report, he told Kenneth Sills that the Medical School was sick unto death and too weak to talk. Now, however, the Overseers had given it a new lease on life. The acting president was not elated at the news. He feared that the impasse in the Boards had merely prolonged the patient's agony, and that he would have to witness the dying gasp.

After the protracted debate about the Medical School, the Boards turned with relief to less controversial matters. They authorized the faculty to award certificates of honor to Bowdoin undergraduates who were called into the service. They approved Kenneth Sills's suggestion that a course in Russian be offered in 1918–19 and they endorsed his proposal that the college reimburse members of the faculty for any loss of compensation during their service in the armed forces. Then, without debate or discussion, and almost as if by an afterthought, the Trustees "voted and chose by ballot Mr. Kenneth C. M. Sills as President of Bowdoin College." On this occasion the Overseers concurred. When the secretary announced the result of the vote, the only ripple of surprise came from a sudden realization that such formal confirmation had actually been necessary. In the eleven months since President Hyde's death, the name of but one man had been mentioned for the office, and that man was the dean and acting president. "While we were waiting for divine Providence to grant us another William DeWitt Hyde," Charles Taylor Hawes '76 remarked to a fellow overseer, "we almost forgot the great blessing we already possessed in Kenneth Charles Morton Sills."

Kenneth Sills was notified of his election by Philip Greely Clifford '03, who hurried downstairs to a telephone in Hubbard Hall as soon as the Overseers adjourned. "May I speak," he asked, "to the *President* of Bowdoin College?" If Kenneth Sills blushed when he heard the jubilant congratulations of his college friend, there was no one present in his bachelor's quarters to observe it. Two days later he scrawled a note to a friend in New York. It began as an apology for his failure to call on May 11 when he had been in the city with only twenty minutes to scurry from Pennsylvania Station to Grand Central. "Perhaps you have heard," he added in a postscript, "that last Tuesday I was elected President of Bowdoin. If not—it's true—strange as it may seem." The note was sent to Miss Edith Lansing Koon, 61 East 77th Street. It was followed the next day by another to the same address in the same scrawl. "Just because I am a college president," he wrote, "I hope you don't think I am to forget my friends: *Quorum pars magna estes.*"

When Professor Elliott greeted his new chief the morning after the election, Kenneth Sills seemed even more diffident than usual. "All it means," he said, "is a chance to help the Faculty do the *real* business of the College without interference or distraction." Then, after brushing some imaginary flecks of dust from the lapels of his coat, he added, "Teaching is our proper business. I'll do my best not to bother you." Meanwhile congratulations began pouring in from all sections of the country. William R. Pattangall, who had managed Casey's campaign for the Senate two years before, confessed to a sense of having been absolved from a heinous sin. "I was afraid," he wrote from Augusta on May 15, "that the fact that you were a *Democratic* candidate for the United States Senate might have injured you with some of the Trustees. I felt guilty in this matter." The president's allegiance to the Democratic party was not the only anomaly in his new eminence. "When as staunch an Episcopalian as you can get elected to a Calvinistic-brimstone college," Theodore Woodberry exclaimed, "it seems the world is making progress." Although the liberal teaching of President Hyde had dispelled all trace of brimstone, his successor's Episcopalianism was not universally palatable, especially to the Brunswick household presided over by Miss Fan Pennell. Miss Pennell, who might have stepped out of the pages of Harriet Beecher Stowe or Sarah Orne Jewett, had a sharp nose for the scent of heresy, even in her own beloved First Parish Congregational Church. Moreover, her worship of John Calvin was equaled only by her pride in the Psi Upsilon fraternity and the Republican party. "Bah! Don't call *that* man *President* Sills," she retorted when a neighbor told her the news. "He's a paltry Democrat, D. K. E., and an Episcopalian."

The old comrades of Kenneth Sills's pillow-kicking exploits at Harvard in 1903 sent a joint letter of felicitations. William Lawrence predicted that his "dear Schwan" would be "as successful in kicking away the troubles of Bowdoin College" as he was in "propelling pillows through the transom in Weld Hall." Chester Greenough and George Chase boasted they had detected signs of future greatness in the pummeling he had inflicted on his battered copy of Behrens' *Grammatik des Altfranzosischen von Dr. Eduard Schwan*. The trio of Behrens-Schwan baiters had not forgotten their friend's desperate literary advice to a Harvard Freshman. "Now that you are a Great Man," they counseled, "please try to be 'a trifle less *bookish* in your writing.' Bookish baccalaureates, dear Schwan, will never, never do. What? Never? Well, hardly ever." K. C. M. S. gravely acknowledged their admonition, but found it difficult to follow in answering a letter from Margaret Ellen, the young daughter of Philip Clifford, who combined two queries with her congratulations. "I hope you will come to see us just the same if you really are president," she wrote on May 21. "And now I wonder if the

President of Bowdoin can answer these questions. Who was the great-uncle of Perseus? After whom was the Hellespont named?"

Other questions were to admit of less ready answers. One of them was raised about the Medical School by Marshall Cram, who had been out of town on May 14. "Got back home full of curiosity to find out what damage the Boards did while I was away," he wrote in his journal for May. "Found they elected Sills president which is a great relief, but the medical school question was not settled so satisfactorily. The Overseers by a vote of two to one refused to agree with the Trustees, so that everything remains as it is. . . . It's a mean legacy for Sills to have as he becomes president." Cram's view was the prevailing one in the faculty with the exception of that of Dr. Whittier, for whom the Medical School was a passion. The new president, who always put the interest of the college first, was disturbed at the constant drain on the general funds. The action of the Overseers, he was convinced, could only defer the ultimate blow, but he resolved to use the reprieve granted the Medical School to seek whatever aid could be found to reduce the embarrassing deficits. More immediate matters now claimed his attention.

Presiding at his first faculty meeting two days after the election, K. C. M. S. recommended the appointment of Professor Paul Nixon as acting dean for the remainder of the term. "It is the hope of all of us," he said, "that in June the Governing Boards will elect him Dean of the College." In his annual report to the visiting committee, the president spoke warmly of his departmental colleague and administrative assistant: "During the past year Professor Nixon has been assistant dean, and has shown unusual executive ability. He is popular with the undergraduates, and is continuing his sound scholarly work on Plautus; indeed he has all the necessary qualifications to take up the duties that are of such importance." Paul Nixon was Kenneth Sills's first official appointment. It was also one of his wisest. Twenty-two years later, in recounting some of the events during his administration as president, he told the undergraduates, "I have always taken what I think is a justified pride that I was given the wisdom to nominate Paul Nixon to be Dean of Bowdoin." It proved to be the happiest of partnerships. The alliance of Casey and Nick soon became a cherished Bowdoin symbol. In 1933, on the fifteenth anniversary of President Sills's election to office, Dean Nixon wrote, "As professor, dean, and acting president, Kenneth Sills has been my superior officer for nearly twenty-five years, without once appearing to be anything but my friend and colleague."

The faculty, wishing to set the earliest convenient date for the inaugural of their new president, voted to combine the ceremony with the Commencement exercises already scheduled for June 20. The decision pleased K. C. M. S. It not only appealed to his modesty, but also accorded with his desire to avoid any suggestion of pomp and ostentation in wartime. Best of all, it would enable him to play a less conspicuous role, even at his own inaugural, than would have been possible were the induction to take place at a special ceremony in autumn. He wanted the delegates and guests to honor the institution rather than its president. Such characteristic self-effacement was a source of affectionate raillery by his friends. "I suppose you'll be looking as shame-faced as usual," Eleanor Vanamee declared, "and you will positively slink around corners—such being your custom when the rewards of virtue materialize!"

Marshall Cram, who was in charge of the arrangements, feared the whole program would fall flat. He counted only thirteen Seniors in line at the baccalaureate services on June 16 and, with so many alumni busy in war work, he foresaw a slim attendance at the inaugural itself. Cram noted glumly that the Yarmouth bridge was closed for repairs and predicted that some of the delegates would get lost in making the awkward detour. To avert this catastrophe, he arose at five o'clock on the morning of the inaugural and traveled to Portland to transport a dozen guests safely to Brunswick. His worst fears, however, went unrealized. All the delegates and guests reached the campus, while the pres-

ence of only a few Seniors to represent a class six times as large
and the absence of one-fourth of the faculty and many alumni
in the armed forces added a poignant footnote to the inaugural
address. "Half of the heart of the College is now in France,"
Kenneth Sills said, "and the remaining half here beats in sympathy,—its thoughts largely over there."

Kenneth Sills was always to be at his most impressive on Commencement Day, and his first official appearance as head of the
college set the standard to be followed for the next thirty-four
years. His first baccalaureate address also achieved the restrained
eloquence, the modest tone, and the concern for the spirit rather
than the fortunes of men which generations of departing Seniors
were to remember as a benediction. "Baccalaureate addresses do
not contain the sum total of human wisdom," he told the members of the class of 1918. "They can only suggest certain avenues
of thought, open new vistas of policy, or bring to mind old
dreams. Certain things, however, ought to be said, things so
obvious that they will strike your minds with the irritating and
haunting quality of old hymn tunes." The time-honored pattern
was followed at the ceremony of induction: a prayer of invoca-
tion by the vice president of the Board of Trustees, an address
for the faculty, the investiture and presentation of the keys of
the college by the president of the Overseers, and "Domine
Salvum Fac Praesidem Nostrum" sung by the choir. The benediction was given by the president's father, the Reverend Charles
Morton Sills.

In his own address, Kenneth Sills recounted the contribution
of men and ideas which American colleges were making in the
conflict for freedom. He refused to believe, even when technology was in the saddle, that the college of liberal arts must change
the whole basis of its training. Seeking the distinctive place of
Bowdoin among the nation's colleges, he said simply, "We have
in the past stood stoutly for a liberal education: we shall continue to stand for it." He promised that the classics would always
have an important place in Bowdoin education because "a first-

rate thing is never dead." The president disavowed any ambition to have Bowdoin become a university or to tack on a technical annex. Although numbers, he said, are not the ultimate test, he hoped Bowdoin would never succumb to the temptation of bigness. He pledged himself to maintain President Hyde's policy of giving the faculty complete independence and a large share in the direction of the college. By substituting comprehensive examinations for course credits, he hoped Bowdoin would emphasize subjects rather than courses. Above all, transcending the complicated machinery of college administration, K. C. M. S. insisted there must be a zeal for honest workmanship and an impelling, driving spiritual force. Education, he concluded, is primarily concerned with the individual. Its object is to free man intellectually and spiritually, to develop a resourceful mind in a strong Christian character.

Although Kenneth Sills had not looked forward to his address with much pleasure, and would continue to have an aversion to a public show on any occasion of personal significance, the response to his inaugural was distinctly favorable. "It must have been, in some ways, an embarrassing position for you," Franklin Payson, a trustee, said after the exercises, "but you met it thoroughly." Those who knew the president best felt that his remarks were characteristic of the man. "Your address is splendid," Wilbert Snow '07 wrote from Camp Zachary Taylor. "In it you express yourself as we know you: constructively, conservatively, and honestly. Your smile shows that you still distrust the Pollyanna world and the Pollyanna people; you wouldn't be *you* if you didn't." Further assurance came from William Lawrence. "The whole day went off exceedingly well," he wrote, "and your part in it was dignified and modest, and what you had to say was characterized by common sense which an inscrutable Providence has not always bestowed upon college presidents."

In the company assembled in the First Parish Church for the inaugural there were those not yet convinced that any man, especially one so young and diffident, could possibly be worthy enough to follow Hyde. Beneath the academic decorum some sharp appraisals and comparisons were being made by the older alumni. Unlike his predecessor who enjoyed public speaking and exulted in the cut and thrust of debate, Kenneth Sills never was entirely at ease on any platform. Hyde spoke vigorously and with a forthrightness which threw off sparks and shocks. From his first sentence, often a precisely stated but boldly unqualified assertion, he challenged his listeners to take sides. The new president, on the other hand, was not immediately provocative. He preferred to wind his way slowly into the heart of his subject, to shy away from authoritatively pronounced opinions, and to concede that "much might be said on the other side." To be sure, the rigors of his senatorial campaign had taken the edge off his self-consciousness and had partially overcome his shyness, but the old uneasiness of manner remained. Although his hesitancy of utterance gradually wore off with each passing year, on June 20, 1918, at the beginning of his administration, many older alumni shook their heads gravely. "President Sills, for all his thoughtfulness and dignity," they said, "will never speak like old Prex."

The more discerning members of that audience refrained from making invidious comparisons. They realized that Kenneth Sills had won his position not by spectacular performance or facile speech but by obvious fitness and downright devotion to every detail of his office. They sensed they had been listening to a scholarly man of innate dignity and first-rate mind. His inspiration would doubtless not be like that of their late president, but it would be inspiration all the same. Even some of the old guard were compelled to acknowledge that Kenneth Sills possessed a certain tone and quality of his own. Wilbert Mallet '91, principal of Farmington Normal School, spoke for many of his contemporaries when he wrote the president after the inaugural ceremony: "Doubtless as time runs on, we old dyed-in-the-wool Republicans who have looked askance at you because you were a Democrat, and were a little shy, too, of one whose ecclesiastical connection was outside the traditional New England fold, will find that one who combines and harmonizes in his own mind democracy in politics and the Apostolic succession in church is the very one to lead a free college." Others who were sure that Bowdoin's greatness was about to enter a mild Indian summer after the flowering period under Hyde were heard to remark after the inauguration, "The young fellow isn't too bad; he did pretty well after all." The majority opinion was put bluntly by Jeremiah Smith, Jr., who read the address in Paris early in July. "The trustees would have proved themselves the greatest set of geese known to history," he exclaimed, "if they had failed to elect Kenneth Sills!"

Brunswick townsfolk were delighted. It was reassuring to see a familiar figure as head of the college, and something of a relief not to have to get used to a stranger. President Hyde, for all his national prominence and public spirit, had remained somewhat aloof from the social and business life of the community. Citizens regarded him with a respect bordering upon awe, but few found him easily approachable, and fewer still ever set foot inside the square, cupola-crowned house at 85 Federal Street. It would be quite different, most people believed, with Kenneth Sills. In school committee, Red Cross, church, and Town Meeting, his activities had already done much to blur the distinction between town and gown. Children and adults from both sides of the tracks spoke to him without a trace of self-consciousness. Many youngsters soon ceased being surprised when he called them by their first names. In any event, the dignity of his new position as president had no terrors for Elijah Boyd, Brunswick's amiable collector of garbage. Whenever they passed each other, Elijah dropped the reins of his unsavory horse cart, raised his battered hat, and called out cheerfully, "Hi there, young fella! How's your college gettin' on this mornin'?"

Meanwhile, the prospect of a bachelor president preparing to move into the huge empty mansion on Federal Street provided Brunswick tea and auction tables with a topic of lively interest.

Although Casey's bachelorhood took on an added dimension after May 14, 1918, it had always been a piquant subject in Portland and Brunswick society. As early as 1900, Mary Sills enjoyed teasing her brother about the current status or availability of his "old flames" back in Portland, especially one "dear young lady as pretty as a picture," whose engagement had just been broken. "She is also very wealthy now," Mary wrote encouragingly. "You'll have my blessing." But neither his sister's raillery, nor the hope of the Reverend Mr. Sills that his son's return to Bowdoin as a professor in 1906 would hasten his marriage, had any discernible effect. Kenneth Sills's membership in The Octopus, a dining club of eight Brunswick bachelors, made him an attractive target for campus wits. In June, 1908, when Gerald Wilder became the third of the Octopi to desert the ranks within less than a year, the *Bugle* hinted that the Winkley professor's friends were beating him to the altar. The squib was captioned, "It's Up to Casey Now!" And the coach of a faculty farce, *The Servant Not in the House,* was accused of type casting when he selected K. C. M. S. for the role of "a cautious bachelor" who was made to exclaim in Act II: "This notion that men always have to depend on the women—well—pray pardon the expression—it makes me tired. It's immoral—positively immoral—as immoral as total abstinence." Despite his ungallant speech, he was assured by a faculty wife that the unmarried members of the Ladies Auction Club thought his performance was "perfectly stunning."

The new president of Bowdoin soon became the blushing beneficiary of a good deal of advice about his future happiness. "You may laugh all you please," wrote Allen Johnson, "but no single man has wisdom enough to serve acceptably as a college president where social obligations must be incurred . . . you're bound to have cares that you can't share with your closest friend." Margaret Hale, wife of Judge Clarence Hale, one of Kenneth Sills's Portland well-wishers, sent him an ultimatum the day after his inauguration: "I'll give you until Christmas to select a wife for yourself, and then I'll choose one for you." His English kinswoman, Beatrice Rice, assumed a miniatory tone: "You are very naughty not to get married; good husbands are very scarce now-a-days. Why didn't you find a nice English girl when you were over here in 1913?" Kenneth Sills's mother, who probably had asked the same question, now filled her letters to her son with praise of the heroism of British women in the war. While the president's single state continued to evoke mingled curiosity and commiseration in Brunswick, Francis Dana, Ripley's brother, threatened to take matters in hand. "Unless you get busy yourself," he wrote in July, "your friends will form an association to select a wife for you." There is no record of a reply. If K. C. M. S. followed his usual custom when confronted with gratuitous advice, he doubtless thanked his friend for making "a highly interesting suggestion." Throughout this barrage the president maintained an inscrutable silence. Little wonder that another friend, Laurence Crosby, could write confidently, "I am wont to think of you as an American type of Oxford don— of the days when dons were dons and not husbands." Mrs. Henry Johnson's observation in 1906 that Kenneth Sills loved women en masse, not as individuals, must have seemed prophetic.

As an administrator, whenever K. C. M. S. was told of a current crop of rumors or gossip, he enjoyed dismissing his talebearers with a favorite quotation from Bishop Berkeley: "They say? What they say? Let them say!" On many occasions during July and August, he must have repeated this axiom to himself with quiet amusement. For he could be proudly confident of what all people would say in the last week of August when his engagement to Edith Lansing Koon was to be announced. "You have furnished the good people of Brunswick with a topic of conversation which for a time will be more interesting to them than the war," wrote W. J. Curtis when he received the news. It is perhaps the crowning evidence of Kenneth Sills's reticence about his own affairs that almost no one "knew." He even kept the secret from his sister Mary whose husband sent his congrat-

ulations from France on September 5: "You are a sly dog to give
us no inkling. I suppose Mary can chaperone you both." William
Lawrence, who was to be his best man, was taken aback delightedly. "Who would have supposed," he wrote from Portland,
"that beneath the dignified and bland demeanor of our last meeting you harbored such designs as these." Few letters left town
without bearing the news to the president's friends. "Eight percent of Brunswick, fifty percent of Portland, and ten percent of
Boston have informed me of your engagement," Philip Meserve
protested in a note from the French front. "How dare you brave
the calumny of Fan Pennell?"

There were, of course, a few intimate friends who were not
completely surprised. Violetta and Harold Berry, at whose Falmouth Foreside farm Edith Koon spent the summer of 1918,
had more than an "inkling." The Berrys had known Miss Koon
since 1912 when she first came to Portland to teach Greek and
English in the high school, and they soon became devoted to the
charming young Wellesley graduate. The friendship continued
after she moved to New York City in 1916, and they often entertained her on her frequent visits to Portland. In New York she
taught Latin at Lenox, the day school of the Finch Boarding
School for Girls, where in 1917, she combined her teaching with
graduate study in comparative philology at Columbia.

In the common chance of society it was inevitable that she
should have met K. C. M. S. long before leaving Portland for
New York. They had many mutual friends, especially the Berrys,
Browns, Cliffords, and Thaxters, who eventually would have
introduced them, and Edith Koon was a vivacious figure in the
affairs of the College Club and an active member of St. Luke's
Parish. Actually they met for the first time at a Cumberland
County teachers' convention on the Bowdoin campus in October, 1913. There in Memorial Hall, following a session on the
ancient languages, Miss Alice Lord, an older teacher at Portland
High School, presented Miss Koon to Dean Sills as a fellow
classicist. "Of course, I was properly impressed," she recalled

later, "and we had a pleasant time together with all the other teachers." A few days after this meeting, both were pleased to find themselves dinner companions at the Portland home of U.S. Senator Frederick Hale. Their host said that he thought a teacher of Greek might enjoy talking with the dean of Bowdoin College who had recently spent his sabbatical in Greece. Thus their acquaintance began.

It soon deepened into friendship as they discovered how much they had in common. Both were children of Episcopalian clergymen, both had been brought up in rectories amid similar interests and responsibilities, both had majored in classics at college, both were teaching ancient languages, and both were eager to maintain the place of Greek and Latin against the inroads being made in the schools by less rigorous disciplines. Notes soon began flying between Massachusetts Hall and Portland High School on a variety of professional topics. The dean sent copies of the Oxford examinations in Greek grammar in the hope they might help her students to prepare for the entrance tests at Harvard. When she wrote of some of her problems in teaching Greek composition, he promised to arrange conferences in Brunswick with Bowdoin's professor of Greek Frank Woodruff. Occasionally he treated her to a few of the bright spots he encountered on his Freshman papers, such as an inspired translation of *cave canem* as "Look out! I may sing."

By the middle of the winter they were seeing each other quite frequently in the homes of Portland hosts where K. C. M. S. was able to share her pleasure in some of his old friends. She was delighted with the urbane and sprightly Dr. James Spalding, a physician-linguist, who returned the compliment by sending her his Latin rendering of "Little Jack Horner." She enjoyed Judge William Putnam's relish of the translation of Horace's *Telephum, quem tu petis, occupavit* as "The telephone when you want it is busy." But her admiration of Professor and Mrs. Henry Johnson pleased Kenneth Sills most of all. After meeting them at tea in Brunswick, she wrote, "I have always felt the greatest reverence for intellect, ever since I can remember. It certainly must be more or less of a Utopia to live in a community where every one has so many things in common with every one else."

Their correspondence was not wholly concerned with pedagogy. The dean contrived ways to combine Miss Koon's afternoon conference with Professor Woodruff on Greek composition with Brunswick dinner parties, lectures, and concerts. There were also the classical collections in the art building waiting to be inspected by a teacher of Greek, if only she would permit a professor of Latin to be her guide. On another occasion he persuaded her that the Brunswick Dramatic Society's production of *Green Stockings* was worth the discomfort of the midnight train back to Portland. In June, 1916, when he learned that the Berrys were planning to attend the Commencement Dance, he volunteered to provide "some agile and youthful partners" on the condition that she would consent to come along. Within a year of their first meeting, his letters had dropped their formal salutation of "My dear Miss Koon" for "Dear Miss Koon" and, by the summer of 1915, he was addressing her as "Dear Edith." Their growing interest in each other seems to have been generally unobserved, but it did not escape the notice of a sharp-eyed matron at a play presented by the Portland College Club in November. She told her husband of the surprising presence in the audience of the dignified dean of Bowdoin, who applauded the acting of Miss Koon with something more than the perfunctory politeness expected at amateur theatricals.

After Edith Koon left Portland for New York in 1916, K. C. M. S. was drawn to the city by more than college business. Between his other engagements, he was usually able to take her to dinner or the theater. His letters reflect a vicarious delight in her enthusiastic responses to the opera, exhibitions of modern art, and volumes of the new poetry. "I am glad to learn that New York is still fascinating," he wrote in December. "I should like to see some of the modern poetry magazines. I've got to be converted to *vers libre*, but I'm game, I hope, and open-minded."

He confessed to a lack of tolerance, however, when she reported that her fellow teachers were excited about self-expression in the Latin classroom. "Don't let them fool you with educational theories," he warned in October, "or the nonsense about being in tune with the Infinite and the Child. You know quite as much about your job as the other ladies—I'll bet a hat." Kenneth Sills, who had been brought up on a diet of gerund-grinding, was gently quizzical about the "natural method" of instruction. "How do you like it?" he inquired early in October. "A teacher can very easily be carried away by it and forget the hard and narrow path of *hic, haec, hoc*. A little of it is a good thing—but too much of it leads to superficiality." His sense of humor saved him from playing the part of an academic Sir Oracle. "Hear Old Wise Acre spout!" he exclaimed. "I never taught in school and lower Latin is Greek to me. I should be very much up against it if I were to teach the elements."

Brunswick gossipers were unaware of the flurry of letters between the dean's office and New York, but one of the messages ultimately reached a wider circle of readers than was contemplated. Since the two classicists occasionally enjoyed writing to each other in their favorite languages, it was natural enough for Edith Koon to accept an invitation to dinner and the theater by sending K. C. M. S. a telegram in Anglicized Greek letters. The wire was dispatched after the United States entry into the war, and a telegrapher, who had been instructed to pounce upon all communications in code, promptly reported his suspicions to the precursor of the F. B. I. Security agents began an investigation at once, but instead of discovering a dangerous enemy alien operating from 61 East 77th Street, they found a charming young woman who not only was able to establish her innocence, but also to persuade them that even an elementary knowledge of Greek had some value.

Letters in any language, even telegrams in the best Greek, do not speak as eloquently as a living presence, and the return of Edith Koon to Maine made the summer of 1918 the happiest in

Kenneth Sills's life. Falmouth Foreside was near enough to Brunswick to enable them to spend many hours together during July and August. It was there, during the last week of the summer, that she accepted his proposal of marriage. They would always associate the beginning of their happiness together with evening walks along the shore, the dark woods behind them, and the sound of a bell buoy across the starlit waters. "This week has transformed me utterly," Kenneth Sills wrote her from Montreal a few days later. "At breakfast this morning in the Canadian Pacific Station I thought that any one would say, 'Who is that ordinary-looking man over there with his neck-tie awry and his absent-minded air?' 'Why,' I would reply, 'that is no ordinary man: he is the most extraordinary man—the most utterly fortunate and happy man I know—because for no other reason except her own good will, the loveliest lady in the world loves him and told him so.' "

With the wedding date set for November 21, Edith Koon resumed her teaching, and the correspondence—now almost wholly in English—continued between Brunswick and New York. "Just think," he wrote, "a few weeks more and you won't have to write to me at all. Marriage will have some compensations."

Meanwhile the president had his hands full in preparing the college for its new military status. After a conference with the War Department in Plattsburg early in September, he told an anxious faculty, "It certainly does not look as if there were going to be very much left of our colleges except as military institutions." As September 26, the opening date of the fall term, approached, K. C. M. S. expected to see Bowdoin turned inside out and upside down at the request of the government. That the college was able and willing to do so would, he hoped, prove its flexibility and justify the public confidence in American institutions of learning. In any event, tests of the flexibility of the faculty were not long in coming. Between September 5 and the first day of classes three weeks later, the War Department issued and revoked three programs for the Student Army Training Corps. On the afternoon of the president's return from Plattsburg on September 5, he summoned the faculty to work out the details of the army's rigidly prescribed schedule of military French or German, mathematics, chemistry or physics, and a course in war issues. The contract stipulated that textbooks were to be provided by the college. When the president reached his office the following morning, he was notified by the War Department of a change in the program, and he asked the faculty to reconsider its plans. "Nothing much was done at this meeting," Marshall Cram noted. "We expect further orders, so do not dare to take anything we may hear now as final." His fears were confirmed on September 9, after the texts had been ordered, when another directive announced that the books would be furnished by the War Department. On September 24, two days before the opening of the term, a new order from Washington called for a third rearrangement of the curriculum to include, among other things, courses in military law, map-making, and surveying. "This plan leaves us completely at sea," Cram remarked. "We have no one to teach military law, and the only hope for map-making and surveying is the new instructor in mathematics." K. C. M. S. attempted to cheer his colleagues by predicting optimistically that a new order would probably arrive to cancel any preparations that had been already made for the opening day. On the eve of the first classes he wrote Edith Koon, "I am sure the old woman who lived in a shoe did not have any more troubles than yours truly."

A bewildered faculty which by this time had become thoroughly flexible met on September 25 to be told that a naval unit was to be established at Bowdoin, the reversal of a policy formulated at the Plattsburg conference. Kenneth Sills was undismayed, even by the news that the syllabus for the S. A. T. C. program promised by the War Department had failed to arrive. He told the faculty that it would have much in common with the greenest Freshman: both would be ignorant about the program on which they were to embark the next morning. Only one provision seemed to be immutable: reveille was to sound at 6:40 A.M. and taps at 10 P.M. Whatever else might happen, the president added, Bowdoin students would get up and go to bed earlier than at any time in man's memory. As for the faculty— perhaps they might be comforted, he said, by reading an essay in a recent *Atlantic Monthly* in which the author observed: "The professor was reputed to be fossilized; but he has turned out to be almost embryonic in his modifiability and capacity for growth."

Although the academic year opened on September 26, the formal establishment of the S. A. T. C. and the naval unit was delayed until October 1. Normal campus life, of course, would be "out" for the duration, but President Sills encouraged the fraternities to initiate as many Freshmen as possible. He believed such additional ties to the college, tenuous as they were, might induce more students to return to complete their courses after the war. By October 10, 273 men, including seventy in the naval unit, were in uniform under military discipline. Eighty-eight others, who were either physically ineligible or too young for the service, were enrolled in the regular college program. This remnant, with the sympathetic support of the president, continued to publish the *Orient* and to maintain at least some semblance of fraternity life. Bowdoin was now a wartime college and, as the *Orient* observed on October 15, "With the coming of the S. A. T. C., instead of the happy, carefree atmosphere which has characterized it in the past, we see determination and serious purpose." Yet the student body had hardly become accustomed to the strange routine of inspections, drills, military instruction, and supervised study when the armistice was signed on November 11.

The experience with the S. A. T. C. convinced President Sills that military and academic education do not mix. "Educationally it was indeed a failure," he wrote after the demobilization, "for men interested in military drill and discipline found it irksome not to have the full amount of time for such work, and men interested in the theoretical side of the training and in their academic studies were consequently and necessarily handicapped by military duties." Although the financial settlement made by the government was satisfactory, Kenneth Sills had no wish to see an R. O. T. C. program at Bowdoin except in a national emergency. Administering a combined military and academic curriculum was beset with constant difficulties and frustrations. Too often it seemed that when the War Department asked anything of the college, it regarded Bowdoin as a military post, but when the college requested anything of the War Department, it took the position that it was not a military post. The president's considered opinion was stated in his official report to the War Department in which he held that "the proper conduct of military training demands a man's entire time; proper conduct of college work demands the same thing; and both the army and the college are to be esteemed more highly because such is the case."

The sudden signing of the armistice and the government's decision to withdraw the S. A. T. C. units as soon as possible brought the welcome responsibility of preparing for the return of students from the service. In order to enable many veterans to complete their course with their classmates, President Sills divided the period from January through June into two college terms. This accelerated program was successful. "Of our many undergraduates who were in the service," he wrote in May, "I personally know of only two who have not returned to college or who do not plan ultimately to return, and only two of the men who have returned have fallen down badly in their studies as a result of their experiences in the army." As the veterans trooped back to resume their studies, Kenneth Sills told them of the pride of the college in their gallant response to their country's call. "She is equally proud," he said, "that they return to the duties of college life, as so many of their mates have returned to the duties of civil life, with added zest and with serious attitude."

Kenneth Sills's administration had begun formally with his inauguration on June 20, 1918, but he preferred to date its real beginning from the time 85 Federal Street would become the home of the president and his wife. Early in October, Mary Sills Robinson, whose husband was in France with the Canadian Army, came to Brunswick to assist her brother in getting the house ready. "Mary and Marshall Cram helped with the shades and stair carpet," he wrote Edith Koon on October 6, "while I hung some pictures." K. C. M. S. enjoyed his role of the comically helpless bachelor who was permitted to dust bookshelves while more important business was afoot. He reported his sister's dismay as she watched the large rooms swallow up his few pieces of furniture. "This is the first letter from *our* house," he wrote the day after the moving. "I am writing from our living room upstairs furnished now only with some pictures and my desk. You should see me running the furnace! Mary says to tell you that the simple life is surely lived in Brunswick." Not so simple, however, were the inquiries put to him by society editors from the Portland newspapers. "I was asked today for a description of your wedding dress," he wrote on November 13. "The reporters have promised to be good at least until the ceremony. But could you send me a *feminine* description of said raiment?" He repeated with glee a remark made by his family's old cook at St. Andrews when she was told of the coming marriage. " 'It's a fine thing,' " he reported Effie Byrne as saying. " 'He needs someone to push him socially.' So you see that you have *that* task." K. C. M. S. also forwarded other comments to give fair warning that the lot of a president's wife would not be a sinecure. "Miss Koon will be a distinct asset to Bowdoin College," Kate Douglas Riggs predicted. "I have even a hope that without her saying anything, the students will blacken their shoes more frequently and cease to wear tan ones at commencement." Kenneth Sills took special delight in quoting Robert Hale's letter of congratulations: "I know she'll be a good wife, and I dare say if you want to take a week off, she can run the college as well as you can."

Kenneth Sills was married to Edith Lansing Koon on November 21, at St. Luke's Cathedral in Portland, near the deanery where he had spent his boyhood on State Street. His father, the Reverend Charles Morton Sills, performed the ceremony, and the bride was given away by Harold Lee Berry. Only the demands of military service kept Ripley Dana from being present. It was a "Bowdoin wedding," and William Lawrence, the best man, said he was tempted to emulate Mark Twain and appear in his Bowdoin doctoral gown and hood. Mary's husband was still in Europe, and the bride's only sister was doing war work in France, but the other members of the immediate families were there, as were virtually all the Governing Boards and faculty. "Adjourns" were issued right and left, the *Orient* noted, so that the faculty might see the president and his wife start on their new life together. The reception following the ceremony seemed almost like a Bowdoin Commencement. Perhaps Mrs. Kenneth Charles Morton Sills thought she had just been married to Bowdoin College. After the Thanksgiving recess, when Edith and Kenneth Sills crossed the threshold of 85 Federal Street, Bowdoin also entered a new era. From that time forward no one would ever think of one without thinking of the other.

# 9

## *ADMINISTERING BOWDOIN*

## *IN THE 1920s: I*

On December 2, 1918, when classes were resumed after the Thanksgiving holiday, passers-by may have noticed a new American flag flying from the staff on the front lawn of 85 Federal Street. Its significance had not escaped the sharp eyes of Marshall Cram. "The Sillses are at home!" he exclaimed earlier that morning as he watched the president and his wife leave their house together for the first time. They were carrying a carefully folded flag which Mrs. Sills helped her husband attach to the halyard and raise to the top of the pole. "Togetherness" had not become a part of the Brunswick vocabulary in 1918, but this was the first of the many engaging examples of it which the Sillses were destined to provide, whether in the form of their delivering Christmas wreaths, entertaining undergraduates, or presenting toys to faculty children. From across the way, Professor Manton Copeland who had also witnessed the scene, hurried over to greet his neighbors just returned from their wedding journey. The Sillses' friends realized that this was not an ordinary homecoming. The whole college community, rejoicing in the personal happiness of the president and his bride, agreed with Mrs. Roscoe Ham that it also had many reasons to congratulate itself. Now that the uncertainties of the acting presidency were over, and the college, like the rest of the nation, was being demobilized, the faculty could look forward to a long administration led by a colleague in whom it had absolute trust. Professor Wilmot Mitchell spoke for both town and gown when he predicted the beginning of a new era of good feeling.

Following the opening chapel exercises, an Alpha Delta Phi

Freshman was overheard to remark, "Casey spoke very *credibly* this morning." When this ambiguous compliment was repeated to the president, he shifted his green cloth bookbag from one hand to the other and tried to repress a grin. "Perhaps, in the fullness of time," he said, "I may even learn to speak *creditably*, too." K. C. M. S. remembered hearing President Charles Thwing of Western Reserve warn a young president that he would need four years to become familiar with the duties of his new office, and that the experience would be like entering college all over again. If this were true, Kenneth Sills felt that at least he had survived a rigorous orientation. As dean during Hyde's illness in the trying spring of 1917, and later as acting president, he had learned the war and peacetime specifications of his job. His first few months were enough to convince him of the truth of Ellery Sedgwick's definition of a college presidency as "the impossible profession." Casey reflected that impossibility is at once the glory and despair of all professions concerned with the spirits rather than the fortunes of men, whether in college or church. The son of a Christian minister needed no reminding of that. When he thought of the loyal comradeship of Edith Sills, he knew that for him the profession would no longer be a lonely one.

Unlike most college presidents whose first encounter with the tough realities of administration is mercifully deferred until after the amenities of the inaugural, Kenneth Sills had his initiation beforehand without ruffles and flourishes. The very meeting of the Governing Boards at which he had been elected on May 14 had ended in a discouraging impasse about the Bowdoin Medical School. Feelings ran high on both sides, but the president believed no good could come from persistent and acrimonious agitation over the difficulties of the school. The question of its continued support by the college would, he foresaw, be the first major crisis of his administration. If this were to prove his baptism by fire, he would face it manfully. Yet, as always, he knew there was "much to be said on both sides." For years annual deficits had made the Medical School a "poor relation" of the college, and as Dean Addison Thayer remarked, "The discovery that a poor relation is also a very near one, naturally arouses mixed emotions."

President Sills was peculiarly susceptible to the force of these conflicting feelings. He was proud of the honorable history of the school, the sixth oldest in the nation. Its maintenance since 1820 he regarded as one of the great services Bowdoin College had performed for the state of Maine. From his boyhood days in Portland, he knew the esteem in which one of its graduates and teachers, Dr. Frederick Gerrish '66, distinguished anatomist, was held by patients and colleagues alike. Two of his earliest friends, Dr. Israel Dana, Rip's father, and Dr. James Spalding, had been highly regarded members of the medical faculty. As dean of the college, Kenneth Sills knew that many promising boys from rural Maine had been encouraged to enter Bowdoin by influential medical graduates, most of whom were beloved family physicians practicing in small towns. His friend the indefatigable Dr. Frank Whittier pointed out that the closing of the school would leave Maine, an area equaling the combined size of the five other New England states, without an institution for the training of doctors. As the school approached its centennial in 1920, K. C. M. S. was convinced that with proper financial support it would be able to continue its good work. If adequate funds were not forthcoming, he was equally convinced of the folly of maintaining what would inevitably become a second-rate institution.

Money, of course, was the crux of the whole question. Deficits and financial crises in the Medical School had been regularly recurring nightmares as far back as Kenneth Sills could remember. In 1897 President Hyde had deplored as "primitive in the extreme" the practice of medical professors dividing up student fees among themselves, and recommended that the Boards assume responsibility for all appropriations and salaries. At a later critical juncture in 1912, a Boards' committee urged the faculty, alumni, and friends of the school to undertake a campaign for endowment enough to make the institution self-supporting. Meanwhile the college continued to meet all deficits. Yet five years later, despite zealous efforts to attract additional funds and more students, the results were neither satisfactory nor reassuring. Enrollments had declined while expenditures mounted. In June, 1917, the visiting committee reported an impending deficit of more than $7,000, "the largest within the period of this attempted revival," and threatening "to jeopardize the welfare of the College itself."

Kenneth Sills, who had helped to prepare the budget in 1917 in the absence of President Hyde, shared the committee's view that so heavy a draft on the funds of the college was unjustifiable. He was reluctant, however, to recommend that the Medical School be immediately discontinued, a radical measure strongly favored by a majority of the Trustees and a few Overseers. His hesitancy was natural enough. Only a few hours before, he had been appointed to discharge the duties of President Hyde during what was then hoped would be only a temporary disability. With so many perplexing contingencies to be considered, and with the desperate shortage of doctors in wartime, the acting president advised against taking drastic measures at the Commencement meeting in 1917. He approved as a wise compromise the Boards' decision to empower a new joint committee to make a final attempt to determine how the Medical School might be adequately maintained. In the event such determination failed, he concurred in the vote to submit the whole problem to the Boards at Commencement in 1918, or at an earlier special session.

The story of that fateful special meeting which was convened on May 14, 1918, to settle once and for all the future of the Medical School, but instead proceeded to defer the decision and to elect Kenneth Sills to the presidency has now become a twice-told tale to the readers of the preceding chapter. When the meeting adjourned, a new Bowdoin president was left with an old Bowdoin problem. The vexing question remained: to close or not to close one of the most useful institutions in Maine.

Now in full command of the college, President Sills watched solicitously as the school struggled to stay alive. In 1918 the entire entering class numbered only seven men in a total registration of but forty-four medics. K. C. M. S. realized that both school and college were contending with the same difficulties. The drafting or volunteering of students had resulted in decreased enrollments everywhere. He also knew that the drop in numbers was due in part to the commendable steps taken by the Medical School to raise its own standards. A sharp falling off had followed the requirement in 1912 of at least one year of college work for admission. The size of the entering classes in 1916 and 1917 was drastically affected by a further raising of the admission requirement from one to two years. Kenneth Sills vigorously supported both these measures which had not only done much to improve the quality of the candidates, but also helped to retain the school's precarious Class A rating by the American Medical Association. He feared, however, that Dean Thayer was unduly optimistic when he reported in 1918 that "The wounds of war appear to have left us vigorous and cheerful,—strengthened by the visions of our opportunities for future service."

K. C. M. S. promptly offered the dean his "whole-hearted support," but warned of the need of a large increase in the number of students. In his efforts to recruit additional candidates, Dr. Thayer emphasized the value of individual instruction in laboratory, out-patient service, and at the bedside. In Portland, where the third- and fourth-year clinical work was done, he was able to promise that "forty-seven doctors were ready to take a direct personal interest in twenty-nine Bowdoin medical students." Indeed, Dr. Whittier could boast that the faculty was larger than the student body, and that the lecturers outnumbered the lectured. These advantages were obvious enough, but as the president wrestled with the budget, he discovered that each student was being educated at a cost of $500, of which $170 was coming from the limited funds of the college. Such an imbalance, however necessary for the present emergency in 1918, he could not regard as a sound permanent policy. Its continuance, he said, would "in the long run be disadvantageous both to the Medical School and the College."

Dean Thayer was confident that the tide had turned in the autumn of 1919. Cheered by the admission of a first-year class of nineteen men, he declared at the opening of the October term, "The fight for individual work has been won, and the School has a bright future." The centennial year which began with such brave hopes was, however, soon to be overshadowed by a renewal of the agitation to influence the Boards to abolish the school. On May 10, 1920, fifteen graduates of the college, of whom twelve were physicians, sent a circular letter to many alumni to solicit their "opinion of the proposition to discontinue the Bowdoin Medical School." The letter was written by Dr. Lucien Howe '70, a distinguished scientist who had studied under Lister and Helmholtz and was then director of the Howe Laboratory of Ophthalmology which had been named in his honor by the Harvard Medical School. He and his cosigners informed the alumni of a recent decree of the Council on Medical Education that "No medical school should expect to secure admission to, or be retained in Class A which does not have an annual income of at least $25,000 in addition to the amount received from students' fees." To meet this standard, Dr. Howe warned that "Bowdoin alumni must soon raise each year $17,000 for the School alone." Directing his appeal to the Overseers, he asked whether the school should be "voluntarily discontinued while still in Class A, or later be relegated to Class B, or perhaps Class C, and then die an ignominious death?" With its present scanty income, Dr. Howe wrote, the college "is utterly unable financially to do justice to itself and the School." As for the non-medical faculty of the college, he predicted that "unless some further increase can be made in their salaries, several will probably go elsewhere." In support of his position, he cited "Bulletin Number Four" of the Carnegie Foundation for the Advancement of Teaching in which Abraham Flexner questioned why Bowdoin, a college of liberal arts, should be concerned with medicine at all.

Although this document voiced some of his own misgivings about the wisdom of continuing the school, President Sills was disturbed by its timing. He had hoped for a lull in the controversy, especially when the Medical School was making what might be its last effort to become self-sustaining by enlisting public support. To strengthen Dean Thayer's attempts to save the school, the president had sought and received from the Council on Medical Education in May, 1920, assurances that no step would be taken in the coming year to relegate the school from Class A to Class B. This twelve-month period of grace, K. C. M. S. believed, should give the friends of medical education in Maine sufficient time to demonstrate their ability to put the school on a firm basis. Dean Thayer told the president that the school was not ready to commit "hari-kari" for the only crime alleged against it—that of poverty, but that he would favor "immediate discontinuance" if it lost its Class A standing. The officers of the school were looking forward to its centennial on June 23, 1920, as an appropriate occasion to appeal to the public for an adequate endowment. Certainly it was no time, Dean Thayer remarked, for the Governing Boards to show infanticidal tendencies toward their one-hundred-year-old offspring.

The circular letter, promptly followed by a spirited rebuttal by Dr. Gerrish, Dr. Whittier, and Dr. Thayer, provoked a lively and at times a bitter debate in the newspapers. K. C. M. S., who had been warned by Hyde to avoid controversy as he would shun poison, was now faced with an issue on which loyalties were sharply divided. On one side were those who felt that financially the school was "an open sore," eating into funds intended for the proper work of the college. Edward Stanwood '61, editor of *The Youth's Companion,* and his classmate Lucilius Emery, chief justice of Maine, told the president in 1920 of their unwillingness to contribute to the college if any part of their gifts would be "swallowed up by that leech, the Medical School." Others held that the school, far from being a burden, was actually a financial boon. They reminded President Sills of the bequest of almost $400,000 in memory of Seward Garcelon and Samuel Merritt, both of them medical graduates, and neither an alumnus of the college. Friends of the school pointed out that the only reason any of the money was bequeathed to the college was the donors' gratitude to the Medical School.

Throughout the controversy, K. C. M. S. refused to overstate the case of either side. As a result, his fair-mindedness won the confidence of Dean Thayer as well as that of Dr. Howe and the signers of the circular letter. Their differences of opinion, he wrote in his conciliatory report for 1919–20, were more apparent than real. He praised the heroic efforts required to run a medical school on a budget of less than $21,000 a year. "No one," he declared, "wishes the School to continue unless it can be maintained as a Class A school, worthy of its past history and of its association with Bowdoin College." He cited the inability of the college to provide either the income or the number of eight full-time teachers needed to maintain Class A rating. An application for state aid, he said, was not possible under the provisions of the college charter or in accordance with Bowdoin traditions. "The only solution," he concluded, "seems to be the raising of a fund of half a million to a million dollars; or the relinquishment by the College of its responsibility."

A month later at the centennial exercises, on June 23, 1920, Kenneth Sills allowed others to recount the past glories of the school. "Today we ought not simply to look backwards," he said. "If we stand still we perish." Appealing to all those interested in the cause of medicine, he declared, "If the School is to survive and hold its place of usefulness in the future, it must have far more than it has now, the support, financial as well as sympathetic, of the people of Maine." If the funds are received, he promised that Bowdoin would gladly continue the school entrusted to it by the people of the state a century ago, "but we

shall not maintain a School that is not first rate." Later that evening after reviewing the situation, the Governing Boards agreed
that the Medical School was entitled to do what it could to improve its financial position while it still had a Class A status, although time was fast running out. K. C. M. S. advised against
taking immediate action, but he warned that unless solid support
were forthcoming within the next six months, a decision to close
the school would have to be announced before the end of the
current year. Arthur Staples '82, whose *Lewiston Journal* had
reported the pros and cons of the question, began writing his
news story of the meeting as he rode home in an open trolley car.
"The Trustees and Overseers accomplished much business," he
noted, "but took no action toward the movement which was
started last spring to have the Bowdoin Medical School discontinued."

Although President Sills had not expected a Maine Rockefeller
to come forward to save the school after the centennial exercises,
he resolved to carry his appeal to the Rockefeller Foundation itself. Phillips Kimball '07, an influential New York banker, had
intimated that Dr. Wallace Buttrick, president of the Foundation,
would welcome an interview. "He likes to have such men as
yourself drop in to see him, if only for a chat," Kimball wrote.
"Dr. Hyde never called to see him and he noticed it, so it might
be well to cultivate the habit of calling every time you are in New
York." Kimball, who had already informed Dr. Buttrick of the
predicament of the school, reported that the response was hardly
encouraging. "I am almost inclined to agree with him," Kimball
confessed, "and have become enthusiastic over the idea of divorc-
ing the school from the college altogether . . . even if such
a move means the end of the Medical School."

Kenneth Sills knew that Buttrick's opinion was held by virtually every member of the college faculty except Dr. Whittier,
but he felt it his duty to present the best possible case to the
Foundation. Accordingly, he submitted its proud record of
graduating 2,121 physicians and of training more than 1,450

others who obtained a large part of their medical education in Brunswick. He cited the school's contribution to the public health and welfare by supplying rural Maine with general practitioners. He also reaffirmed President Hyde's belief in the value of a small medical school, adequately equipped to avail itself of the practical results of medical research, yet primarily devoted to training men to use those results in the actual practice of medicine. Dr. Buttrick's answer was as flattering to the college as it was damaging to the medical school. He conceded that the school had done "fairly good work in the past," but that the Foundation approved the tendency to larger schools with their superior teaching and facilities for original research to advance medicine as a science. He doubted whether the demand for a medical school in Maine could justify Bowdoin's jeopardizing her future by attempting to fill it. New England, he said, was pretty well supplied with medical schools. In his opinion, the school added nothing but a burden to the college, and the sooner Bowdoin discontinued it the better. Although Dr. Buttrick declared flatly, "There is nothing about the Medical School that would interest the Foundation in any way at all," he was enthusiastic about Bowdoin College. "I admire it immensely," he told the president, "as one of the best small colleges in the country, but it should not carry anything else on its back but its own work." Discouraging as this verdict was to the friends of the Medical School, it was one with which Kenneth Sills was disposed to agree. In his heart of hearts, he felt Bowdoin's proper destiny was that of a small college whose chief business was to improve the quality of those who teach and learn. In such an enterprise no burden would be too heavy. This was the commitment which he had accepted on his inaugural day when he said, "In the administration of my office I will give my best."

Soon after informing the Boards of Dr. Buttrick's indifference to the plight of the Medical School, K. C. M. S. was compelled to report a second setback. Dr. N. P. Colwell, secretary of the Council of Medical Education and Hospitals, had advised him in

December "that conditions in the Medical School are so seriously
below the Council's requirements for an acceptable Medical
School that the Council has no other alternative than to place
the institution in Class B of American Medical Schools." The
blow was scheduled to fall in June, 1921, unless in the intervening time the school were able to increase its resources. President
Sills, who now estimated the required sum to be at least one
million dollars, felt the prospects were frosty indeed.

The Boards took prompt action at a special meeting on December 17, 1920. Seeing little hope of satisfying the conditions necessary to retain the school in Class A, they concurred in a vote to
close its doors on July 1, and prepared to surrender the charter
and dispose of its property and assets. In his announcement of the
action, President Sills repeated his conviction of the need of a
medical school in Maine, but affirmed his belief that it was not
the business of the college to raise large sums for medical education. "The College," he said, "will not apply for state aid for
the School. But if the citizens of Maine who believe that the maintenance of a medical school is properly a state function desire to
have the School re-established as a state institution under state
control and adequately supported by the State, Bowdoin will
be glad to give all assistance possible to that end."

The president's statement placing the issue squarely before
the public was widely debated in the press. Viewing the problem
as of more than local interest, the *Boston Transcript* praised Bowdoin for the courage to discontinue a service which no longer
could be conducted efficiently, but acknowledged Maine's need
of a school to train general practitioners. Although most Maine
newspapers deplored the decision to close the school, the more
conservative editors rejoiced at the Boards' unwillingness to seek
state aid. "It is encouraging to know," declared the *Bangor Commercial*, "that Bowdoin College is determined to stand upon its
own resources unhampered by political or governmental control." While the academic faculty welcomed a policy which
would enable the college to concentrate all its resources upon

undergraduate education, the *Brunswick Record* feared the closing would not only be "a severe blow to the Town of Brunswick and the State of Maine," but would seriously damage Bowdoin's prestige.

Meanwhile, Dr. Whittier took to the road to address alumni clubs, granges, chambers of commerce, and county medical societies from Kittery to Calais, returning with a sheaf of bristling resolutions begging the Boards to reconsider. In some quarters the American Medical Association was accused of "outside interference" and ridiculed for imposing "unreasonable technical exactions." Edgar Oakes Achorn '81 asserted that "by utilizing all that is best in the State, you will not have a School that the American Medical Association will put in Class A, but you will have an A-1 school that will conform to the genius of American institutions and will meet the requirements of the people." In other quarters Kenneth Sills was charged with sympathizing with those members of his faculty who for years had "disparaged the medical department of their own college." Another critic complained, "Casey was all too prone to regard with polite condescension Bowdoin's medics as socially uncouth and narrowly vocational unless they happened to hold degrees from colleges of liberal arts." "Science and the Medical School were both alien to him," another medical graduate remarked. "He treated us as though we came from the wrong side of the intellectual tracks." There were moments during the controversy in the spring of 1921 when the president felt the Boards' decision had produced almost every response except money.

As the prospect of unexpected gifts grew increasingly dim, friends of the school turned to the legislature for help. They threw their support behind a bill introduced on February 9 by Representative Tudor Gardiner to incorporate the trustees of a Medical School of Maine, and to provide a subsidy of $100,000 for the first two years. Bowdoin loyalties, as well as popular and medical opinion, were split upon the merits of the proposed legislation. At the public hearings late in February, former Gov-

ernor William T. Cobb '77 testified that the loss of the Medical
School "would be a public calamity to the State." His view was
shared by many rural legislators who had grim memories of the
scarcity of doctors during the influenza epidemic. These solons,
complained the *Lewiston Journal,* believe the state should edu-
cate doctors "no matter how much it costs. . . . This doesn't
look much like keeping the tax rate down." Much of the opposition centered in Portland where both the *Herald* and the *Press*
objected on the grounds of expense. Robert Hale '10 insisted at
the hearing that the cost of supporting a Class A school would
be double the sum proposed in the Gardiner Bill, while Owen
Brewster '09 doubted whether the rural areas would be benefited. President Sills was careful to state the position of the
college: "Bowdoin believes that the Legislature should determine
whether it is a proper function of the State to maintain the School
as a Class A institution. It would be most unfortunate to open
the medical school and then not be able to get a desirable rating."

Members of the appropriations and judiciary committees, who
met jointly to consider the proposal, were strongly influenced
by the "strict economy message" read to the legislature by
Governor Percival Baxter '98, and unanimously reported that
the Gardiner Bill "ought not to pass." But Dr. Whittier and his
colleagues had not traveled up and down the state in vain. By
a decisive vote, the House and Senate overruled their own committees by passing the measure. The rejoicing was short-lived.
On April 4 Governor Baxter vetoed the bill for reasons of
"economy." A significant thing about this veto, the *Portland
Press* remarked the following day, "is that Governor Baxter is a
graduate of Bowdoin and if sentimental reasons were to influence
him it is probable that this school long known as the Bowdoin
Medical School would have had some weight with him. But
Governor Baxter isn't intending to govern Maine by sentiment."
Among the telegrams received at the State House while the
governor was writing his veto message was one which may have
caused him to pause. The plea was not impelled by sentiment. It

was sent by his former college roommate, Kenneth Sills, who urged his old friend to sign the Gardiner Bill for the common good.

At the last commencement of the Medical School on June 22, when President Sills conferred degrees upon a class of eight doctors, Governor Baxter witnessed the ceremony. Whatever their sentimental regrets at the passing of the century-old school, neither man betrayed them. Kenneth Sills was moved the day after the exercises to receive a letter from Dean Addison Thayer, who, with Dr. Frederick Gerrish, had fought for the life of the school to the very end. "Our friend Dr. Gerrish has commented more than once," Thayer wrote, "upon the kindliness and square-ness with which you have belied the reputation of college presidents. . . . Few people have been in a position to understand better than I the trying situations in which you have been placed, or the tactfulness and wisdom and persistence with which you have acted. It might be said of you, what someone said of Emerson as an iconoclast, that you shattered our idols so gently that it seemed almost an act of worship."

Commencement in 1921 was not funereal, despite the death of the Medical School. Casey's classmates turned their twentieth reunion into a jubilee in the president's honor. At the alumni dinner, when Governor Baxter told of his prophecy in 1897 that someday K. C. M. S. would become head of the college, the graduates stood up and cheered to the echo, while the president blushed like a school girl. More heartening than the ovation was the election of his old friends William Witherle Lawrence and Harold Lee Berry to the Board of Overseers. Kenneth Sills welcomed them as his own college contemporaries. In 1921 only four of the fifty-four members of the Governing Boards had received their degrees in the twentieth century.

The closing of the Medical School enabled the president to give his full attention to the college. He found it necessary, however, to assure the public that Bowdoin had no intention of using the Garcelon-Merritt bequest for its own academic purposes.

"The College," he said, "will ask the courts to be allowed to establish from the income of the Fund, scholarships for boys who would thus have an opportunity perhaps otherwise denied them, of studying medicine." Such a decree was eventually given by the Supreme Judicial Court of Maine in May, 1922. Thereafter, when the Garcelon-Merritt awards were made, Kenneth Sills often used the occasion to remind undergraduates of the history of the Medical School. "Casey really seems to believe," one undergraduate remarked, long after the odor of formaldehyde had disappeared from Adams Hall, "that we are all a part of everything that ever happened around this place." The boy's observation was a shrewd one. It was a cherished article in the president's creed that in the Bowdoin fellowship all are members one of another.

Even without the Medical School to worry about, college affairs were quite enough to keep Kenneth Sills busy. His mail was filled with advice, especially from older graduates who feared a youthful president might break too sharply from the Hyde tradition. Those who knew him best felt no such alarm. "The things which have given Bowdoin its quality and distinctive place," wrote Chauncey Goodrich, "are in the safest hands now. It is good to know that, as the college develops, it will be along the lines which will hold it true to form." The president needed no prompting to follow one notable Bowdoin tradition: he would continue to teach. "I have often wondered what happened to President Hyde's courses in psychology and philosophy," Rowland Walker '02 asked K. C. M. S. "Something should be done to have them carried along in somewhat the same manner and spirit. Wouldn't it be desirable for you to step into his shoes in that respect?" President Henry Wild of Williams College and Casey's old friend Dr. Spalding urged him to continue teaching Latin. "It gives one a sense of security in these days," Dr. Wild wrote, "to have a classical man, especially yourself, continue the great traditions." Dr. Spalding reminded his friend that the Boards had not only elected him to the presidency but asked him to retain the Winkley professorship of the Latin language and literature.

When Kenneth Sills was an undergraduate, Hyde's celebrated course in philosophy had been required of all Seniors. Twenty years later, with the extension of the elective system, K. C. M. S. had no desire to have a captive audience, yet he wanted as many students as possible to know him primarily as a teacher rather than as an administrator. Were he to offer his former courses in Livy, Horace, and Terence, the enrollment would be limited to a few men majoring in Latin. Even the Greek and Latin classics in translation would be unlikely to appeal to a majority of the upperclassmen. The answer seemed to point to the selection of a field broad enough to interest Juniors and Seniors, yet one embodying his own chief literary enthusiasms. While casting about for a solution, he recalled Professor Fletcher's Columbia lectures in comparative literature. Bowdoin's austere curriculum lacked such a course. It also neglected the literature of the Bible. K. C. M. S. had often heard Professor Roy Elliott lament his students' ignorance, not only of Biblical literature, but of classical mythology. Perhaps these gaps might be filled by a broad survey beginning with the Bible and devoting the rest of the first semester to Greek and Latin literature, the Vulgar Latin, and the Church literature of the Middle Ages, and concluding with the precursors of Dante.

The president's heart glowed at the prospect of making his beloved Dante the center of the course. From Dante he could proceed in the second term to an examination of the writers of the Italian Renaissance, with a more cursory glance at the literature of Germany, France, and Spain. If time remained, it might just be possible to suggest the influence of earlier writers on Spenser, Shakespeare, and Milton. To be sure, it was a large order, but he was not to be deterred by what some of his colleagues would say about mere snippets from an anthology. After all, a college president must be allowed some privileges. "I would not think of permitting any other member of the Faculty to give such a smattering," he confessed cheerfully to one whose scorn for survey courses was cosmic, "but I know very well what I am doing and I intend to do it." The new course was duly listed in the catalogue for 1919–20 as "Literature 1, 2. Elective for Juniors and Seniors, Monday, Wednesday, and Friday at 11:30." There, scheduled for the same hour, it was destined to remain for the next thirty-three years. During that time more than 3,000 undergraduates elected it for at least one semester, but if any of them ever referred to the course by its official catalogue title, the fact has gone unrecorded. Many job-hunting Seniors, scanning the transcript of their Bowdoin courses for the first time, were momentarily puzzled to discover they had received grades in Literature 1, 2. "Why," they exclaimed, "*that* must be Casey's Lit!"

The grades were likely to be "C's." President Sills knew perfectly well that the popularity of his course was not due to a campuswide passion for comparative literature. Many of the regular takers were those bent on amassing a sufficient number of "C's" to ensure their graduation. There was also a sprinkling of science majors who preferred to satisfy the literature requirement by avoiding the rigors of an advanced foreign language or a close reading of Shakespeare. A campus wit, watching the hordes pour out of Adams Hall after an hour exam in Literature 1, cried, "Here come Casey's multitudinous C's incarnadine!" Yet the course usually contained a fair number of men on the Dean's List who soon discovered that the president was quite chary about bestowing "A" and "B" grades. Occasionally he enjoyed goading those who complacently lowered their sights to the level of the "gentlemen's grade" of "C." One glib loafer who had exhausted his knowledge of Petrarch by writing, "He was the first modern man," noticed a scrawled admonition in the margin of his returned exam book. "A cliché is often true," Casey wrote, "but don't repeat it—document it."

K. C. M. S. doubtless chose the 11:30 hour for Literature 1 because it enabled him to get in a full morning's work at his desk in Massachusetts Hall, but he may have had a less obvious reason. Since all the fraternities were represented, he could count on having his comments on college affairs promptly discussed during luncheon at the various chapter houses a few moments after the class scattered at the sound of the bell. More often than not, he used the first five or ten minutes of the lecture hour for a brief homily. The point of departure might be an editorial in the *Orient,* an athletic victory, an instance of undergraduate thoughtlessness, or the publication of an article or book by a colleague. One could never be quite sure. On one bleak Monday following a disastrous Saturday afternoon on Whittier Field, the president surprised his class by fishing a sports page from his green bag and solemnly reading the football scores of a dozen victorious colleges and universities. "None of these institutions," he said quietly, "has ever impressed me as being any great shakes as a place of sound learning, but defeat doesn't make a good college either." Students looked forward to these lay sermons after the president first looked over the class quizzically, recorded the names of absentees, and arranged his lecture notes. His comments were always serious. No member of the course ever heard him utter a facetious remark or invite easy laughter by the use of sarcasm or ridicule. His dignified platform manner was the antithesis of the popular lecturer, yet somehow he turned his shyness and reticence into positive qualities of effectiveness. Even his hesitations and pauses achieved a quiet drama of their own. "It's funny about Casey's lectures," one undergraduate observed. "He always makes you wonder what thing of interest or importance he's going to say next. Nobody watches the clock." There were times, however, when the collective lethargy of a class became almost overpowering. During one such languid period, just before the bell, when K. C. M. S. was describing a complicated political maneuver by Lorenzo de' Medici, he suddenly asked, "All those who approve of Lorenzo's action raise their hands." No hands were raised. "All those who disapprove." Again no hands. "All those who do not care a damn."

Every hand shot up. "I dare say," the president replied as he stalked out of the room.

Although Kenneth Sills sometimes achieved his ends by indirection, he never regarded Literature 1 either as a sounding board for the policies of his administration or as a medium of self-expression. The ancient classics were his first love and the writers of the Italian Renaissance his chief literary passion. In his lectures he wanted to communicate the best things he had to say about them. When students came to review their notes before an examination, they were surprised to find how many facts had been packed into a single hour. "If you take full notes in Casey's Lit.," a wiseacre remarked ruefully, "you'll end up with a bag of solid buckshot." It was not until the cumulative impact of the course began to be felt that the more perceptive students realized they had been listening to overtones which the president had no intention of including on his examinations.

K. C. M. S. was not perturbed when his course sometimes failed to attract all the able students planning to enter graduate schools of arts and letters. Nor did he expect to encounter many men for whom a liberal education was the goal of life itself. He was out for bigger game—the majority who were headed for business careers, and for whom Literature 1 was likely to be their only course in imaginative literature. He sought constantly to have them share and retain some measure of his own delight in books. "Many of you will soon have your first jobs," he told a class in May, 1926, "and perhaps some will live in dingy hall bedrooms in Boston or New York, but life need not be drab if you reserve space on your shelves for a few really good books." Conservative in his own literary tastes, as were Longfellow and Lowell whose teaching he admired, Kenneth Sills strove to conserve the humane values. Since his conception of a liberal education was largely derived from classical sources and their interpretation by the humanists of the Italian Renaissance, "Casey's Lit." was an expression of his educational philosophy. Again and again he quoted Dante's ideal in *Of Monarchy:* "The proper business of the human race as a whole is to actualize constantly the total potentiality of the possible intellect." For Kenneth Sills, as for Dante, the possible intellect meant the human mind. Whatever else his students may have remembered of his lectures, they never forgot the president's admiration of those individuals who most nearly attain the limits of their mental powers. Few ideas were examined more minutely than *virtu*, the ability "to get there," a quality prized by Renaissance man. No one regarded it more highly than K. C. M. S., especially when Bowdoin students exemplified its spirit by seeking constantly throughout their college course to achieve intellectual disinterestedness.

Teaching three hours each week provided a pleasant interlude in the president's schedule, but even these few hours were encroached upon. Several times a month when he was compelled to ask colleagues to meet his class, he chose lecturers who in themselves possessed some measure of the qualities under discussion. Preceding their appearance, he usually spent a few minutes to cite the reasons for his choice. Perhaps his favorite "guest" was Professor Charles Clifford Hutchins, whose scientific accomplishments included the invention of a thermograph for measuring the heat of the moon, and a device for "blind flying" of heavier-than-air machines. "At the next meeting," he told a class in the winter of 1921, "you will hear a lecture by Professor Hutchins on Leonardo da Vinci. The speaker would have been at home in the Renaissance. He reads Latin, French, Italian, and German. He is a talented musician; his skilful hands carve lovely objects out of wood; he is a worker in brass and clay; he writes witty light verse; he is the author of a monograph to show that Galileo knew the secret of the curved ball in baseball and of the cut in tennis. You may not remember all that he will say to you, but at the end of the hour you will know that *virtu* is not confined to the Renaissance."

By inviting such lecturers, Kenneth Sills brought his class into contact with faculty members whose special interests might otherwise have been unknown to many students—William Albion Moody on mathematics, Thomas Van Cleve on political theory, Charles Livingston on the *fabliaux*, Stanley Smith on Lucretius, and Stanley Chase on Chaucer. The president was aware of the objection that an annual parade of visitors gave his course the aspect of a Chautauqua program, but he knew exactly what he was about. He believed that fresh perspectives and different points of view would fully compensate for an occasional lack of continuity. When he was sometimes told that Literature 1, 2 was regarded as an "easy" course, he said he could trust his colleagues to offer enough "hard" ones to correct the imbalance. Professor Nathan Dane, a colleague and former student, remarked, "The President was under no illusions that his course equated Organic Chemistry in difficulty; he was dedicated to its humanizing effects. Faculty members can be superb, but they are free to 'cut out' and shrug off any responsibility for humanity in education. K. C. M. S. knew that in this respect a President or a Dean can never do so."

Another sympathetic colleague, Professor Thomas Van Cleve, who watched the course from its inception in 1919, saw in its methods and aims a reflection of Kenneth Sills's view of the function of the college of his day: "To his mind even a brief or occasional exposure to the substance of liberal studies was advantageous to the individual character as it was useful to good citizenship. It was perhaps this attitude that led him to attach what many of us felt to be undue importance to the 'browsing student.' Perhaps even a momentary glimpse into a great book could make him more sympathetic to the artistic or intellectual life. In some measure he conceived of his course in Comparative Literature as a gateway to intelligent browsing. Thus he saw in the liberal arts college an institution essential alike to the future scholar and writer, on the one hand, and the future executive of a wholesale grocery or fertilizer manufacturer, on the other."

Kenneth Sills knew that "browsing" was a poor substitute for the study and reflection necessary for proper intellectual leadership of a college, but his first years in office allowed him time for little else. In his report to the Governing Boards in May, 1920, he noted, "When a man is called upon to make formal addresses on all sorts of subjects in all sorts of places, he may become a facile speaker but he is pretty sure not to have much to say." He told his friend Roscoe Ham that he had to abandon all hope of keeping up with the scholarship in the learned journals. In acknowledging an article by William Lawrence at Columbia, he declared that after writing seventy addresses in 1919–20 he saw no chance of realizing his ambition to be a scholar as well as an executive: "Apparently even the president of a small college must give up all thought of scholarly activity and devote himself to the multifarious duties of business and direction."

Of these duties, the one which excited him most was concerned with attracting and retaining an able faculty. "Now that you are no longer Casey at the Bat, but in the pitcher's box," Lawrence wrote, "remember the sweating team. Look with consideration on the toiling professors." K. C. M. S. hardly needed his friend's playful admonition. Indeed, his understanding of their difficulties was so sympathetic and his concern for their welfare so constant that some alumni occasionally accused the president of allowing "the toiling professors" to run the college. Kenneth Sills regarded such criticism as a high compliment. He knew that the success of his administration would depend largely upon his ability to provide his colleagues with the proper tools and best conditions for their teaching. Above all, he wished to help create a climate of emotional and intellectual sympathy in which the youngest instructor was made to feel that he belonged to a common enterprise, that Bowdoin was his college, and that its reputation depended upon him. Kenneth Sills identified himself so thoroughly with his faculty that in the early years of his administration when honorary degrees were conferred upon him by Bates, Colby, and Dartmouth he was

ing the war, the growing popularity of courses in English had
severely taxed the resources of the three men responsible for all
the instruction in composition, literature, and speech. K. C. M. S.
had just persuaded the Governing Boards to strengthen the
department by adding a fourth member, when Professors
George Roy Elliott and William Hawley Davis resigned to
accept more remunerative posts at Amherst and Leland Stanford.
Their resignations not only dramatized the need for higher
salaries, but led the president to study the future program of a
department whose sole surviving member was Professor Wilmot
Mitchell. The loss was a grievous one. Elliott had a touch of the
poet, a graceful style, and the rare quality of inspiring enthusiasm for a union of scholarship and literature. His intuitions
excited the ablest students, and sometimes puzzled, but always
impressed the others. Under his direction, the courses in the
Renaissance, Shakespeare, and nineteenth-century poetry and
prose gained a remarkable hold on the undergraduates. Davis,
who shared the teaching of speech and rhetoric with Professor
Mitchell, was a conscientious teacher of exposition and argumentation, inaugurating at Bowdoin the discipline of the daily
theme which he had admired in English A at Harvard. As coach
of debating, he prized straight thinking and intellectual candor
above victory. More often than not his students achieved both.

The senior and for a brief time the only member of the department was Wilmot Brookings Mitchell, Edward Little Professor of Rhetoric and Oratory, a living embodiment of the older
New England literature of which he was one of the pioneer
teachers. It is a measure of his intellectual suppleness that he
immediately recognized the need of combining the dignity of
his beloved tradition of rhetoric and oratory with the new enthusiasm for courses in the novel, drama, criticism, and contemporary letters. "I love to teach Jevon's *Logic* to freshmen," he
told a colleague somewhat wistfully, "but I'll see what I can do
with *Winesburg, Ohio* without abandoning *The Country of the
Pointed Firs*." Working together with complete tolerance of

each other's points of view, K. C. M. S. and Professor Mitchell decided to fill Elliott's chair by calling to the faculty Dr. Stanley Perkins Chase '05, who had a ripe teaching experience of fourteen years at Union College. An admired student and friend of the great Kittredge and Robinson at Harvard, where he had taken his doctorate, Professor Chase brought to the department a vast erudition in the history of English literature, a sensitive critical intelligence, and a strong ambition to develop the program of comprehensive examinations which was then in a formative stage. In considering a successor to Professor Davis, K. C. M. S. broke with tradition by urging the appointment of a teacher trained in literature rather than speech and argumentation. The president also recommended adding as a fourth member of the department a young instructor who could combine teaching composition and debate.

In 1925, as he helped to shape the future pattern of the offerings in English, Kenneth Sills may have recalled his keen disappointment in 1904 when President Hyde's appointment of William Trufant Foster had weighted the department heavily on the side of forensics. Now, twenty-one years later, he sought to correct the imbalance. During this interval English had gradually replaced Greek and Latin as the backbone of the humanities at Bowdoin, and literary studies had helped to train the sensibilities of a majority of the undergraduates. K. C. M. S. was convinced that whatever the variety of methods employed, it was important that literature be successfully taught. In Charles Harold Gray the president found the qualities of intelligence, warmth, and commitment that he was seeking. A native of Oklahoma, Gray was graduated from the University of Washington in Seattle and had studied at Lincoln College, Oxford, as a Rhodes Scholar. After a few years of brilliant teaching at Reed and St. John's, he continued his studies at Columbia where, despite his gay irreverence for the graduate school pieties, he won the admiration of William Lawrence. A single interview was enough to persuade the president that Harold Gray was a liter-

upon ideas, followed by lively conferences, now made factual quizzing, formal recitations, and drillwork seem curiously old-fashioned. These trends received the quiet but warm encouragment of the president who felt there was too much teaching and too little learning and studying. "Bowdoin *is* a conservative college," he told the Portland alumni in April, 1921, "but the College has never been afraid of making changes and trying experiments within reason." In announcing the appointment of Professor Daniel Stanwood, he said, "We do intend to make the course in International Law a regular part of the curriculum. It is designed to study, not only such things as modern diplomacy and the League of Nations, but to present a point of view that is essential for American undergraduates to have, namely, that we must realize as a nation our increasing international obligations." As further evidence that Bowdoin was aware of its proper function in the postwar world, the president cited new courses in contemporary history and politics given by Professor Bell and the training in the Russian language offered by Professor Ham.

A more spectacular experiment which attracted nationwide comment, including a letter of congratulations from the President of the United States, was the Institute of Modern History, initiated in April, 1923. K. C. M. S. invited eight eminent authorities, seven of whom had occupied positions of importance at the Paris Peace Conference, to give a series of thirteen lectures and conferences on world politics. Their public lectures drew audiences from every corner of the state, but most effective in the president's opinion were the conferences conducted solely for undergraduates. "I felt as though I had a reserved seat at the League of Nations," one student remarked. "It was exciting to hear K. P. Tsolainos, Secretary to Premier Venizelos of Greece, mutter imprecations while Professor William Westermann was speaking about Turkey, and then jump up to challenge him to a debate upon the situation in Eastern Thrace." The success of the Institute persuaded the president to seek the resources needed to make such programs biennial events. A month later he was able to announce plans for a second institute, on modern literature, in 1925, to celebrate the centennial of the graduation of Hawthorne and Longfellow. By having the college sponsor an institute every two years on a subject of broad, general interest, K. C. M. S. told the undergraduates, every student would benefit from the lectures and roundtable conferences twice in his college career. "Bowdoin," he said, "may seem to you to be at the end of the line geographically, but it will never be permitted to become an intellectual dead-end."

Thus begun in 1923, the institutes continued to be popular and dramatic events on the Bowdoin calendar. President Sills was pleased by the lively interest they aroused, but he knew that the really significant innovations in educational policy, like the quiet happenings in the life of a scholar, are neither outwardly stirring nor newsworthy. Of these advances, he always considered the new system of comprehensive examinations to be the most important. In his inaugural address he had declared, "We ought to supplement our instruction by providing not only for tests in courses but for general examinations in subjects." A year later, in May, 1919, he urged the faculty to adopt "a system by which there shall be, at least in the major subject of every student, a general examination covering the whole field, and not limited to work done in courses." When the program got underway with the class of 1921, the president made a point of dropping in on the oral examinations given by the various departments and asking a few questions himself. "Attendance at the examinations," he informed the Boards, "gives an admirable opportunity to test the kind of teaching being done in the College." If such visits, which were usually unannounced, produced occasional consternation for the examinee and some nervous apprehension on the part of the examiners, they also had their rewards. Kenneth Sills was delighted when a candidate in philosophy, asked to tell what seemed to him the most interesting reading he had done recently, replied, "Kant—it's like chopping wood when you don't have to." K. C. M. S. considered the general examinations to offer the

tion that must always be made in speaking of the campus," the editor of the *Quill* wrote in January, 1925, "is the distinction between the *mass* and the *slice*, between college men and that very small, very choice coterie of intelligent college men. The two groups mingle in their daily life, but intellectually they are worlds apart. . . . One has to speak of them in two entirely different tones of voice." Viewing "the slice" with a mixture of admiration and amusement, Professor George Roy Elliott described the Bowdoin Intelligentsia as sharing "a common love of literature, uncommon intelligence, and the Oxford manner." In their hands the *Quill* had become, by the mid-1920s, a monthly irritant concocted to outrage the sensibilities of the "mass," which included an overwhelming majority of the faculty. But if the *Quill* columnists hoped to ruffle the president, they were disappointed. When he was criticized for permitting an editor to pillory "the average football-loving, send-our-sons-to-Bow-doin-in-the-fall alumnus as the most arrogant ass in the world," K. C. M. S. replied mildly that whatever else might be said about the observation, it proved there was no attempt at Bowdoin to repress freedom of speech. As the president opened each new issue of the *Quill,* his only uncertainty was where the next bomb would fall. The editors described a proposed war memorial as "an utterly unthinkable scar on the landscape," useful only as "another place to park Ford cars." The librarian was charged with having bought nothing "since Stevenson died," and interested only "in economics reference books and Cape Cod novels." As for the library itself, it constituted a "sufficient reason for doubting Bowdoin's claim to being an educational institution." Few campus idols remained unscathed by the debunkers. Wearers of the Phi Beta Kappa key were distinguished only by their skill in avoiding hard courses. To the alumni who protested to the president at these manifestations of the new freedom, Kenneth Sills remarked that he was reminded of the saying of Benjamin Jowett, Master of Balliol College, who, in a walk through a quadrangle littered with broken windows and other debris, said cheerfully, "Well, after all, the mind of the College is still vigorous."

Although Casey's Lit. was rarely elected by the Intelligentsia, the president knew that any comments he made about them to the mass would soon be reported to the slice. He made the most of his opportunity. On one occasion, when "the happy few" published a broadside urging the student body to refuse to pay their activities fee on the grounds of taxation without representation, K. C. M. S. began his homily by solemnly quoting Alexander Meiklejohn's aphorism: "What undergraduates have to say to us is always interesting, sometimes important, but not necessarily conclusive." The president also enjoyed making forays into the coterie's own province of literary criticism by citing Samuel Johnson's contempt for the snobbery of cliques and his preference for the common sense of readers uncorrupted by the refinements of subtlety and the dogmatism of learning. The president was diverted by a bit of undergraduate fooling on this subject in the spring of 1925 while the college was celebrating the anniversary of the graduation of Hawthorne and Longfellow. A campus Puck, bent on discomfiting the Intelligentsia, copied one of Longfellow's distinguished sonnets, signed it with the initials "H. W. L. '25," submitted it to the *Quill*, and waited for the fun to begin. A few days later, to the glee of the unregenerate mass, the manuscript was rejected haughtily as unworthy of print. On a more sophisticated level, Professor Elliott also delighted Kenneth Sills by an experiment in his class in poetry. Elliott asked his students to discuss the quality of several poems, including the first stanza of Longfellow's "In the Churchyard at Cambridge," which he submitted without indicating their authors. Although the class was chiefly composed of the elite who habitually condescended to Longfellow as "a children's poet," they hailed his stanza as refreshingly "new" and as an expression of "modernity." K. C. M. S. reported the experiment to his own class with a reminder that the poems most people are unwilling to forget are usually those worth remembering. *Vox populi,* he said, is not necessarily *vox humbug.*

Kenneth Sills never ceased to regard the college as a family, but he noticed that its manners were changing rapidly in the decade following the Armistice. Students seemed strangely hard to get hold of, less responsive to appeals to old loyalties, more casual about accepting the privileges of an education, and less likely to be grateful for scholarships and financial aid. "Under the present conditions," K. C. M. S. informed the Governing Boards in 1924, "it is by no means easy to guide and control the younger generation which is used to so much freedom." This new generation was certainly more urbane, yet the president was uneasy in the face of "smoothness." "Superficial good manners are worse than rudeness," he warned in a chapel talk in February, 1922. "Bad manners in a college destroy entirely the idea of a family in which we like to dwell." A few years later he told the Boston alumni, "You no longer see on the campus the young, raw-boned, unsophisticated boy from the country. The radio, the automobile, the movies have changed all that." Although Kenneth Sills had his moments of discouragement and doubt, he was cheered by the persistence of the "Bowdoin type": "We still have the earnest, hard-working students who are either working their way through college or are being sent by their families at a considerable financial sacrifice."

As a means of tempering the new mood of restlessness and indifference, the president planned a series of talks to acquaint the sons of the college with the heritage which so many of them seemed disposed to take for granted. Every Wednesday morning in chapel, he devoted his remarks to some aspect of the history, organization, and government of Bowdoin, especially to the careers of her great teachers and other "worthies." Beginning in February, 1925, the talks were designed to be repeated once in each four-year cycle. Their cumulative effect, K. C. M. S. hoped, might make students more aware of their indebtedness to an institution which had been made possible only by the sacrifices of generations of Bowdoin men. At least one thoughtful Senior sensed the president's purpose. "He started off this morning on James Bowdoin himself," Athern Daggett '25 wrote in a letter to his parents on February 9. "I think it is all a very good idea, and it should be interesting. It is striking how quick in condemnation college boys are. They are hair-trigger in their estimations, condemn both things and personalities right and left at very slight provocation or at none at all."

Kenneth Sills knew that disillusion can be a creative force, but he was saddened by the then fashionable cynicism. In his baccalaureate address in June, 1924, he lamented the disappearance of the word service from the student vocabulary except in a pejorative sense. Its place, he noted, was usurped by such terms as self-expression and debunking. And he was dismayed when the editor of the *Orient* asserted that a college need seek no other justification for its existence than its teaching "that many of the bigwigs of the college world are charlatans." "If one emerges from college with such a point of view," the editor remarked, "and with a certain cynical aspect toward the world, his four years have been profitable ones." Against poses of this sort, the president used all his powers of reasonableness. "There is current at Bowdoin a healthy spirit of instructive criticism," he said in chapel on March 15, 1925, "but when it reaches that stage where youth thinks that its ideas are always right, even when in conflict with mature minds, it is time to call a halt." In a series of Sunday chapel talks on the Christian virtues, he frequently pointed a moral by references to student behavior. "We should all observe our own actions very closely before we attempt to criticize others," he counseled on May 12, 1923, "for in all probability we are as guilty as they. Such considerations bring us to the question of charity to our neighbors." Prophetically enough, at the very beginning of the decade, K. C. M. S. urged the cultivation of intellectual humility. "As you start the college year," he said on September 23, 1920, "remember that a very large part of the world's work is done by men and women who have never been to college; and that often they are superior not only in their contributions to society, but in their intellectual attainments to college graduates." Two years later, at the opening chapel service, he repeated the admonition. "The intellectual snob, the man who thinks because of his more formal education he will become *ipso facto* a superior being," he warned, "will not be long tolerated, even should he succeed in escaping from college."

Daily chapel was a popular target of the campus critics, but they invariably made an exception of the services conducted by President Sills. "He is not an extraordinary speaker or anything like one," Athern Daggett wrote in May of his Junior year, "but there is a certain quality about him that is compelling. I would rather listen to him than to any of the preachers, bishops, and other dignitaries that are invited here to speak." The quality which the upperclassman felt but left unnamed was perhaps a constancy or steadfastness. In the unstable world of the 1920s, Bowdoin undergraduates found in their president the stability they lacked. His steady light made the Roman candle wit of their smart coteries seem garish. When he spoke in chapel they heard what goodness, faith, and wisdom really sounded like. His kindly voice, serene brow, and friendly upturned face invested him with a kind of academic sainthood which was not less real because it was felt rather than analyzed. To those who entered Bowdoin in the 1920s, the great William DeWitt Hyde was not even a memory. For them Kenneth Sills seemed somehow always to have been part of the college fabric, as durable and as timeless as the granite walls of the chapel. Thus it came as something of a shock for undergraduates to discover that many of the older alumni regarded the president as an untried "youngster." When Athern Daggett, then a Freshman, remained on campus after the June examinations to attend his first Bowdoin Commencement in June, 1922, he was startled by a greeting from DeAlva Stanwood Alexander '70, the venerable president of the Board of

Overseers. "Well, how's the young fellow getting on?" Alexander asked. The seventeen-year-old Freshman was momentarily flattered by this solicitude from a patriarch, but he soon sensed that he was not the object of the inquiry. Mr. Alexander, who had received his degree from President Samuel Harris, simply wanted to know how Kenneth Sills, aged forty-two, was behaving.

Later that afternoon at the Commencement dinner, young Daggett heard speaker after speaker from the reunion classes arise to extol the "great days" of President Hyde. The Freshman learned for the first time that when an alumnus thinks of his alma mater the image evoked is not that of the present-day college, but the one he remembers of his own student days. Daggett was conscious of bridling at so much talk about past glories and the good old days. He hoped to hear at least a word or two about President Sills's "great days." He wanted to say that the present time was also a good time, and that for Bowdoin, perhaps the best days of all were those which lay ahead.

Mr. Alexander of the Overseers might have found a partial answer to his question about the behavior of "the young fellow" in the reports of the visiting committee of the Boards. During its annual inspection of the college, the committee was favorably impressed, not only by the high morale of the faculty and the excellence of the teaching done by the new instructors, but by the cordial relationship between the students and their teachers. The *Orient* noted that this spirit of friendliness was perhaps the most important accomplishment of the new administration. "At the close of the War," the editor recalled, "the undergraduate was apt to need strict restraint, and regarded the Faculty as antagonistic. But President Sills has built up a decided spirit of coöperation between students and administration." This era of good feeling was all the more remarkable an achievement at a time when crackling criticism was rife, and the campus wits were making their monthly genuflections to H. L. Mencken in the *Quill*. "The critical attitude is with us in abundance," K. C. M. S.

told the students in a chapel talk. "More stress is laid upon it than upon the creative attitude to life."

Accepting this critical temper as the spirit of the age, President Sills resolved to put it to work for the good of the college. No one, he assured the student council in May, 1925, wishes to encourage irresponsible sniping and misinformed carping, but instructive criticism can become truly serviceable. Accordingly he invited thirteen Seniors of the class of 1926 to study the needs of the college, pledging them a free hand in their inquiries, and promising publication of their report. This self-study, finally submitted to the president in February, 1926, was a startlingly able document. Its most striking recommendations were concerned, not alone with physical resources and externalities, but with the hidden processes which quicken and enrich the inner life of the college. The committee vigorously opposed adding "practical courses" to the curriculum, advocated bringing athletics under institutional control, and urged a further strengthening of the faculty as the best means of maintaining Bowdoin's tradition of effective teaching. "I should be perfectly willing," K. C. M. S. declared, "to submit our undergraduate report to any fairminded body of alumni or to others interested in education, as a sample of the kind of training that is being given at Bowdoin today."

The student report also impressed the Trustees and Overseers who asked K. C. M. S. to appoint two undergraduates to serve on a Boards' committee to improve the procedure of allotting financial aid to nearly one-half the student body. Noting that it was "a radical departure in the management of affairs at this College to have two undergraduates on the proposed committee," the Boards remarked, "They have not only earned the right to participate, but proved that the College itself is fortunate if it can enlist their service." This experiment in undergraduate participation in the councils of the college exceeded all hopes. The students' suggestions were all adopted, including the award of fewer but larger scholarships based primarily upon need, with further provision that candidates for financial aid be interviewed by a faculty committee and required to submit itemized budgets. Their recommendations, which became effective in 1927, silenced criticism of the former methods, and resulted in a more equitable distribution of scholarship and loan funds. It was not until after the Boards had expressed their admiration of the statesmanlike contribution of the students that Kenneth Sills revealed his topsy-turvy method of selecting them. One of the two Seniors he had chosen for the assignment stood at the head, the other at the foot, of his class. The president took a mischievous delight in the Boards' inability to distinguish the top from the bottom. "I have never underestimated the quality of the average, or even of the below-average student at Bowdoin," he said. "Grades are not an infallible index."

Kenneth Sills often succeeded in disarming his critics by an invitation to assist in solving the problems which brought them scurrying to his office. When in the spring of 1926 a delegation called to complain about the neglect of contemporary writers in the section of books for the proposed "browsing room" in the library, he asked gently whether they had brought with them a list of significant authors whose works had been overlooked. Their objection would have been more compelling, he remarked, had they checked the librarian's list of recommendations. Would they be good enough to compile a bibliography of important current titles? Perhaps they would permit him to add a few of his own, even though he was woefully "behind in his reading of the exciting new books"? The next autumn, when the new reading room was opened, all the titles recommended by the students were found on the shelves. The dissidence of dissent rarely survived the first five minutes of an interview in Massachusetts Hall. "You enter as a rampant critic," Paul Palmer '27 observed, "but before you know what has happened you leave as a collaborator." Bowdoin students tried to measure up to the high regard their president had for them. They knew he meant every word when he said in chapel, "I number among the greatest privileges

of being President of Bowdoin the close association with undergraduates." His office, usually unguarded by a secretary, was
easily accessible. Freshmen who visited it for the first time when
they signed the registry book on the opening day were made to
feel they had a right to return whether or not they had any
special business. Mrs. Clara Hayes, the college secretary, was
sometimes irked by what she regarded as interminable calls by
undergraduates, but she seldom succeeded in shortening the interviews. On more than one occasion, when she stuck her head in
the doorway to remind the president a trifle waspishly that he
had many letters to sign, she was told, "After all, the College
really exists for the students."

The president's accessibility was not limited to his generous
morning and afternoon office hours in Massachusetts Hall.
Neighbors who saw students and other visitors stream in and out
of the front door of 85 Federal Street often wondered how the
Sillses ever found any time for themselves. "Kenneth and I read
a canto of Dante every night," Edith Sills remarked to a faculty
wife in 1919. "I wish we had more time for such camaraderie,
but the days are so full and busy." From the beginning of their
married life, they were at home to undergraduates on Tuesday
and Friday afternoons and Sunday evenings. "We try in this
way to come into more personal contact with them," she explained, "and also to keep them in touch a little more with home
life." In addition to having students for tea, the Sillses always
tried to reserve at least one evening a week for entertaining a few
members of the faculty for dinner. In 1919 they began the
custom of having each Freshman class, in groups of twelve or
fifteen, come to the house on Sunday evenings for talk and
refreshments in the fall semester, and similar delegations of Seniors in the spring months. The Senior dinners were "state occasions." "I use our best china and silver and everything else that I
would have for the most distinguished visitor," Mrs. Sills remarked, "because there is no one we would wish to honor more
than our Bowdoin seniors." Several thousand Bowdoin men

cherish the memory of these dinners, which were usually preceded by a walk through the garden and concluded by their
standing around the long table in the ball room singing "Bowdoin
Beata." Perhaps most memorable of all was the talk following
the dinner, when K. C. M. S. invited his guests to pull out their
chairs and sit around the table for a frank discussion of the needs
of the college. Often their suggestions and hopes were later
embodied in his reports to the Boards. Few Seniors ever left these
affairs without feeling a real sense of the partnership they had in
their college.

On such occasions the mistress of 85 Federal Street recalled
her father's hospitable rectory where guests were always coming
and going. "I have often thought that much of our pleasure in
entertaining derives from my experience at home," she wrote in
1956. "To 'break bread' in our home, no matter how simple or
informal, has a special grace, and both Kenneth and I felt that
such occasions are among the happiest memories of our life at
Bowdoin." During their retirement their thoughts often returned to these evenings in the Bowdoin springtime. "As we
watched them leave our house to stroll across the Delta on the
beautiful June evenings," Edith Sills recalled, "we thought of
their coming and their going and how quickly four years have
sped away, and tears are very near and we remembered that
wonderful line of Virgil, 'There are tears of things and mortal
affairs touch the heart.'"

The Sillses soon learned the hard facts about entertaining
undergraduates. One was the futility of issuing general invitations. They discovered that announcements of an "at home at
85 Federal Street" were not likely to be taken very seriously
except by two or three students and a few members of the faculty. To avoid being confronted with mountains of uneaten
sandwiches and cakes, it proved more practicable to invite specific fraternity delegations or student groups with interests in
common, such as the classical club or the staff of the *Quill*. With
them conversation flowed easily and naturally; diffident Fresh-

men, however, often taxed the ingenuity of their hosts. Edith
Sills quickly sensed that shy youngsters would rather have almost anything happen to them than to be made conspicuous.
"When I was first entertaining them," she confessed to a friend,
"if I found one among the group whom I had known for a long
time, I would say, 'Why I have known this boy ever since he
was a baby, and he was a darling.' *That*, I am told, the boy never
quite lived down." The president, who was shy even in the
presence of equally shy Freshmen, was grateful to have Mrs.
Sills fill lulls in the conversation. In such moments, K. C. M. S.
blushed happily, chortled, and busily tamped down the tobacco
in his pipe. "To watch Casey try to keep his pipe going," one
student guest observed, "was to witness one of the indecisive
battles of the world. He actually smokes *matches*." Edith Sills
encouraged her young guests to talk about anything which she
thought might take the edge off their constraint. "Years ago,
when I was less experienced," she told Mrs. Helen Chase, "a
freshman got started on the subject of shaving which led all the
others to tell of their first experiences, and it was only an heroic
effort by Mr. Sills which prevented that topic from going on all
afternoon."

The presence of a boy from Aroostook County invariably
provided the hostess with a welcome conversation piece, because
she had lived in Houlton before moving to Portland in 1912. "I
can expatiate on the beauty of endless potato fields in blossom,"
she boasted gaily, "but even on this topic I don't always get the
coöperation that I might. One freshman from Idaho was un-
moved by my praise. 'Aroostook potatoes may be prettier to
look at,' he said judiciously, 'but Idaho potatoes are better to
eat.'" Upon another occasion, during an awkward pause before
tea was served, Edith Sills remarked desperately that she had
heard Benny Goodman described as the "father of swing," and
what did the boys think of that? Her gambit was immediately
countered by a *sotto voce* rejoinder which might have been
politely translated as, "Mother, how ridiculous!" "Perhaps it

would be better to say," one youngster remarked, "that Benny Goodman is the *master* of swing." From that point forward there were no more moments of silence. "When boys settle down to explain swing music," the astonished hostess observed, "their expositions sound more intellectual to me than a learned doctor's thesis in physics or philosophy." One never knew just what might become the point of departure for animated talk. The Sillses' cocker spaniel, Byng, often did yeomanly service to thaw out an especially uncommunicative group, as did an old silver Georgian candlelighter for cigarettes. Occasionally it was a set of French sandwich plates with innocent-looking mottoes which K. C. M. S. said it was fortunate that none of his guests could translate.

If self-conscious Freshmen sometimes found tea-table conversation difficult, it was even harder for them to know how to leave. "It used to embarrass me dreadfully," Edith Sills told an alumnus, "when I heard Mr. Sills say, 'I am sure you have a great deal of studying to do for tonight, and we don't want to detain you any longer.'" She was touched when a departing guest said frankly, "Good evening, Mrs. Sills, I have had a much better time than I expected to have." The Sillses felt a certain pathos about homesick Freshmen who had so recently been Seniors in high school and leaders in all sorts of activities. They made a special point of having them at 85 Federal Street in the first few weeks of their Freshman year when they were most impressionable. "I like to think," Edith Sills once said wistfully, "that they may come to look upon Mr. Sills and me just as two older friends such as they might find in their parents' homes. Here they meet us more or less as adult equals."

Official academic summonses as well as social invitations brought students trooping to 85 Federal Street. At the middle and end of each semester, the president insisted upon conferring privately with every undergraduate who failed to achieve passing grades in two or more courses. Known grimly as "Casey's house warnings," these interviews took precedence over all other college engagements and conscripted a disconsolate company to await their turn to see K. C. M. S. in his study in the southwest corner of the second floor. Below, in the reception rooms, Mrs. Sills's ministrations of sandwiches, tea, and small-talk were not available to soothe the anxious breasts. A Portland friend who called on one of the "warning days" was surprised to find the front rooms filled with a dozen painfully quiet boys sprawled in attitudes of dejection while Edith Sills hurried her caller to the rear of the house. The scene resembled, she said, a "Party in the parlor; All silent, and all *damned.*" "Long ago, I used to try to cheer them up," she explained to her guest, "but I learned another lesson from one particularly forlorn boy who told me all he wanted was to be 'let alone.' Since then I merely provide magazines—those with lots of pictures—and cigarettes." Upstairs the president was unsmiling but solicitous as he greeted the delinquents. "He *knew* that I *knew* I was just loafing," one student reported after his interview. "And he made me feel that I had let my family and the College down." To "slow" students and those handicapped by poor training, the president always spoke sympathetically. "Discouragement," he said, "is often a more dangerous foe than dissipation." He invariably promised Freshmen that they would not be dropped from college at the end of their first term, but would be given a full year in which to make good.

The hospitality of the Sillses made the president's house so integral a part of the college that the Governing Boards voted in 1920 to heat 85 Federal Street from the central steam plant on the campus. Economical as he was about expenditures of college funds for physical equipment and mere "creature comforts," K. C. M. S. accepted the boon gratefully. His manful struggles with the old furnace were not unlike his efforts to keep his pipe lighted, but failure in the cellar, as his friend Professor Hutchins remarked dryly, was likely to have graver consequences. The president also welcomed the gift of a commodious room for dances, receptions, and large formal dinners. This addition built on the north side of the house just behind a suite of two living rooms permitted large-scale entertaining without destroying the atmosphere of a private household. Brunswick's lack of adequate hotel facilities had made 85 Federal Street an inevitable place for entertaining visiting dignitaries and lecturers. K. C. M. S. realized that Bowdoin's out of the way location needed to be offset by bringing in a succession of interesting people from the world outside. His answer was to increase the number of public lectures and invite students and faculty to his house for talk and coffee following the events. These informal gatherings were managed with such seeming effortlessness that only Kenneth Sills knew that his wife had been feverishly cutting sandwiches in the kitchen until the first guest arrived. Few visitors were aware that the Sills household was without a maid to wait on the tables, except for the service of the peripatetic Lena Coffin whose help was also in demand by the entire college community. Her unfailing presence at faculty dinner parties led Hamlin Garland to remark to his hostess during a three-day visit, "There must be a large family of sisters who serve in the various families here. Everywhere I go the waitresses all look alike." Edith and Kenneth Sills allowed the apostle of realism to depart with this romantic illusion intact.

The Sillses' first important guest, William Howard Taft, was also one of the most delightful and considerate, but the prospect of entertaining him only a short time after they had moved into 85 Federal Street was not without its terrors. "In those days in our guest room," Edith Sills recalled with a shudder thirty years afterwards, "we had a very small bathroom with a very small tub. As a nervous hostess I was terribly worried lest our famous guest might get stuck." Her apprehensions were hardly allayed at dinner when the former President told of his horseback expedition to survey the island when he was governor-general of the Philippines. "I reported my safe return at once to Secretary of War Stimson," Mr. Taft said. "And Stimson promptly cabled, 'Glad you are all right, but how is the horse?' " Later that eve-

ning in the First Parish Church, while Taft was speaking eloquently in support of the League of Nations, the mind of his
hostess was less concerned with international crises than with a
possible domestic calamity. Her fears proved groundless, however. The next morning Mr. Taft emerged for breakfast unscathed, unstuck, and eager for a tour of the campus. As the pair
walked down Federal Street, Kenneth Sills waved to his friend
Elijah Boyd, who was driving his dump cart toward the campus.
The greeting, much to the president's surprise, was stonily
ignored. "Oh, I seen both you and Mr. Taft all right as big as
life," Boyd explained a few days later, "but my cart was filled
with horse dressin', and I didn't want to embarrass you none by
lettin' on we know'd each other while I was in so delicate a
condition."

Not all visitors who were entertained at 85 Federal Street
possessed Mr. Boyd's exquisite delicacy. It was the Sillses' custom, when they were not personally acquainted with a prospective guest of the college, to suggest that they would be happy
to entertain him at their home where there was likely to be more
quiet than at a commercial hotel. Even this knowledge did not
deter Lord Dunsany from behaving callously during his twenty-
four hours at 85 Federal Street. The six-foot-four Irish baronet
complained of the lack of a valet; at dinner he immediately blew
out the candles because they hurt his eyes; he banged shut all
doors to avoid possible drafts; he told Zetta Jordan, the Sillses'
faithful cook, that her meal was abominable. After the lecture
he complained to Kenneth Sills, "If you had invited a plumber
to come here and talk about art he might have been understood,"
and the next morning he insisted upon having his bags packed
and his boots polished after having been informed no one was
available for such services. His hosts were discreetly silent about
the experience, but Miss Jordan, whose cooking had been
scorned, was not so reticent. A few hours after Lord Dunsany's
departure, Marshall Cram was reporting gleefully that the Sillses
had mistaken the Irish Renaissance for another Irish Revolution.

The long social annals of 85 Federal Street were rarely punctuated by such explosions. Virtually all their guests were charmed by the Sillses' informal hospitality and looked back on Bowdoin as an academic Eden. Kate Douglas Wiggin, who bequeathed her library to the college, became a friend of Zetta Jordan and atoned for Lord Dunsany's behavior by presenting the cook with *The Birds' Christmas Carol* inscribed, "I hope you will like my work half as much as I have enjoyed yours." When Hugh Walpole was told of Miss Jordan's delight in his fiction, he visited the kitchen to tell her of the new novel he was writing which he later sent her with a note to "My friend, Zetta Jordan." Robert Frost, an old friend, became an annual visitor, often staying for several days, sharing the hospitality of the Sillses and the Burnetts, and occasionally teaching classes of Casey's Lit. "All college presidents *officially* endorse poetry," he told one class, "but Kenneth Sills has a *weakness* for it." Perhaps the Sillses' most glamorous guest was Edna St. Vincent Millay at the height of her fame in 1925. The undergraduates greeted her rapturously in Memorial Hall, where an admirer described her as looking like "a tiny, slender Bunthorn lily," wearing a satin medieval gown resembling "the inside of a million-dollar limousine." When the Sillses asked for several volunteers to wait on the table at the dinner party, they were swamped with candidates. Professor Cram, who was alarmed at the poet's reputation for Bohemianism, was horrified at a campus rumor that students were to serve her breakfast in the president's guest bedroom.

Even if Kenneth Sills had been temperamentally capable of leaving his college worries on his desk when he left his office in the late afternoon, the accessibility of 85 Federal Street gave him little protection. The college was always with him. He had neither the time nor energy for tennis after his election in 1918, but whenever a lull in his office routine permitted, he enjoyed a round of golf on the Brunswick course, usually with his friends Fred Brown and Orren Hormell. On these outings he did more listening than talking, although his intense interest in people often prompted him to inquire about the welfare of the families of his colleagues and staff. No new babies arrived in the college community without receiving a present from the president and a call from Edith Sills. "How do you suppose Casey knew," a college workman once asked, "that my daughter won a spelling match yesterday at Longfellow School?" Perhaps because of his own awkwardness with his hands—he never was able to fill his own fountain pen—K. C. M. S. was enormously appreciative of the manual skills of others, and he was never too preoccupied to compliment George Higgins, the college carpenter, upon some piece of repair work.

The routine of his day which began with scanning the newspapers after breakfast at 7:30, and included calls on patients in the Coe Infirmary after morning chapel, rarely ended without a dinner engagement in the evening. His schedule left him almost no time for the kind of general reading he liked. For this reason he never seemed fatigued by the many trips necessitated by his outside activities. "I manage to do a good deal of reading on trains," he told a colleague who marveled at the president's freshness after an ordeal of several nights on a sleeper and a succession of college dinners and speeches. Conductors on the Boston and Maine noticed that he preferred day coaches to parlor cars between Brunswick and Boston, and that he usually found an inconspicuous seat where he immediately began reading. One trainman occasionally tried to protect him from intruders. "There's President Sills," he said, "slumped down in his seat so as not to be noticed." Although trips provided relaxation and some privacy, he usually had to meet vexing problems immediately after coming back. "I never seem to go away," he once told William Lawrence, "without getting home to find a baby on my doorstep."

The lustiest of these babies was wrapped in a varsity sweater and had a disconcerting habit of bouncing back again and again. Indeed no single problem was to prove as bothersome to Kenneth Sills as that of the proper control of athletics. The full-scale resumption of intercollegiate sports after the war compelled him to face what he called the grim fact that "not only the alumni, but also the general public are more interested in sport than in scholarship, and in spectacular sport at that." "We can hardly blame the undergraduate for losing his sense of proportion," K. C. M. S. told the New York alumni in 1922, "when graduates of the College more often care about the retention of a successful football coach than of an inspiring teacher." His review of the situation at Bowdoin convinced him that "The chief trouble is the over-emphasis upon gate receipts." As a first step toward a sound policy, he proposed in 1919 that "The College ought before long to include the running of athletics on a sane basis in the college budget, and pay all coaches and trainers from college funds." "We now have this vicious circle," he said in his first address as president at a dinner of the influential Bowdoin Club of Boston in January, 1919. "In order to have a good coach we must have large gate receipts. In order to have large gate receipts we must have a good team. The coach in order that his salary be increased is interested financially in having a good team so as to get good gate receipts. And so the thing goes."

At the end of his first year in office, Kenneth Sills recommended to the Governing Boards that all expenses of athletics should be assumed by the college and should form part of the college budget. "Gate receipts," he conceded, "would be for a little while necessary, but could be gradually lowered and ultimately done away with. It is as logical to pass the hat among the alumni to help hire a football or a baseball coach as it would be to do the same thing for an instructor in History or Physics." He further urged the abolition of "everything that tends towards professionalism, such as scouting, seasonal coaching, training tables, and long trips." In commenting upon these recommendations, the *Boston Herald* observed prophetically that "any college president who undertakes revolutionizing athletics is likely to find that he is taking hold of live wires whatever may be the merit of his plans." Kenneth Sills soon felt the force of the editor's comment. The next autumn when the Bowdoin football team suffered a 93–0 defeat by the Army, many alumni who witnessed the massacre at West Point decided that Casey need have no worries about professionalism.

If the debacle of the Army game had confirmed Bowdoin's lily-white status in athletics, the fact contained small solace for the president. His mail was filled with sharp reminders that in football, at least, the college reputation was black and blue. Amid the demands for a new coach, K. C. M. S. found himself in an anomalous position. As head of Bowdoin he was held responsible for everything pertaining to the college, yet the athletic system of divided responsibility left him without real power. As he studied the situation, he realized that the Governing Boards had failed to exercise their undoubted authority over athletics. In the absence of action by the Boards, the Athletic Council, dominated by its seven alumni members, had assumed virtual control and was not, in any formal way, responsible to anyone. The arrangement was a thing of shreds and patches which had grown up gradually during the last twenty-five years. Some of the coaches were paid entirely by the college; some were paid partly by the college and partly by the Athletic Council; others were paid entirely by the Council. In addition, the instructors in the department of physical training were appointed and paid as other members of the faculty. In so skimble-skamble a system confusion was inevitable. "It is remarkable," Kenneth Sills observed, "and speaks well for the loyalty of instructors and coaches that there has not been more friction."

But now, still smarting from the humiliating trouncing at West Point, the Athletic Council asserted its power by engaging Fred Ostergren, Holy Cross star and All-American, to replace Major Greene, who had coached the team for the last two years. In offering a contract to Ostergren, the Council disregarded a strong preference for Greene, not only by the team and a large majority of the students, but also by the faculty committee on athletics and Dr. Whittier, the director of physical training. During the whole affair which the *Bangor Daily News* predicted would "become something of a college political issue" when the Boards met in June, Kenneth Sills was helpless. He knew that as long as the Athletic Council held the purse strings and the power of appointment of coaches, even the president of the college lacked authority to intervene. In his report to the Boards for 1920–21, K. C. M. S. protested that "the administration of the College has practically no voice in the selection of coaches." "I desire to repeat the recommendation made two years ago," he wrote in May, 1921, "that as soon as it is practicable and possible the salaries of coaches should be placed on the college budget and the appointment of coaches should be ratified by the College." Despite the urgency of his appeal, the Boards took no action at their meeting in June, 1921. The president could not be sure which was the more formidable—live wires or vested interests.

Convinced that no improvement in the control of athletics could come without united action, K. C. M. S. welcomed an invitation to discuss the problem with the presidents of Amherst, Wesleyan, and Williams on March 25, 1922. A fortnight later, on April 10, in Springfield, he helped draw up a resolution in which the heads of eleven New England colleges agreed to urge their trustees and faculties, beginning in the fall of 1923, "to appoint all coaches in the same way as are members of the Faculty and other officers of the institution." Woodbury Howe, sports editor of the *Portland Press Herald*, noted that "The plan, if adopted, will mean placing control of athletics and coaches in the hands of the colleges themselves, and will deprive alumni councils of the power they now in many cases exercise." Howe, who was familiar with the situation at Bowdoin, doubted the effectiveness of the presidential resolutions: "What *real* changes in the athletic policies of the various colleges this conference will result in is problematical." The editor of the *Orient* also foresaw that Casey would have a battle on his hands. In reporting the reforms adopted in Springfield, he added: "This hits alumni control very hard."

His hand strengthened by the joint action of his fellow college presidents, K. C. M. S. renewed his appeal to the Boards in May, 1922. "The whole problem lies in this one fact," he reported. "The College must run athletics or athletics will run the College." With the Athletic Council carrying a considerable debt and the cost of intercollegiate athletics amounting to more than four times the budget for physical training, the president declared, "It is high time that a halt be called to unreasonable expenditures. At present we are paying more than we can afford for the support and coaching of our teams." The consideration dearest to his heart he reserved for the end of his report. "At Bowdoin," he wrote, "we are paying our coaches on a higher scale and our professors on a lower scale than is the case at Amherst, Wesleyan, and Williams." At the Commencement meeting in June, 1922, some members of the Boards voiced their concern, but no action was taken. Alumni control remained intact. Kenneth Sills, however, saw some grounds for hope in the appointment of Professor Thomas Means as graduate manager of the varsity teams and to regulate the schedules of games.

Professor Means was succeeded a year later by Lyman A. Cousens '03, a member of the Athletic Council, who abolished the separate sport treasuries and pooled all funds under the control of the graduate manager. These cautious steps toward fiscal reform ended some diffusion of responsibility, but were far from ideal. Meanwhile, the president kept hammering away. When Bowdoin won the New England Track and Field Championship in the spring of 1923, he reminded the alumni that college control of athletics does not mean defeat. "It may interest the alumni to know," he wrote in the *Orient* on June 11, "that the coach of the track team has been paid by the College in full for the past two or three years, and that his duties are assigned to him by the President of the College after consultation with the

Athletic Council. What is possible in track may be possible in other sports." Two weeks later, K. C. M. S. was encouraged when the visiting committee recommended the appointment of a committee to devise an athletic policy "that shall reflect the reasonable desires of the student body, the Faculty, and the Alumni and eliminate confusion." The Boards, however, were not fully persuaded. At a special meeting called on February 1, 1924, to receive the committee report, neither the Trustees nor the Overseers believed that conditions at Bowdoin justified their assumption of full responsibility for the direction of athletics. "It is thus clear," the president wrote in his annual report for 1923–24, "that for the present the control of athletics is vested in the Athletic Council, subject of course to the authority which the Governing Boards undoubtedly have over all phases of college life." He could point to only a few gains. "Several important forward steps have been taken this past year," K. C. M. S. wrote in May, 1924, "such as the institution of the rule barring freshmen from 'varsity athletics in the first semester, and the centralization of financial responsibility in the graduate manager's office."

The first real test of strength between the president and the Athletic Council came following the sudden death on December 23, 1924, of Dr. Frank Whittier, director of physical training. Dr. Whittier had opposed the Council's appointment of Coach Ostergren in 1921 and shared the president's ambition to bring all athletic activities under institutional control. He also deplored the Council's increasing demands for funds which threatened to cut into the budget for physical training. Dr. Whittier's death now gave Kenneth Sills an opportunity to coordinate the work in physical training and athletics, and he sought a coach of football who believed that athletics are an integral part of physical education. Although the newspapers reported that a poll of the Athletic Council indicated that Ostergren was to be reappointed, the president wished to end the policy of seasonal coaching and to make the new coach primarily responsible to the administration rather than to the Council. While the matter was hanging fire, K. C. M. S. received considerable, if somewhat embarrassing, support from the students. In the preceding term, an anonymous pamphlet entitled "Don't Pay Your Blanket Tax" had objected to a procedure whereby "A small section of vociferous, misguided alumni, through their representatives on the Athletic Council . . . run athletics to suit themselves and support them out of the students' pocketbooks." The authors ridiculed "The idea of paying the football coach $4,000. . . . For nine weeks work—during which he does not even reside in Brunswick—he receives a sum equal to that paid for nine months work to the highest paid member of the faculty as a teacher." In a letter to the *Orient*, Walter K. Gutman '24 pointed out, "Neither the Faculty or students have any control over the Athletic Council, but if the blanket tax money is withheld until a reform is either accomplished or definitely promised, the end will be achieved through mere lack of funds."

Sports writers had enjoyed picturing President Sills as being "as much in the dark as the next fellow as to who will be selected as the next football coach," and Bud Cornish in the *Portland Herald* had depicted him standing cap in hand at the door of the Council to receive the news. K. C. M. S. acted promptly to spike such allegations by recommending John M. Cates, a former Yale star under Walter Camp, to become director of athletics and coach of football. He was accorded the rank of professor of physical education with supervision of the entire program of physical training and athletics. "The action of Sills," a surprised sports editor wrote on February 18, 1925, "presents the somewhat unusual situation of an athletic council being asked to confirm the individual choice of the president. It may not be a precedent, but it is not usual for a college president to take special personal charge of the appointment of coaches." Kenneth Sills had no apologies to make. In his report to the Boards for 1924–25, he wrote, "The reply to *that* is that the coaches have so much to do with the development of the character of our boys that the choice of a coach is a matter of great importance, and no college president would be worthy of his hire if he were *not* interested in such appointments." He told an incredulous reporter, "In the next few years, all athletic instructors should be placed on an equal basis with members of the Faculty and with prestige equal to that of the teacher of science and art."

The appointment of Professor Cates was heralded by Philip Clifford, of the Overseers, as "the greatest forward step in athletics which has been taken for a long time," but the president cautioned his friends not to expect the advent of a millennium. Actually, the forward step had been achieved by a compromise. Only one-half of the new director's salary was to be assumed by the college; the other half, for his services as coach of football, was to be paid by the Council. The old problem of divided responsibility remained unsolved. K. C. M. S. also feared that many alumni were expecting the new coach to turn out winning elevens as regularly as John Magee's track squad captured the state championship. Ostergren's adherents scoffed at Professor Cates's first public pronouncement that "As Director of Athletics, football will be just an incident in the year with me. Whether we win games or lose them is not so important as playing them well, or in the education which the games will give the players." In the fall of 1925, when the varsity lost all three games to its opponents in the climactic state series, there were charges that athletics-for-all was merely an academic synonym for "defeatism."

In the winter of 1925–26, Kenneth Sills expected that the "reforms" in the athletic policy would be as predictable a fixture at alumni dinners as the menu of chicken à la king, green peas, and bricks of warm ice cream. At the annual meeting of the Kennebec Association, in Augusta, he heard Judge Sanford Fogg '89 assert roundly, "I don't believe a great majority of Bowdoin graduates believe athletics . . . as they have existed should be curbed." To such criticism, K. C. M. S. had a detailed answer. On February 23, in Bangor, he conceded, "So far as

victories are concerned, our football season may not have seemed
a great success, but I think all alumni will be interested to know:
(1) at the end of the season there were many more men out playing football than at the beginning; (2) that Mr. Cates refused to
allow a man to play if there were any chance of his being badly
hurt; (3) not a direction was given by the bench during the
whole season. The boys on the field did their own playing. We
at Bowdoin . . . are in the vanguard of an important educational movement."

President Sills's memories of his tour of the alumni-dinner
circuit were still fresh when he addressed the New England
Federation of Harvard Clubs on July 23, 1926. "I don't object
to alumni talking about athletics," he said. "It is a good starting
point for conversation like the weather, but if the talk continues
in that line as in the other, it denotes a certain intellectual thin-
ness that is discouraging. If an alumnus is to be a valued critic
of his college, he must first keep his intellectual life vigorous and
alive." K. C. M. S. was heartened by the undergraduates' responses to the new regime. Unlike some of the alumni, the students were not ready to prejudge the whole program on the
basis of one disappointing football season. "The new physical
training program," the *Orient* remarked on December 9, 1925,
"which permits a large portion of the men in college to select
their own form of required exercise in place of the usual stereo-
typed gymnasium work is worthy of sincere commendation."
Welcome support also came in June from a committee of responsible alumni appointed to study the needs of the college.
"We think that the views of Mr. Cates," the report concluded,
"are sound and correct, and that they have the endorsement of
the alumni body." Professor Cates's position was further
strengthened by a successful football season in 1926 when the
team defeated Bates and Colby, and compiled a record of five
victories, one tie, and only two losses. The *Orient* went so far
as to boast on January 13, 1926, "We believe that the policy
pursued in recent years at Bowdoin has come just about as near

the ideal as it is possible to get." Cheered by the turn of events, the president continued his appeal to the Boards in his report for 1926–27. "I strongly recommend," he wrote, "that the salaries of *all* coaches and instructors be carried on the regular college budget with such contributions from the funds of the Athletic Council as may be desirable."

The president was beginning to see his dream of institutional control of athletics come closer to realization when the success of the program attracted the attention of Yale. On March 17, 1927, he was compelled to announce that Professor Cates had submitted his resignation to become director of athletics at Yale University. "I wish to remark with all possible emphasis," K. C. M. S. told the students in chapel, "that the College intends to continue along the lines of athletic policy instituted these past two years, a determination in which the Governing Boards, Faculty, and Athletic Council are united." The departure of Cates for wider opportunities in New Haven left another problem child on Casey's doorstep. At a special Boards' meeting in April, the president recommended the appointment of Malcolm Morrell as acting director and coach of football. "Very frankly," he told the alumni, "many of the arrangements for next year are experimental." In the emergency he was compelled to accept the Athletic Council's appointment of an assistant coach for the football season only, but he assured the faculty, "It is not our intention in the future to have any part-time coaches and instructors." K. C. M. S. hoped to salvage as much of the athletics-for-all policy as possible, but he knew that much would depend upon the success of the 1927 football season. He told William Lawrence that in a small college all educational problems also become athletic problems. "Fortunately for Bowdoin," his friend replied, "along with other virtues, your fairy godmother endowed you with an uncommon stock of patience."

Kenneth Sills needed all of it in the last few years of the decade. He had foreseen that the emotional climate of the college would be profoundly affected merely by the way a pigskin chose to bounce on a few autumnal afternoons on Whittier Field. And the ball bounced perversely. Between 1927 and 1929, the team won only two of its nine games with the other Maine colleges and failed to achieve a single winning season. The *Orient* bemoaned Bowdoin's status as "the weak sister of the Maine athletic group," while the *Quill* grew more querulous than ever. Its editor charged that the athletics-for-all policy had been ignominiously "subordinated to the interests of varsity athletics which any moron knows are more and more showing signs of dying a natural death." It is getting more difficult for a Bowdoin team to win, he continued, because it is impossible "to maintain athletic standards equal to those of our neighbors whose scholastic standards are far below ours." Readers of the president's report for 1928–29 felt that Casey was guilty of an understatement when he wrote, "The lack of success of several of the major athletic teams added to the restlessness of some undergraduates and the unhappiness of many alumni." To critics who sought to make a scapegoat of the requirements for admission, K. C. M. S. said bluntly, "The College has always held that it is better that some should fall in the ditch than that every clodhopper should clear it." With Bowdoin in the athletic doldrums, alumni enjoyed only cold comfort in her high standards or in the fact that their alma mater was among the twenty-eight North American colleges and universities where no indication of subsidized athletics was found by the Carnegie Foundation. "The Carnegie report stated," the *Orient* observed on October 30, 1929, "that the only inducement Bowdoin had to offer any student was a good education." President Sills vowed to keep it that way, even though a week later he watched Bowdoin lose to the University of Maine, 25–6.

Following the disastrous season, when Coach Morrell resigned to devote his full time to the office of director of athletics, K. C. M. S. was faced with another reorganization of the harassed department of physical education. Again he appealed to the Boards to put an end to "the present anomalous situation of divided authority." "No coach in any sport should be appointed," he declared, "without the approval of the College; the policy of athletics for all should be heartily supported, and the best coaching within our resources should be given to all teams, major and minor." In the meantime, some sports commentators scented signs of change. "There is more in the Bowdoin gridiron situation than meets the eye," Burt Whitman wrote in the *Boston Herald*. "We understand there is a real move to get an outstanding man for the position." Bud Cornish predicted in the *Portland Press Herald*, "With the adoption of a new policy, the Polar Bear is expected to come back to its own in the athletic world of New England." Cornish hinted that the Athletic Council was still supreme, and the *Quill* exclaimed despondently, "We are back where we started from. The old ideal of an athletic aristocracy has resumed full sway." President Sills, however, said flatly that there would be no "big time" athletics as long as he was head of Bowdoin. He told the Governing Boards in 1929 that "The athletic staff should realize their responsibility belongs not so much to the public or to the alumni as to the College itself. In Professor Morrell, the new Director of Athletics, he had an unflinching ally. Together they would continue the battle, despite the fact that the choice of Charles Bowser, the new coach from the University of Pittsburgh, was dictated by the Athletic Council. To a younger colleague, who sensed the president's concern, Kenneth Sills quoted a couplet from his favorite ballad: "For I will stand by and bleed but awhile, And then will I come and fight again."

The furor over athletics convinced the president that his chief problem was one of emphasis. American society, he remarked, must not be permitted to make over the college in its own image. He had no wish to preside over an athletic association or a country club. Amid the strident materialism of the 1920s, he held that "The greatest need of the College is a proper understanding on the part of graduates and the public of its true function as an institution of learning. The College cannot fulfill its high and important duties in this respect if there is a feeling abroad that learning and intellectual training are unimportant." To keep Bowdoin serene and strong was proving to be a struggle even in the best of times. And in October, 1929, there were portents foreshadowing times which were fully as critical as those which existed when Kenneth Sills was inaugurated in the midst of the First World War.

# II

## *LIGHTS AND SHADOWS IN THE 1930s*

Kenneth Sills at first was disposed to regard the market crash in October, 1929, as only another periodic crisis which would mainly affect a lunatic fringe of speculators. In the next few months, however, when every brief rally was punctuated by a violent collapse, he was not entirely reassured by those who kept insisting on the soundness of the national economy. At a faculty meeting in December, he warned of future financial stringency for the college even though Maine was suffering far less than the heavily industrialized states. Department budgets, he said, must be cut to the bone. He failed to share the amusement of his colleagues when Professor Wilmot Mitchell mildly rebuked the librarian for allowing a twenty-five-watt lamp to burn all night long in an upper corridor of Hubbard Hall. Yet there were encouraging signs. In 1929–30 the college had been able to add more than $600,000 to its resources and, in the following year, benefactions amounted to $825,000, bringing the Bowdoin endowment over the five million mark for the first time. Gratifying as these increases were to the president, he told the student body not to be complacent. "This is hardly a time for any trace of self-satisfaction or smugness," he said in chapel. "Lean years are likely to follow."

In the preceding spring, K. C. M. S. was deeply troubled about a more immediate depression faced by the senior members of his faculty. Although he remembered having heard President Nicholas Murray Butler predict that the pensions granted by the Carnegie Foundation would prove to be pitifully inadequate, he was not prepared for the drastic cuts announced by the Founda-

tion on May 1, 1929. When the Carnegie pension plan was
instituted in 1908, shortly after his return to Bowdoin as an
adjunct professor, the retirement age was set at sixty-five with
an allowance of $3,000. The fifteen members of the faculty who
were appointed prior to 1915 had been relying upon the Foundation to make good its promises and had looked forward to pensions of the same amount as those received by their predecessors.
Suddenly, however, with virtually no warning, the age of retirement was advanced to seventy, and the annual allowance reduced to $1,500. To make prospects even more bleak, the Foun-
dation intimated that after 1932 the pensions for those totally
disabled and for widows would amount to no more than $500 a
year. There was little comfort in the fact that the Carnegie
allowances were outright grants rather than legal contracts.

President Sills acted at once to relieve the anxiety of his older
colleagues by appealing to the executive committee of the Governing Boards. "This is not the place to criticize the management
of the Foundation, although many winged words might profit-
ably be let loose," he reported, "but in accepting the provisions
as laid down by the Foundation, the College to a very real degree, morally, at least, underwrote the transaction and should, in
my judgment, find some way to make good the reasonable expectations of the members of the Faculty affected." Henry Hill
Pierce, of the Trustees, who was appointed by K. C. M. S. to
head a committee to study the problem, was in full sympathy
with the president's views. Together they persuaded the Governing Boards in June, 1929, to provide a supplementary allowance equal to the original terms of the Carnegie commitment,
with more generous provisions for total disability. This concern
for the welfare of the faculty induced Cyrus H. K. Curtis to
send the college in 1929 a Christmas gift of $115,000 in support
of pensions for the older teachers. The problem of the younger
men appointed after 1915 had already been met by a contributory plan for those willing to allot 5 percent of their salaries to
pay a portion of the premium on deferred annuity contracts.

Later, at the president's suggestion, participation was made mandatory for all members of the faculty with more than two years of service.

The president's solicitude about decent remuneration was not limited to retirement allowances. At the beginning of his administration in 1918, the maximum salary for a full professor was $2,750. Ten years later the figure had reached $6,000. "It must, however, be remembered," he reported to the Boards, "that this advance hardly covers the increase in the cost of living and while respectable as compared with other institutions, is by no means lavish. There is no reason why a professor should sacrifice the comfort of his wife or the education of his children simply for the sake of being in the teaching profession. The maximum salary for a professor is not yet so large as it ought to be." In 1925 when the top salary of $5,000 had been insufficient to retain the services of Professor Roy Elliott, K. C. M. S. considered asking the Boards to provide funds to enable him to offer bonuses to reward distinguished teaching and scholarship. Reluctant as he was to lose Elliott, one of the most inspiring teachers on his faculty, the president was even more reluctant to give up the uniformity in the salary scale which had helped to make the morale of the Bowdoin faculty the envy of many colleges. Although he saw merit in a system flexible enough to attract and to keep the most effective teachers, he was convinced that a fixed scale would, in the long run, be best for the college. In the meantime, he told the Governing Boards, it was their duty to raise the scale for every rank. "The proper payment of teachers," he said, "is in reality an act of public service."

A step toward such service was made possible by another unexpected gift from Cyrus Curtis in the summer of 1930, when he gave the college 5,000 shares of Curtis Publishing Company preferred stock valued at $594,000, the income to be used "exclusively for additions to the salaries of such professors as the Boards think best entitled to increases." No gift could have been more welcome to the president, not only because it enabled him to add to the fixed salary scale at all levels, but because it constituted an endorsement of his educational policy. Mr. Curtis had been watching the college sympathetically ever since 1921, when he had been impressed by the courage shown by the Governing Boards in closing the Medical School rather than conducting it as a second-class institution. He was also enthusiastic about Kenneth Sills's efforts to maintain Bowdoin as an undergraduate college of liberal arts, and saw in its wisely limited curriculum a source of strength. The donor congratulated K. C. M. S. for holding out against academic fads by seeking not to offer "new" courses but to give the existing ones more effectively. He was delighted when, at the president's recommendation, the Boards voted to use the income from his gift for additional compensation, not on a percentage basis, but as a flat sum which would especially benefit the younger teachers.

As the shadows of the Depression lengthened in the autumn of 1932, Kenneth Sills told the alumni that the state of the nation compelled him to think more seriously than ever of the real purpose of the college. "Suppose," he asked on November 5, "that Bowdoin's funds were so far reduced that we had to cut out everything that was unessential—what would be left? One can well imagine a college run without administrative officers; a college could certainly be run without a president . . . it would still be a college if there were no athletic fields, no fraternities. When you come right down to the bare necessities of the college you are driven to the conclusion that the college consists of those who teach and those who study together. The essential equipment can be confined to the library and the laboratory, with a few classrooms thrown in for good measure."

These words were spoken at an alumni luncheon just before the state series game on Whittier Field with the University of Maine. Unfortunately for the happiness of many in his audience, football success was far from being unessential, and their unhappiness was intensified later that afternoon. Nor was it lessened on the following Saturday when their team ended the season by losing to Wesleyan. In the preceding year, despite the brave hopes cherished for the new coaching regime of Charles Bowser, Bowdoin had failed to win a single game. "I suppose that intercollegiate athletics were invented to keep every college president in a state of humility," K. C. M. S. wrote to Harvey Dow Gibson at the end of the hapless season. "They certainly furnish more trouble than all the rest of the College put together."

The tenor of much of the mail addressed to the president did nothing to dispel such an impression. As he read some of the criticism he often recalled Lawrence Lowell's exclamation, "Sometimes I wish I were the head of a penitentiary. Then I should have no trouble with parents, and none with alumni." Professor Charles Livingston encountered the president in an unusually discouraged mood on an afternoon train to Boston in December, 1932. "Here I am, trying my best to conduct a respectable educational institution in difficult times," he protested to his colleague, "yet certain prominent alumni seem quite ready to judge my efforts solely on the basis of the success of the athletic teams." Struck by the despondency of his admired chief, Livingston feared that K. C. M. S. might be tempted to resign. Such moods were, however, rare. Although Kenneth Sills continued to the end to worry about the exaggerated emphasis upon football as a melancholy indication of the chief interest of many Americans, including hundreds of Bowdoin alumni, he never lost faith in intercollegiate athletics as a valuable accessory to an education which includes "the whole man." Even in the winter of his discontent in 1934, after another winless football season, he was cheered by the way in which undergraduates accepted defeat more philosophically than the alumni and public. "The sane and healthy attitude which most students display in all matters of athletics," he remarked, "is often a lesson to their elders."

Many alumni, misled by the president's criticism of football as a public spectacle, and by his alarm at the growing expense of intercollegiate athletics, had come to believe that he lacked a genuine interest in sports. The great majority of undergraduates were not so deceived. They noticed that he often walked to Pickard Field to watch varsity practice, that he frequently spoke at pregame rallies, invariably attended home contests, and more than occasionally visited the team in its dressing room to lend the encouragement of his presence. Unlike some of his faculty colleagues, he was unconvinced that athletics seriously interfered with study. His experience as dean and president in talking with hundreds of students in scholastic difficulty led him to believe that the athletes who neglected their work would have done so whether or not they played on the teams. He knew of many instances where participation in sports helped rather than hindered scholastic endeavor.

When the athletic situation grew steadily more acute between 1930 and 1934, Kenneth Sills refused to look for a convenient scapegoat. Characteristically, he was disposed to blame himself for having failed to assert proper leadership. He now saw clearly enough that in the past there had been no consistent policy. He had been content to believe that "so far as intercollegiate athletics are concerned, it is the duty of the College to furnish good coaches and let other matters take care of themselves." Amid the resulting confusion, he had watched a procession of coaches come and go under an authority divided between the Governing Boards and the alumni Athletic Council. He also reproached himself for not having given adequate support to his director of athletics. As a consequence, the physical education program with its emphasis upon intramural sports and the coaches striving for victory in intercollegiate contests were often at odds with each other. Football was threatening, in the president's judgment, to become merely a means for the alumni to enjoy a Roman holiday. Despite the previous work of conscientious committees of the Governing Boards, alumni, faculty, and undergraduates, no workable plan had emerged for bringing all aspects of athletics and physical education into a wholesome relationship with the intellectual life of the college.

The disappointing season in 1934 only added fuel to flames which had been smoldering for some time. In 1930, with the appointment of Bowser as head coach, fresh from "big time" triumphs under Dr. Jock Sutherland at the University of Pittsburgh, the president had yielded to the wishes of the alumni Athletic Council. If the "Pitt system" could cure Bowdoin's chronic gridiron woes, K. C. M. S. was willing to give it a fair chance. The Council was elated at the choice. William R. Crowley '08, a member, assured his fellow alumni, "Bowser has no sentimental illusions about sport for sport's sake. No pupil of his has ever been taught an unethical dodge, yet no coach strives more persistently to fire his charges with the will to win." Unfortunately, the desired victories were not forthcoming, and when the team failed to win a game during Bowser's second season in 1931, the critics were again in full cry. Kenneth Sills winced at the prospect of a repetition of the athletic "crises" of the 1920s, but this time there was less disposition to find fault with the coach than to carp at the organization of the department of physical education and at the college itself. "All factions seem to agree," wrote Al Buck, sports editor of the *Portland Press Herald,* "that Bowser has made the best of a bad situation." Kenneth Sills was told that since Bowdoin had a reputation for being "the grave-yard of able football coaches," the fault must lie elsewhere than on the coaches' bench. Jack Magee, the doughty director of track and field athletics, carried his grievance to the president. "Why don't some of these professors who say, 'You ought to give us a winning team, you're the coach,' go out and arrange a test of their own ability by a contest between their classes and similar ones in other colleges? Then we'd hear the *profs* complain of lack of good material." Later, when Magee was asked whether K. C. M. S. approved his proposal, he replied, "Casey said it was an interesting suggestion." Those better versed in Sillsean semantics than the track coach knew that when the president labeled a proposal interesting, it was the kiss of death.

The intramural program soon became a favorite whipping boy. Following the dreary season in 1931, the *Lewiston Evening Journal* attributed Bowdoin's poor showing to "stiffer entrance requirements and an excess of intramural athletics," while the *Kennebec Journal* predicted that any further stress on intramural sports would make a farce out of intercollegiate competition. Back on the campus, Coach Bowser found a welcome ally in Magee in blaming interfraternity games for the decline of zeal in varsity sports. Later that winter, in talks to alumni clubs, they repeated the indictment, equating the falling off of candidates for varsity teams with a decrease in loyalty to the college, and urging the abolition of all intramural sports. Subversive forces of a more ominous kind were hinted at by George B. Chandler '90 in an open letter to the student body. "To laud the spineless substitute of interfraternity schedules while the varsity languishes," he wrote, "seems so utterly incompatible with the spirit of Young America that one is tempted to speculate on what influences may be at work in Bowdoin College." Aroused by such charges, the students held a mass meeting in Memorial Hall on December 8 to deplore any attempt to sacrifice intramural sports on the altar of more football victories, and to endorse the Sills policy of athletics for all. The president's faith in the common sense of the undergraduates was confirmed the next day when the editor of the *Orient* remarked, "despite the temporary gloom which follows defeat, the course of the sun remains unchanged and graver problems linger on the horizon."

Kenneth Sills stoutly refused to hedge in his stand on the benefits of intramural sports. "Some time ago I announced that the policy of the College was athletics for all, and to this policy I firmly adhere," he promised the students in a chapel talk on January 6, 1932. "It seems to me that the natural rivalry furnished by fraternity groups is the best method of conducting many of these contests. The main thing is to have as many students as possible take part in sports and games. When that takes place, naturally the boys of superior athletic talent will find their way to the so-called major team. Intercollegiate competition is necessary, desirable, and important; but a sane and sensible program of intramural sports is just as important and to such a program nothing should be sacrificed." Two days later, when a sports columnist on the *Kennebec Journal* warned K. C. M. S. that he could not eat his cake and have it too, and that it was naïve to champion intramural games and at the same time expect a reasonable share of intercollegiate victories, the president told an *Orient* reporter that he had no intention of permitting sports writers to run the college. Such forthright statements from the president, however often he repeated them, did not deter several of the coaches from continuing their campaign against interfraternity athletics. When they succeeded in persuading six of Bowdoin's eleven fraternities to curtail their sports programs, the *Orient* flatly charged them with violating a sound educational policy "without consulting any higher authority than themselves." "Athletics today are properly a part of the college curriculum," the editor concluded, "and their control should be vested in the Faculty."

Kenneth Sills often wondered precisely where the control actually resided. Although the alumni Athletic Council had been made directly responsible to the Governing Boards in 1931 and the director of athletics was nominated by the president of the college, this nomination, as well as those of the coaches, was subject to the approval of the Council; moreover, the duties of the director had never been clearly defined. Theoretically the coaches were under the authority of the director of athletics, but they all knew that his appointment as well as their own depended upon the approval of the Council. Past experience had shown that the Boards were too preoccupied with other concerns to take a sufficiently active interest in athletic affairs. To be

sure, the visiting committee in the spring of 1933 was urged by
the faculty to give the director of athletics "supreme authority
in every branch of his work," and to make the functions of
the Council advisory rather than executive. In its report to the
Governing Boards in June, however, the committee confessed
that it had been unable to "study the interlocking complications
of the Athletic Department and hesitated to express an opinion
on this subject." Lack of decisive action thus created a power
vacuum in which the Council, as the president had observed,
was "not in any formal way responsible to any one." The *Orient*
went so far as to charge in a front-page editorial that a small
group of influential alumni, having gained virtual control of
athletics, was able to bypass both the president and his director
of athletics. "Never, perhaps," the editor asserted, "has such a
rank exhibition of political method been perpetrated in the history of the College." Although K. C. M. S. deplored the editorial
as "rather lurid," he knew that the situation was far from being a
happy one.

The president was particularly irked when he learned that
the head coach of football flatly refused to supervise intramural
sports, even though the director of athletics requested him to
share in the program at the end of the football season. This
anomalous state of affairs, the director told the Bowdoin Club
of Portland, "invites the playing of politics to secure power
through courting the votes of poorly informed Council members." "No member of the Department," he said after the miser-
able 1934 season, "can feel that honest and good work assures
him of security in his position. Rather, he invariably feels that
he must entrench himself with voting members of the Athletic
Council in various ways." The difficulties were further complicated by an inconsistent representation of the department of
physical education on the faculty. Although three of its members enjoyed faculty status, none of them coached a major sport,
while the head coach of football and the spectacularly successful
director of track and field athletics were without faculty rank.

This imbalance resulted in a divisive spirit of mutual recrimination and distrust, and led the coaches of major sports to seek allies in the Athletic Council. Jack Magee said bluntly, "If major sports coaches were allowed on the Bowdoin College faculty, as are the minor sports mentors, a great deal of good would result and more football games would be won."

Meanwhile, football victories, for whatever the reason, were slow in coming, and the question of the renewal of Bowser's contract attracted more than local interest. At the end of the 1933 season, sports writers pounced upon a rumor that the varsity squad had refused to give the coach a vote of confidence as early as the second game of the schedule. Bowser, they predicted, was through. Some days later, however, they reported that the team had reversed its position on a second ballot. In the midst of the confusion, the Athletic Council met to consider Bowser's future at Bowdoin. Although the team had done creditably in the past season, defeating three of its four out-of-state rivals, in the all-important state championship series it had failed to win a game, losing to Colby and Maine, and playing a tie game with Bates. "The most that the campus supporters of the coach hoped for," the *Orient* noted, "was a one-year term." This was precisely the recommendation submitted by the director of athletics who believed, in the circumstances, that future embarrassment might be avoided were Bowser offered a single-year contract. The Council knew that this proposal also had the endorsement of President Sills who regarded it in the same way he treated all recommendations from the chairmen of other departments. The members of the Council, however, hoped that the season's record of three victories might be the happy augury of a renaissance in Bowdoin's football fortunes. They were also swayed by the team's reconsidered vote of confidence and by assurances from the two faculty representatives on the Council that in the event of another unsuccessful season Bowser would not hold the college to the strict terms of his contract. In their eagerness to express their own confidence in the coach, the

Council finally disregarded the wishes of both the president and the director of athletics by offering Bowser a contract for three years. Imperturbable as always, Kenneth Sills somehow managed to keep his disappointment to himself. It is perhaps significant, however, that in his annual report to the Governing Boards in June, 1934, instead of following his custom of devoting a section to a review of athletics, he merely remarked, "The undergraduate members of the Athletic Council have shown a good deal of restraint under some critical conditions."

The deepening of the economic depression dwarfed the difficulties of the athletic situation, but the president was not ready to agree with the *Orient*'s view that "The whole absurd incident seems now to take on all the aspects of a tempest within a small campus teapot." K. C. M. S. realized that even though athletics were subordinate to the main purpose of the college, they had a disconcertingly explosive way of affecting it. At Bowdoin athletic problems invariably became educational problems as well. Reluctant as the president was to interfere actively with the cumbersome existing system, he knew that he could not postpone much longer the decisive action needed to bring the whole athletic program under educational control. For the time being he resolved to do some watchful waiting. In any event, he reflected grimly, he could not be accused of failing to give the Council ample time to muddle through. When Professor Morgan Cushing, a faculty representative on the Council, spoke hopefully of a turn for the better in athletics, K. C. M. S. was not optimistic. "We'll see what we'll see," he said glumly. After classes were resumed following the Christmas recess, a few discerning students in Casey's Lit. observed that the president seemed tired and depressed. "He talked about the *Inferno* in class this morning," one of them said, "just as though he had actually felt the flames."

Amid the acrimonious bickering over athletics, Kenneth Sills found it necessary to remind students that their woes were comparatively trivial. "Every period of crisis is also a period of criticism," he remarked in a chapel talk on the virtue of charity. "An unsuccessful athletic season is in this respect like an economic depression. Criticize with charity and with a sound knowledge of the facts. This is no time to regard life in college as a fool's paradise, untouched by the distress and suffering that are going on in the world outside. Your brothers of the same age, cut off from their ability to earn a living, ask you to find the road to a better state of affairs." In the meantime, the president promised that Bowdoin would set an example by practicing the old-fashioned New England virtue of "making things do." He was touched by the encouragement proffered by Horace Litchfield, a veteran college carpenter. "Any old fool can work with good tools," he told K. C. M. S., "but a real workman is the feller who can do things when he has to use his head." In 1931–32, by the exercise of rigid economy, and by the postponement of all projects except the most needed repairs of buildings, a threatened deficit of $38,000 had been averted. By January, 1933, however, the treasurer reported that the income of the college had fallen off so seriously that more drastic steps were needed. On January 16, the executive committee of the Boards asked members of the faculty and all college officers receiving salaries in excess of $2,000 to contribute 10 percent of their salaries to the alumni fund. A month later a similar cut was made in the wages of all other college employees. The request came at a time when the income of the faculty was further reduced by the omission of the dividends from the Curtis fund. Additional hardship was also caused by the closing, in some instances permanently, of banks in Portland and Brunswick. "It can therefore be seen," the president reported to the Boards in May, "that the members of the Faculty have not been without the experience so common elsewhere."

Kenneth Sills kept his faculty fully informed of the financial plight of the college. His colleagues, as always, sensed instinctively that their chief identified himself with their best interests. He made clear that the 10 percent contributions were to be regarded as "voluntary," and that the Boards were eager to keep the base rate of salaries intact by putting the contributions on a percentage basis rather than jeopardizing the entire structure of compensation which had been built up slowly in more prosperous days. Above all the president refused to reduce the effectiveness of Bowdoin as "a teaching college" by cutting down the number of assistant professors and instructors. Such a policy, when adopted elsewhere, he deplored as a great disservice to American education. Responding to the contributory plan unanimously and cheerfully, the faculty assured K. C. M. S. of their readiness to make still greater sacrifices as an alternative to terminating the appointments of the younger instructors. Professor Roscoe Ham heard the news in Göttingen, Germany, where he was spending his sabbatical. "Bowdoin has come through the storm in much better condition than I believed I had any right to expect," he wrote on June 4, 1933. "Frankly I didn't believe you could possibly pull through without a very large permanent cut in salaries and staff. I shall have to regard you and Roosevelt as on the same level—*un magico prodigioso*." Dean Paul Nixon attempted to mask his admiration and affection for the president by resorting to mock abuse. "What do you mean by refusing advances in salary while all the rest of us took them?" he asked. "And by turning over fifteen percent of your current salary to the Alumni Fund while the rest of us are contributing only ten percent of ours? And by making bigger contributions to charities than you should? Things of that sort hardly check with your going without a car all these years and buying a Ford—on time, too, we suspect." Kenneth Sills was profoundly moved by the spirit of his colleagues. "The morale of the College as a whole is the best that I have known for some years," he wrote in a letter to the alumni in April, 1933. "Despite the economic distress there is a feeling of unity when all of us—undergraduates, faculty, and working staff—are all in the same boat, and realize that cheer and courage are the best sailing companions." It never occurred to the modest and self-effacing president to recognize how much this cheer and courage owed to his personal example.

Kenneth Sills finished writing his report for the academic year, 1932–33, on May 14, the fifteenth anniversary of his election to the presidency of the college. Inevitably, his thoughts went back to the spring of 1918, in the midst of the First World War, when students were leaving the campus every day, some never to return. Now, in the trough of a great depression, he found a different kind of restlessness. In 1933, as in 1918, many undergraduates were wondering whether they had any right to be in college at all, but their latter-day uncertainty was of quite another sort. For them there was no conviction of leaving to join a high adventure or to share in preserving a prized social order. Faced with dark prospects of employment, many were questioning the worth of an economic system which seemed to have no place either for their training or their ideals. As the president reviewed the changes wrought in the undergraduate temper by postwar disillusionment and the materialism of the 1920s, he saw much to encourage him. "Today, unless I am greatly mistaken," he wrote, "the undergraduate has even less use for that kind of life which has been designated as that of the rich and successful business man. He wants to be independent, to earn a decent competence; but he does not care to be included among those who have in his eyes, rightly or wrongly, brought the world to its present pass. And with a good many others, he feels that our human instruments, the church, the school, the college, and the home have somehow failed in the development of character and personal responsibility." In that attitude and in that feeling, K. C. M. S. felt anew the urgency of Bowdoin's mission as a college of liberal arts: "For it means that in the getting of knowledge we must not forget wisdom; and that if we develop the intellectual life well, we must not delude ourselves by believing such training is sufficient. Without character it is as tinkling brass or a sounding cymbal." Whatever crises lay ahead, the president could think of no better preparation for them than the development of a resourceful mind in a strong

Christian character. He had voiced this conviction in his inaugural address in 1918, and now, after fifteen years of stewardship, he was only more sure of what he had always known was true.

To those colleagues who congratulated him on the anniversary, he confessed to feeling a desolate sense of loss and change. Of the twelve Trustees who had elected him to office, only one, the venerable Governor William Titcomb Cobb, remained; of the forty-two Overseers, only thirteen were members of that Board on May 14, 1918; of the fifty members of the present faculty, less than one-third were at Bowdoin when his presidency began. "I do not believe," K. C. M. S. said, "that any college president in the country has had finer men to direct and advise him than has fallen to my lot." During his fifteen years in office he had also witnessed many changes in the administrations of all the colleges in Maine, Vermont, New Hampshire, and Connecticut. His seniors in the presidencies of the New England group of men's colleges were reduced to three: Lowell of Harvard, Hopkins of Dartmouth, and Garfield of Williams. When his grateful faculty gave him a dinner to mark the anniversary, telling him they could not imagine Bowdoin without his leadership, he remarked that he was living on borrowed time because the average tenure of an American college president is only five years. He capped the observation by quoting the *Rubaiyat:* "We are no other than a moving row, Of Magic Shadowshapes that come and go."

When Paul Nixon asked, "How is it that those four factions —alumni, undergraduates, faculty, and trustees—that usually draw and quarter college presidents, have left you pretty much intact?" K. C. M. S. escaped from his embarrassment by recalling a remark of President Roberts of Colby at the inauguration of Dr. Clarence Cook Little as president of the University of Maine. "Too bad," Roberts had said, "he seems like such a promising young man." There were times, Kenneth Sills told his faculty, when his job was an intolerably lonely one, and when his chief function seemed only to give and receive pain. He was quick to deny that he had brought to his office any unique qualities. "There are hundreds of potentially good college presidents lying around perfectly competent to handle the job," he said. "For we Americans take naturally to business. Executive competence is common rather than rare. The rare thing in any college is the good teacher. A good executive has got to be ready to make decisions when necessary, and to make decisions promptly, and if sixty per cent of his decisions are right, he gets away with it. But a good teacher has got to be right nearly all the time, and that is a far more difficult matter." Whatever distinction Bowdoin may be said to possess, the president added, is owing to the quality of her faculty. "As for my own function," he said, "it is not unlike that of a housekeeper, who must give his days and nights to seeing that the house is in order so that the other members of the household may have the best conditions for work and play." On the whole and in the main, he concluded, "my job has been great fun, and I would not willingly exchange it for any other kind of work in the world. But I know it is not so easy on the family, and I am acquainted with a certain lady who is quite sure that her second husband, whatever else he may be, is not going to be a college president."

Kenneth Sills remembered hearing President William Faunce of Brown University once say that a college president at least had the consolation of knowing he would never go crazy brooding over one difficult problem, because long before that was settled another would arise to make him forget the first. Although Kenneth Sills knew that the unsettled athletic situation might flare up again at any time, he was relieved to be able to turn to matters closer to his heart. Not the least of these was his concern for recent graduates of the college seeking academic appointments after a year or two of graduate study. He was pleased to learn in 1932 that Bowdoin with thirty-six representatives was second only to Harvard in the number of its alumni in the Harvard Graduate School of Arts and Sciences. Yet these young scholars, fresh from advanced training, enthusiastic about

their subjects, and eager to impart their knowledge were finding
that for every vacancy there was an overabundance of candidates.
With the cordial endorsement of the faculty, the president persuaded the executive committee of the Boards to authorize the
appointment of five recent graduates as teaching fellows in the
autumn of 1934. "Like every other profession," K. C. M. S. told
the committee, "the teaching profession needs apprentices."
The fellows, whose salaries were paid out of the general funds
of the college, and later from special gifts, were assigned various
tasks. They conducted conferences, served as laboratory assistants, and helped to direct students preparing for their comprehensive examinations. Begun as an experiment, the venture was
so successful for the college as well as for the fellows themselves
that the program was continued for the remainder of the decade.
Virtually every department of instruction benefited from the
fellows' enthusiastic teaching, but the chief value, as the president had foreseen, was the opportunity it offered young scholars
to begin their careers in a friendly environment at a time when
the academic world was discouragingly difficult to enter. For
the great majority of the fellows, this experience confirmed
their interest in teaching and enabled them to obtain positions
elsewhere with the confidence derived from having taught successfully at their own college. One of them, Nathan Watson
'35, a teaching fellow in French in 1937–38, was later to recall
his year at Bowdoin, working closely with the senior members
of his department and with his students, as the most helpful
single year in his career.

Although Kenneth Sills remembered the scant regard students
had paid to the moving events in the spring of 1917 before the
United States entered the First World War, he was surprised
to observe how very little the life of the undergraduates was
immediately affected by the depression. "To a certain measure,
the college undergraduate lives in a world of his own which he
and his comrades create," K. C. M. S. told a reporter on the
*Boston Herald* in March, 1933. "It is a very busy world where

he is much intent on the affairs of the moment and where it sometimes seems as if he passes his time without paying much heed to the world outside." Certain signs, nevertheless, were becoming apparent in the early 1930s. The president noticed with amused relief the eagerness of the *Quill* to disavow any appearance of preciosity. "Flickering candles and tea-drinking are barred at the meetings," the editors solemnly announced after the bottom had dropped out of the stock market. "We have no intention of encouraging *poseurs*." Above all, K. C. M. S. sensed a restlessness different from anything in his experience. He attributed the surprisingly large vote for Norman Thomas in a student poll in 1932 to a feeling of helplessness on the part of those who were worried about conditions at home, but knew there would be no work for them if they returned. "They know that something ought to be done," K. C. M. S. said, "but they do not know just what, and this increases their restless spirit."

When Newton Chase described the feelings of his contemporaries in his address on Class Day in June of his Senior year, the president listened sympathetically. "We became freshmen in September, 1929, when the outlook was bright," Chase said. "Then in October came the first crack of thunder that warned of the approaching storm. For nearly a year the deluge held off, but by the middle of our sophomore year it was felt at home, if not on the campus. As seniors we have few illusions about the difficulties of employment." K. C. M. S. had shared the hope of many optimists that business was beginning to revive in 1932. "Industry is like a man who has been knocked unconscious," he said at the opening of college in September of that year. "He is still out, but his fingers are beginning to twitch, and there are signs of reviving life." Such optimism, however, was not confirmed by the income yield on college investments which fell from a high of 5.4 percent in 1930 to 3.7 in 1934–35. "For the fourth consecutive year upper classmen are seeing their friends graduate without very definite assurance of employment," he reported to the Governing Boards in 1933.

"Each year they have been told that prosperity is just around the corner . . . and each year they have seen their hopes dashed. All their young lives they have followed the advice of their parents and elders; many have worked hard and saved money, now to see their efforts frustrated and much of their earnings dissipated by the mismanagement of banks. . . . But no matter how hard they have worked in college . . . there is no more place for them in our present social order than for a graduate of a second-rate high school. Is it any wonder that youth all over the land is seriously questioning the worth of our present social order?"

Kenneth Sills attempted to counteract this tendency toward pessimism by reminding his students that they were not so helpless as they assumed, even in the depth of the depression. "If from all our colleges men and women could go forth this year intent, not so much on reforming the world, as on living lives of high honor and integrity," he said in his baccalaureate address in 1933, "what a fresh breeze of inspiration and confidence might sweep across the nation." The president never tired of devoting his chapel talks to the stirring examples of personal integrity in the careers of Bowdoin alumni. At a time when the newspapers were filled with reports of unethical business deals, he told of General Thomas Hubbard's refusal to make a huge profit by selling out the rights of the minority stockholders of a western railroad in which he held controlling interest. A generation of Bowdoin undergraduates were made familiar with the saga of Harry Oakes '96, whose British partner was called to the colors in 1914. "For four years," the president said, "Oakes carried on a large business enterprise alone and at the end of the period divided all the profits fifty-fifty though he could have legally and with consent bought out his partner at any time and doubled his own gain." K. C. M. S. also cited the careers of Bowdoin men serving their country in public office. "One way to throw off the depression," he said in May, 1932, "is to work for a better social order by entering politics." In February, 1933, he begged the new members of the Dartmouth chapter of Phi Beta Kappa not to succumb to the indifference to politics prevalent among undergraduates. "That indifference is engendered by a kind of defeatism unworthy of the younger generation," he told the scholars in Hanover. "They look upon the world so confused and bewildered that they put the blame on their elders, shrug their shoulders, and dwell largely on the corruption and inefficiency of American life." Back home, in an aside to his class in Casey's Lit., he objected to an editorial in the *Yale Daily News* which had denigrated politics as too corrupt a vocation for college-trained men. "There is far too much defeatism and cynicism in certain academic circles concerning democracy and democratic institutions," K. C. M. S. remarked. "Such an attitude is a good deal like that of the small boy who defined water 'as that stuff that turns black when you put your hands in it.' " The president told his class that he bore some honorable political wounds himself. "More than once I have been castigated for pretending to be a Christian," he added, "and at the same time asserting that I was going to vote the Democratic ticket. But there has been a gain in tolerance, even in Maine."

Rumors that the Maine Democratic State Committee had sought to persuade K. C. M. S. to become the party's nominee for governor were sufficiently persistent in 1931 to compel him to deny that he had been approached on the subject. In a statement to the *Portland Press Herald* he said flatly, "Under no consideration nor in any circumstances will I consent to become a candidate." His clear and present duty, he told inquiring reporters, was to remain at his own job. The dimensions of that job, however, continued to be wide enough to permit him to voice his opinions on a variety of controversial issues. When he was warned of the inevitable criticism likely to ensue, he replied that in becoming a college president it had never occurred to him that he should cease to do his duty as a citizen. Less interested in abstract political theory than in practical decisions, he was chiefly concerned with the quandary of the man in the street who often on scant evidence must make up his mind on complex issues. In an address on the Eighteenth Amendment to a group of Auburn businessmen in February, 1930, he remarked, "I have no patience with those who are all one way or the other. It is plain that there was great good in Prohibition and that there are great evils in it. It becomes us to weigh these and make up our minds." Thousands of ordinary citizens came to regard the president of Bowdoin as a fair-minded presiding justice at the court of public opinion, one who was never accused of having his own axe to grind. As Arthur Staples, editor of the *Lewiston Evening Journal*, noted, "Whatever the issue, we expect from Dr. Sills a very fine judicial summing up, much as the Judge sums up for the perplexed citizen after a long trial." The president was moved when his Greek friend Louis Zamanis, proprietor of a Brunswick restaurant, told him, "If I were on trial for my life, I would be content to have my fate decided by you alone."

World conditions in 1930 confirmed Kenneth Sills's lifelong support of the World Court, the League of Nations, and its precursor, the League to Enforce Peace. In a series of radio broadcasts early in January, he pointed out that every secretary of state for thirty years had worked for the creation of a world tribunal, yet the United States had delayed its adherence to the Court since its establishment in 1922. Those who oppose our joining, "like Senator Moses of New Hampshire, are still living in the dim and distant past," he charged. "Others, like some of the editors of the Hearst papers, seem to me to be acting like demagogues." In his ardent advocacy of the Court, President Sills forgot the risk of employing historical allusions. In his radio speech on January 13, he exclaimed, "The great American public, some day before long is going to say to timid, reluctant, and hesitant senators, 'Go hang yourselves, brave Senators, we won the victory for the World Court and you were not there.'" The following morning he was startled to read in several headlines that he had recommended the "gallows" for recalcitrant U. S. senators, especially for Moses of New Hampshire. The editor of the *Lewiston Evening Journal*, an Overseer of Bowdoin, hastened to exonerate the head of his college. "We believe as a matter of fact," Arthur Staples wrote, "that President Sills is opposed to hanging or any other form of capital punishment. He was simply indicating a fondness for historical example. When a certain general arrived late on the field of battle, the King said, 'Go hang yourself, brave Crillon. We fought at Arques and you were not there.' "

Again and again, K. C. M. S. lamented that the League of Nations had become a partisan issue. "The Senate can raise as many objections when subjects of this kind are discussed," he said, "as a small boy can when giving reasons why he should not go to bed." "The highest tribute that can be paid to the vision of Woodrow Wilson," he wrote on the tenth anniversary of the League, "is that nearly everyone now agrees that if the League of Nations did not exist, we should be obliged to create it." To the Wilson Club of Portland, he regretted that his own Democratic party had sidestepped the issue in its last two national platforms. In 1932, when he learned of the defection of Governor Franklin Roosevelt of New York, who had campaigned gallantly for the League in 1920, he protested sorrowfully. "It seems to me," he wrote F. D. R. in February, "that those who feel that the only real progress the world can make must be through international cooperation have lost a real leader when you have given up the fight for the League. . . . To have a man so prominent in the party as yourself absolutely go back on the League is a very great shock." In his reply, Governor Roosevelt recalled gratefully Kenneth Sills's campaign for the Senate in 1916. "I wish much that I could have a chance to have a good long talk with you about the League and its objectives," F. D. R. wrote on February 15, ". . . you and I have exactly the same objectives but the immediate methods we advocate are different. Perhaps I can put it best by using the simile of the man who is seeking to saw a piece of wood and finds that he cannot do the job properly with one saw, and as a result tries another saw."

When in 1932 President Sills joined with Lowell of Harvard and scores of other college heads in urging President Herbert Hoover and Congress to boycott Japan if she were proved to be guilty in Manchuria, he encountered fiery differences of opinion among his own alumni and drew a sharp rebuke from the leader of a neighboring college. In an address to the Portland Rotary Club in March, President Clifton Gray of Bates disparaged as "amateur diplomats" those college presidents who suggested the boycott. "This boycott," Dr. Gray charged, "proposed paradoxically by those who are theoretically opposed to war, contains more dynamite than all that is now lying loose in the Japanese occupation of the Shanghai area." Colonel George Fogg '02, after commending Gray's stand, remarked pointedly in a letter to the *Orient* for March 23, "few, if any of the 120 college heads fought in the World War or would be called upon to do so in the future event. They can withdraw into scholarly seclusion. . . . They are in reality *amateur diplomats*, without authority but, what is more to the point, without responsibility." These and other protests reminded K. C. M. S. of his campaign in 1916 when opponents had derided him for leaving his "scholarly seclusion" to meddle in practical politics. It was like running for the U. S. Senate all over again. In the intervening years, Kenneth Sills had found "scholarly seclusion" to be a rare commodity indeed. He told his faculty colleagues that he envied them for whatever share they had of it. "No one realizes more keenly than I," he said, "the lack of time for reading, study, and reflection. The old question is constantly burned into me: *And friend when dost thou think?* No one suffers more from the busyness of American life than does the college executive."

In declining to run for public office in 1931, the president remarked that he believed his influence on legislation might be greater if he remained in his favorite role of "a disinterested outsider." His fellow citizens, however, would not permit him to stay on the sidelines. No sooner had he retired from the Brunswick school committee in 1932, after serving as its chairman for sixteen years, than Governor Louis Brann named him to head the Maine commission on school finance. K. C. M. S. welcomed the assignment, promising that his report "would give the next Legislature something to think about." "It is certainly a reversal of good old New England form," he told reporters, "to put anything ahead of school and church, yet a thousand Maine teachers are paid as little as ten dollars a week or less. It is a great deal easier in Maine to interest people in a program for State highways than it is in a program for State schools." Appropriately enough, he began his fight on the home front at the Brunswick town meeting on March 6, 1933, when the finance committee and the tax payers association recommended a 10 percent cut in the woefully low salaries of teachers. Reminding his fellow citizens that the range for grade-school teachers was from $750 to $1,000, and that the top salary for a teacher in the high school was only $1,400, K. C. M. S. said, "Roads can wait, bridges can wait, buildings can wait, but you cannot interrupt the education of a child without permanent damage. It is the children who are going to suffer." Although the *Brunswick Record* conceded that the president's long service on the school committee lent weight to his words, the editor approved the cuts as being in line with those adopted by other Maine communities. Two days after Brunswick voted to reduce teachers' salaries, Kenneth Sills told the Pomona Grange in North Chesterfield, "Popular support of education in Maine often stops with 'talk.' " "Economy! Economy!," he exclaimed. "What crimes are committed in thy name." When a local merchant attempted to console him by observing that the cuts would affect only those with salaries of $1,000 or above, the president flushed angrily. "I daresay," he replied, "but it's a scandal that so few teachers *are* receiving $1,000."

Ironically, the influence of President Sills, which was spurned as "too idealistic" by many of the town's businessmen when he spoke in behalf of public school children, was anxiously sought by the same interests during the protracted moratorium on Brunswick's two commercial banks. Following the bank holiday, the *Brunswick Record* on March 9 had boasted of "ample and convincing proof" that the Fidelity Trust Company and the First National Bank were "in the soundest condition" and would "open shortly." A week later, citizens were assured by the same newspaper that "At no time has there been any question of the soundness of these particular banks." Brunswick people refuse to be disturbed, the *Record* noted comfortably, and are taking the bank holiday lightly. Early in April, however, the Supreme Judicial Court, sitting in on equity proceedings, decreed the liquidation of the Fidelity Trust Company. Public confidence was further shaken by the failure of the First National Bank to reopen, while week after week its officers strove to formulate an acceptable plan of reorganization. The mood of its depositors was constrained but noticeably edgy and unpredictable when, at the bank's invitation on May 2, nearly 1,200 citizens jammed the Town Hall to learn of the conditions to be met before the bank could resume its normal functions. The gathering listened impassively as President Samuel Forsaith and the bank attorney asked depositors to accept trust certificates for 20 percent of their deposits. Further conditions, they explained, included a contribution of $75,000 by common stockholders to provide a necessary working capital, and the sale of $125,000 of preferred stock. The final step, Forsaith announced, was approval of the plan by depositors whose holdings totaled 75 percent of the total deposits on March 3, 1933. Such action, he promised, would result in prompt restoration of complete banking and credit facilities for the town; it would also, he added, be a welcome vote of confidence in the management.

When the meeting was thrown open for general discussion there was a long and uneasy moment of silence. Many of those present had accounts in the Fidelity Trust Company. Others lived next door to people who had preferred to entrust their life savings to the banks rather than to invest in stocks promising double the interest rate. If any latent hostility existed, it remained inarticulate, yet the public temper was coolly if not sullenly skeptical. For weeks the metropolitan papers had been filled with astonishing instances of mismanagement by men once respected as the very pillars of society. As the meeting wore on, Kenneth Sills sensed that the spirit of the majority in the hall was puzzled and bewildered, rather than revolutionary. He realized the necessity of approving the reorganization plan as speedily as possible, and he listened sympathetically as four or five substantial merchants and businessmen arose to testify to the integrity of the bank officers and to urge acceptance of the proposed reorganization. Their testimony, however, produced no discernible effect. For the generality of those present, especially the "little people," small depositors, shopkeepers, clerks, and mill workers, something more was needed, some additional assurance from one not closely allied with the mercantile or banking interests, someone above the faintest suspicion of self-interest. As the meeting lapsed into another awkward lull, President Forsaith asked a bit plaintively, "I wonder whether, if Mr. Sills is in the audience, he would care to say a word or two?"

President Sills had gone to the meeting without any intention of participating actively, but he responded simply and persuasively. He was unable to agree, he said, with one of the officials of the bank who had attempted to minimize the amount of the trust certificates on the grounds that the losses would have been much heavier had the depositors invested their money in common stocks. K. C. M. S. insisted that the bank owed a special obligation to those who sacrificed the expectation of larger returns for the security of a savings account. Doubtless some mistakes had been made, he conceded, but no one questioned the good faith of the bank officers. He had accepted their invitation, he said, to serve as a trustee of those assets which at present were unacceptable to the Federal Reserve authorities. He promised that when these funds were converted from time to time they would be applied to redeeming the trust certificates. He also volunteered to assist in soliciting those depositors whose approval was still needed before full banking services could be available. The college finance committee, he said, was ready to subscribe generously to the new preferred stock. Above all, he assured the gathering that in the reorganization plan the depositors, not the stockholders, would be given first consideration. The president's words were what the meeting had been waiting for. "It's sort of funny," a businessman remarked after the adjournment. "Casey probably doesn't know very much about banking, and there was nothing new in what he said. But *he* said it, and that seemed to make all the difference. People trust him." To those who tried to thank him, K. C. M. S. replied that the only people who deserved commendation were "workingmen with families dependent on them, not knowing in the least where the next job is coming from, or indeed if there is to be a next job. They have shown such patience and restraint and self-control as would put to shame those other members of society who because they have to exchange a Rolls Royce for a Packard wail as if the end of the world had come."

The attitude of the students was all the president could have desired. "No undergraduate," he reported to the Boards, "has come to ask for help without making it clear that he did not wish to receive such aid if any other boy in college needed it more." Although not a student was compelled to withdraw between February and June, 1932, for financial reasons alone, K. C. M. S. soon foresaw the impossibility of maintaining the cherished tradition of never losing an undergraduate who came to Bowdoin with enough money to see him through the first semester of his Freshman year. A dozen men were forced to leave in the following term when the president's loan fund was exhausted early in 1933. Even with the improved economic conditions in 1937–38, student needs continued to be acute. Of the 281 applicants for financial aid during that winter, 154 were boys whose parents stated they had annual incomes of $2,000 or less. "It is one of the glories of the small college," K. C. M. S. wrote, "that it takes into the fullness of its life, socially and intellectually, so many boys from homes of modest incomes. It would be a calamity of the worst kind, if through the diminution of endowment, or loss of large gifts, the College could not continue to render this important public service." Always believing that Bowdoin should be something like a large family, it was natural for him to keep its members informed of the way the college was faring during the depression. "We are sailing pretty stormy seas under double reef with the hope of riding out the storm," he wrote on April 4, 1933, in a letter to all alumni. "In these days the College would not urge a single one of its sons to contribute if it meant a real sacrifice or withdrawal of aid from more needy institutions." Thus far it had been possible, he said, to keep the college organization pretty well intact and not to cut down the staff. The cost of administration has been kept to a minimum: "I do not believe now, and never have believed, in expending an undue portion of money on the administrative side." The president was almost apologetic in suggesting the desirability of having separate offices for himself and for Dean Nixon. "For the past thirteen years," he noted, "the President and the Dean have been playing Cox and Box, and while their relations are still amicable, the strain on the Dean has been quite heavy. Perhaps some changes can be made in Massachusetts Hall that will provide more office room."

Strains of a more serious kind were detected by Dr. Henry Johnson, the college physician, in the autumn of 1933. For several years Kenneth Sills had persistently disregarded his physician's advice by remaining at his desk rather than taking his customary vacations in St. Andrews. Dr. Johnson begged him to heed the maxim which President Hyde had offered to another college executive: "Strain and rest, strain and rest—*but don't bunch your strains.*" K. C. M. S. was perhaps not fully conscious of the cumulative strains implicit in administering an intimate, family college where every problem became at once a personal one. His reluctance to delegate authority and his dislike of adding administrative assistants or secretarial help were beginning to exact their toll. The college was just small enough to make it possible for him to have a detailed knowledge of its manifold operations and he was constantly being asked about data which he alone could supply. His secretary, who was really a maid of all work to the entire administration, did her best to protect him from the endless line of callers each of whom wanted "only a few minutes of the President's valuable time." The president himself was not notably cooperative. Such interruptions, K. C. M. S. once told her after she had glowered at an unannounced visitor, "may result and have resulted in beautiful buildings for the college, in friendship with very unacademic members of society, and in renewed confidence in a despondent student." Mrs. Hayes finally gave up in despair. "President Sills is glad to see anybody at any hour," she snapped to a faculty member who had been kept waiting on a hard bench in the hall for an unconscionable time. "Why can't *you professors* teach him to be perfunctory to his callers?" Fearful that the president might suffer a nervous breakdown unless he were granted a respite from his duties, Dr. Johnson suggested to members of the executive committee of the Boards that they prescribe an enforced vacation, "preferably in Timbuctoo where nobody has ever heard about Bowdoin College." Instead, the Boards ordered a Mediterranean cruise.

Kenneth Sills complied with the directive cheerfully, but when he informed the faculty of his unprecedented holiday, he blushed as though in some obscurely reprehensible way he was failing the college. Before sailing on March 7 on the *Aquitania*, he accepted an appointment by President Roosevelt to the Board of Visitors of the U. S. Naval Academy, promising F. D. R. to return in time for the first meeting at Annapolis in April. Edith Sills assured anxious friends that in the meantime she would see that her husband did nothing but loaf irresponsibly and read frivolously. K. C. M. S., however, had not forgotten to leave a farewell message for the students. "With Dean Nixon in charge," he said, "I feel confident that the College can get along without its President even better than the President can get along without the College." The undergraduates, who had casually assumed that all college officers are eternal, became suddenly solicitous about their president's health and showered him with affectionate bon voyage greetings. Characteristically, he acknowledged all of them promptly in his familiar but barely decipherable scrawl. The "Mustard and Cress" columnist in the *Orient* volunteered to keep him accurately informed of all the campus doings with a reminder that he once had said, "Because you see it in the *Orient*, it is not necessarily so—unless you see it in Mustard and Cress." The *Orient* itself predicted that the professors of English would have a field day when they took over Casey's Lit. for six weeks.

Whatever feelings of "guilt" the Sillses may have felt at leaving Brunswick in midterm were soon softened by shipboard routine. Mustard and Cress congratulated them on missing a nasty March blizzard. "So you'll be in Naples when you get this," the columnist wrote on March 14. "You don't know how lucky you are. They located the gymnasium under several feet of snow the other day, and are now taking soundings to find Hyde Hall." When they reached Monte Carlo they were cautioned to be careful, "The cable address is 'Bowcol,' in case you need any money. If you see Sam Insull, don't speak." Meanwhile, faculty households were able to chart the Sillses' itinerary by a steady stream of postcards and small gifts. The trip was really a condensed version of the 1912 sabbatical. At Athens they inspected the Acropolis with Professor Thomas Means who was spending a year at the School of Classical Studies and visited the English School conducted by John Spanos '26. K. C. M. S. noted with satisfaction how well the city had absorbed the refugees from the First World War, and was pleased to hear high praise of the archaeological work done by Professor Stanley Casson who was currently holding the Tallman professorship at Bowdoin. In Istanbul, where K. C. M. S. rejoiced to observe that the city "now faces the west instead of the east as formerly," the president and his wife were guests of Robert College, founded by Cyrus Hamlin, a Bowdoin worthy of the class of 1834. They reached Palestine just before Easter, landing in Haifa, motoring through Nazareth and Samaria to Jerusalem where they worshipped in the Church of the Holy Sepulchre. In the Holy Land they spent an evening with John Dinsmore '83, who told them of his botanic researches in Palestine and accompanied them to the Mount of Olives. On their way to the port of embarkation at Naples, the Sillses spent three days in Cairo and sailed down the Nile to Port Said. They were back in Brunswick on April 12, two days after classes had been resumed following the spring recess. The president promptly gratified an *Orient* reporter seeking some "colorful anecdotes" by disclosing that he was singled out as an opium smuggler in Egypt by a suspicious customs official, but found the experience "exhilarating." As for returning a bit late, K. C. M. S. said the dean had allowed him "travelling time" so that not even double cuts could put him on probation. The holiday had done the Sillses worlds of good. Charles Taylor Hawes, the president of the Board of Overseers, greeted them in Boston and remarked, "They both look finely."

K. C. M. S. often enjoyed telling those of his faculty on sabbatical leave that "in the main and on the whole" the college had prospered in their absence. They now replied by reporting that everything had gone smoothly while he was away. The president was pleased to find fewer students in financial difficulties because of the aid granted by the Federal Emergency Relief Administration. When he had applied for this federal assistance in February, K. C. M. S. assured the Governing Boards that no work would be assigned that would ordinarily have been done by the regular working force. "As this is, in most cases, the first experience that any of the students have had with the government," he reported, "particular care has been exercised that the work should be done thoroughly, without any soldiering, and under proper supervision." Although some members of the Boards were averse to applying for any help from the F. E. R. A., they were impressed by the industry shown by the fifty-eight students on the payroll. Fully aware that the New Deal had few champions among the Trustees and Overseers, Kenneth Sills was at pains to explain, "There has been a good deal of misunderstanding as to the purpose of this aid. . . . The aid did not go to the College but to the individual student. . . . There has not been in any way, shape, or manner the slightest indication of dictatorial authority over educational standards and methods, and there has not been the least evidence of the slightest desire on the part of the government for interference in college affairs. During a period of economic stress a good deal can be said for this policy." Three years later, in June, 1937, when the Boards voted to refuse further federal aid, K. C. M. S. reminded them, "Inasmuch as an emergency still exists, it will clearly be our duty to provide from our own income a still larger amount than was available this year, even if we have to cut down elsewhere or lower salaries."

Refreshed from his trip abroad, Kenneth Sills promised his physician to avoid bunching his strains, even though nation, state, and college seemed to be conspiring to bunch his duties. He was amused to see that *Time* magazine saluted him as a patriot for consenting to serve again on the Board of Visitors at the U. S. Naval Academy. "Not for him are battleship junkets, dress parades, honorariums," the editor noted. "For his annual trips to Annapolis he receives only his travelling expenses." K. C. M. S. had been sharply critical when he was president of the Board in 1921, charging that midshipmen in the nontechnical courses failed to receive "as good teaching as students get in the best colleges and universities." He now found a marked improvement. "Although a dozen years ago midshipmen were not encouraged to use the library because it interfered with their studies largely confined to textbooks," he reported in 1934, "today the circulation and general use of library facilities compares very favorably with the practices in our good colleges."

Of more immediate concern was the consistent failure of the
Maine legislature to provide adequate support for the public
schools. As chairman of the state commission on school finance
appointed by Governor Brann in 1933, K. C. M. S. found the
schools suffering from drastic economies enforced during the
depression. "There are places in Maine," he told a group of
thirty members of the 87th Legislature, "where school facilities
are as inadequate as they are in some of the poorer mountain
districts of the southern states." After devoting most of the summer of 1934 to the study, he reported his findings in a statewide
radio address on October 4. "A great many business men desire
drastic cuts in school appropriations," he declared, "yet a century ago Maine paid more for public instruction than today. In
1915, thirty-nine cents out of every dollar raised by the state
budget went to education. In 1931, only sixteen cents was devoted to schools." He warned the Governing Boards that the
situation was affecting the number of Maine boys at Bowdoin.
"Until there is better support for Maine public high schools
from towns and state alike," he said, "we cannot expect pro-
portionately as many candidates from Maine as we have had in
the past, unless we are willing to lower our standards of admission below those of colleges of our class."

The president's service on the commission soon involved him
in the thorny problems of taxation. "The improvement of schools
in Maine is closely bound up with the improvement of the system
of taxation in the State," he told Governor Brann. Describing
the department of taxation and assessment as "the little Cinderella of the State House, poor, destitute, and inadequately
equipped," he demanded a reorganization of the department and
a plan for the equalization of assessment. At a meeting of the
Maine municipal officers association in Augusta on October 24,
he predicted, "Sooner or later Maine is going to come to a sales
tax or, perhaps, an income tax to relieve the burden now carried
by real estate. After all, the only source of taxation is wealth, and
wealth in all forms must bear the burden, and not, as at present,

one form of property alone to pay more than its fair share." His recommendation of the establishment of minimum educational opportunities for all pupils in the state was vigorously opposed by James Barlow, Portland's city manager, who feared that his community would pay a disproportionate amount of the taxes. At the legislative hearing, K. C. M. S. retorted that such objections "tend to drive a wedge between rural and urban areas." "The Commission has tried to keep in mind the common interests of the people of Maine," Kenneth Sills testified, "and to look upon the problem of equalization of school funds as a state problem. Every fair-minded citizen must admit that wealth should be taxed where it is found, and that there is more wealth to be taxed in the larger centers." As the vote on school appropriations approached, he was not optimistic. "One encounters too often these days," he complained, "the old Yankee philosophy which insists, 'I'm right because I know I be.' You will see in the coming session of the Legislature all sorts of objections raised to any form of tax levies and objections also to legitimate state expenditures."

The president's worst fears were confirmed by the 87th Legislature in March, 1935. Disregarding the commission's proposals for improved schools, the Maine House of Representatives passed a bill providing for a state lottery to finance an old age pension plan. "Instead of facing frankly the necessity for new sources of taxation, and the desirability of securing revenue from income, sales, and excise taxes," K. C. M. S. lamented on March 22, "the House substituted this fantastic legislation which offends the moral sense of thousands of Maine people." His fight for decent support of schools did not end with his report for the school finance commission in 1935, but continued during the preparation of every biennial legislative budget. In 1937 he reminded the 88th Legislature of Maine's parsimonious treatment of education. "Maine spent $12,000,000 for public schools in 1929," he said as the session convened, "but in 1935 and 1936 only about $9,500,000 was spent. We act as if we thought that on the whole our teachers are pretty well paid and have pretty easy jobs. If an attempt were made to have the State improve our schools as it does our roads on bond issues, a howl would be raised that could be heard from Kittery to Fort Kent." His hopes were again disappointed by the inadequate provision of $200,000 for education by a special session of the legislature in October, 1937. "The action is a stopgap of the usual compromising kind," he said in a statement to the press, "and is disappointing to those who feel the $500,000 appropriation for equalizing educational opportunity is the absolute minimum." Such an example of reaction against reason in Augusta, he told a Brunswick audience, "should only spur on to greater efforts those who believe inevitably and finally reason will hold sway in the affairs of men." Kenneth Sills's sustained interest in public education made him eager to improve the whole structure of state government. "I am not a bit afraid of giving the Governor more power," he said to those who wished to retain the Governor's Council as a check on executive authority. "The tendency in all administration nowadays is to centralize responsibility. Nominate and elect men whom you can trust and then trust them. To centralize power in the Governor's hands is more desirable than dangerous."

Kenneth Sills had expected to devote the summer of 1934 to a preliminary study of public school finance, but he was soon caught in the midst of an even more controversial issue. On July 1, President Roosevelt encouraged Governor Brann to appoint a commission to report on the desirability of developing the enormous latent electrical energy of the tidewaters of the Bay of Fundy. "With my summer home so near Eastport for so many years, I have been interested in what is known as the 'Quoddy project' for a long time," F. D. R. wrote the governor, "and it has been my hope that eventually the State of Maine would become not only a great industrial center of the nation, but that its agricultural population would be among the first to enjoy the manifest advantages of cheap electrical power on the farm as well." In view of the magnitude of the project, Roosevelt told the governor, "I think such a commission should have on it men whose reputation for judgment and the disinterestedness of whose motives cannot be questioned. . . . I will await the report of such a commission in case you decide on taking such action with the greatest interest and can assure you that you will have a sympathetic ear in Washington for whatever recommendations may result from their studies." Armed with so compelling a directive from the White House, Governor Brann needed no further prompting. He at once thought of Kenneth Sills's reputation for disinterested public service. Would the president of Bowdoin, Brann asked, accept the chairmanship of the Passamaquoddy Bay Commission with a mandate to report as promptly as possible upon the economic feasibility of harnessing the tides of the Bay of Fundy to create electrical power, and to indicate possible markets for that power?

Much to the surprise of the governor, K. C. M. S. replied by saying that his imagination, like that of President Roosevelt, had long been stirred by the racing tides of Passamaquoddy Bay. He recalled a favorite boyhood walk from St. Andrews to Minister's Island on a road which at high tide was really the bottom of the sea. If the governor had not appointed him to head the school finance commission, he said, he would now be playing golf on the shores of the Bay of Fundy instead of fuming in Brunswick. Was not one commission enough for a single summer? Would Governor Brann allow him a week to consider so formidable an assignment, and might he have some intimation of the identity of the other members to be appointed? What technical assistance would be available for the many legal and engineering problems? Would the cautious governor's council be likely to provide an adequate budget? He had his own responsibility to Bowdoin College to think about, but he promised his answer within a week. It was not until the governor had left 85 Federal Street that Kenneth Sills remembered Hyde's warning about bunching one's strains.

# 12

## FROM THE DEPRESSION
## TO THE SECOND WORLD WAR

Maine people were so used to regarding the president of Bowdoin as a public servant that his acceptance of Governor Brann's invitation to head the Passamaquoddy Commission surprised no one. In Brunswick everybody knew that K. C. M. S. was not the man to urge others to engage in public affairs without first setting a personal example, but some members of his faculty were more concerned with their president's store of energy than with the kilowatt hours latent in the Bay of Fundy. Electricity might be exported, they protested, but his supply was needed for domestic uses. The linking of his name with a New Deal project raised political eyebrows in a state which had given President Herbert Hoover a thumping majority in 1932, and four years later was to vote even more heavily for Governor Alfred Landon. The *Bangor News* branded the enterprise as "a downright plunge into State Socialism," the brain child "of economic adventurers deriving their inspiration from Moscow." Other papers scented a mixture of crazy economics and blatant politics. With the governor seeking reelection in September, the *Boston Herald* charged Harold Ickes, public works administrator, with a cynical attempt to buy votes. "The Maine project is ludicrous, enormously expensive, utterly indefensible, and reeks of the pork barrel," the editor observed. "But why not josh the Down East Boys a little? . . . $47,000,000 is loose change for Uncle Sam as things are going now . . . and our Maine brethren would not be traditional Down Easters if they did not try to get their share."

Partly because the press kept insisting that President Roosevelt's interest in Quoddy was motivated by his desire to help Brann's candidacy in a strongly Republican state, K. C. M. S. decided to limit the activities of the commission until after the Maine election on September 10. Certainly his fellow commissioners could not fairly have been described as "boon-doggling New Dealers." The governor had obeyed Roosevelt's injunction to name citizens of impeccable probity in appointing the following men: Edward S. French, of the Boston and Maine, Wingate F. Cram, of the Bangor and Aroostook, William N. Campbell, president of the Goodall Worsted Company, and Harry B. Crawford, master of the state Grange. Kenneth Sills regarded them as constituting a judicial rather than a political body. Such a concept enabled him to welcome expressions of opinion both from those who favored and those who opposed the project without giving any hint as to the verdict. To scores of inquiries from reporters, the chairman had but one answer: "As the Commission has a judicial function of passing upon the evidence submitted to it, I do not feel like making any further statement at this time." His nonpartisan attitude disappointed the more zealous proponents, especially those citizens of Eastport and Lubec whose brains were boiling with visions of boom times. "We would be interested to learn where the Commission has been hibernating—and why—since its appointment three months ago," the editor of the *Eastport Sentinel* demanded on November 15. "The Commission has evidently gone into the Great Silences to await the ultimate blast on Gabriel's trumpet.'

Kenneth Sills was tempted to reply that Gabriel himself was likely to be heard from before either the Maine legislature or the governor's council voted to supply the needed funds. "Up to the present moment the Commission has worked without any funds at all," he protested to the governor on October 2, 1934. "The members have paid their own expenses and we have not even had a stenographer." Mrs. Clara Hayes, the president's secretary, complained during the opening week of the fall term that she was beginning to confuse kilowatt hours with credit hours on students' records. "Half the time," she said, "I don't know whether I am working for an educational institution or a Democratic dam." Soon after the organization of the commission, K. C. M. S. assured Governor Brann that although its members were ready to give their services without compensation, "They feel very definitely that if they are to continue the work . . . they must have an initial and immediate appropriation of $25,000." "In order to inquire intelligently into the many questions upon which the Public Works Administration must have information, particularly the vexing problem of marketing power," he wrote early in October, "it is imperative that the Commission employ some expert advisers and secure some technical assistance." The all-Republican council was, however, in no mood to encourage a project threatening the profits of public utility companies. It was not until the third week in November that the council grudgingly appropriated $5,000, barely one-fifth of the requested sum.

The delay gave Kenneth Sills time to review his own sketchy impressions of the Quoddy project. Although one of his early boyhood memories of St. Andrews was the spectacular ebb and flow of the tides, he had never dreamed of the possibility of harnessing them. Later, in the 1920s, he had heard the American hydraulic engineer, Dexter P. Cooper, describe his grandiose plan of building two huge storage pools in Passamaquoddy Bay by constructing a series of dams between Eastport and the mainland, the upper pool to be filled from the outside sea at high tide. K. C. M. S. was bewildered but impressed as Mr. Cooper explained how the water from the mechanically controlled upper pool would be run through turbines into the lower or receiving basin, while a power-storage reservoir would make it possible to conserve any surplus energy. The scheme appealed to Kenneth Sills's imagination, but when he was told the cost would approach $100,000,000 he was unable to believe, for all of Mr. Cooper's enthusiasm, that the engineering dream could be realized in the present century. When some of his St. An-

drews' friends became alarmed at the prospect of their picturesque town becoming an industrial center, he thought their fears
were chimerical. Even when Cooper's original plan was modified after Canada withdrew because of possible damage to her
fisheries and the cost was scaled down to $47,000,000, K. C.
M. S. continued to be skeptical. His doubts seemed confirmed in
the spring of 1934 when Secretary Ickes, after receiving adverse
reports from the Federal Power Commission and the P. W. A.
Board of Review, refused a loan to Dexter Cooper's private
corporation.

President Sills assumed that the project had finally been
crushed under the weight of economic fact but, as *The New
York Times* noted, "The Passamaquoddy project does not
down." Certainly its undaunted sponsor Dexter Cooper continued to make converts of almost every visitor to Eastport. He
had no difficulty in convincing Governor Brann that it would
do more to relieve employment presently and provide industrial
prosperity eventually than any other project. It was rumored
that President Roosevelt, Cooper's summer neighbor on Campobello, was sympathetic. Even critics of the plan agreed that from
an engineering standpoint the project was feasible, although the
*Boston Herald* remarked that the same thing might be said of a
project to level Mount Washington. The adverse reports in the
spring of 1934 had been based largely on the lack of a market
and doubts as to whether the impounding of the tides could produce cheaper power than steam. Whatever his motives, F. D. R.
was now ready, despite unfavorable reports from his economic
advisers, to revive the issue by asking the governor to appoint
a commission to make a further study. "If the Quoddy project is
feasible as an engineering proposition, and if a market can be
found for the power," Roosevelt wrote Kenneth Sills on September 18, 1934, "it would then be possible for the Public Works
Administration to put this project on its list for early consideration and action when funds are available."

Down Easters made a holiday of August 21 when Secretary

Ickes and Major Philip Fleming, P. W. A. engineer, accompanied the governor and his commission to inspect the proposed location of the dams and the site of the generating station between Lubec and Eastport. Dexter Cooper was preternaturally eloquent as he translated his blueprints for the benefit of the laymen, and his eyes shone when Mr. Ickes declared, "It is not often that the great dream of an engineer comes true in his lifetime, but I hope for your sake that Quoddy will go through as one of the greatest engineering feats in the world." Hopes soared as the secretary said, "You know of President Roosevelt's interest in the project; the whole administration is interested in it, and you have a Governor who knows his way to Washington and how to get things for the State of Maine. The one big question standing between the plan and its possible construction is the practicality of utilizing its developed power at a salable price." When Kenneth Sills was introduced as chairman of the commission, he assured the expectant gathering in city park, "We are going to do our best to fulfill your wishes," but he cautioned them to remember that "the Commission is a non-political, non-partisan body." Later in the program, as he listened to the cheers when Eastport's Republican mayor Roscoe E. Emery hailed Franklin Roosevelt as a divinely appointed leader, K. C. M. S. remembered his senatorial campaign in August, 1916, when from the same flag-draped platform he had defended the idealism of Woodrow Wilson to a handful of Democrats and a hired fife and drum corps. The whirligigs of time, he reflected, bring curious ironies.

Kenneth Sills felt more comfortable a week later in Augusta where, without political fanfare, federal engineers told the commission that its critical problem was to find markets for the abundance of electrical energy contemplated in the engineering plans. It was the failure to find customers for power, they reminded the commissioners, rather than any technical difficulties, which had compelled the P. W. A. to deny Cooper's application for a federal loan in April. Major Fleming and K. E. Kingfield,

P. W. A. finance officers, suggested that aluminum and stainless steel plants as well as phosphate and fertilizer manufactories might be attracted to the area. Convinced that the fate of the project would depend upon the finding of markets, Kenneth Sills again pressed the governor for funds to engage expert consultants. He was compelled to explain to a delegation of impatient Eastporters who had come to Augusta expecting an immediate decision that the commission's investigation needed to be carried to far greater lengths before a final report could be made.

While waiting for sufficient money to enable the commission to begin its work, K. C. M. S. found himself concerned with falling tides of quite a different kind. Unlike the wondrous water levels of Passamaquoddy Bay, those of Bowdoin's football fortunes never seemed to rise. After the team had failed to score in the first three games of the 1934 season, the *Orient* noted on October 24, "No one now in college has ever seen Bowdoin win a state series game. And if the squad continues to play as it played against Wesleyan and Williams, no one ever will." The doleful prediction soon received melancholy confirmation. At the end of the state series in which Bowdoin went virtually scoreless, the *Boston Evening Transcript* reported, "Maine gave Bowdoin its sixth straight defeat. . . . Charlie Bowser's teams have won only one Maine game in five years." Sports columnists filled reams of copy in attempting to diagnose the athletic ills of the college. A writer in the *Portland Sunday Telegram* attacked the scholarship committee for turning away "many brilliant students simply because they are blessed with the bodies and the initiative to become great athletes," while the *Press Herald* remarked, "One or two members of the Bowdoin faculty should begin to realize by this time that there is such a thing as a student-athlete." Distressed by such misinformed criticism of his admissions and scholarship policies, President Sills was pleased by the sanity of the *Orient* which reminded sports editors that an educational institution is not to be judged by rumors emanating from "belligerents around the gymnasium and from the more vociferous alumni." Members of the Athletic Council had refused to talk for publication following a twelve-hour session in Brunswick on December 8, but two days later, in an article headed, "Bowdoin Athletic Council out on a Limb," a *Press Herald* reporter asserted, "The Bowdoin Athletic Council . . . asked for the resignation of Bowdoin's football coach, Charles W. Bowser, and Mr. Bowser refused to resign. Since his contract has two years to run, the Council is rather up against it." When the story was picked up by the metropolitan papers, K. C. M. S. replied on December 12, "The resignation of Mr. Charles W. Bowser has not been demanded either by the Athletic Council or by the College. The College with the cooperation of the Council is seeking to improve the athletic situation." While the Bowser affair was still hanging fire, Kenneth Sills observed in his annual New Year's greeting to the alumni that even an unsuccessful football season is not an earth-shaking matter. "It is a satisfaction to be able to state unqualifiedly that we are having a very excellent year indeed," he wrote on January 1, 1935. "The College has not had a single withdrawal for any reason from the 580 students enrolled—a unique record. . . . Except for the utterly disappointing football season, athletics are in a healthy condition. And the College is perfectly willing to be judged by the general tone, temper, and morale of the student body."

The outer serenity of the president belied his concern about the explosive situation. He felt that somehow his administration was answerable for the excessive number of defeats, and he shared the *Orient's* exasperation that "The maddening thing about the situation is that the team *has* potentialities." When the council failed to reach any conclusion at its protracted session in December, K. C. M. S. was finally convinced that it could no longer be trusted to act for the Governing Boards in athletic affairs. There was an uncomfortable measure of truth in the demand by the *Orient* for an end of what the editor described as "a vacillating policy of silence." As eager as President Sills was to avoid crises, he was forced to concur with the editor that "If the authorities hope, by maintaining silence, to wait the matter out and let it blow over without disturbance, they are very wrong." It was with relief that K. C. M. S. could finally tell the press on January 19, 1935, that "Mr. Bowser felt his resignation was to the best interest of the College and himself," but the president knew that the problem was too complex to be resolved by a mere change of coaches. "I have asked for the coöperation of three committees," he announced early in January, "representing the faculty, undergraduates, and alumni to make independent reports on the general athletic problems of the College, and—easier said than done—to suggest improvements." Sensing that the president was really determined to bring athletics under institutional control, a special committee of the Governing Boards named to receive the reports in April told K. C. M. S. that "the time has come for the Boards themselves to recognize more fully that athletics is a part of college work and to exercise the same direction over the Department of Physical Education . . . as is maintained over other departments of instruction." Faculty skeptics complained that earlier committees had voiced the same pious sentiments, but the president made it clear that he was sick and tired of his former policy of watchful waiting which had merely resulted in a succession of athletic "crises."

Meanwhile, President Sills was not permitted to confine all his worrying to the management of athletics. Quoddy enthusiasts kept prodding him with reminders that he had a report of his own to prepare in time for Governor Brann to submit it to Roosevelt early in January. Forgetting that the commission had been forced to mark time until late in November because of the lack of funds, the *Eastport Sentinel* demanded, "If the members of the Commission, all busy men, are too busy to attend to its duties, they should resign. President Roosevelt said he wanted an early report and undoubtedly would appreciate being taken at his word." K. C. M. S., however, refused to be perturbed. Despite the burden of administrative duties at Bowdoin, he continued to preside over frequent sessions of the commission and in the intervals between meetings to puzzle over technical reports on the operation of great dams in the south and west. He was amused to discover how quickly he acquired a vocabulary of engineering terms, but he refused to pose as an expert when he was invited to write an article for the *Public Utilities Fortnightly*. "I feel," he told the editor, "that someone with more engineering experience would be better able to present the facts." Yet he conscientiously answered hundreds of inquiries from citizens interested in all aspects of the project. In rereading his response to a series of questions from an industrialist, the former classicist blinked his eyes incredulously at the strange language: "The total estimated installed capacity 234,000 k.w. The first peak power available 139,000 k.w. Mean output on basis of 40% load factor, 487,000,000 k.w.h. per annum, on basis of 44% load factor, 533,000,000 k.w.h. per annum." "I have looked up these figures quite carefully," he scrawled at the bottom of the page, "but I hope they mean more to you than they do to me."

Since Kenneth Sills believed a function of the commission was "to deal with broad underlying principles," the members followed his suggestion to accept "as reasonably feasible" the engineering conclusions reached by Dexter Cooper and the government experts. At the beginning of their deliberations in August, they had attempted to arrive at a detailed estimate of the cost of production per kilowatt hour, but they were soon bogged down in the question of interest charges. It became clear early in their discussions that Maine would be unable, even if the state were willing, to assume control of the project because it was prevented on constitutional grounds from borrowing a sum of money large enough to finance the undertaking, and in the present economic situation private capital was unavailable. For these reasons the commission was unanimous in its recommendation that Quoddy "must be undertaken, if at all, by the federal government and financed by federal funds under federal control." When funds were belatedly made available in November, the commission engaged the Maine planning board and consulting experts to study the problem of potential markets. Although the board's 256-page report held out some hopes, K. C. M. S. refused to be optimistic. "It would require," he wrote, "a prophet of the first order to predict the possible use of power a few years hence."

Unable to marshal enough evidence to prove that the project would be self-liquidating, President Sills urged the commission to emphasize its social desirability. The tactical advantage of such emphasis became apparent when a delegation from Secretary Ickes' office, meeting with the commission on November 23, intimated that the P. W. A. was as much interested in the "social factors" of Quoddy as in the market for power. While the commission was debating the wisdom of stressing the social argument, unexpected support came from U. S. Senator Wallace H. White of Maine. In an urgent letter to K. C. M. S. on December 13, White asked, "Is there anything you can tell me about the attitude of your Quoddy Commission towards the project? I have some ideas that I should like to go over with you before your Commission reaches its conclusions." White's inquiry arrived while Kenneth Sills was working on a rough draft of the report, but he replied at once. "The Quoddy Commission hopes to have its recommendations in the hands of the Governor by the first of the year," he wrote on December 14. "So far we have been maintaining a judicial attitude leaning toward sympathy." Senator White immediately telephoned to arrange a meeting in Boston. "I feel so strongly that I want to talk with you about the report," he told K. C. M. S. "I don't know whether what I want to say to you will make any impression or not, but I cannot justify not contacting you before your report goes in." When they met two days later at the Copley Plaza, the senator reported on the current crop of Washington rumors about the attitude of the W. P. A. toward the project. He had received, he said, strong intimations from the White House that if the case for Quoddy were made on the ground of social welfare and the public interest, F. D. R. would look upon it with more favor than did the P. W. A. when the unsuccessful application for a loan was made by Cooper's private corporation.

In his memorandum on the interview, Senator White noted, "President Sills made no commitments. He was a sympathetic listener, and at the close of our talk I felt that he was sympathetic with the view I presented." The senator's impression was not unlike that of many members of the faculty after a consultation in Massachusetts Hall, but they were not always as shrewd in estimating the measure of presidential sympathy. Back in Brunswick on December 22, with only a fortnight in which to complete the report, Kenneth Sills informed the commission of his talk with White and arranged for a full meeting with the governor on January 4. In a note to Edward French on December 27, he wrote, "I had a long talk with Senator White last Saturday who gave me some interesting information right from Washington. He seemed to feel that we would do well, as we had already planned, to emphasize the social desirability of the Quoddy project and regard the engineering, legal, and other problems as subsidiary." Actually, the lack of funds for technical assistance had induced the commission to stress the social aspects of the enterprise in planning the format of its report in November. This shift of emphasis was doubly welcome to the chairman whose chief interest in Quoddy had always been in its promise of benefits to the people of Maine. His admiration of their self-reliance had not blinded him to the economic changes which made it impossible for the state to prosper alone without the central, energizing power of the government. Senator White's counsel of political expediency only served to confirm Kenneth Sills's main contention that the development of Quoddy would be in the public interest, not only by relieving the immediate problem of unemployment, but in renewing the industrial and agricultural life of one of the most hard-hit regions in the United States.

Only minor changes were made in the report when the commission met in Augusta on January 4, 1935. At Governor Brann's suggestion, it was agreed, for tactical reasons, to modify a statement which read originally, "It is our opinion that Quoddy power would not be very cheap power but that it would be cheap enough to act as a yardstick and to be an important factor, if properly developed, in the whole problem of power in New England." The sentence smacked of Sillsean caution, but K. C. M. S. revised it cheerfully to become, "It is our opinion that Quoddy would prove to be an important factor, if properly developed, in the whole problem of power in New England." The recommendations of the commission were unanimous: (1) that the Quoddy project can only be constructed at this time as a federal project, and (2) as a federal project it should be undertaken at once and carried to completion as promptly as efficiency in construction will permit.

President Franklin D. Roosevelt received the report from the governor and his commission at the White House on January 21, 1935. K. C. M. S. had expected the delegation to be questioned closely about the problem of markets and was prepared for a stiff cross examination, but F. D. R. merely thanked the commission for its devotion to duty. His courteous, noncommittal reception may have reminded Kenneth Sills of his own behavior when waited upon by undergraduates bearing petitions, and he was relieved when President Roosevelt did not describe the report as "interesting." All Bowdoin had learned how to interpret that label. With the submission of the document, the commission considered its responsibilities were ended. The chairman's last official act was to mail copies to the Maine congressional delegation. Senator White's response was "altogether favorable." He told K. C. M. S., "I am getting spanked occasionally for my newspaper statement in behalf of the project, but I guess I shall have to stand it." Conservative Senator Frederick Hale, was something less than ecstatic. "I have read the report with interest," he replied, "and find it a very fair one." The chairman needed no help in translating "with interest." His friend Robert Hale was characteristically forthright; he simply noted, "It seems to me an unfortunate document." Congressman Owen Brewster, however, who represented the northeast section of the state, promised his support. "I think you have wisely placed the emphasis on social questions," he wrote K. C. M. S., "and it is these that we shall urge in consideration of the project here."

Kenneth Sills thought his duties were over, but he was soon besieged by architects, engineers, and contractors seeking employment. The host of applicants increased after May 16, 1935, when F. D. R. made $10,000,000 available from relief funds for the first stages of the work. K. C. M. S. patiently referred all job-seekers to Major Fleming's office. "Since January, 1935, when the report of our Commission was filed," he wrote again and again, "I have had nothing to do with the Quoddy project and know very little about it except what I have read in the papers." This "little" was enough to convince him that until Congress actually appropriated funds for construction, any celebrations Down East would be premature. He was not present in Eastport on June 28 when jubilant citizens tendered a testimonial dinner to Dexter Cooper, who said nothing to dispel the notion that Congress was on the verge of appropriating all of the $36,000,000 now estimated as the cost of the tidal development. Nor was he among the 10,000 cheering Eastporters on July 4 when Vice-President Garner touched off the work by pushing a button in Washington, D. C. Although K. C. M. S. never doubted Roosevelt's warm interest, he questioned whether Congress would appropriate further funds when the relief money was exhausted. He also foresaw the reluctance of the Maine legislature to create a state authority for the disposing of the power. He was not surprised when dwindling relief funds reduced the Quoddy allotment to $5,000,000 in October, 1935.

By the end of the following year, the project which had once employed over 5,000 men had less than 350 on the payrolls and further cuts were imminent. Through these and later political vicissitudes, the former chairman of the Passamaquoddy Commission refused to comment. Whatever the measure of his disappointment, it was the less keen because his hopes were never high. From the outset he had considered himself as a judge rather than advocate. Just as he had consistently refused to prejudge the merits of the case before hearing all the evidence, he now shied away from discussing the verdict. "You picked out the right word, *arbiter*, when you referred to my Quoddy job," he told his friend, Roy Marston '99. "I suppose the primary function of an arbiter is to listen with what intelligence he possesses to both sides." This is what Kenneth Sills had tried to do, and since his considered conclusion was embodied in the commission's report, he said nothing more.

President Sills's public service during the autumn and winter of 1934–35 was done so quietly that most undergraduates and many colleagues assumed that all his waking hours were being devoted to the college. He continued to meet Casey's Lit. regularly every Monday, Wednesday, and Friday morning and to correct all the papers himself, although he often had to hurry from his lecture in Adams Hall to catch the noon train for Augusta. Only rarely was he compelled to miss conducting chapel services on Monday and Wednesday. How he managed to be in his office three afternoons each week for apparently unhurried consultations with faculty and students remained a mystery to his secretary and the dean who knew his crowded schedule. The college problems to which he returned often seemed fully as complicated as those of kilowatt hours, but they were closer to his heart. In the spring of 1935 the committees at work on the pesky athletic situation were not the only critical investigations, both from within and from without, of the policies of the college. "In a world where change is the order of the day," he wrote in May, "it is inevitable that present practices, particularly in a college that strives to follow the traditions of liberal education, should be rigorously examined, and by some vigorously assailed." K. C. M. S. knew that Bowdoin's conservative curriculum would be attacked as contributing to the lack of success in football, and he was prepared for the assault. "Many colleges are not only accepting candidates who have little or no formal preparation in mathematics, the classics, and the modern languages," he told the Governing Boards in 1936, "but are also broadening their electives so as to permit students to go through freshman and sophomore years without work along these lines." When such changes were recommended by a number of Bowdoin alumni teaching in the secondary schools, the president refused to abandon the requirement that all Freshmen study Latin or Greek or mathematics and either French or German. To critics of Bowdoin's limited Freshman electives, he replied, "To substitute for such courses that give training in accuracy and in dealing with facts, subjects that deal very largely with questions of opinion, seems to me to be putting the educational cart before the horse."

The president was also prepared to defend Bowdoin's traditional policy of refusing to award prematriculation scholarships. With the exception of four $500 grants to Maine boys passing the best competitive examinations, the college withheld all financial aid to Freshmen until after their February examinations. In his report to the Boards in 1936, K. C. M. S. declared, "We believe that it is much better for a student to show his quality and to prove himself worthy before any scholarship aid is granted to him. . . . This policy, which has now been in effect for at least forty years, is on the whole and in the main, beneficial both to the College and to the student." He knew that his attitude was unique, and he was troubled each autumn by the loss of a few promising boys from families of moderate means because they were offered scholarships elsewhere. He also counted on being informed whenever one of them turned out to be a half-back who later wreaked havoc on Whittier Field.

He realized, too, that students sometimes failed to do good work when dogged by financial worries at the beginning of their Freshman year. These and other disadvantages induced him to reconsider his policy, but he moved cautiously. Advertising the college by dangling fat scholarship aid before high school Seniors was as repugnant to him as any form of self-advertisement. Even college publicity, unless it were handled with the greatest restraint, was distasteful to him. "I am quite content," he said, "to have Bowdoin judged as she should be judged—solely by the quality of the men who have been trained here." When strong pressure was put upon him by the directors of the alumni fund to allocate a portion of the annual income for prematriculation scholarships, he reminded them of President Hyde's remark that "Since all scholarships are awarded on the basis of good scholarship, good character, and need . . . any one who is confident of his ability to meet these three requirements can promise one to himself." The present policy, K. C. M. S. said, "makes it impossible for any one to charge that the College is using its scholarship funds to induce boys to come to Bowdoin."

Reluctant as he was to abandon this position, he was ultimately compelled to yield. Some years before his retirement in 1952, an increasing number of Freshmen were entering Bowdoin each year with awards ranging from $400 to $700 and assurance that these stipends would be sustained for their undergraduate career. K. C. M. S. was also forced to recognize the need of appointing an admissions officer. During his own seven years in the dean's office, he had recruited and chosen, with the help of a faculty committee, each entering class. His successor, Dean Nixon, continued to direct admissions policy. Years before the unsatisfactory athletic situation had intensified criticism of Bowdoin's requirements, President Sills had been concerned with the growing difficulty of many schools in preparing students for college. Only his aversion to adding to the administrative staff made him hesitate to appoint an officer to maintain effective relations between the college and the schools. He was also unwilling to recommend substantial changes in the requirements for admission for candidates for either the A.B. or B.S. degree. As a concession to those who advocated far more sweeping changes, he persuaded the faculty in May, 1935, to authorize the recording committee to waive or modify specific subject requirements for a limited number of individual candidates of exceptional ability. A month later he announced the appointment of Edward Sanford Hammond, Wing Professor of Mathematics, as Bowdoin's first director of admissions. Dr. Hammond's appointment was in accord with the president's belief that the problem of selecting candidates most likely to profit from college work can best be solved by a member of the faculty actually engaged in teaching and intimately associated with classroom duties. Unfortunately, however, K. C. M. S. failed to provide his new officer with adequate secretarial assistance. This neglect was due less to the president's failure to estimate the scope and complexity of the office than to his inveterate dislike of diverting college funds to non-teaching functions. Unusual, understandable, and, often, from the faculty point of view, laudable as this prejudice was, it resulted in later embarrassment, not only to the admissions office, but to other departments. Don Potter, the superintendent of grounds and buildings, needed all of his Yankee ingenuity to keep the plant in decent repair. Glenn McIntire, the bursar, performed managerial miracles for the finance committee of the Boards, some of whose members, accustomed to relying upon ample personnel in their own businesses, were perhaps unaware of how many details were handled by the bursar himself.

Despite the gloomy football season and the need to continue the reductions in salaries and wages, Kenneth Sills considered the sessions of 1934–35 to be "perhaps, on the whole, the finest year since I became President in 1918." He might, indeed, have omitted his cautious "perhaps" had he been able to foresee the remarkable improvement in Bowdoin's football fortunes which followed the reorganization of athletics in June. At their meeting on June 18, 1935, the Trustees by a unanimous vote, and the Overseers by a decisive majority, gave the president a clear mandate to assert once and for all his rightful leadership in the control of athletic policy. The Boards abolished the old Athletic Council which had enjoyed the power of veto over the acts and recommendations of the director of athletics and, by giving special weight to the faculty and student reports, further voted to concentrate full power in the director and to confer faculty status upon all the full-time coaches. Harry Shulman, the astute Brunswick correspondent of the *Portland Press Herald*, echoed the overwhelming sentiment of the college when he reported: "As members of the Faculty, the coaches may sit in at meetings and have a voice in the proceedings. They are no longer dependent on their popularity with the alumni. There will be no need for suspicions or petty jealousies. All coaches are now on an equal basis. All will have an opportunity to discuss their problems at faculty meetings and will not have to run to influential alumni. It should be smooth sailing from now on." Although K. C. M. S. knew that the supply of athletic utopias was strictly limited, he was destined to inhabit one for the remainder of his administration. The advent of Adam Walsh as head coach of football, an appointment recommended by Malcolm Morrell, director of athletics, and approved by the president in the spring of 1935, heralded the beginning of a new era. In the first season of the regime, Bowdoin won its first state football championship since 1921. "We rejoice with those who rejoice, and we weep with those who weep," Kenneth Sills said at the victory dinner in 1935. "We've been weeping for some time, so let's rejoice for a change."

The rejoicing seemed permanent. In winning four successive state titles between 1935 and 1938, the team won in four years as many games as all its predecessors had won in the last fourteen. In 1939 the president was almost apologetic in reporting to the Boards "the abnormal success in football, golf, and track, and creditable records in swimming, tennis, and baseball." Casey's football headaches were never to recur. The pre-1935 disasters soon became old, unhappy, far-off things, and battles long ago. The president, however, never lost his antipathy for superlatives. "Things are going pretty well in the athletic department," he said in 1941, after Walsh's seventh championship season. "The teams have compiled pretty good records." Sons of the college were not deceived by the understatement. They recalled that once in a moment of pride, K. C. M. S. had gone so far as to boast, "On the whole and in the main, Bowdoin is a pretty fair college." The renaissance of athletics was all the more gratifying because it was accompanied by heightened academic achievement. "Each senior class," the president reported in 1936, "seems to have the laudable habit of beating the scholastic record of its immediate predecessor." Not only was he able to announce that four men in the class of 1936 had won highest honors and that nine had "straight A ranks," but that the average grade of the state championship football team was above that of the fraternity that won the scholarship cup in the preceding June. "If our friends or our foes expect any fundamental change in our policy so far as athletics and scholastic standards are concerned," he told the student body in chapel, "they are doomed to disappointment. And the same applies to the provisions for admission."

Kenneth Sills devoted most of his efforts in the 1930s to strengthening the curriculum and the faculty, but his best energies were lavished upon those who taught. In William Witherle Lawrence, the chairman of the Boards' committee on educational policy, he had an ally who shared his conviction that alterations in the curriculum are of secondary importance in maintaining a high standard intellectually among faculty and students. Without the best of teaching, they agreed, no rearrangement of courses or modification of requirements will make a college successful; men and not methods are of permanent importance. Kenneth Sills always considered his most vital function to be that of attracting and holding able teachers. Although he never made a promotion without the consent of the department concerned and the advice of the senior faculty, he accepted the final responsibility as his alone. In considering promotions he was always sobered by the reflection that a college president can no more remove a man of professorial rank than a governor can remove a justice of the Superior Court. "The wise college president like a wise governor," he said, "must bear in mind that he is building for the future." "Whenever I believe I have made a promising appointment or a deserved promotion," he once told a colleague, "I feel justified in retiring to my study at 85 Federal Street, lighting my pipe, and thanking God I've done a good day's work."

The president's major appointments during the mid-1930s enlivened the teaching of the creative arts. In naming Robert Peter Tristram Coffin '15 to the Pierce professorship of English in 1934, he inaugurated the policy of reserving at least one of the endowed chairs for a man of letters who would spend such time as he could spare from the teaching of poetry to the writing of it. K. C. M. S. was fully aware that the appointment of a practicing poet was a calculated risk, but it was the sort of risk he was eager to take. He was delighted when Professor Coffin warned his students not to expect the Monday-Wednesday-Friday brand of academic orthodoxy. "I shall say round things and quick things and bold things, and in a style closer to poetry and life than scholars can afford to come," he promised in his opening lecture. "I am going to talk like a particular person, not like a dozen well-bred scholars at once. For what you may miss of the history of poetry, I may make up to you in my exploration of poetry." Coffin's success in the classroom, and the prestige he conferred upon the college as a Pulitzer Prize poet, emboldened the president to quicken the teaching of music and the other fine arts. The death in 1935 of Dr. Edward Hames Wass, associate professor of music, had left the college without full-time instruction in a subject that never had been accorded major status at Bowdoin. When discussing the medieval quadrivium in his course in comparative literature, Kenneth Sills reminded his class that in the Middle Ages music had lightened and adorned the liberal arts, while in the Renaissance it was an essential part of the education of a gentleman. "It's high time," he said, "that the College recognizes as a real princess this neglected Cinderella of the curriculum." Faced with the problem of creating a new department, he enlisted the help of a faculty committee in examining the credentials of more than sixty candidates. There were doctors of philosophy galore and dozens of musicologists with bulging bibliographies to choose from, but K. C. M. S. wanted above all other qualities enthusiasm and skill combined with a warm sympathy for youth. When he found these virtues in Frederic Tillotson, a remarkable concert pianist lacking even the formal qualification of a bachelor's degree, he promptly offered him a full professorship, the first such position in the history of the college. To Tillotson's inquiry about the president's concept of the job, K. C. M. S. said, "I merely want you to affect the minds, hearts, and souls of your students, and to transform Bowdoin into a singing college. If you can perform this miracle, I'll never ask how." He never did.

By other judicious appointments in the 1930s—those of George Quinby in drama and Philip Beam in art—the president gave further emphasis to the creative side of curricular and extra-curricular activity. Problems of theater and museum differed, but Kenneth Sills sought in each the same objective: a wider participation by undergraduates in those arts which make for more humane living. In creating the position of director of dramatics under the aegis of the department of English, and by calling to the post a graduate of the Yale Drama School with experience in the professional theater, the president hoped to stimulate the writing as well as the production of plays, and to underscore the need for a well-equipped playhouse on the campus. Handicapped by the lack of adequate facilities, Professor Quinby gratified his sponsor by an imaginative use of the chapel, Moulton Union, auditorium, and athletic cage for the staging of plays, many of them in the arena style.

The high competence of these performances and the increasing numbers of students participating in them were ultimately crowned, in the last months of the Sills administration, by a bequest providing for the Pickard Theater in Memorial Hall. Its construction was far enough advanced in the autumn of 1954 for Kenneth Sills to inspect the building and to rejoice with Professor Quinby in the realization of their dreams. The situation in the art department was of another kind. "The College has been very proud of the Walker Art Building and of the collection it houses," K. C. M. S. told the Governing Boards in 1936, "but we have not, I think, as a college, either been fully aware of the importance of the collection or awake to the educational value of the building and its contents." For this neglect, the president assumed a large share of the responsibility in failing to provide proper assistance to Professor Henry Andrews, the director, who, since 1918, had been teaching all the courses in the fine arts as well as administering museum affairs. With Professor Andrews' support, K. C. M. S. persuaded the Boards in May, 1936, to increase the staff by adding an assistant director to begin his duties in July. The work of Professor Philip Beam was soon reflected in the separation of the masterpieces from items of historical rather than artistic value, in the increased number and variety of exhibitions, and—most gratifying of all to the president—in the creation of an atmosphere in which students were made to feel at home in a museum which many of them hitherto had regarded with awe, but rarely visited. Students were also encouraged to use an improvised studio for their own work with crayon, water colors, and clay. Their enthusiastic response delighted the president, who gave his blessing to a regular course in drawing, painting, and sculpture which was instituted in 1938. By the end of the decade, K. C. M. S. could report, "There seems to be from the undergraduates more and more appreciation of what the Department of Art is striving to do for them."

As Kenneth Sills watched these developments leading to a revival of interest in the creative arts, he regretted that the curriculum of the 1930s was not equally hospitable to religion or religious studies. Although he knew that the college was not a substitute for church, he never ceased to be surprised that the spiritual side of college life was seldom discussed, either at meetings of his own faculty or in larger academic circles. The president realized that the Christian character of the college could not be ensured by the organization of a department of religion or by the imposition of formal requirements. He respected the faculty view that attempts to confound church and college too often resulted in both an inferior church and an inferior college. Yet he was troubled by the secularity of college life and the tendency of many teachers to take a neutral attitude toward Christianity. Convinced that Bowdoin's mission as a Christian college was not so much to teach religion as to teach all subjects in a religious spirit, he believed that even if the word religion was never mentioned in the classroom, by virtue of the teacher's character, the college would become unmistakably Christian or agnostic or pagan. In all this thinking about the problem, he was guided by Hyde's concept of education in which the opportunity "to form character under professors who are Christians" was regarded as not the least of Bowdoin's offers. Yet K. C. M. S. was haunted by a fear that the college was not doing enough for religion, and especially for orthodox Christianity. When his appeal in 1933 for funds to endow a chair in religion were unheeded, he induced the Board to provide for instruction in Biblical literature, and subsequently appointed the Reverend John Schroeder, D.D., of Portland, who offered an elective course from 1934 until he was called to Yale Divinity School in 1937. Dr. Schroeder's success in emphasizing religion as a cultural force was continued by Dr. Henry Russell, who augmented the offerings to include the history of religions and studies in major Christian authors. Courses alone, however, even when supplemented by daily chapel services, did not entirely meet the president's ideal of a religious spirit which should permeate and energize every aspect of college life.

Seeking to bring the college closer to this goal, he was on the verge of recommending the appointment of a college chaplain in 1938, but was deterred by the difficulty of finding the right incumbent. A year later, when he thought he had discovered a promising candidate, he hesitated again for fear that the very office itself might defeat its purpose by seeming to be overspecialized in function. Kenneth Sills was concerned with the essence rather than the form of religion. For him it was not a "way," a pedagogical method, or a professional career, but a spirit. He felt that religion, like happiness, when pursued for its own sake is likely to be lost. Only his closest friends and colleagues like Charles Burnett and Roy Elliott, who shared his spiritual concerns, were fully aware of the president's brooding on the problem. They sensed his conviction that to divorce religion and education in a college of liberal arts is to fall prey either to blundering goodness or arid intellectualism. The emphasis in many of his chapel talks fell upon the tendency in the academic world to lay undue stress upon the intellectual side of religion to the exclusion of conscience and imagination. He wanted the college, in Roy Elliott's words, to dispel "all polite ambiguities, all smirk and murk, from her treatment of Christianity." Instead of unduly exalting the intellect, he urged students to submit humbly to a higher power and to value the mystic and devotional elements of religion. Although such exhortations often moved his hearers deeply, he sometimes confessed to a sense of failure. "Perhaps because yesterday was Ash Wednesday with a call to repentance," he wrote to his wife on February 23, 1939, "I was thinking of all the things I do badly. I don't really give much time and thought to the Church. I fail in my duty to the community. . . . I am aware how lacking I am in ideas." Such a mood was rarely voiced except to those who knew him intimately, but he was never wholly free from a sense of personal inadequacy. Freshmen meeting their president for the first time, fully prepared to be awed by his learning and dignity, were impressed instead by his shy friendliness and humility. Christian humility was as close to his very being as the throb of his pulse.

The British reticence which made it difficult for K. C. M. S. to discuss his own deepest religious convictions disappeared whenever the virtues of the small, undergraduate college came under attack. When critics from the universities, like Professor Thomas Wertenbaker of Princeton, condescended to small colleges as "graveyards" of scholarship, Bowdoin's president was quick to reply. He bridled at the assertion that "a graduate school is an indispensable adjunct to every first-class American college." He had known too many able young Ph.D.'s who preferred appointments in colleges like Haverford, Hamilton, Swarthmore, and Wesleyan to positions in the larger universities to believe for a minute that smaller colleges lacked intellectual stimulation. He recalled with pride the unsuccessful attempts of many universities to lure away members of his own faculty. In 1938, when Dr. Robert Lightfoot, a visiting scholar from Oxford, asked "how Bowdoin happens to have so many on its staff who are active in research and well known outside for their scholarship," K. C. M. S. replied, "It just happens; but probably the policy of the College in encouraging research by reasonable teaching hours and frequent sabbaticals is bearing fruit."

Kenneth Sills felt that President Robert Hutchins of the University of Chicago must have been writing "on a very rainy day" when he charged that small, independent colleges had outlived their usefulness, and that a college education should have little or nothing to do with the building of character. He reminded Hutchins "of the danger always present in academic circles of failing to see the distinction between intellectualism and moral intelligence." Equally unpalatable to K. C. M. S. was President Hutchins' opinion that the four-year course was an anachronism. Replying in a radio address in 1938, he submitted that "Experience of over a century has shown that for the average college man four years give the best opportunity for intellectual, social, and moral development. Compression might be feasible if the only object of education were the advancement of the intellect. Let other educational institutions experiment with a truncated collegiate course, and let degrees be given elsewhere in a year or two if the brain of the student can be crammed in that time, but Bowdoin will stick to the four-year course and demonstrate its value in American education."

The president was also adamant in his refusal to concede there was any virtue in mere numbers. Bowdoin needs but cling a little longer to her policy of limited numbers, he told the New York alumni in 1939, to find herself leading in the newest movement in education. "Twenty-five years ago," he said, "virtually all the small colleges were doing their best to become large, and today all the large colleges seem to be doing their best to become small." K. C. M. S. regarded the house plan at Harvard and the college system at Yale as great compliments to the small college. "Bowdoin," he promised, "will remain small enough for every student to feel that he is a recognized and potentially desirable part of the whole institution. The small college has an unusual opportunity to develop the character of the individual student which is far more important than molding his character with the mass." The examining committee of the Boards, after a visit to the campus in the spring of 1937, congratulated the president upon providing better teaching for the Freshman than larger colleges and universities were able to afford, and recommended "that Bowdoin be not allowed to grow into a college of more than six hundred men." "Bowdoin at present has a rather special atmosphere of general friendliness, a rather unusual family atmosphere," the committee reported in June. "Were the College any larger, we feel that there would be more forgotten men in the college body than there are now, and far more frostiness in the campus air."

Many instructors whose academic fortunes later took them

elsewhere often looked back at the Bowdoin of the 1930s as a sort of collegiate utopia, while visiting professors rubbed their eyes in astonishment at the absence of the professional jealousies and intradepartmental feuds which they had come to expect as normal hazards of faculty life. "Bowdoin is the sort of place," remarked Chesney Horwood of Oxford, who held the Tallman professorship in 1938–39, "where colleagues actually have a good word to say for each other's books." Burdensome committee assignments which would have brought indignant protests from a later generation of instructors were accepted cheerfully because President Sills made even the youngest teacher feel he belonged to a common enterprise. Such a happy state of things was largely a result of the Sills policy of rewarding good teaching and refusing to regard a faculty member's bibliography as the sole measure of his value. "President Sills wants both productive scholarship and vital teaching," Dean Nixon told a youthful instructor, "but he'll often settle for effectiveness in the classroom." To colleagues with scholarly books afoot, he often granted sabbaticals at full pay or out of turn. For promising but Ph.D.-less instructors, he frequently arranged leaves of absence for the completion of their graduate study. Faculty members soon came to regard Kenneth Sills as a fellow teacher rather than as an administrator. In 1941, when Yale made Bowdoin's president a doctor of laws, Arnold Whitridge, the university orator, cited him "as the loyal friend of every man on the faculty." Faculty children, hearing only affectionate praise of the president at home, sometimes gave unwitting but incontrovertible testimony to the aura surrounding him. When one such youngster, five-year-old Clive Tillotson, was complimented by his parents for his strangely hushed behavior at a presidential dinner party, the boy exclaimed, "He's the father of his country, isn't he? First in war, first in peace, and first in the hearts of his countrymen!"

The gradual fading of the depression, the increase in the number of candidates for honors, the unparalleled success of the football team, and the renewed interest in the creative arts all contributed to the president's felicity. In his report to the Boards for 1936–37, K. C. M. S. wrote, "Perhaps as old Izaak Walton remarked of the strawberry, 'Doubtless God could have created a better berry, but doubtless God never did.' I can say that perhaps there is somewhere a finer body of undergraduates than that now on the Bowdoin campus, but at least I would not know where to find them." He surprised the alumni who were schooled to expect only qualified optimism from their president by saying in 1937, "The College has had an extraordinarily happy and uneventful year."

While counting Bowdoin's blessings, K. C. M. S. did not permit friends of the college to forget her most pressing needs. In 1936 he set alumni, faculty, and undergraduate committees to work putting together suggestions for improvements to be achieved before the observance of the sesquicentennial in 1944. In the meantime, he reminded alumni of immediate needs. "To mention but one," he wrote in 1939, "our classrooms and their equipment do not compare favorably with those of many a good preparatory school." If any one believes, he added, that Bowdoin is prone to put emphasis on the log rather than on Mark Hopkins, he should remember that Adams Hall, the most recent classroom building, was built in 1860 and is neither a thing of beauty nor a joy forever. The president was also troubled by the number of students—more than one-fifth of the student body in 1938— who were living off campus. "I have long advocated a dormitory for seniors," he wrote in 1939, "whereby seniors would have some individual quiet and perhaps slightly more comfort. It would emphasize college and class rather than fraternity. It would release places for sophomores, too many of whom now live off campus."

Less tangible but no less important to President Sills were other proposals for the strengthening of college work. He encouraged and watched solicitously the plan for freeing gifted Seniors from formal course requirements to enable them to do independent work, and he supported, against mounting pressures, the requirement of at least one classical language for the A.B. degree. Speaking in chapel on the 2,000th anniversary of the birth of Horace, he remarked, "I don't know of any better way of paying tribute to the greatest lyric poet of all time than by noting that in the last fifteen years, of the 950 candidates for the A.B., 900 were graduated; of the 1100 B.S. candidates, only 500 were graduated. The time has passed when you couldn't be a gentleman without having read Horace. But you'll be a better gentleman and a better scholar if you read him." To schoolmen who saw no loss in dropping Greek and Latin from the high school curriculum, K. C. M. S. predicted they would soon be equally indifferent to the value of modern languages. Bowdoin, he said, will continue to require an elementary knowledge of both French and German, as well as an advanced proficiency in one of these languages for the bachelor's degree. "We do not intend," he warned, "to give up our birthright for the cheap mess of pottage that consists in lowered standards and slovenly work."

The collective affection of Bowdoin undergraduates for their president was made vocal in 1938 on the twentieth anniversary of his election to office. Whenever he was in Brunswick on May 14, he always conducted the morning chapel service, although the special significance of the date was realized by only a few. In 1938, however, he was surprised to find the chapel crowded with students and faculty who arose spontaneously at his entrance and sang his own college song, "Rise, Sons of Bowdoin." Kenneth Sills reminded the congregation that although twenty years is a short span in the annals of a college soon to celebrate its 150th anniversary, yet none of the twelve Trustees who had chosen him in 1918 and only eight of the forty-four Overseers who had confirmed the vote were now alive. Of the faculty of thirty in 1918, he said only twelve were still in active service, including his teacher Professor Wilmot Mitchell. He recalled with pride his first appointment, that of Paul Nixon, his only and incomparable dean. The *Orient,* noting that President Sills was now junior in service only to Hopkins of Dartmouth and Neilson of Smith, and recounting the increase in endowment and the number of buildings, remarked that impressive as these physical assets were, they were dwarfed by the president's sympathy and understanding which brought him "closer to the heart of the student body than most presidents ever hope to attain."

The twentieth and later anniversaries brought sorrows as well as joys. Except for four years as a graduate student at Harvard and Columbia, Kenneth Sills had been intimately associated with Bowdoin since 1897, and each passing year now meant a series of changes and losses. As he chronicled the deaths of the elder statesmen of the college in his annual reports, he wrote, "There is something about the men that we produced at Bowdoin two or three generations ago that seems to be lacking today, a certain simplicity and directness, a ruggedness, perhaps a result of direct contact with forest and sea." In 1937 the death of Governor William Cobb '77 marked the passing of the last Trustee who had elected him to office. "It is impossible to put into adequate words," K. C. M. S. wrote, "what his support and advice and helpfulness meant during the last twenty years." Early in 1939 he was saddened by the loss of Charles Taylor Hawes, president of the Board of Overseers, and of Professor Henry Andrews, director of the museum of fine arts. Later in the same year, in the deaths of his mother whose last years were spent at 85 Federal Street, and of Ripley Dana '01, his oldest and dearest friend, he sustained the heaviest loss of all. The president was unable to remember the time when he had not known and loved Ripley Dana, his boyhood companion and classmate, "the best friend that ever a man could have." The melancholy list was lengthened in the following year when K. C. M. S. mourned the passing of Henry Hill Pierce '96, the senior Trustee, Arthur Staples '82, of the Overseers, and, from the Faculty, Professors Charles Hutchins and Philip Meserve. "In no single year since I have been President has the College been called upon to mourn so many valued officers, each one of whom was to me an old and dear friend," he wrote. "If in these trying days the College has been able to hold its own and has continued in its strength, it is due in no small measure to these men."

As Kenneth Sills began his third decade in the presidency, he found American domestic affairs and the international situation almost equally discouraging. Normally sympathetic with labor, he now felt that many union leaders were just as ruthless as the lords of industry had ever been. In his baccalaureate address in 1938, he asked the Seniors to extend into commercial and industrial life something of the democracy of the small New England town early in the century where "There was a spirit of real neighborliness, where people knew and respected one another, and were interested in each other's fortunes." His admiration of F. D. R. was also becoming clouded. The growing asperity of Roosevelt's attacks on the "horse-and-buggy" doctrines of the Supreme Court was deplored by K. C. M. S. as a dangerous invitation to government by men rather than by law. He was apprehensive about the likelihood of F. D. R. seeking a third term. Speaking to the Kiwanis Club of Portland in July, 1938, he declared, "A third term, no matter how strong the popular sentiment for it, is undesirable not only for Mr. Roosevelt, but for any president under any circumstances." It would require a good deal of effort, K. C. M. S. told his wife, to resist the temptation to be "a bad citizen and go fishing on election day."

President Sills's chapel talks in the spring and autumn of 1938 were increasingly concerned with the threats to peace in central Europe where he saw "force taking the place of reason and good will in the dealings of nations one with another." His fear of isolationism and his support of the League of Nations were constant themes of his addresses on and off the campus. He had noted in 1935 "that the two nations which of late have done the most to disturb the tranquility of the world, Japan and Germany, have both withdrawn from the League and have insisted on substituting their own individual plan for coöperation." In an address in May, 1938, he observed, "No less significant are the desperate efforts of certain great nations to preserve the peace by giving in to force, and the surrender of principle by the Council of the League of Nations." He was saddened by the failure of the government to invoke the Kellogg-Briand Pact against the aggression of Japan in China. "We as a country are responsible for many of the troubles that afflict the world today," he charged. "Our policy may have saved our skins, but it has not helped the world much." On June 20, 1939, he urged Cordell Hull to enlist the immediate support of the State Department to pending legislation to prohibit the export of war materials to Japan. Beset by discouraging developments on every hand, K. C. M. S. tried to salvage some remnant of hope following the Munich agreement. "Hitler was treated as a spoiled, petulant child who must be allowed for the time being to blow his trumpet and make a noise," he told the students at the opening of the term in September, 1938. Hoping against hope that the cheers of the people of Munich for the British Prime Minister "showed how deep in the hearts of the German people is the desire for peace," President Sills ventured the opinion "that Munich may witness the beginning of the end of Hitler's power."

Eight months later he continued to believe that war could be avoided, but he told a Patriots' Day audience in Camden in 1939, "The United States is not without responsibility for the present world conditions. When we refused to join the League of Nations . . . we lost a great opportunity to help the rest of the world. It ill becomes us to find fault with quarreling nations in Europe." He listened incredulously at the Commencement dinner on June 17, 1939, as Maine's Governor Lewis Barrows cheerfully assured the graduates, "There is no cause to worry." When the college reconvened in September, three weeks after England and France had declared war on Germany, K. C. M. S. warned the student body, "The days are as critical as in 1815, 1861, and 1914. You will soon find that the war going on in Europe will affect you directly or indirectly every day of this term." Deploring the fashionable cynicism about democratic institutions only because they lacked perfection, the president declared, "The fault of democracy lies not in the system itself, but in ourselves. Although the part a single individual can play in the defense of democracy is infinitesimal, it is absolutely essential that he play that part." As a practical, immediate step, he advocated opening the nation's doors to European refugees: "It would be a mockery if we, as a democratic nation, should shut our doors to refugees. If we could allay our religious prejudices, if we could be of some help to other peoples, we could keep our heads up and speak of our country as a democracy."

The effects of the European war on education dominated the discussion of the Association of the Colleges of New England which met in Brunswick on October 11, 1939. As the presiding officer, K. C. M. S. reported, "At least ninety-five per cent of Bowdoin's undergraduates are firmly opposed to the United States entering the war abroad, but no American equivalent of the famous Oxford oath 'never to fight for king or country' exists on the campus." A few weeks later, in response to questions at an alumni luncheon on November 4, the president said that a majority of the students sympathized with England and France without seeing any reason why the United States should send them abroad to fight. He told the alumni that many undergraduates confessed to having a fatalistic sense that the war would eventually call them, but they were maintaining a skeptical attitude toward all propaganda. Recalling the apathy toward international affairs between 1914 and 1917, he was convinced that the present generation was far more interested in the events in Europe. In his review of the year for the Governing Boards in June, 1940, the president found undergraduate opinion to be greatly confused. "There are a few boys of high calibre who are sincere pacifists," he reported. "There are also a few who feel strongly that we ought to support the democracies of the world at once and in full measure. But the great preponderance of undergraduate opinion is a good deal like that of the American people, hoping that the Allies may win, but feeling that under no circumstances should the United States take any active part in the war."

Although K. C. M. S. obeyed his own injunction to avoid fear and hysteria, he made no attempt to conceal his warm support of the British and French democracies. To insist upon complete intellectual objectivity where a moral issue is at stake seemed to him to disregard the very nature of man. For Kenneth Sills, the defense of liberty and the rights of the individual was essentially moral. If, as some members of his faculty believed, the repeal of the arms embargo would be tantamount to entering the war, he was ready to take the risk. He deplored the view of Colonel Charles Lindbergh that the United States would be able to preserve her democratic institutions, even with a Hitler-dominated Europe. In an address in Portland on May 20, 1940, he asserted, "Hitler wants to smash to bits the British Empire and to establish all over Europe a great national socialistic state under German military rule. Evil as war is, there may be alternatives that are worse, such as the loss of liberty, or the reign of tyranny." He dismissed as the cant of a spurious liberalism that the war is "only a clash between different forms of imperialism." By the end of June, 1940, after the dismemberment of France, K. C. M. S. still found the great majority of students "confused, frustrated, besought, and perhaps a bit frightened and ashamed," but in a statement to the *Boston Herald* on June 30, he noted signs of change: "More and more undergraduates expressed themselves as being in favor of sending aid to the Allies (now, alas, to England alone) and of doing what they could to help, short of going to war."

Beneath the pomp and ceremony of the 1940 Commencement were signs of tension between youth and age. In his baccalaureate address on June 9, President Sills urged the country to throw its economic and moral weight to the Allies. "Frankly, I have no patience," he said, "with those who profess to see no difference to individuals whether they live under a totalitarian regime or a democratic state. I have much sympathy for the almost universal hatred of war prevalent among American undergraduates, a hatred, I need not remind you, that has been prevalent in many another country now fighting for its life or already a country no longer." The president knew he was talking to a generation brought up to believe that war is futile, and that the Treaty of Versailles and the bungling of their elders were responsible for the present situation. As the editor of the *Orient* remarked, "Students learned their opposition to war from the faculty and are now putting what they learned into practice." What they learned was set forth a few days later in a special edition of the college newspaper: "It is youth that supplies the materials for every war, and as long as it refuses to hearken unto its supposedly wiser elders, we can't be dragged into the European conflict. Let the pulpit and the lecture platform produce their war enthusiasts and mock patriots. They swayed public opinion two decades ago, but they are going to have a difficult time doing it again."

As the autumn term opened, a writer in the *Orient* sensed "an air of unrest that is almost a presentiment of the future. . . . The results of next week's game, the subjugation of freshmen, and fraternity pledging sink to positions of relative insignificance." At the first chapel service, President Sills called attention to the presence of Thomas H. Eaton, of the class of 1869, who remembered Bowdoin students returning from the Civil War in his Freshman year. "We would not wish the colleges of the country today," K. C. M. S. said, "to be safe and careful havens of refuge unaffected by what is happening in the world outside." The mood of insecurity and suspense was intensified early in October as the 168 eligible undergraduates prepared to register under the Selective Service Act. As a symbol that the duties of citizenship are common duties, Kenneth Sills arranged to have the registration take place, not on the campus, but in the Brunswick Town Hall. "There was some laughter and a little kidding," the *Orient* noted on October 16, "but it was of a strained sort. The tenseness of the situation was reflected in every action." Meanwhile undergraduate columnists warned against "the rising war fever." Remarking that songs like "I Am an American," and motion pictures like "The Ramparts We Watch" were gaining popularity, the *Orient* warned, "As college men, let us not be drawn in by these expressions of patriotism and things leading to mob hysteria." An *Orient* news commentator wrote, "We wonder whether our educational leaders possess any of that prized 'detachment' which is supposed to temper their learned ideas and decisions . . . . Obviously, not even our professors and college presidents are exempt from the subtle effects of propaganda. Isn't it fine how generous we can be when someone else is asked to make a personal sacrifice!"

Undergraduates were impressed by the personal sacrifice of one young alumnus, Arthur Mills Stratton '35, who returned to the campus in November to recuperate from severe wounds suffered while driving an ambulance in France. The first American to be decorated with the *croix de guerre* for bravery under heavy machine-gun and artillery fire, Stratton told the *Orient*, "I believe the professors thoroughly when they say we must get into the war." K. C. M. S. observed that students listened intently to this graduate's account of the war, but seemed confident that such experiences would never be theirs. Their confidence was reflected in a student poll on May 14, 1941, when 233 men voted against intervention, and 159 opposed aid in any form to Great Britain. In commenting upon the results to his class, the president read a letter from Lieutenant Colonel Stanley Casson, professor of classical archaeology at Bowdoin in 1933–34, and now with the British Army. "American opinion is much in the same condition as was British opinion in 1937," Casson wrote. "But the speed of events in the last half year will speed your views faster than ours. Self-preservation is an instinct which produces immediate reactions once it operates." His prediction was soon to be confirmed. Although the *Orient* continued to snipe at "the idealistically bellicose opinions of the President of the College," by the middle of May the editor discerned a change in campus opinion. "How was public opinion so rapidly reversed?" he asked on May 14. "Some of us are still marvelling at the swiftness of it all." A month later in his valedictory editorial he wrote: "The Class of 1941 should leave the campus with a firm conviction that there are other things worse than war. Our exasperation with those 'anything-but-war' exponents has grown with tremendous vitality during the past few weeks as 'the handwriting on the wall' has become clearer."

During the summer of 1941, amid multiplying signs that the war was closing in, President Sills urged the parents of prospective Freshmen to encourage their sons to get as much formal education as possible. In a radio address in August, he found himself virtually repeating the advice he gave in 1916–17. "Boys of high school age will make a great mistake," he warned, "if they go into industry or postpone their college education. It seems to me not only individually desirable, but in every sense of the word highly patriotic for each boy to stick to his school or college tasks until the government calls him." K. C. M. S. hoped there would be no repetition of the Student Army Training Corps experience of the First World War. "It is unwise to combine military and college training," he told the faculty. "The mixture of scholarship and army service is a mishmash." As evidence of a far more sensible policy, he welcomed the request of the U. S. Navy to provide laboratories for the training of young naval officers under the direction of Lieutenant Noel Little, U. S. Naval Reserve, professor of physics. The first contingent arrived in mid-June, 1941, and until the officers donned their uniforms at the outbreak of the war, they were often mistaken for undergraduates. Known as the Naval School of Radio Engineering before the mysterious word radar was permitted to be used, it ultimately trained 2,500 naval officers under the direction of Lieutenant Little. In greeting the arrival of the first unit six months before Pearl Harbor, Kenneth Sills remarked, "Were it not for the specialized and important scientific work in the laboratories of England before 1938, England would have been conquered in the summer and autumn of 1940."

The World War was still a European one when Bowdoin reopened on September 25, 1941, but President Sills often feared that he would wake up some morning to learn that the United States had been in it for months. In his first chapel address, he called on the undergraduates "in spirit and in work to be ready for any test that may come, praying that it will be a test of peace, but ready for any fiery trial." Beguiling as were the traditional excitements of athletic and fraternity activities, the president did not permit the student body to forget that its agreeable, self-contained little world was hovering in a dread twilight zone between peace and war. Although he believed that young men should go to college, he was unwilling to ask for their favored treatment in the draft. His democratic instincts were aroused by the proposal of President Seymour of Yale whereby college students would be allowed to take their year of military training in 3 four-month installments during summer vacations. "We must have as little distinction as possible raised between college men and their fellows in other walks of life," he declared. "Warfare nowadays is total warfare." The president had no sympathy, however, with those who held military training to be a valuable aid to education. "Selective service must be accepted and carried through as a necessary evil," he said. "It is better to have it even if it should not be needed, than to need it and not have it." He had been appalled in August, 1941, by the narrowly averted catastrophe when the House of Representatives, by the margin of a single vote, passed the measure to keep the army together for another eighteen months.

In addition to his regularly scheduled chapel talk every Wednesday, K. C. M. S. often spoke two or three times each week as the autumn wore on. Recalling the pessimistic tone of many Commencement addresses in June, including a few graduation essays by his own Bowdoin Seniors, the president declared in October, "I am sick to death of hearing that democracy is not so efficient as dictatorship. The passage of the Selective Service Act and of the Lend Lease Bill, the quick seizure of sabotaged ships—all these show that a democracy under proper leadership does and can work." He was, however, dismayed on November 13 by another scant margin in the House of Representatives where, by a vote of 212 to 194, the Neutrality Act was amended to permit American merchant ships to be armed and to sail into combat zones. Convinced that so formidable an opposition to extending selective service and amending neutrality legislation could only be attributed to a failure to understand the gravity of the crisis, Kenneth Sills continued to insist that if civilization is to survive, force must be checked with greater force. "We must not allow our hatred of Bolshevism to prevent us from aiding the Russians," he urged in another chapel talk, "nor must we let our hatred of war keep us from seeing that there are worse alternatives. Belgium, Holland, and Norway also abhorred war."

On Tuesday, December 2, 1941, President Sills left Brunswick for a series of meetings in New York and Boston. Just before his departure, he learned that a student poll conducted by the *Orient* on December 1 revealed that only 112 votes were cast for a declaration of war as against 357 opposed to such action, and 365 votes were cast against the use of American troops in Europe. On Wednesday and Thursday, K. C. M. S. attended sessions of the national council of the Episcopal Church, and on the evening of December 4, he addressed the Maine Society of New York. In Boston the following day, he presided over the committee on athletics appointed by the presidents of the New England colleges, and on December 6 he took part in the annual meeting of the New England Association of Colleges and Secondary Schools. The war in Europe had cast its shadow over every topic and informed every discussion during the last few days whether it was concerned with school, college, or church. He was preparing to return to Brunswick when he learned of the attack on Pearl Harbor. As his train carried him back to the college, he may have recalled listening as a Freshman to President Hyde's words in chapel at the outbreak of war with Spain in April, 1898, and perhaps remembered the words of the same president nineteen years later after the declaration of war in April, 1917. Hyde had said in 1917: "Rather than live ourselves, or leave our brothers of the European democracies to live, in such a world as a victorious enemy would make, we throw into the fateful scales of war the whole weight of our resources; the full strength of our sons." It was those and other sons of whom Kenneth Sills was thinking on his way to Maine.

# 13

## THE PRESIDENT
## AND THE SECOND WORLD WAR

The chapel bell was tolling when President Sills reached the campus late in the afternoon of December 7, barely in time to preside at the thinly attended vesper service. Much to his surprise, the visiting clergyman, Dr. Robert Cummins, did not mention the crisis in either his sermon or his prayers. When informed of the news after the benediction, he explained that he had motored to Brunswick without learning of the attack. K. C. M. S. was not surprised at the presence of only a scattering of students. He knew that most undergraduates would remain at their radios listening to the bulletins trickling in from Pearl Harbor. Remembering the restlessness in April, 1917, he scrawled a notice which he posted himself on the bulletin board on Sunday night. The message simply said: "The door to my office and the door to my house are open to you twenty-four hours a day." His first duty would be to urge students to continue their courses until the nation called them. "This is easy to say," he confessed to an *Orient* reporter the next morning, "but hard to do."

When he faced the crowded chapel following the declaration of war against Japan, Kenneth Sills found himself repeating, almost word for word, the advice he had given a generation of Bowdoin men twenty-four years ago. "It is perfectly clear," he said, "that the duty for most of you is to remain where you are until your country needs you. Regular academic work in library and laboratory, and daily studying may not seem to be of national significance, but the nation is going to need men with adequate training. Think what a generation would be like without men who had been to college. There has been a surprising unanimity during the past few days, and there will be need of as much stamina and fortitude in the days to come."

Inevitably, the president's mind raced back to the scenes of excitement in Brunswick after Woodrow Wilson had read his war message to Congress in 1917. "To one who saw the undergraduate body through the first World War," he told the Governing Boards, "there are some contrasts to record. There is far less flag waving, less emotionalism, less talk, than there was in 1917. The students are well aware that the war is closing in on them, as on us. There is no enthusiasm for war; service is accepted as a necessary duty." To a worried alumnus, who had deplored the lack of military ardor on the campus, K. C. M. S. replied that he welcomed it. He sensed that the overwhelming number of undergraduates, despite the threatened dislocation of their lives and the apathy reflected in their recent poll in the *Orient*, were ready to face the war with a deep feeling of its importance for human liberty and for the future of civilization. He remarked on other differences in students' attitudes when he met his class in comparative literature on December 10. "While there seems to be the same hatred of Hitler as there was of the Kaiser, there does not seem to be the same unreasoning hostility to German letters and music. Students today are more concerned with the war and its issues than they were in 1917; motion pictures and radio have shown what participation really means."

One sign of this involvement was immediately visible on the campus. The eighty members of the naval preradar unit, whose civilian clothes made them difficult to distinguish from Bowdoin upperclassmen before December 7, were now in uniform. Their commanding officer, Professor Noel Little, of the department of physics, was becoming accustomed to returning the salutes of his students. Lieutenant Little, U. S. Naval Reserve, was the first member of the senior faculty to join the armed forces, although he was destined to retain the command of the unit at Bowdoin for the duration. Radar had not become a public term in 1941, but as a columnist on the *Orient* observed, "anyone eavesdropping on the campus can hear a lot said about 'electronics,' 'vacuum tubes,' 'electrostatics,' and a score of mysterious terms." The editors of the *Orient*, whose issue for December 10 had been virtually in type before the attack and was filled with stories of the coming Christmas house parties, apologized for the lack of war news. Readers were directed to consult the college bulletin board for announcements. There they found that K. C. M. S. had summoned the student council to organize committees for civilian defense. "Business as usual is going out of the window," he warned student leaders, "and there will be profound changes all along the line."

As a veteran college administrator in the last war, President Sills was invited to speak to the faculty of the University of New Hampshire where, on December 15, he advised against repeating the unsatisfactory experiences with the Student Army Training Corps. "We learned in 1917–1918," he said, "that scholarship and army service do not mix." College teachers, he advised, would be most valuable in their present positions: "Were it not for the highly specialized and important scientific work in the laboratories of England before 1939, England would have been conquered in the summer and autumn of 1940." In the present crisis, he told his audience at Durham, "an important role of the college and university is to uphold the morale and preserve the democratic spirit." Back on his own campus, he reminded undergraduates of the significance of the 150th anniversary of the Bill of Rights. In his last chapel talk before the Christmas recess, he urged students to visit the Walker Art Museum to look again at the Gilbert Stuart portraits of Jefferson and Madison, "men who were in large part responsible for the Bill of Rights." "As you go home for the holidays which will be very different from any you have ever known," he declared, "do not forget to carry with you a message of the abiding faith and confidence of a fuller understanding of what this country stands for, and a resolution to do all you possibly can to extend the liberties of the Bill of Rights so that ultimately the world will not only have freedom of speech and expression of worship, but freedom from care and freedom from fear."

During the Christmas season, for the first time since 1918, the cupola on the president's house was without a gaily lighted Christmas tree. One undergraduate, who had been air-raid warden on Federal Street that first winter when only imaginary bombs fell, later wrote K. C. M. S. from Omaha beachhead that he thought of the darkened cupola at 85 Federal Street while his LST went back and forth over the English channel amid real bombs. "I hope to see your tree lighted again," he wrote two weeks after D-Day. "The thought of the College and of you and Mrs. Sills in your friendly house helped to keep me going."

In his New Year's letter to the alumni, the president promised that Bowdoin would take her full part in the national defense. "Thus far," he wrote, "we have been host to two hundred young officers in the U. S. N. R. Under the auspices of the C. A. A. we have trained sixty-one men to serve as pilots, twenty of whom are now in the Army, Navy, or Marine Corps." "The great task of the College for the moment," he told the graduates, "is to help the students who may soon be engaged in active service to make the most of their precious days here, to hold the College together as well as we can, and to keep constantly before the undergraduates the abiding principles of the democratic and Christian way of life."

From Baltimore on January 3, where K. C. M. S. attended an emergency three-day session of the Association of American Colleges, he wrote a troubled letter to Edith Sills: "One realizes here how terribly serious war is to everyone, not excluding the colleges. There is still much confusion." Less than a year ago he had told the Governing Boards, "It is not perhaps utterly fantastic to foresee under certain conditions that we may be obliged to keep the College in session all the year." At the time, both he and the Boards had felt such a contingency to be remote, but now, with students leaving on short notice, at unexpected intervals, and at various times of the year, he was convinced that Bowdoin must revise its calendar to enable undergraduates to advance their training as far as possible before their selection for military service. At a special faculty meeting on January 6, plans were initiated for an accelerated course, an earlier Commencement, and a twelve-week summer trimester to begin on June 22. The word trimester was alien to the Bowdoin vocabulary and K. C. M. S. winced as he pronounced it. "The term is a horrid but a necessary one," he told the faculty clerk who had looked up inquiringly before entering it in the minutes. The president foresaw that among other losses acceleration would mean the abandonment for the duration of his beloved system of comprehensive examinations. Although the financial problems for an institution not budgeted for year-round instruction would be formidable, he was more concerned with less tangible qualities. He lamented that there was no substitute for the mechanism of orderly, tutorial work, for the leisure needed for wide reading in, around, and above one's subject, and, above all, for unhurried reflection. He also shared the fear of his colleague, Thomas Van Cleve, that in responding to the demands of national defense, small colleges of liberal arts might lose their unique characteristics. No matter how burdensome the administrative difficulties or how high the cost, Kenneth Sills vowed that Bowdoin would keep alive the flame of liberal education.

This dilemma had been voiced by President Franklin D. Roosevelt to the college administrators in Baltimore in January, when he warned that while winning the war was imperative, it was no less essential to preserve those aspects of American life for which the war was being fought. How these two goals might be achieved at Bowdoin was the problem which K. C. M. S. placed before the Governing Boards and faculty. At a special session on February 7, the first such meeting since the one which had named him to the presidency in May, 1918, the Boards adopted the accelerated program and authorized the awarding of degrees at the end of the fall, spring, and summer trimesters.

They also followed the president's recommendation that members of the faculty and staff leaving to enter the service through draft or enlistment be fully compensated for the difference between their Bowdoin salaries and their pay received in the service. At his further suggestion, it was voted that the college assume whatever costs were required to prevent members of the faculty, while in their nation's service, from suffering any loss in retirement allowances.

Kenneth Sills's total identification of himself with his college led him to take for granted a similar commitment on the part of all his colleagues. Probably he had not even thought of additional compensation for those who were asked to teach in the summer trimester of 1942, but they responded unanimously and cheerfully, undertaking the extra instruction without salary. "The faculty adopts this obligation," reported Professor Edward Kirkland, chairman of the committee on summer plans, "not only because of its loyalty to Bowdoin, but also because of its devotion to higher education." He reminded the president, however, that "the present arrangement should be regarded as temporary." K. C. M. S. heeded the admonition. After the summer of 1942, members of the faculty received one-sixth of their base salary for six weeks of teaching in the summer trimester. Professor Roscoe Ham, who volunteered to offer a course in Russian, and Professor Wilmot Mitchell, who emerged from retirement to teach American literature, were surprised to receive checks for their services. "I thought an error had been made by the Bursar," the latter remarked to a colleague. "I've come to regard teaching at Bowdoin under President Sills as compensation in itself."

Proud that Bowdoin should have been the first college in Maine to announce plans for an accelerated program, K. C. M. S., in a broadcast from station WGAN on April 2, urged "those parents who are thinking of helping their sons to get a college education to consider most seriously enrolling them for the summer trimester." To his smaller audience of undergraduates in chapel, he promised that the college would provide "a maximum of information with a minimum of advice." This policy was welcomed on the campus where but a few months before there were objections to appeals from "arm-chair patriots" and gratuitous counsel from men too old to fight. "President Sills is keeping his door open to students at all hours," observed the editor of the *Orient*. "His judgment regarding the war, and the College during the war, has proved to be extremely accurate and wise. He is a fine leader and we are doing well in following him with all the cooperation we can give." Earlier a columnist had noticed some occasional "I-don't-like-the-draft" sniping by a few undergraduates, but such talk was rarely heard in the wartime college. Speaking in chapel on February 16 to students preparing to register for the draft, Kenneth Sills declared, "This is one of the darkest periods of modern history. If anyone here on December 7 had predicted that in less than ten weeks Japan could have overrun Malaya, captured Singapore, threatened the Dutch East Indies and Australia, and rendered us impotent to aid our valiant army in the Philippines, he would have been deemed a false and hysterical prophet. The peril is real and urgent, and those who register should feel it is not only a duty but a privilege to place themselves thus at the call of their country."

History was now repeating itself almost daily in Massachusetts Hall. In mid-March when a Sophomore, Walter F. W. Hay, Jr., called to say good-by before joining the Marines, the president told the youth that his father had come on the same errand just twenty-four years ago and returned to be graduated with his class. To all those leaving, K. C. M. S. promised to reserve places for them after the war. Dr. Daniel Evans, who visited the campus on April 16 as chairman of the Boards' examining committee, noted "much restlessness in the underclasses, and an eager desire on the part of upperclassmen to get into some branch of the service." The restlessness was not confined to the students whose uncertainties were often shared by their teachers. Philip Wilder

'23, the alumni secretary, after serving with the Red Cross since January, was commissioned by the Army in April. He was soon followed by Professor Boyd Bartlett '17, a physicist who had directed the C. A. A. pilot-training course, and was now called to West Point in June to teach electronics. A month later, when Professor Thomas Van Cleve, medievalist and veteran of the First World War, accepted a commission in military intelligence, the president reminded him, "This is the second time I have given you the blessing of the College in time of war." By the end of the spring trimester, K. C. M. S. had said farewell to ten of his colleagues headed for the armed forces or other forms of service.

Although the accelerated program meant the end of general examinations, and reduced the modern language requirements to an advanced knowledge of only one foreign language, K. C. M. S. rejoiced that the government had not requested the college to offer more specialized courses. When asked what provisions were being made to fit men for the armed forces, he could reply that Bowdoin had always given the fundamental training in mathematics, physics, and chemistry now so desperately needed by the Army and Navy. "We *are* shifting the emphasis in certain courses," he assured a group of alumni in Portland, "rather than introducing a number of new and fancy courses largely to attract public attention." Although the president conceded that techniques of rapid computation were essential, he said, "We are not offering a course in 'Swift Mathematical Computation 1'; instead, the Department in its regular work is giving special training along these lines. The same thing is true of the work in astronomy and navigation. The instructor makes in the old courses the necessary changes, and within the framework of the familiar tasks makes his students see the relation between what they are studying and their future work. This seems to many of us sounder educational policy and one way of preserving the essentials of a liberal education." Even the traditional requirement that all Bowdoin Freshmen study Greek or Latin or mathematics, which had often been cited as a mossy symbol of Bowdoin's stubborn conservatism, was now being hailed as "realistic" and "progressive." Those Freshmen who had elected mathematics, if only to avoid ancient languages, discovered when they reached camp that they possessed an open sesame to officers' training school.

Before the bombs fell on Pearl Harbor, Kenneth Sills had dreamed of a celebration of the 150th anniversary of the founding of the college to take place in 1944, but the war compelled a change in his cherished plans. "It will be impossible to put up the new buildings that we had contemplated, or to ask for any large sums of money," he told the Boards in May, 1942. "We shall probably have to be content with celebrating our birthday by emphasizing the things of the spirit, those characteristics, principles, and qualities that really count, by honoring the great teachers of the College, past and present, and by re-studying what we are trying to do and by adapting our educational policy to the strange new needs of the times." Bowdoin men were, however, unwilling to permit their president to forget that he had an anniversary of his own coming up. The Boards' excessive caution in delaying his election until after a probationary period as acting president had long been forgotten. For twenty-five years, ever since the illness of President Hyde in the spring of 1917, Kenneth Charles Morton Sills had been entrusted with the destinies of Bowdoin College. His grateful students, many of whom realized that they were living on borrowed time, wanted to show their affection here and now. Formal recognition could come later on the anniversary of his actual induction in 1943, but neither the faculty nor the student body was disposed to wait another year.

On the evening of May 1, 1942, while seventy-five faculty colleagues were paying their tributes at a silver anniversary dinner in the Moulton Union, several hundred students staged an impromptu rally of their own on the terrace outside with songs and cheers. "One of the most sincere and spontaneous demon-

strations in Bowdoin history took place last Friday evening," the
*Orient* reported. "The singing of 'Rise, Sons of Bowdoin,' written by the President, and the prolonged shouts of 'We Want
Casey!' certainly were enheartening in these times." When the
chants for "Casey" reached a crescendo that could not be denied,
the president appeared at the door to acknowledge their greeting.
He covered his embarrassment by remarking that it was sometimes a relief to be called away from a faculty meeting. After the
war, he said, there would be many more merry parties, but he
begged them not to remember him merely as "the President from
war to war." "Perhaps I should not detain you any longer from
your studies," he said. When the howls subsided, he concluded
solemnly, "I want you to know how happy your generous tribute will make Mrs. Sills. We are both proud to have a college
as fine as Bowdoin to serve as best we can."

Upon his return to the dinner, K. C. M. S. became increasingly
uncomfortable as the dean read congratulatory letters and tribute followed tribute. He fidgeted in his chair when Professor
Charles Burnett spoke of "the little nameless unremembered acts
of kindness and love" which had endeared him to the whole
community and helped to make his faculty a true fellowship. He
played fantastic tricks with his napkin when Austin MacCormick
praised the president's modesty and friendliness coupled with a
mind so good that it would have justified A-plus arrogance and
aloofness: "Some people forget how good 'Casey's' mind is because his character is so darned good. I used to think that there
could never be anything wrong with him until I remembered
that he is that most spectacular of all Nature's errors—a Maine
Democrat." He busied himself with his intractable pipe and
matches while Roy Elliott described him as a salutary mixture
of practicality and spirituality: "He has worked for the present
good, but at the same time he has stretched forth his hands toward
the Good that is beyond." It was only when Dean Nixon read
Professor Herbert Bell's words about Edith Sills that K. C. M. S.
appeared to be wholly at ease. Of the grace and charm which she

lent to Bowdoin life, of her sacrifices on its behalf, and of the impossibility of thinking or speaking of the president without thinking of her too—these were truths Kenneth Sills could endorse happily. Later that evening when he described the affair to Mrs. Sills, it was only by persistent prodding that he could be persuaded to recall any of the words that were said about him. "Everybody was very eloquent and generous about my administration," he finally reported, "but their praise, in a very real sense, was for the College."

Admiration of his leadership during the mounting student restlessness in 1942 was not limited to faculty and students. The Governing Boards, noting with surprise that K. C. M. S. was approaching his sixty-third birthday, recognized that the task of carrying the college through one world war was all that should be asked of one man. Yet they counted confidently on his continued service. "I hope that President Sills will have no more wars to interfere with the splendid routine he has established at Bowdoin," declared Judge John A. Peters of the Trustees, "and that after this is over he can carry on his fine work for many years." In commenting upon the recently established mandatory retirement age of seventy for all officers of the college, Judge Peters told Dean Nixon in April, 1942, "I am glad we reserved the right to continue a man beyond that age in 'special cases!' President Sills is a most 'special case.' It is fortunate that we have a head of the institution so competent to handle the administrative difficulties in this crisis."

Such difficulties would come soon enough, but the expected drop in enrollment did not occur in 1942. The student body of 578 men in March was actually increased to 585 when the fall trimester opened in September, enabling the college to close its books with a balanced budget. Although some members of his faculty complained that the president seemed to mope excessively over the annual budget, the threat of deficits concerned him less than the problem of morale. To a greater degree than was true of most of his contemporaries, Kenneth Sills sympathized with the distrust of glib slogans and emotional appeals held by a generation which had been disillusioned by the depression and brought up on the ideal of a warless world. The campus mood was voiced by a Senior, Donald Sears '42, who had listened to an address by Governor Sumner Sewall of Maine. A veteran of the First World War, the governor had told the Seniors they were fortunate to be living in "a grand world and one worth fighting for." "Yes, we agree with you," Sears replied, "but we don't dare admit idealism even to ourselves. This war we want to fight with a sullen collected anger. We want ideals kept to a minimum. That way it will hurt less to see them shattered." K. C. M. S. also understood the implicit aspirations in Richard Bye's Class Day oration in May. Directing his remarks to the older generation, Bye disgruntled some of them by asserting, "I can tell you that we are not going to fight to bring back *your* dreams. We shall be fighting with all our strength to have a chance to replace them with our own." President Sills, who had long been an advocate of lowering the voting age to eighteen, welcomed the views of the "angry young men." "It is a matter of simple justice," he said, "that those old enough to fight should have the privilege of exercising the franchise. Youth is unafraid of change and we live in a changing world. I have no fear of a Youth Movement. Young men between eighteen and twenty-one are better informed than many of their elders."

Whatever youth's reservations about the advice proffered by their elders, Bowdoin students made an exception of the counsel of their president. It is a measure of the cumulative influence of the character of Kenneth Sills that they crowded the chapel whenever he was scheduled to speak. They rarely hesitated to seek him out in his office or his home when they were troubled. As one of them was to write later, "Casey became a benign father image to me. It was hard for anybody to be untruthful or insincere in his presence. Perhaps his understanding and sympathy came from his passion for fairness; perhaps, although he never mentioned it, his strength derived from his religious faith. Amid our doubts and confusions, he seemed as rugged as the rock of ages. He was always *there*." Undergraduates also sensed that K. C. M. S. understood, perhaps because he had once shared them himself, their feelings of helplessness in the face of demands for vocational skills not provided in the Bowdoin curriculum. To those who asked what earthly good a liberal education would do a man behind a machine gun, he answered that "an education in principles and ideals gives the reason for his standing behind the machine gun for it explains why such action may be necessary." The president's humanistic training made complacency impossible for him. All his wartime utterances were impelled by what he believed to be his students' most desperate need: a sense of the things which, under whatever outward guise, are really enduring and imperishable.

Kenneth Sills was elated by the undergraduates' earnest work in the 1942 summer trimester, but he grew gloomy about the fortunes of war, fearing that the success of the Axis Powers in Egypt would prolong hostilities at least two or three years. "It has all been rather *grim*," he wrote Edith Sills from Washington on August 28. "There is a general feeling, along with a good deal of contradiction and confusion, that the draft age is going down to eighteen; the immediate future of the College is none too bright. The day is not too far off when every able-bodied individual must regard his days in college as pre-induction training." At the fall Commencement on September 12, when, for the first time in the memory of the alumni, Bowdoin baccalaureate degrees were awarded at a time other than in June, K. C. M. S. told the sixteen Seniors not to be misled by the current emphasis upon the useful as distinguished from the liberal arts. "I would not have you for a moment underestimate the worth of the education you have received in this college of liberal arts," he declared. "One of the contributing causes of the chaos in our modern world has been the fact that in so many nations, due to the first World War, thousands of young men and women grew to maturity without the kind of education that is rightly called liberal, and without having received in their early days the emphasis on the spiritual and ideal side of life."

Both the faculty and student body thought the president was unduly pessimistic in September when, despite a larger enrollment than was anticipated, he predicted that within a few months, probably by November, only a few regular students would be left on the campus. "In one way they were right," he conceded later. "I expected the change in November; it did not come until February, or in full force until March. Nevertheless there were signs and omens all about that college-as-usual was coming to a close." One such sign was the approval of the teenage draft bill by President Roosevelt on November 13. Three days later, in discussing the legislation in a chapel address, K. C. M. S. remarked, "One reason why the government did not grant deferment to college students was that the students themselves had not convinced the public of the value of a college career in wartime. The public believes colleges are places of special privilege." This impression, he feared, had been strengthened when President Seymour of Yale pleaded for the deferments of college men. "The colleges are going to be the last institutions to ask for special privileges," K. C. M. S. promised, "and Bowdoin will be the last of all to do so." As for the undergraduates, he said their responsibilities were plain: "It is only by living up to our conviction that what we are doing here is worth-while that we may avoid the tragedy of popular loss of faith in the value of a liberal education, the true education of free men in a free state."

Kenneth Sills would look back upon the mid-winter Commencement of January 25, 1943, the third graduation in eight months, as a symbol of the unprecedented times in which the college was doing unprecedented things. He attended the Class Day exercises in the morning, then hurried from Memorial Hall to conduct the Seniors' last chapel, and from thence to his lecture in Casey's Lit. At high noon he presided over the Commencement luncheon, and two hours later he conferred eighty-five degrees in a double-decker ceremony combining the graduation exercises with the James Bowdoin Day citations in honor of the ranking scholars. These duties over, he prepared to welcome the sixty-seven new Freshmen who arrived to join those who had entered in June and September. It was only with some effort that he remembered that the June Freshmen had already become Sophomores by completing two trimesters. His next task was to wrestle with the administrative problems brought on by the threatened dissolution of the student body in the coming spring trimester. K. C. M. S. spoke with his usual understatement when he told the New York alumni on January 29, "For every major problem to be decided twenty-five years ago, there are twenty-five to be decided today."

The enrollment of 471 at the opening of the term in January had fallen to 366 by February 24, and within the next six weeks sixty more reservists were called to active duty. Further withdrawals of men in the Naval Reserve and Marines led K. C. M. S. to predict that the civilian population of the campus would be reduced to about 150 for the summer and autumn trimesters. His estimate proved to be accurate: the average enrollment of civilian students for the academic year 1943–44 was 152 men. It was this slender band of those unable to serve in the armed forces, Freshmen under eighteen years of age, and reservists awaiting call that Kenneth Sills regarded as the group maintaining the continuity of the college. For them, he promised that Bowdoin would continue to give courses of its usual standard and scope in the liberal arts, not neglecting extracurricular activities and fraternity life, even though these would be in skeletal form. To be sure, the football team added another state championship to its record by defeating the University of Maine in 1942, but thereafter athletics were largely on an informal basis for the duration. With the departure of 316 men between December, 1942, and April 1, 1943, President Sills sought to preserve at least some semblance of fraternity life. "The welfare of the College and the welfare of the fraternities are bound together," he assured the students in chapel on March 1. Here, as in so many other matters, his experiences in 1917–18 stood him in good stead. Twenty-four years ago he had observed that men returning from the service, by resuming their places in their fraternities, became rapidly readjusted to college life and had not, as in many other colleges, formed divisive veterans' groups. "I am recommending to the Governing Boards," he reported in April, "that from June 1 the College will agree to pay all the carrying charges such as insurance, taxes, and interest on mortgages, and to return the houses at the end of the war in as good condition as we found them." He hazarded the hope that the war might help to democratize the fraternities, but reaffirmed his conviction that "In a college of our size, the division into fraternities, both from the standpoint of administration and from the social benefits to be derived, is on the whole satisfactory."

Although the shutters on Massachusetts Hall were tightly closed, campus air-raid wardens often detected lights burning late during the spring of 1943. Since the preceding October, K. C. M. S. and the bursar had been negotiating with the Army Air Force for the establishment of a basic premeteorology unit. The first detachment finally arrived in February, but only after the first letters of intent were substantially changed, courses drastically modified, and dates of arrival postponed. Meanwhile, additional burdens were placed upon Professor Nathaniel Kendrick, who had succeeded Professor Van Cleve as military adviser to civilian students. "The difficulties of his duties may be realized," President Sills remarked, "when it is remembered that from the time of our entrance into the war, December 7, 1941, until April 1, 1943, the government changed its collective mind twenty-seven times so far as undergraduates were concerned." For the inadequate administrative staff there were records to compile for men leaving for the service, rebates of term bills, the combining of fraternity dining clubs, the equipping of dormitories to serve as barracks, and the recruiting of additional teachers. Professor Edward Hammond, the academic director of the military training programs, was compelled to enlist the entire college departments of mathematics, physics, English, and history, with numerous borrowings from other fields of instruction. Amid this flurry of activity, Kenneth Sills was too busy to register more than mild consternation when he was asked to appoint several well-trained women to the faculty: Mrs. Marguerite Little and Miss Ruth Judkins in physics and Mrs. Marion Holmes in mathematics. There were, however, limits to Sillsean flexibility. The president's jaw was set when he warned the bursar, "I'm not going to have any WAVES or WACS around here!" K. C. M. S. who believed in running a small college with a genial margin of inefficiency, came to rely more and more upon his able bursar. "I do not know how we should have come out," he confessed in June, 1943, "had it not been for the patience, the attention to infinite details, and the business acumen of Mr. Glenn McIntire." There were moments, however, when the bursar had to ask his chief plaintively, "Am I the Comptroller or the Business Manager?"

In helping to formulate the curriculum in English and history for the premeteorology program, K. C. M. S. gave his blessing to the inclusion of books emphasizing the vitality of American institutions and American culture. He also found time enough to participate in the course of lectures, speaking to each successive detachment on Woodrow Wilson and the League of Nations. "It is wise to listen to well-reasoned prophecy," he told the soldiers in one of his talks. "In 1917 President Wilson predicted that a war more terrible than the one in which the world was engaged would be fought by your generation unless some organized plan of peace were inaugurated, but his predictions were ignored by the American people. In 1923 Wilson sorrowfully acknowledged that we turned our backs upon our associates at the close of the war by drawing into our shell of selfish isolation."

The establishment of the naval school in radio engineering in June, 1941, had encouraged the president to hope the Navy might choose Bowdoin for its well-planned V-12 program, but the presence of one naval unit on the campus made the college ineligible. There were, however, many reasons why he welcomed the detachment in premeteorology. "In the first place," he reported to the Boards in May, 1943, "the age is right, 18 to 21 years; in the second place, the unit is here for a full year; in the third place, probably sixty percent of the men have had college experience; and finally, the material studies are of college grade and may well be counted for college credit." Many members of the unit, despite a crowded forty-nine-hour class schedule each week, and a rigorous physical training program, managed to accept President Sills's repeated invitations to attend college lectures, plays, and concerts, and to snatch a few hours for browsing in the library. K. C. M. S. never lost his conviction that even a slight contact with humane studies might induce soldiers to begin or resume college education after the war, a belief which was confirmed when a number of the "pre-Metes" who had gone into the Army directly from high school were admitted to regular standing at Bowdoin in 1946. The men in uniform were quick to realize that President Sills's interest in their careers was neither perfunctory nor "official." Arthur Jaffe, editor of *The Meteor*, a mimeographed newspaper published by the unit, spoke for the whole contingent when he said of the president: "More men of his ability and foresight would make a world where men would not need to mix war and learning."

K. C. M. S. had less opportunity to judge the success of the army specialized training program. When the first unit of 200 men reached Brunswick in August, 1943, and the college was asked to prepare for a second detachment in March, he remarked to the bursar, "Only the Marines are needed to make Bowdoin an all-service college." The exigencies of war forced the Army to cancel the second unit, and on March 1 the whole program was abandoned. A week later the 200 men were ordered to a Southern camp for infantry training and thence to Europe where many of them were lost in the Battle of the Bulge. K. C. M. S.

had expected some curtailment of the Army plans, but he was unprepared for so drastic a measure. In three months the enrollment in the various training units had been reduced from 850 to 330 men. If 1942–43 had seemed the most critical of the war years for the college, the period from 1943 to 1944 certainly presented more problems. "Like business concerns, we have to convert and reconvert," the president reported to the Boards, "to build up organizations to instruct and to house and to feed all these trainees; and then to see such organizations dissipated with the possibilities that in a few weeks we may be asked to undertake instruction again or to receive another unit." These and subsequent uncertainties were recognized by Kenneth Sills as comparatively minor inconveniences to be borne cheerfully, but there were times in the spring of 1944 when he appeared tired and depressed. The strains showed when occasionally he set several staff members doing identical tasks, and he had to be reminded to include the names of the associate professors on the salary list for 1944–45. The bursar noted on his desk pad, "K. C. M. S. blue," "K. C. M. S. fretful," yet he marveled at the president's resilience. A night's rest or a round of golf seemed all that was needed for him to regain his vigor.

The perplexities of administration, however frustrating, were dwarfed in the president's consciousness by his grief at the lengthening roll of Bowdoin men lost in the war. Each of his annual reports was prefaced by the list of casualties, and each death was announced with heavy heart in chapel. When he was inaugurated in 1918, the gold stars on the service flag numbered twenty-nine; now, in November, 1944, there were forty-three, and the number would soon become ninety-four. Bowdoin's sons had long been accustomed to look to Kenneth Sills as the head of a closely knit family who shared their joys and sorrows. Throughout the long war years, as in 1917–18, he wrote letters in his own hand to all the bereaved parents. Invariably he found time to call upon the families of boys who died in camp or in action. "President Sills did a perfectly characteristic and wonderful thing while he was in Newark," wrote Andrew Rollins '19 following an alumni dinner in New Jersey on December 9, 1944. "A local Bowdoin boy was reported lost, and with all the things that the President has to do, he called upon the boy's parents. He didn't tell us, but all knew it, and I don't need to tell you the impression it made." His solicitude followed Bowdoin men everywhere. Gerhard Rehder '31, who was stationed in Italy in the closing days of the war, was not surprised to be asked by the president, "If you ever get to Rome, would it be possible for you to call on Senor Manfredi Azzarita, father of Manfredi Azzarita, of the Class of 1932, at Via Emmanuelo Gianturco? You may remember that Manfredi was slaughtered by the Germans in the caves outside Rome." To these sorrows were added the deaths of old friends on the Board of Overseers: George Cary '88, Wilbert Mallett '91, John Clair Minot and Sir Harry Oakes, of the class of 1896, Brooks Leavitt '99, and Lyman Cousens '02. In the more intimate circle of his faculty colleagues, the president mourned the passing in 1943 of the scholarly Arthur Gilligan, professor of French, and, in 1944, of Gerald Gardner Wilder, who was the same age as the president and who had been associated with the college library for forty-four years. K. C. M. S. could only reflect again on the strength of an institution able to continue its work in the face of so many heavy losses.

Shadows of war and bereavement conferred a special solemnity, but could not entirely darken the Commencement in May, 1943. Travel conditions and the scarcity of accommodations in Brunswick forced the president to urge all but local alumni to postpone their reunions until happier times. Hopefully, he said, the sesquicentennial in 1944 might also mark the end of hostilities and make next year's Commencement a triumphant homecoming. Those who did manage to return saw acceleration in full swing. The Seniors shared their Class Day program with those in the class of 1944 who were scheduled to receive their degrees in September and February. Of the 119 members of the class of 1943, fifteen had already been graduated in September, 1942, and seventy-eight others in February, 1943. The remnant was now augmented by twenty-eight men of the class of 1944, beneficiaries of the accelerated program who were enabled to complete their college course in three years. Bowdoin was continuing to march in double-quick time. The president reported that only sheer inspiration could have prompted an eager Freshman to write the dean of his desire to register for Bowdoin's "exhilirated course."

If the absence of Bowdoin men deployed around the globe gave the Commencement of 1943 its seriousness, the recognition of the twenty-five years of service of the president and the dean indicated that alumni had not forgotten their leaders on the home front. Kenneth Sills felt that his own silver anniversary had received more than enough attention, but he welcomed the privilege of conferring an honorary doctorate on Paul Nixon, citing him as a "Dean of Deans, witty, incomparable, understanding." Indeed, K. C. M. S. looked forward to presiding at the Commencement luncheon with more than his usual relish because he knew further tributes were in store for the fellow classicist he had appointed in 1918 to share his administration. These came in full measure, but the president soon discovered there were plans afoot to remind him of his own quarter-century of leadership. With growing apprehension, and discomfort, he was compelled to listen to scores of grateful letters assembled by his faculty from Bowdoin's far-flung family now extended from Brunswick to Buna, New Guinea. Although tributes poured in from the White House, the Supreme Court, and Congress, perhaps the most eloquent came from recent graduates now in the front lines, as if to confirm Robert Hale's remark that Kenneth Sills had helped "Bowdoin's brash blindmen of 1940 to become her heroes today." When the president was permitted to say a word himself, he responded simply by stating that the last twenty-five years had been happy ones because of the devotion of all those who shared his labors for the college. Of nothing was he more confident, he concluded, than the conviction that "the best days of Bowdoin College are clearly the days ahead."

His present concern, however, was with the next week rather than the next decade. Fluctuations in enrollment and the uncertain future of the army training program in 1943–44 strengthened his reluctance to plan for more than immediate needs. "The administration must keep its options open as never before," he told the faculty, "and simply cross the bridges as it comes to them." The fear, often voiced in academic circles, of winning the war and losing the peace failed to impress him. "We must remember that one of the most effective ways to lose the peace is to lose the war," he replied to an impatient undergraduate. "For the present and for the immediate future all our energies should be bent on winning the war." K. C. M. S. was especially cautious about yielding to the popular demands for postwar plans, despite some restiveness in his faculty. "I think it is well not to be too precipitate along these lines," he told his critics. "It is clearly too early to make definite blueprints or very clearly defined plans for postwar education, but it is not too early to be thinking of some problems that will be upon us after the victory is won." The urgency of one of these problems induced the president to change his mind about the need of appointing a college officer to assist undergraduates and alumni in finding positions in business, industry, and teaching. For many years such placement work had been carried on by the dean, who now estimated that while one-third of the alumni in the armed forces would resume their positions after the war, and another third would return to Bowdoin or enter graduate schools, the remainder had no idea what they would like to do and would be in need of expert help. Faced with this situation, K. C. M. S. finally agreed on the establishment of a placement bureau, and by April, 1944, its director, Samuel Appleton Ladd, Jr., was in communication with all Bowdoin men in the service.

Cautious as the president was about promising revolutionary changes in the postwar curriculum, he was convinced of the validity of a liberal education and its increasing importance in the future. "The college of liberal arts all over the country is showing both its vitality and versatility in the many ways in which it is contributing to the war effort," he reported to the Boards. "When the war is over there will be just as important service to render. If the mind is to be kept free, if intellectual curiosity and resourcefulness are to be encouraged, if idealism, not materialism, is to rule, and finally, if the past and present are to be properly interpreted in their relation to the future, liberal studies must not only be maintained but extended throughout the whole wide world." In the meantime, he strove to preserve both the quality and scope of instruction in the liberal arts even when the college numbered fewer than 150 men. While the emphasis was placed on the sciences for premedical students and for those expecting to enter technical branches of the service, K. C. M. S. made it clear that the exigencies of war did not demand that an undergraduate force himself to study mathematics or physics if nature clearly intended him to study the humanities. No matter how scanty the registration for any one subject, courses continued to be given in the ancient languages, and at least a handful of men were reading Homer, Plato, Dante, Chaucer, Molière, and Goethe in the original languages. Looking ahead to the postwar period, the president recommended that Bowdoin sponsor an institute for the appraisal of liberal education as one suitable way to observe the sesquicentennial in 1944. "It seems appropriate," he told the Boards, "to devote the Institute lectures to a consideration of what liberal education means, not so much to the College itself, as to the community, and as a symbol that we must be ready for peace in time of war."

Convinced of the value of continuity not only of the curriculum and of daily chapel but of all things connected with the college, K. C. M. S. encouraged the maintenance of many extracurricular activities. In the bleakest of the war years, musical and dramatic interests were sustained; athletic competition was kept alive, although Bowdoin often was the only college represented by teams composed wholly of civilians; fraternities continued to initiate new members, sometimes with delegations of only one or two neophytes; and the *Orient*, not infrequently with the desperate help of the faculty, preserved its record of continuous publication. "All this evidence points to the fact," the president assured the alumni, "that rarely has there been on the campus a happier group of undergraduates." He counted it as especially fortunate that the college itself was kept intact with no mixing of civilian and service men in the same classroom. Sometimes, he conceded, "the civilian and military do get confused," and he recalled an undergraduate going to a rehearsal of *A Bell for Adano*, in which he played the part of a lieutenant, being briskly saluted by an ensign in the naval unit. "To one unfamiliar with youth it would seem extraordinary that undergraduates now in college could get so much out of college life and work," he wrote in the spring of 1944. "It is a statement well within the bounds of accuracy to say that no other college has during the past year done more for its civilian students than has Bowdoin."

Acceleration's relentless pace slackened only momentarily as Bowdoin paused to observe its sesquicentennial on June 24, 1944. Kenneth Sills preferred to have it that way. Uncomfortable amid academic pomp and, as the Amherst delegate noted, "never one of the loud speakers of the American collegiate tribe," the president was pleased that the notable anniversary convocation met just as the work of the summer trimester was getting under way. A recital of Bowdoin's resourcefulness in confronting the changes of a century and a half would indeed have seemed to him hollow without evidence of her present contribution in the crisis. War duties prevented all but ten members of the class of 1944 from being present to receive their degrees, while seventy-one certificates of honor, one of them posthumous, were awarded to those who ordinarily would have been graduated. For the first time in Bowdoin's history, the Seniors were outnumbered by the recipients of honorary degrees. One of these guests, the

Earl of Halifax and chancellor of the University of Oxford, found a reassuring answer to this anomaly in the fact that more than 2,000 Bowdoin men were in uniform in all parts of the world. "The task of education," he said, echoing the words of President Joseph McKeen at the opening of the college in 1802, "is not, as I see it, to make good lawyers or good doctors or mechanics or chemists or businessmen; it is to make good citizens." Of all the tributes, perhaps the most memorable was not in the speeches or on the scrolls presented by the emissaries from sister colleges and universities, but came from a young Bowdoin soldier in Italy. "It is fitting," he wrote, "that a college that has grown up with our Republic should mark its anniversary with so many scattered over all the world fighting and working for the preservation of the ideals which the Republic and the College exemplify." Kenneth Sills carried this V-mail message in his waistcoat pocket throughout all the ceremonies commemorating Bowdoin's 150th birthday. It seemed to him somehow to justify the sesquicentennial celebration.

The remainder of the summer and the first few months of the autumn term followed what had now become a familiar wartime pattern. With an October enrollment of 196 men, a slight increase over that of the preceding trimesters, hopeful undergraduates began looking forward to the time when they would outnumber the 220 members of the surviving naval unit, but by April 1, 1945, the registration dropped to 160, a quarter of the normal size of the student body. Returning alumni, many of whom spent a day or two of their precious furloughs to visit the campus for a few hours, were astonished to see fraternity initiations held in faculty homes or the president's ballroom, to notice students seated in chapel with scant regard to class membership, and at the special Commencements, to watch degrees being conferred upon Seniors representing classes ranging from 1941 to 1946. Yet even casual observers were impressed by the camaraderie among Bowdoin students. "Perhaps it was the breaking down of class and fraternity distinctions," remarked the *Orient*, "perhaps the realization that Bowdoin's numbers were pitifully small led to a natural desire to stick together. 'Cal' classes and central dining rooms brought large segments of the student body, upperclassmen and freshmen alike, into close contact. An *esprit de corps* was bound to result."

The president was especially pleased at the results of his fraternity policy. He sent his congratulations to the three Bowdoin chapters which celebrated their centennials in the war years. "At Bowdoin we believe in the fraternities," he wrote in April, 1945. "Organizations do not last for so many years unless they have some good in them." In his report to the Governing Boards for 1944–45, he noted, "While in many other colleges there has been much excitement about the fraternity problem, and in some places agitation about the abolition of fraternities, at Bowdoin we have been quietly going along, helping the fraternities to maintain their continuity, and encouraging them to be ready for the postwar world." There was a large measure of truth in his assurances of the happiness of the student body, but all was not quiet on the home front as the winter of 1945 slowly wore into a reluctant spring. Kenneth Sills's invincible respect for tradition and his efforts to maintain the continuity of Bowdoin institutions did not go unchallenged by a generation which prized contemporaneity more than continuity. Crawford Thayer '44 was gently quizzical in the *Orient*. "The big impression left by the Sesquicentennial," he wrote, "was not how much the College has changed, but how little it has changed during the years."

Other campus critics wrote sharply about the lack of postwar planning. "What has Bowdoin got to show?" asked Philip Hoffman '45 in the *Orient*. "So far, just an eight-page report on what system of priority should be used in admitting students after the war, always assuming that we shall have more applicants than we can handle. We won't have unless we have something to offer them. Bowdoin seems very proud of its being very slow to make changes. There are even those starry-eyed alumni who would like to see Bowdoin 'just like it was before the war.' It's about time we saw some specific proposals on how to make Bowdoin qualitatively superior to its rivals in the postwar era." The *Orient* reflected the general discontent: news from Europe continued to be bad in January, twenty-five men had left college since the Christmas recess, and the 4-F students fretted over their books while defense plants clamored for workers. The restiveness produced a bumper crop of letters to the editor, bristling with demands that K. C. M. S. institute courses in general education, establish a publicity bureau, add a psychiatrist to the staff, and plan for an expanded enrollment which would be less predominantly New England. The dissidents who beat a path to his office were reminded more than once that while student opinion is always interesting and sometimes valuable, it is never conclusive. To those urging curricular changes, K. C. M. S. replied, "Changes will not be so revolutionary as in some other colleges because for many years the core of the curriculum has been planned so as to furnish an introduction at least to the important fields of knowledge." As for expansion, he promised a policy of "utmost flexibility," but warned there were reasonable or practical limits. His insistence that Bowdoin remain a small college drew support from the press. "We think Dr. Sills shows an informed solicitude," wrote the editor of the *Springfield Union*, "in resisting unwonted and unwanted changes and expansion for Bowdoin. . . . Perhaps too many of us confuse physical immobility with stagnation."

Problems of future expansion were far from the president's mind on May 4, 1945, when he left Brunswick to address the Bowdoin alumni in Washington, D.C. Wondering where students for the next fall would be found, he had planned to tell the graduates of the difficulties of keeping the college alive and of his worries about finances and prospective deficits. On the morning of Monday, May 7, however, Congressman Robert Hale '10 brought news of the collapse of Germany, and in the afternoon they went to the Senate chamber hoping to hear President Truman announce the end of hostilities. That evening, at the Bowdoin dinner, K. C. M. S. tempered his rejoicing over the momentous events. "With the terrible war in the Orient still going on, and with the selective service act still in force," he said, "it is difficult to foresee any great change in the College next year." The principles of continuity and flexibility upon which he had relied during the trying years of the war still seemed viable. "In the present confused state of education," he remarked, "we are still obliged to plan for next week as well as for next year." At midnight, Dean Paul Nixon telephoned to describe the mood of the students as one of gratitude, but "a strange gratitude, qualified and somber." On his trip back to Brunswick, K. C. M. S. recalled he had also been away on December 7, 1941. Perhaps on V-J Day he would be on the campus to hear the chapel bells himself.

Three weeks later, at Bowdoin's fourth wartime Commencement, there were solemn reminders that the nation was still at war. Only ten Seniors of a class originally numbering 152 could be present to receive their degrees from the president, who awarded 135 certificates of honor, including six posthumously. His tribute to Bowdoin's war dead, now numbering sixty-five, and Admiral Ernest King's warning that mountains of men and supplies must be moved long distances to end the war in the Pacific were sobering intimations of past sacrifices and future losses. Yet there were hopeful signs. In his state-of-the-college address, K. C. M. S. promised that the college would continue its year-round program as long as veterans returned from the service in any large number. He foresaw "more emphasis upon those studies that make for gracious living, such as art, music, and the drama." The coming summer term, he predicted, would be characterized by a sober optimism.

The session began normally enough on June 18 with an enrollment of 154 men. The president came as close to optimism as he was ever to come when he discussed finances, conceding that despite his earlier fears, the deficit for the past year was "only slightly in excess of $15,000," and that the Boards had made no provision for a possible reduction in faculty salaries. Indeed, there were times, in the few weeks before V-J Day on August 14, that he almost succeeded in persuading himself that he was presiding over a college functioning quite normally. Undergraduates were back in their own chapter houses for the summer, there were petitions to resume intercollegiate football in the autumn, the yearbook was revived as a paperback, and the *Orient* began printing—an infallible sign of normalcy— the usual number of protests against compulsory chapel and the lack of adequate campus drainage, lighting, and college publicity. "We are having a very normal summer session here, with a good deal of activity one way or another," K. C. M. S. wrote Lieutenant Rehder, hungry for Bowdoin news in Italy, "but there is nothing of great importance to report. Blessed is the college whose annals are uneventful!" Normal, too, but in the president's opinion hardly newsworthy, were persistent rumors that the State Democratic Committee had chosen him to head the party ticket in 1946. "I am not a candidate for Governor—now or anytime," he informed the political editor of the *Portland Sunday Telegram*. "Furthermore, I am not even eligible for the Governor's post as I was born in Halifax, Nova Scotia. Under Maine law, the Governor must have been born in the United States." If the summer days had seemed to slip by uneventfully, their placidity ended with the mushroom clouds over Hiroshima and Nagasaki. This time, unlike that fateful December 7, 1941, the president was in Brunswick. "Peace must be the result of human understanding, and not fear of eventual annihilation," he told the student body in chapel. "The atomic bomb itself should be placed under the jurisdiction of the Security Council of the United Nations so that we may prevent its wanton use by some wanton power."

On August 16 he summoned the college community to a service of thanksgiving to mark the end of the war. "This is an occasion to which Americans have been looking forward for almost four years, our British cousins for nearly six years, and our valiant Chinese allies for more than eight years," he said. "With the final and complete surrender of the Japanese, we can say with the Psalmist, 'This is the day the Lord hath made. We will be glad and rejoice in it.' Never has so much been due to so many. Yet after all our deepest gratitude goes out to the men not returning. Here at Bowdoin we think today of the seventy-seven sons of the College who have given their lives that we and our sons may enjoy the blessings of liberty. And so it is with very sober and with very thankful hearts that we approach the end of the combat, dedicating ourselves to the cause of peace and national unity with as much devotion as we as a people have shown from Pearl Harbor to V-J Day."

# 14

## CONTINUITY AND CHANGE
### 1945-1952

Kenneth Sills had not only brought the college through two world wars, he had also witnessed, after the first one, the collapse of Wilson's foreign policy and the rise of isolationism. Amid the jubilation following V-J Day, he told the student body that his experience in the 1920s had taught him that the nation would find it much harder "to maintain unity of thought and effort, and to put aside selfish aims than it was during the combat." To those eager to hear about postwar plans for Bowdoin, he replied that he was more concerned with avoiding postwar complacency than with planning a postwar curriculum. Earlier, at the memorial services for Franklin D. Roosevelt on April 15, he had pointed to "the disastrous consequences of the reactions that came after the death of Abraham Lincoln and after the close of Woodrow Wilson's administration." "We must not," he warned, "let the same thing happen a third time." In his Commencement address on October 6, he cited the failure of the council of foreign ministers in London and the industrial strife at home as melancholy evidence that "we still are very far from any real cooperation, either national or international." "Nations, including our own," he charged, "are still seeking their own interests, apparently without regard for the good of the whole. Certainly we should not shrink back to a situation where isolation will play the dominating role. Young men completing their college course this fall must feel bewildered indeed."

Outwardly, however, Bowdoin's first peacetime Commencement since 1941 did not vary from the interim graduation exercises during the war. Of the sixteen Seniors, nine received their degrees *in absentia*, one being awarded posthumously to William Muir '44 who was killed on Okinawa in June. K. C. M. S. welcomed the brief interval between the summer and autumn terms in 1945 as the only period in four and a half years when instruction had not been going on without interruption except on Sundays and at Christmas. "The buildings themselves," he said, "seemed to give a sigh of relief." For a few days the campus was strangely quiet. On October 1 the departure of the last detachment of officers in the naval radar school left the college without men in uniform for the first time in almost four years. The air of strangeness persisted when the new term began on October 15. The enrollment of 312 men included 103 veterans, many of whom had been away for several years instead of the few days between semesters. For them, the falling acorns and the scent of smoke from the burning leaves on the campus paths—sweetly remembered Bowdoin symbols in far-away places—were now poignantly real. While some servicemen expressed doubts about their ability to do good college work, the president soon discovered that all they really needed was encouragement. He now felt justified in having shrugged off as premature proposals that he appoint a psychiatrist to meet the needs of the veterans. "The experience of the College," he assured the Bowdoin teachers club a month after the start of the term, "is that the veterans constitute no administrative problem, and are in need of nowhere near the aid that some college people thought would be necessary." Indeed, many veterans greatly improved the standard of their preservice grades, and the acting dean, Professor Nathaniel Kendrick, reported that the wives of servicemen were proving to be attractive and persuasive "assistant deans." One such wife, Edith Sills delightedly told the president, excused her absence from a party at 85 Federal Street by saying ingenuously, "*We* had to study for an hour exam that evening."

K. C. M. S. knew he would be unlikely to see another student body approaching in its constituency the college of 1939. "Conversion will be a long and difficult process," he predicted to the Governing Boards. "It will be long because probably for a decade veterans will form a very substantial and very influential part of our undergraduate body. There will be difficulties because we do not yet know whether there will be a universal military service law. Consequently it is easy to understand that there will be the same need of flexibility in educational matters after the war as has been manifest during the war." In looking ahead for the next ten years, he envisaged a college calendar of three terms—fall, spring, and summer—with men entering Bowdoin three times a year. Such a prospect, he confessed to the faculty, was a discouraging one, noting that "The number of honor students had declined under the accelerated schedule, a decline undoubtedly due to the fact that the students had not enough time for reflection and sustained study and independent work." Yet the president promised, "Whether the College is on a two-term schedule, an accelerated program, or a combination of both, we shall endeavor to maintain standards; we shall avoid cutting corners, and we shall insist upon no diminution of the work required for the bachelor's degree." Meanwhile, as the world moved from a fighting war to an inconclusive peace, the pressures for admission seemed to Kenneth Sills little less than fantastic. The handful of ten veterans in the 1945 summer session was joined by 103 in October, and by 335 more in April, when they constituted more than three-fifths of the student body, a proportion which was to increase with each succeeding term. This influx of servicemen was accompanied by an unprecedented demand for admission by high school graduates, who overwhelmed the office with 850 applications for the 150 places available in the entering class for the fall of 1946. If the president believed that only those colleges with uneventful annals are truly blessed, Bowdoin was hardly enjoying a state of grace. He counseled the Boards and faculty to be of good cheer. "Whatever the difficulties, however complex the problems," he wrote in May, 1946, "one can repeat the well-known words of

Winston Churchill after Dunkirk, 'No matter what may come nor how perilous the times may be, I find the situation exhilarating.' "

Exhilaration, however, was not his prevailing mood. There were times when Kenneth Sills felt depressed and lonely. With President Ernest Martin Hopkins' retirement from Dartmouth in November, 1945, he was startled to realize that he had become, in length of service, the senior college president in New England, and he had seen every New England college change its leadership, several of them more than once. "Dr. Hopkins has been my close friend and one of my chief counsellors over the years," K. C. M. S. told an *Orient* reporter. He continued to grieve over the growing number of Bowdoin's war casualties. By November 11, eighty-two were known to have died, and those reported missing would ultimately bring the total to ninety-four. At the memorial service, now called Veterans' Day, he read the names of all the sons of the college who lost their lives in both world wars. Commenting upon the impressive ritual which K. C. M. S. had inaugurated in 1918, the *Orient* remarked, "Probably we all silently resolved as President Sills read the list of Bowdoin's dead in World Wars I and II that this time we should establish not just an Armistice but a peace." The president's seniority also meant changes which were no less sorrowful because they were inevitable. Of his former Bowdoin teachers from 1897 to 1901, only the *emeriti*, William Moody and Wilmot Mitchell, were still living. The death of Professor Charles Burnett in January, 1946, removed the last of those colleagues who had welcomed him to the faculty in 1906. Retirement also thinned the ranks of the president's old and intimate friends in the active faculty. Professors Roscoe Ham and Frederic Brown became *emeriti* in 1945, and were followed a year later by Manton Copeland and Phillips Mason. "The ties that bind together the members of a small college faculty are different from those of any other calling," Kenneth Sills said. "We see one another almost daily; we are intimately associated in the work we share in common; we are a closely knit community. Such ties are not easily broken." On more than one occasion, K. C. M. S. may have wished he could grant the plea of a young graduate on duty in the Pacific, begging him to preserve intact the prewar college. "Don't you let anybody change it," he urged. So human a desire touched the president, but his answer was firm. "One thing seems clear to me," he wrote, "it is wishful thinking to believe that we shall return to the situation that existed before the war. We must gird ourselves for new tasks, new problems, new responsibilities."

Of these problems, the most immediate was that of admissions. The enrollment of 655 men in the 1946 summer term already exceeded the normal size of the college in prewar years. The fall semester began in October with 966 students, four-fifths of whom were veterans. At the first chapel service which had to be moved to the First Parish Church to accommodate the student body, the president recalled that he had once vowed he would never permit Bowdoin to become a college of more than 600 men. But, as he had said wistfully to the Boston alumni in the preceding April, "Normal college years as we have known them will perhaps never be seen again." Happily, by a combination of what K. C. M. S. described as "good luck and foresight," the college was able to lease the officers' barracks at the recently deactivated Brunswick Naval Air Station. There, 150 veterans were housed comfortably, while many of the 110 married students found quarters in apartment houses and at Jordan Acres, a housing project made available when naval families were transferred from Brunswick. "So we have not had to double up students in dormitories," the president reported to the Boards, "nor to bring on to the campus unsightly, temporary buildings, nor to house students miles away. Anyone who has been at different institutions of learning . . . will easily understand how fortunate we are in this respect."

Kenneth Sills regretted that he had not shown similar foresight or been equally as fortunate in anticipating the mounting pressures on the admissions office. His promise of priority to former students in the service and to those who had been formally admitted but were prevented from entering Bowdoin after their graduation from high school left little room for the usual number of Freshmen coming up each year from preparatory and high schools. "Next fall the demand for admission is likely to reach a peak," he told the alumni council on March 8, 1946, "and the College is frankly puzzled how to meet it." The problem was plain enough. Since Pearl Harbor about 800 men had left Bowdoin with a varying number of credits. Some had been in college only a year, and many for even shorter periods. "Clearly these men will have first claim on us," K. C. M. S. stated in the autumn of 1945. In addition to this considerable group, the college was committed to accept at least 150 high school graduates who had certificates of admission but were inducted into the armed forces before they could begin their Freshman year. Furthermore, the president knew it was essential for Bowdoin to keep her contacts with the schools from which the college usually admitted from 175 to 200 Freshmen each fall. These pressures were intensified by the enthusiasm of the alumni who were persuading more and more promising boys to apply for admission. "Alumni are placed in a somewhat difficult position," Walter Emerson '11 told the Bowdoin Club of Chicago in April, 1946, "by being urged to persuade boys to attend Bowdoin while being compelled to inform these boys that they probably could not be admitted." Other graduates, who had moved outside of New England and were eager to have their Alma Mater better known in their areas, were asking the college to admit more students from the South and the Middle and Far West, even if this meant an expanded student body. Still others, equally devoted to the college, were critical of Bowdoin's "old-fashioned curriculum" with its larger number of required courses than at other institutions, and the reluctance of the administration to appoint guidance and publicity experts to the staff.

President Sills addressed himself manfully to these and related questions during his appearances at alumni dinners throughout 1946–47. He urged alumni to continue their recruitment of able candidates, even though not a few were bound to be disappointed. "We have always encouraged our graduates to send their sons to Bowdoin in the fall," he said. "For the past ten years about one-sixth of each entering class was composed of such sons. In truth, we are perhaps guilty of extending to these applicants an unfair amount of consideration. We all want to have the family tradition continued, but we must find room for boys who will begin a new Bowdoin line. Here, as in so many other instances, the alumni must show patience and understanding." Replying to those who asked why Bowdoin could not safely expand the normal size of her student body to 800 men, K. C. M. S. defended his plan to have the college return to the prewar limit of about 600 by a gradual reduction in numbers after the emergency. The present suspension of the policy of limited numbers, however necessary as long as veterans were returning in droves, could not, the president insisted, be extended beyond 1949 without seriously diluting the quality of a Bowdoin education. "Although there is nothing sacrosanct about numbers," he remarked in 1946, "standards count for more, and I am sure that no Bowdoin graduate would wish to see this flag lowered. The college can do its best work if the numbers are nearly commensurate with facilities. We believe in Bowdoin as a small college of liberal arts with reasonably high standards. We have no desire to become 'big.'" As for the danger of fostering a Down East provincialism in a college composed predominantly of New Englanders, the president conceded that an increase of students from outside New England would have a valuable leavening influence. "But it should be kept in mind," he said proudly and perhaps nostalgically, "that Bowdoin is the one small college for men only in the country that is New England in its location, New England in its tradition, and New England in its constituency."

One element of this New England heritage was a Yankee-like

aversion to spending income on nonessentials. "The modern college is expected to render so many services unheard of in earlier days," K. C. M. S. protested to the Boards in 1948, "such as the work that is carried on in the alumni office, the placement bureau, and whatever is done in public relations, that too often the teacher is the forgotten man." Although the president had finally yielded to persistent pressures from the alumni council when he established the placement bureau in 1944, it was only after he had fought a long delaying action. Two years later, under even more intensive pressures from the Boards and many alumni, he was compelled to abandon his cherished policy of assigning a fair share of teaching duties to virtually all administrative officers. He confessed that he had been remiss earlier in failing to provide adequate assistance to the director of admissions, an error in judgment for which he made partial amends in 1947 by appointing an officer to devote his full time to this work. Within the short space of a year, the admissions problem had grown so exacting that the full energies of two administrative officers were barely sufficient to cope with the flood of applications, interviews with candidates, and visits to schools. The president continued to guard against the dangers of a top-heavy administration. "Whenever I see on a college campus the administrative building occupying too much space," he warned the Boards in 1948, "I wonder a little about the teaching being done at that college. It must never be forgotten that the college in actuality consists of those who teach and of those who are taught, and that the only way to improve a college is to improve the quality of the teaching and the quality of the students."

The president's policy drew criticism from alumni who felt the college should provide its students with more counseling, especially vocational guidance. Although he recognized an element of justice in these views, he preferred to err on the side of too little rather than too much. "The College may very easily furnish too much counsel," he told the Boards' committee on educational policy, "and thereby prevent the student from de-

veloping his own powers of initiative and judgment. I am somewhat skeptical even of the battery of tests that some institutions require. . . . In school there is much need of such guidance; in college a man has got to stand on his own feet, learn to be responsible
for his own decisions and profit by his own failures." K. C. M. S.
was even more doubtful about the value of establishing a public relations office. "Publicity of the right sort is certainly desirable," he
told the Alumni Council, "but the College must be very careful not
to expand too rapidly in departments that are not vitally concerned
with instruction." When the editor of the *Orient,* unimpressed
by budgetary considerations, demanded "a public relations office
which will tell the nation the daily story of Bowdoin," the president remarked that "the daily story" of any good college is neither
sensational nor newsworthy. Prodding by the *Orient* continued,
however. Complaints about the lack of college publicity became
as perennial a topic for editorial crusades as the paucity of promising halfbacks in the Freshman class. Eager to goad K. C. M. S.
into action, a reporter asked Harry Shulman, the Brunswick correspondent of the Associated Press, "What are some of the important changes you have noticed at Bowdoin?" "That is one of
the big troubles," Mr. Shulman replied. *"It doesn't change.* There
is a remarkable lack of appreciation of the college for favorable
publicity." To this criticism, the president had an invariable reply: "A new administrative officer means a new office, a new
secretary, and all other expenses that go with the necessity of
conducting affairs satisfactorily. We must be very careful in
balancing the different demands upon the college appropriations
to see that teaching is strengthened above everything else."

The primacy of teaching had long been of central concern to
the president whose preference for "great teaching in wooden
halls to wooden teaching in marble halls" was his most frequently
quoted aphorism. Although equally concerned with what is
taught, he foresaw no need of a brave new curriculum for a brave
new world. "Unless we have been decidedly off the track in the
education given here in the past," he said to the alumni in October,

1945, "we need no general revision of the curriculum or radical changes, though we must, of course, as in the past plan for new courses and perhaps from time to time for the introduction of new subjects." Kenneth Sills was proud of the remarkable stability of the Bowdoin curriculum. For almost thirty years, despite many alterations in details, the requirements for admission and for graduation, the Freshman program, the distribution requirements, and the regulations governing the field of concentration had remained essentially unchanged. K. C. M. S. was aware that such adherence to familiar patterns could be dismissed as merely resistance to change. He had watched sympathetically while countless faculty committees had fashioned the curriculum over a long period, and he was convinced their work was sound. At a time when many institutions were rushing into print with brightly labeled innovations, he was delighted to encounter an unexpected tribute to Bowdoin's conservative tradition from Yale's distinguished anthropologist, Dr. Albert Keller. After praising the Hyde-Sills policy of getting good teachers and then letting them alone, Professor Keller wrote, "Education runs to quantity and ostentation, but I think Bowdoin has stuck to quality. No fads that I know of, and no *education by sprawl*." Yet Kenneth Sills would have been disappointed had Bowdoin not shared the seething introspection common to all colleges after the war. Fully a year before V-J Day, he had set committees at work to determine what Bowdoin's obligations to the national demands and to her own standards should be in the next decade. "We must make sure," he told the faculty, "that our educational policy is adapted to the changing conditions."

A few months after the war, K. C. M. S. gave his blessing to a recommendation that beginning with 1947 the college discontinue granting the degree of bachelor of science. "The distinction between the A.B. and the B.S. has long been obsolete," he advised the Boards. "The B.S. does not denote knowledge of science; it merely expresses ignorance of Latin. It is indeed incongruous that a graduate might have as his major field economics, history,

government, philosophy, romance languages or English literature, and because he had not pursued Latin for four years is
*mirabile dictu* given a degree of Bachelor of Science." The
faculty, however, stoutly refused to abandon the requirement
that all Freshmen elect mathematics or Latin or Greek. Perhaps,
the president remarked wryly to the Dean, this rule may salvage
something of the value of the classical languages. In the teaching
of modern foreign languages, he persuaded the Boards to provide
for additional emphasis on oral and aural training as one of the
lessons gained from the Army-sponsored Language and Area
Studies during the war. He also supported the retention, despite
pleas by the proponents of courses in general science, of the requirement of at least a year's study of a laboratory science—
biology, chemistry, or physics. He further urged that as soon
as funds were available courses in geology and geography be introduced. With only a mild hope of its adoption, he appointed
a special committee to formulate proposals for a course in general
education.

Perhaps the most striking evidence of Bowdoin's attachment to
the conservative tradition was the hesitation of the faculty to
embark upon any program of general education even at a time
when the excitement attending such innovations was presented
in impressive documents by Columbia, Harvard, and Dartmouth.
The committee's first proposal, a two-semester sequence of lectures involving all departments and designed to interpret Western
civilization, was approved by a margin of only three votes. "I am
unwilling," K. C. M. S. told his colleagues, "to bring before the
Governing Boards a proposal upon which the Faculty is so evenly
divided." Seeking more decisive support, the committee submitted, after a year's deliberation, three new proposals: a Fresh-
man-Sophomore survey of world history, a year course in problems of the twentieth century, and an interdepartmental offering
entitled "Centers of Culture." The faculty, however, again failed
to agree when a core of twenty-four of its members voted against
any form of general education. Later in the spring, with prodding

by the president, a compromise proposal of a course on some unifying theme to be presented by lectures from outside as well as within the faculty was endorsed "in principle" but without enthusiasm. Throughout the protracted discussions extending intermittently over two years, Kenneth Sills had given his faculty free rein. Professor Keller's remark that Bowdoin's president had "no yen for dictatorship" was an understatement. Finally, on January 19, 1948, when the committee asked to be discharged, K. C. M. S. showed no signs of disappointment. He knew that academic graveyards were crowded with decently interred educational programs which once had been heralded as ideal. He had retained his faith in the Bowdoin curriculum, which provided students with training in the basic skills and an acquaintance with several important areas of learning in the first two years, and in the upperclass years with an opportunity to gain a reasonable mastery of a single, integrated field. He believed that the indecisive wrestling with the various proposals in general education had not been entirely futile. Emerging from the faculty discussions were hopeful signs of the breaking down of departmental lines and the promise of programs in such fields as American civilization. "There is general agreement," he reported to the Boards in May, 1948, "that in every course more of an effort should be made to interpret the present in the light of the past, and to emphasize the importance of preserving all that is good in Western civilization and culture."

These developments, however, would depend upon a reduction in the size of the student body. When the autumn term began in 1947, with a registration of 1,086 undergraduates, the *Orient* grew impatient. "We had fully expected that Bowdoin would withstand pressures from all sides and maintain her high standards," the editor lamented on October 1, "but we find that she has succumbed to the popular demand and abandoned her advantages." President Sills refused to take so dim a view. Noting that veterans now constituted a minority of the entering students, he assured the faculty that "The period of expansion is over

and the period of contraction has begun." The swollen enrollment proved to be scarcely less embarrassing than the reduced
numbers had been after the cancellation of the military programs
in 1944–45. K. C. M. S. warned in February, 1948, that if the
present rate of admission were continued for a few years, the
college would become twice the optimum size of 600 men which
had been contemplated by the Governing Boards. Accordingly,
the Boards set a strict limitation on the number of Freshmen for
the next three years, in order to achieve a student body of about
750 men by the fall of 1950. So stringent a policy added to the
dilemmas of the admissions office, which had only 185 places for
more than 1,200 applicants, but it was welcomed by the president
even though he was compelled to revise his conception of Bowdoin as a small college. "A normal Bowdoin," he told the faculty,
"may mean about twenty-five per cent more members than the
pre-war limit of 600." Perhaps he found some comfort in recalling that when his friend President James Phinney Baxter faced a
similar problem at Williams, he remarked, "A small college is
whatever size Williams is!"

Meanwhile, K. C. M. S. reminded students that despite its un-
wieldly numbers, Bowdoin still sought to maintain the atmosphere
of a small, friendly college. In his opening address on October 1,
he urged undergraduates to get to know their teachers in and out
of the classroom. Warning that comprehensive examinations
would be resumed with the class entering in 1948, he declared,
"With so many eager to enter college it is not fair for those of
you who are here to abuse your privileges. The College will
gladly accept the resignation of any student who feels dissatisfied
or who for any reason is unable or unwilling to work." Perhaps no
one in his audience suffered more keenly from the burden of excessive numbers than the president himself. He found it difficult to
preserve the atmosphere of an intimate college when many students did not know their teachers and often did not know each
other. He was also pained to see the fraternities become mere
eating clubs, rather than the closely knit social groups which had

meant so much to their members in less hectic days. Although accustomed to large enrollments in his own course in comparative literature, he was dismayed to learn that a colleague, after teaching more than 100 students of the English novel, in the next hour lectured to a class of 170 men in American literature. Other sources of concern were the overcrowded dormitories and chapter houses. Even though the housing arrangements at the airport were better than the temporary quarters at many colleges, K. C. M. S. fretted at the anomaly of calling Bowdoin a residential college while a substantial number of students were forced to live off campus. While he had no wish to place the convenience of the college ahead of its obligations, he was convinced that the double strain of continuous operation and an awkwardly large student body could be justified only by the emergency.

The disproportion between the size of the college and its resources of personnel and equipment was worrisome enough, but Kenneth Sills was more distressed by less tangible consequences. At times he felt as though he were presiding over a strangely impersonal institution. It was disconcerting to cross the campus without being able to greet most students by name, or to award diplomas to Seniors he seemed to be meeting for the first time at the moment of their graduation. Since the system of comprehensive examinations could not be combined with the accelerated program, he felt that the Bowdoin degree often meant little more than the amassing of requisite credits, rather than the logical ordering of knowledge during a two-year study of an integrated field. The president also deplored the changing pattern of faculty life. The increased number of teachers and the rapid growth of Brunswick made it impossible for most of the faculty to live near the campus, where they would always be accessible to students. Nor was it any longer feasible for Kenneth and Edith Sills to continue their charming custom of walking from house to house and leaving a wreath at the door of each member of the college community at Christmas time. K. C. M. S. was happiest when he was able to share the joys and problems of all those associated with Bowdoin, but he was now compelled more than occasionally to rely upon card files for details which hitherto he had absorbed unconsciously. Heads of larger institutions often envied Bowdoin as small enough to enable its president, by the cumulative force of his own character, to touch intimately the lives of almost every one of its members. K. C. M. S. hoped he would not be the last of such presidents. As he approached his sixty-ninth birthday in 1948, he sometimes wondered whether he would ever be permitted to see the return of the old Bowdoin he knew best where, in the words of President Hyde, "small groups of students . . . according to the original meaning of the word *college*, live together in mutual good will, in friendly helpfulness and in earnest study."

Not so the Governing Boards who had come to regard Bowdoin's presidents as indestructible. Had not William DeWitt Hyde served for thirty-two years, while his successor had been in office for a mere thirty? Yet all the Trustees, and forty-two of the forty-five Overseers had been elected during the administration of Kenneth Sills, and only a thinning remnant of alumni could remember Bowdoin under any other leadership than that of Hyde and Sills. For sixty-three years every diploma had borne one of these two names. But Bowdoin's presidents are elected for five-year terms, and the examining committee, in May, 1948, reported that President Sills's current term of office would expire on June 30 when the bylaws decreed, "he must be reappointed or dropped." Such reappointments had been made every five years since 1918, but in June the Boards were aware that at the end of another term of five years, Kenneth Sills would be more than three years above the retirement age of seventy. The Trustees and Overseers, however, had their eyes fixed upon a different and more compelling calendar. September, 1952, would mark the 150th anniversary of the opening of the college. "Even to suggest retirement," remarked William Witherle Lawrence, "would be like retiring Massachusetts Hall or the Chapel." When K. C. M. S. took his usual place to preside over the Trustees' meeting on

June 4, he found a note awaiting him. It contained a single sentence: "The best interests of the College unquestionably require that President Sills be continued as its President so long as his health and strength will permit him to discharge the duties of that office, and that it may properly be left to him whether he shall continue to serve the College until the expiration of another five-year term." Clearly, Bowdoin expects a great deal of her presidents, and the Boards, confident of his acceptance, burst into applause as K. C. M. S. called the meeting to order. Later, when he told the faculty of his reelection, Professor Robert Coffin noted, "He reported the good news as apologetically as if he were announcing a cut in our salaries."

Salaries had, in fact, been increased by 10 percent in 1946, and in February, 1948, by an additional grant for the increase in the cost of living, but K. C. M. S. was finding the task of recruiting new members of the faculty more difficult than usual. "There is very much more competition," he warned the Boards in May, 1948, "not only from the government, but from industry, particularly in the fields of physics, chemistry, economics, and psychology. Furthermore, the great demand for college teachers has raised the salary scale in many institutions so that whereas before the war one could estimate that an instructor's compensation on first appointment would be about one-third that of a full professor, today one must raise that estimate to one-half." The need of increased endowment to provide more adequate salaries, although nearest to his heart, was only one of the problems faced by the President as he began the thirty-first year of his administration. There was also a desperate need of funds for modern buildings. Great teaching in wooden halls was doubtless preferable to wooden teaching anywhere, but K. C. M. S. knew that good teachers deserve good tools. "With the increased cost of maintenance and material, with the competition from other institutions that have better buildings and that often strive to lure away members of our faculty," he told the alumni, "this is no time for any Bowdoin man to be complacent." The plain fact was that no classroom or laboratory building had been erected on the campus since the 1890s. The departments of physics, chemistry, and biology were housed, cheek by jowl, in a structure built in 1894, while the most recent classroom buildings, Adams and Memorial Halls, both eighty years old, were creaking with age. Although covered with ivy and suffused with sentiment, neither hall, President Sills went so far as to admit, was a thing of beauty or a joy forever. The library, built in 1902, was uncomfortably crowded. "There is no institution more dynamic than a college," he told the editor of the *Portland Sunday Telegram* in December, 1947. "It is an eternal small boy always outgrowing his clothes."

For many years, K. C. M. S. had kept Bowdoin's most urgent needs before the alumni in his annual reports. The lists were formidable: a classroom building, a chemistry laboratory, a little theater, a new wing to the library, an indoor hockey rink, and funds for the development of the department of music. He also sought adequate endowment of intercollegiate athletics, to avoid dependence upon gate receipts. Above all, he pleaded for additions to the invested funds. Although a cautious optimist, the president never tackled his mountain of daily mail without hoping that one of the letters might contain a gift to supply a current need. "In my long experience in college administration," he observed in April, 1949, after receiving an unsolicited check for $100,000 from a benefactor who had never set foot on the campus, "I have found that whereas frequently there are no gifts or bequests where expected, just as often they come in from sources that have not been contemplated." When asked to indicate an order of priority among so many needs, K. C. M. S. recommended that each alumnus follow the example of President Eliot who was asked to designate his favorite grandchild. "I have no favorite," Eliot replied, but pointing to one of the dozen youngsters, he added, "*That* is a very nice one." Bowdoin's president made no secret of his own preference. He knew that buildings would come in the fullness of time because the American people were only too ready to put emphasis on the log rather than on Mark Hopkins. He never grew tired of reminding the alumni, "If the College were ever to be stripped to the bone, we could get rid of administrative officers, of all athletics, of all social activities, and if we had left a good library, laboratories, and teachers, we should still have a good college."

Before Bowdoin's energies were devoted to wartime activities, Kenneth Sills had hoped to fill the most pressing needs by means of a major fund-raising effort to culminate with the sesquicentennial in 1944. As early as 1937, he had appointed committees representing the alumni, faculty, and undergraduates to study the project and submit recommendations to the Governing Boards. Although the Boards proceeded cautiously, they needed no convincing about the necessity of initiating a campaign. The international situation, however, soon made it inexpedient to ask for the large sums of money required to undertake a building program. Like so many other Bowdoin dreams for an elaborate celebration of the anniversary, the plans for the campaign were postponed for the duration. K. C. M. S. tempered the disappointment by reminding the alumni that "The College is long-lived, and her sons must be patient, content at least with the thought that through the years Bowdoin has gone without until her needs could be adequately fulfilled."

The supply of alumni and undergraduate patience, however, was strictly limited. At its first meeting after V-J Day, the alumni council recommended "that a major fund-raising effort at Bowdoin should no longer be delayed," and asked that the Boards take "positive action" at their June meeting in 1946 to raise the sum of $7,300,000. When "positive action" took the form of a committee appointed to formulate plans, and in April, 1947, when the Trustees voted to inaugurate a campaign to raise $3,025,000 "for the immediate needs of the College, with an ultimate goal of $6,250,-000" there was some disappointment. "The wheels of progress, unfortunately, seem to grind slowly," complained Richard Wiley '49 in the *Orient*. "Of course progress must be cautious, but it need not be at a snail's pace. . . . Experience and age tempers, but it also destroys." To such criticism, President Sills drew upon his inexhaustible store of patience to explain that "when undergraduates and alumni call for reforms and additions that cost money, they should be fully aware of our present financial situation." "Bowdoin," he reminded them, "is not a rich college, nor a rich man's college, only a college rich in service." "It is a fine thing," he continued, "to have ardent advocates of all these improvements, but it is not in the spirit of defeatism to say that each need must bide its time." The Governing Boards, he noted, were only acting with their customary realism in respecting the axiom: "To advocate changes or deplore costs without counting the cost is to evade the problem."

In discussing the work of the college in his annual reports, Kenneth Sills occasionally made a list of activities entitled, "Things Well Done and Things Done Not so Well." In the unlikely event that he ever made a similar appraisal of his own strengths and weaknesses as an administrator, he probably would have given himself a low grade as a joyous and confident money-getter. Indeed, there is no evidence that he ever invaded the office of a millionaire to make an outright request for funds, and he consented to call upon potential benefactors only after they had first indicated their interest in the college. K. C. M. S. had been in office for only a few weeks in 1918 before realizing that he could not possibly perform all the duties that might reasonably be expected of him, and one of those to be neglected was raising money. He preferred the job of really knowing his college, and of attracting and retaining an able and harmonious faculty, even though it often might be composed of mutually repellent particles. The techniques of public relations experts and development consultants always remained a mystery to him. When he was congratulated on the addition of ten million dollars to the endowment during his administration, he quoted the words of the Reverend Jesse Appleton, Bowdoin's second president: "God always has looked after Bowdoin College and God always will." Yet Kenneth Sills underestimated his effectiveness as a money-getter. His reports and addresses on the state of the college are cogent statements of Bowdoin's needs. In speaking for Bowdoin, he impressed his listeners as pleading for all colleges of liberal arts. "Now that we are emerging from the days when all our energies had to be devoted to winning the war," he wrote in May, 1946, "we ought to realize that education should be one of the main factors in maintaining the peace. To that end every good school, every good college, every good university must be strengthened by generous financial support as well as by increased popular interest. It is still a national scandal that American teachers of every rank are very much underpaid." Nor did the president forget the public schools. "In education we are all in the same boat," he told the alumni in New York City in January, 1947. "If the American people realize the necessity of good teaching in the public schools and improve education there, they will also be ready to improve facilities for education in our colleges." K. C. M. S. was always definite about the purpose for which money was to be raised. On the eve of the campaign in May, 1948, he declared, "The real purpose is to improve instruction at Bowdoin in order to make a pretty good college even better."

Kenneth Sills considered the decision to raise upwards of six million dollars a bold and courageous act. The ultimate goal was ten times the amount achieved in Bowdoin's only other large-scale drive for capital funds in 1921–22 when $600,000 had been added to the endowment. Less optimistic than some of his enthusiastic friends, he warned, "It will indeed be difficult to raise the full amount"; but he assured the alumni, "We are all of the conviction that in a fast-moving world Bowdoin must move fast too." Characteristically, he was unwilling to have Bowdoin appeal to the general public for support until those closest to the college had first shown their faith in the enterprise. He was proud to be able to announce from Brunswick over a telephone hookup to 1,000 Bowdoin men gathered at alumni dinners in twenty-four cities, on May 3, that $600,000 had already been pledged by Governing Boards, faculty, and student body to the immediate objective of

$3,025,000. In acknowledging this generous support, K. C. M. S. may have felt that his saintly predecessor, the Reverend Jesse Appleton, was too otherworldly in his total reliance upon providence to supply Bowdoin's needs. In any event, President Appleton's twentieth-century successor added a touch of Benjamin Franklin's practical idealism. "All these heartening contributions indicate," K. C. M. S. said, "that when we go to the alumni in general and then to the friends of the College, we can at least demonstrate the hope that God will help those who help themselves."

The respect and affection accorded the president by the citizens of Brunswick now helped to make possible an indispensable contribution to the campaign which provided for the enlargement of the campus. Prospects of a new classroom building and chemistry laboratory brought the problem of finding advantageous sites for these halls. For years the college architects had chafed at the awkward division of the Bowdoin grounds by Harpswell Street, a public thoroughfare which not only separated the main campus from Adams Hall, but also from the eight-acre plot of land known as the Delta. Generations of undergraduates had become accustomed to trolleycars clanging beneath the windows of recitation rooms in Adams, and had learned how to scurry to and from classes across the busy street. Traffic hazards were, however, less bothersome than aesthetic, and quite practical considerations. With Harpswell Street forming its northeastern boundary, the central campus resembled a misshapen triangle, lacking a seemly approach from either the Bath Road or Federal Street. It was also cut off from a sizable area containing many of Bowdoin's lovely pines. In studying plans for the expansion of the college, Professor Morgan Cushing envisaged closing that portion of Harpswell Street which split the campus, and in its place building a new road to skirt the eastern end of the Delta, thus unifying the campus and opening up a valuable space for new buildings. Realization of Professor Cushing's imaginative plan, however, hinged entirely upon the consent of the town to close a frequently traveled street.

Brunswick during the Sills administration was free from the uncouth fracases between "town and gown" which had ruffled tempers in the earlier and less urbane years of the century. Ominous grumblings were still often heard at town meetings as the tax-free property of the college increased. During the grinding days of the Depression, envious glances were cast at "the professors on the hill" who enjoyed comparatively secure incomes, long summer vacations, and seemingly short working hours. Yet the town, on the whole, was proud of Bowdoin, and if some of its citizens were disposed to titter when a professor quoted Aristotle or Plato in support of an ordinance to regulate the local clam flats, most townspeople valued Bowdoin as an important element in Brunswick's economy and culture. Early in his career, the president himself had set a pattern for full faculty participation in civic affairs. As chairman of the school committee and Red Cross chapter, as vestryman of his church, and as a member of countless enterprises in the public interest, he proved himself a conscientious citizen. Indeed, his identification with Brunswick was so complete that he consistently refused to patronize chain stores or markets. Local housewives knew that Tondreau's grocery furnished all the provisions for the generous table at 85 Federal Street, with its endless round of dinners and receptions. Most of Brunswick also realized that any deserving graduate of the high school could count on a liberal scholarship if he chose to enter Bowdoin. By their wide but unostentatious hospitality, the president and his wife strove to prevent the college community from being regarded as a self-contained social entity "above the tracks." A campus watchman who sometimes directed traffic in front of 85 Federal Street at receptions following lectures and concerts was heard to remark, "I guess there's few people in town who haven't seen the inside of *that* house." Only a newcomer to Brunswick would have been surprised to see youngsters sidle up to the president after a football game to exclaim, "We slaughtered 'em today, didn't we!"

Kenneth Sills had sat patiently through enough town meetings to know that voters were often unpredictable. An article in the warrant to raise and appropriate a few dollars to install an incandescent lamp on a dark corner of the Growstown Road might evoke lengthy quibbling, while a few minutes later large sums were cheerfully approved without objection. Persuaded of the incalculable long-term benefits which would ensue to the college were the town to relocate a small section of Harpswell Street, the president was apprehensive when the moderator read the crucial articles at the meeting on March 6, 1948. Numbered fifty-eight and fifty-nine, they were reached late in the afternoon, and K. C. M. S. noticed with anxiety that few voters had left the bleak hall, acrid with steaming boots and mackinaws. Yankees are shrewd traders, and the president was about to propose a swap: if the town would abandon Harpswell Street from the Bath Road to College Street, the college would build and landscape a new driveway through the Bowdoin pines and deed the new road to the town. Adam Walsh, head football coach and popular member of the Brunswick Fire Department, seconded the motion and was primed to speak in its behalf if he detected any opposition. The simple and earnest endorsement of the president was, however, all that was needed. During his forty years in Brunswick, no one ever doubted that Kenneth Sills's word was his bond. The town passed both articles without a dissenting vote. Later, in reporting the action to the Boards, he modestly praised Professor Cushing as "the original and persistent promoter of the plan." Bowdoin's triangular campus had now become quadrilateral, with plenty of room to grow.

Seven months later, when the president formally presented the new driveway to the town, he hailed it as a symbol of the amity between Brunswick and Bowdoin. "I challenge any college executive," he said on October 13, "to name a community where there is more mutual understanding, forbearance, and

patience between town and gown." Following the brief ceremony, he invited those citizens who in their childhood had walked
through the pines on their way to primary school to have places
of honor in the first caravan of motor cars to ride over the new
thoroughfare. The compliment was promptly returned. At the
next annual town meeting, his fellow townsmen voted to name
the road Sills Drive. Once again there was no dissenting vote.

The unified campus was the first step toward a new Bowdoin.
It meant the addition of valuable space for sorely needed facilities, and on May 20, 1949, K. C. M. S. announced the Boards'
authorization of plans to build and equip a classroom building
from the first appropriations from the sesquicentennial fund. By
a happy disposition of a bequest not connected with the current
campaign, it was also possible to add a wing containing an auditorium seating 210 people. Of the $1,500,000 received during the
first year of the solicitation, one-half was added to the endowment and the income applied to faculty salaries. The other half
was allocated for the building program, in which the chemistry
laboratory had priority. Meanwhile, the Boards authorized a
rehabilitation of the classrooms in Memorial, Adams, and Ban-
ister halls which Mr. Harvey Gibson, chairman of the fund, had
described as "super-antiquated." With the new classroom building in use since September, 1950, and with subscriptions approaching $2,500,000, ground was broken for the laboratory in
October. "The raising of this sum has been a splendid achievement equal to our expectations if not our hopes," the president
told the alumni. He warned, however, "The next million will
come with a great deal more difficulty and will require even more
united effort, even more generous support." Welcome as these
additions were to the plant, his chief concern, as always, was not
with the physical aspects of the college. "On the more intangible but no less essential side," he informed the Boards in May,
1951, "we have by no means raised salaries to meet expectations,
to say nothing of hopes; but the Sesquicentennial Fund has aided
much in financing the bold increases made two years ago when

funds were not in hand, with the result that . . . the median of our salaries is higher than that of many of our sister institutions. But this should not for a moment make us complacent; competition is becoming keener. . . . The answer is not merely to be found in higher salaries, but in the necessity for more general regard of the importance of the teaching profession."

Although the president was confident that the goal of $6,250,-000 would be reached ultimately, he refused to believe that more than the first phase of the venture could be completed during the remainder of his administration. "As it took eight years from June 24, 1794, the date of our charter, to the admission of the first class in September, 1802," he remarked, "so it will take the same period of eight years, from 1944 to 1952, to complete the Sesquicentennial Fund of $3,025,000." If such a reflection was tinged with personal disappointment, his days were too crowded for regrets. Each morning he paused to watch the construction of the chemistry laboratory on what was already being called "the old Delta," but physical changes impressed him less than other signs pointing to the end of an era. Paul Nixon's retirement as Dean in 1947 had ended a relationship which was coextensive with the president's own administration. K. C. M. S. conferred the Winkley professorship, a chair he had held since 1907, on his fellow Latinist as a token of his affection. Each succeeding year now brought heavy losses to the Governing Boards and faculty. Within a few years, death removed from the Board of Trustees Frederick Pickard, Albert Gould, and Harvey Gibson, each a warm friend for more than forty years. From the Overseers, he mourned the passing of Harold Ashey, Adriel Bird, William Ingraham, and Wallace White. The losses suffered by the faculty were no less grievous: his revered teacher of mathematics, William Moody, and Frederic Brown and Daniel Stanwood among the *emeriti;* from those on the active list, Stanley Chase, senior professor of English, and Henry Johnson, the college physician. "One can scarcely imagine," K. C. M. S. said, "what it means for me to attempt to carry on without the counsel of these devoted friends." The president's trips to St. Andrews were also saddened by the illness of his sister, Mary Sills Robinson. Since December, 1949, he had known she could not recover. Her death in June, 1950, cut the last intimate tie which had bound him to the summer home of his parents in New Brunswick.

Kenneth Sills had welcomed the Boards' action in extending his term of office partly because he disliked the thought of retiring before the immediate objectives of the campaign had been met. An unfinished drive for funds was hardly the sort of present to toss into the lap of his successor. Above all, he looked forward to presiding once more over a truly residential college with a student body living in dormitories and fraternity houses. He also wished to see again the intellectual exhilaration generated by the system of major examinations. Yet K. C. M. S. had known several otherwise successful presidents whose powers faded toward the end of their terms. To be sure, the Boards had trusted him to decide for himself how long he cared to serve, but he was reluctant to impose upon their kindness. In the circumstances, he resolved to submit his resignation when he reached his seventieth birthday; it then could be accepted whenever the Boards deemed it wise to do so. In the meantime, he would continue to rely upon the principles of continuity and flexibility which he believed had, "on the whole and in the main," proved viable.

At the outset of the sesquicentennial campaign in 1948, the *Portland Press Herald* predicted that President Sills would witness more physical changes on his campus than ever before in Bowdoin's history. K. C. M. S., however, was confronted by more striking transformations than those arising from new buildings. Time-honored values and attitudes seemed to be dissolving rapidly in the postwar era. In scouting for new instructors, he now encountered increasingly sharp competition, not only from government and business, but from the bourgeoning state universities and community colleges. The Bowdoin salary scale which he had described as "not so bad" in 1948 was now barely good enough. He also noted that the new generation emerging from the graduate schools often inquired closely about "fringe benefits," "released time" for research, secretarial assistance, and opportunity to offer highly specialized courses. Observing their devotion to a discipline rather than to an institution, he wondered whether these entities need be mutually exclusive. His experience had convinced him that a teacher must not only be devoted to his subject, but should also identify himself with the best interests of his academic community, and show more than an impersonal interest in his students. Although K. C. M. S. was impressed by the high professional competence and ambition of many candidates, he was puzzled by their fear that burdensome committee assignments would interfere with their advancement. When he replied that somehow or other most Bowdoin professors were able to be both effective teachers and reasonably productive scholars, he was met with a look of polite disbelief. Nor was he entirely successful in convincing all candidates that his faculty enjoyed complete academic freedom and "permanent" tenure despite the absence of any statutory provisions guaranteeing them.

The college bylaws stipulated that the president be elected for a five-year term and all professors for terms of three years, but K. C. M. S. assured those who raised the question that it was the established practice at Bowdoin to reelect associate and full professors, so that actually permanent tenure prevailed. So profound was the faculty's confidence in the integrity of Kenneth Sills and of the Governing Boards that few of its members were troubled by the ambiguity in the bylaws. The president, however, fearing the adverse effect on desirable candidates who assumed that an institution of Bowdoin's rank would have explicit, statutory safeguards of tenure, sought to persuade the Boards to codify their long-standing and consistent practice. Although his efforts were unsuccessful, he saw no threat to the freedom of speech and inquiry of the faculty. "I have personally known of no single instance of interference on the Bowdoin campus with the rightful privileges of academic freedom," he declared in May, 1951, "and having for many years enjoyed the privilege of expressing my own views on public and political matters, which often have been minority views, I know that the same freedom exists for my colleagues."

K. C. M. S. kept a solicitous but hopeful eye on the effect of changing student mores on the fraternities. Long convinced that what was good for the fraternities was good for Bowdoin, he had welcomed their management by the college during the war to preserve the twelve chapter houses as Bowdoin's basic living and social units. In returning them to their respective owners in the fall of 1946, he tried to increase their democratization and effectiveness. Speaking at the eightieth anniversary of the Bowdoin chapter of Zeta Psi, in 1947, he declared, "We should regard fraternities as handmaidens of the College. The more independence local chapters can have the better for all concerned." But Kenneth Sills urged a policy of "gradualism," believing "that reforms in fraternity matters should come slowly, and from the fraternities themselves." "We try to give the chapters every possible chance to exercise responsibility," he assured the Boards in May, 1949. When the Bowdoin Christian Association demanded that the administration take immediate action to eliminate restrictive clauses from fraternity charters and constitutions, he cautioned that "greater tolerance in racial and religious matters would not be achieved by legislative action," and reaffirmed his belief in the autonomy of individual chapters. In an address to the New England conference of the Delta Upsilon fraternity in January, 1948, he said, "Just as the college never tells a fraternity to take or not to take any boy, the national body should likewise refrain from dictating to the chapters. The undergraduates are entirely capable of selecting their own members." Two years later, after the Bowdoin chapter of Delta Upsilon was suspended by the national council as a result of pledging a Negro student, and the chapter voted to secede and form an independent group, K. C. M. S. said bluntly, "I do not see how the chapter could have done anything else."

Meanwhile, the president commended the three fraternities

whose charters contained restrictive clauses for their zealous efforts to have them removed by constitutional means, and reminded those which were free of such restrictions to pay more than lip service to their ideals of brotherhood. He also encouraged the formation of a new independent fraternity, Alpha Rho Upsilon, by assisting the chapter to acquire an attractive house facing the campus. Praising its motto, "All Races United," K. C. M. S. reiterated the college policy of prohibiting the establishment at Bowdoin of any group having restrictive clauses in its charter. He was quick to give moral and financial support to another heartening example of imaginative fraternity leadership when Joseph Wheeler '47 proposed that each chapter contribute to international understanding by providing room and board for a foreign student, and that the college remit all tuition charges. They began in 1948, with nine fraternities as hosts, and in the following year all twelve chapters cooperated in bringing to Bowdoin students from Austria, China, Denmark, England, France, Greece, Hungary, Korea, The Netherlands, and Spain. Known as the Bowdoin Plan, the idea spread rapidly to more than fifty colleges and universities. K. C. M. S. hailed the venture as an undertaking conceived and carried out by undergraduates without any prompting by the administration. It was at least one answer, he said, to critics who maligned fraternity behavior as entirely irresponsible. He also rejoiced at certain benefits not anticipated by the sponsors of the plan. "Some of the boys brought up on the Continent of Europe and elsewhere are perhaps two years older intellectually than Americans of equivalent age," he remarked in an interview in the *Boston Herald* for March 27, 1949. "This is sometimes a bitter pill to swallow. Privately, some of the Americans are a bit peeved when they find out that many of the foreign lads who speak English abominably, and hence *seem* stupid, are tough rivals in the classroom."

When Kenneth Sills reached the age of seventy on December 5, 1949, he submitted his resignation as president of the college. "I am, of course, mindful," he wrote, "of the generous action of the Governing Boards in extending my term until June 1, 1953; but it seems to me that the Boards ought to have the chance of saying now when they wish me to retire." The resignation was promptly tabled. At their meeting on February 4, 1950, the Trustees, with a unanimous concurring vote of the Overseers, cited their earlier vote electing him to another five-year term in 1948, and reminded the president that now, as then, they meant exactly what they said. Two weeks later, K. C. M. S. expressed his doubt that the wisest decision had been made, but he told the alumni council he had bowed to the wishes of the Boards, and would attempt to serve at least until 1952, when he hoped to see the attainment of the first objectives of the sesquicentennial fund. Perhaps by that time, he said, Bowdoin would have witnessed the last of the interim Commencements, summer sessions, and year-round operation. Events in the next few months, however, were destined to upset even the most cautious predictions. "I am sure that my batting average as a prophet," K. C. M. S. confessed, "is way below .150." Once again he would turn to his emergency policy of continuity and flexibility.

At its first meeting of the semester, on February 13, 1950, the faculty was asked to consider a request by the Army to institute a reserve officers training corps in transportation. With considerable reluctance, K. C. M. S. decided that international tensions made it the plain duty of the college to accept this small part in the national defense. He feared, however, that members of the faculty would be almost evenly divided on the issue, especially at a time when they were eager to resume the normal work of the college. Although an answer was required by the Army on February 15, the president presided over the debate without attempting to apply arbitrary pressures or to influence the decision. He simply noted that other New England colleges of liberal arts had found it feasible to accommodate army or naval units, and suggested that a study of transportation problems might be useful to men majoring in economics. As to the danger of Bowdoin becoming militarized, he declared that uniforms worn only at

drill one day a week by a small portion of the student body would
not change the nature of the college. When an informal vote was
so close as to be indecisive, K. C. M. S. deferred the decision to
the next day. On February 14, just twenty-four hours before the
deadline set by the Army, the faculty finally gave its approval by
a vote of 40 to 28, a majority which the president deemed substantial enough to justify the experiment. If he had any misgivings, they disappeared on June 25, when the Communists attacked
the Republic of Korea. "How unlucky we would be now if the
minority had won," he exclaimed after President Truman declared a state of national emergency. "Nearly every college that
does not have an R. O. T. C. unit is making desperate efforts to
secure one. We may well thank our lucky stars, and no one should
be more glad than the faculty, that we were wise enough to accept
the offer of the government."

Added confirmation of the wisdom of the action came in the
fall of 1950 while Congress dallied over provisions of the selec-
tive-service legislation. "Uncertainty pervaded the campus,"
K. C. M. S. reported, "but the undergraduates have been remarkably steady. . . . There is no question but that the R. O. T. C.
has been a salutary stabilizing force." Despite the growing seriousness of the Korean situation, the autumn term began with some
signs of a return to normal conditions. Only a few veterans remained in a student body now reduced to 845 men, and the
fraternity groups were slowly regaining their prewar homo-
geneity. The president was, however, pessimistic about prospects
for 1951–52. "If universal service, military and civilian, is adopted,
colleges, particularly those for men only, will experience a radical change," he told the Bowdoin teachers club on October 26.
"Enrollment may be reduced between twenty-five and forty
percent, acceleration will return with periodic graduations, bringing the disruption of normal progression from class to class,
and the abandonment of the recently resumed comprehensive
examinations." Less than a year before, K. C. M. S. had predicted
hopefully the end of summer sessions. On January 1, 1951, how-

ever, when the Communists started a major offensive, and three days later when the United Nations forces withdrew from Seoul, he asked the faculty to plan a summer program as a national duty. "At the present moment we have no idea how many will be enrolled," he admitted to the Boards, "but our principal concern should not be for the faculty, nor the administration, nor the College itself, but for the young men who in all probability before too long will have to undergo military training and very possibly sustain the chances of conflict."

For the next few months, Kenneth Sills's public utterances often seemed to him like the repetition of a twice-told tale. History, he reflected, was repeating itself with dismaying rapidity. In a letter to the alumni on May 15, 1951, he wrote: "The immediate future of the College is as uncertain as is the national scene or the international situation. . . . Consequently we are going step by step, crossing the bridges as we come to them and, though under pressure, refusing to be forced into premature decisions." He also reported the temper of the campus in phrases reminiscent of those he had used a decade ago: "It seems to me that there is little enthusiasm for military service, that there is a certain amount of fatalism in the air, and most students desire to get as much education as they can before receiving the call . . . young men can better serve in military capacities after some college training than with none at all." Once again, as in 1918 and 1941, K. C. M. S. asked for no special favors for undergraduates. He told the alumni in Boston, on April 12, of his opposition to the recent executive order calling for mass deferment of college students. "I much prefer the present plan," he said, "whereby a student who has started a year of college may finish that year, but must then enter the service like the others." The president's democratic sympathies were offended by the proposal to defer students on the basis of academic rank. "If the plan is adopted," he warned, "the college student must not think himself in any way superior to his brother outside the college wall. His brother may be just as useful to his country." K. C. M. S. held the col-

leges and universities partly responsible for the popular ignorance
of the reasons our soldiers were needed in Korea. "Temporarily
on some battlefields we may be outfought," he declared at the
February Commencement, "but let us not forget that more important conflicts are those of the mind, and we must not be out-
thought."

Despite the president's forebodings about the uncertain prospects, the fall term in 1952 opened with more than 800 students.
"Unless the international scene gets much darker," he said with
unwonted optimism, "the college course for the usual four years
will be available to many more undergraduates than was thought
possible a year ago." Indeed, the armistice and cease-fire nego-
tiations in Korea and the negligible number of students leaving
for the armed forces led him to hope that the 1951 summer session might really be the last. There was no question, however,
that this was to be Kenneth Sills's last year in office. In the preceding June he had been authorized to appoint a committee to
select his successor. Eager to avoid an interim between the out-
going and incoming administrations, he had told the Governing
Boards, "The year 1952 will be an admirable year during which
the present President of the College should and will retire . . .
so that a new President may begin his administration sometime
after commencement, when the College starts on its one hundred
and fifty-first year."

Fittingly, in 1951–52, the sun on the college seal beamed as
brightly on the fortunes of the College as if he were a Bowdoin
graduate. Princely legacies from the Moulton and Pickard estates,
and generous gifts to the Gibson and sesquicentennial funds made
possible not only the realization of the immediate objectives of
the campaign, but also the dreams of a theater and music building. In his final report to the Boards, K. C. M. S. was able to announce larger additions to the endowment than in any other year
in Bowdoin's long history. The era of good feeling even reduced
the traffic of student disciplinary cases in the dean's office, a startling phenomenon which Dean Kendrick was unwilling to attribute solely to good fortune. "In the field of student conduct,

the year has been a very quiet one," he wrote in May, 1952. "I believe it is true that the student body has been genuinely anxious that the closing year of the President's service should be a smooth and pleasant one, and the student leaders made a special effort to bring this about." The president himself, without spoiling his record for habitual understatement, observed, "The past year has been indeed *Annus Mirabilis*," and "the gratitude of the College is beyond expression."

Bowdoin men found their own expressions of gratitude difficult to put into words as they made a triumphal procession out of Kenneth Sills's final round of alumni dinners in 1951–52. In Portland, Boston, New York, and Philadelphia, where he made his thirty-fifth annual appearance as head of the college, they showered the Sillses with affection and gifts. When the latter took the form of substantial checks, the president and his wife were ordered to squander the money self-indulgently, if not frivolously. Alumni had not forgotten that in 1948 K. C. M. S. had turned over the full amount of his Bowdoin Prize to the sesquicentennial fund, his second large contribution. He was warned there must be no such nonsense again. Back in Maine it seemed as though everybody from the governor of the state to the selectmen of Brunswick sent him resolutions of regard. Brunswick's Fire Department made him its honorary chief and gave him a gold badge which he wore at the weekly Rotary luncheons. The Colby College faculty tendered him a dinner at which Dean Ernest Marriner introduced him as "the only Casey who never struck out," and President Seelye Bixler cited him as a champion of all colleges of liberal arts. From the student senate of the University of Maine came a scroll listing his activities in support of public education. His own faculty, with vivid memories of 85 Federal Street spilling over with books, established a library fund in honor of the president and his wife. Meanwhile, colleagues calling at Massachusetts Hall on routine errands or dropping in for tea at the president's house, tried bravely but unsuccessfully to forget that each visit might be the last one.

Nothing in Kenneth Sills's long administration of thirty-five years better revealed his wisdom than his conduct during and after the search for the man to succeed him. Before appointing the committee entrusted with the choice, he resolved that the less he had to do with choosing his successor, the better. The committee itself, composed of three trustees and an equal number of overseers, was selected to represent different classes, localities, and professions. Its geographical provenance included Brunswick, Portland, Cambridge, New York, Haverford, and Wilmington; its occupations were business, industry, the law, and college and university teaching. Once the committee had thus been constituted, and K. C. M. S. had assured the alumni and faculty that it would welcome their suggestions, he limited his own cautious advice to proposing a few names of those in positions to know of promising men. Although he was in full agreement with the qualities to be desired in the incoming president and was kept informed of the committee's progress, he remained aloof from all its deliberations. No committee ever had a freer hand. Kenneth Sills had no wish to have the new head of the college return to or imitate his own practices. He had carried forward the program initiated by President Hyde with modifications of his own, tempering the provisions of the elective system and emphasizing the mastery of a single field. The duties he knew best combined those of teacher and administrator in a college small enough to enable its chief executive to conduct chapel regularly, to correct papers, to confer with students in scholastic difficulties, and to become the counselor and friend of several thousand students over nine college generations. During this time, many characteristics of the nineteenth-century New England college had survived vigorously into the first half of the twentieth. As Bowdoin prepared to begin its 151st year, K. C. M. S. was prepared to welcome whatever changes would best enable it to meet the demands of a new era.

The identity of the president-elect had been a perfectly kept secret. Besides the committee, only Kenneth Sills and Philip Wilder, his administrative assistant, had been informed of the choice before the special session of the Governing Boards, on the morning of April 5, to act upon the nomination. "There were tears in members' eyes," the *Boston Herald* reported, "when Dr. Sills read his resignation to both the Board of Trustees and the College Overseers." Early that afternoon, before the news of the election appeared in the evening papers, K. C. M. S. summoned his faculty to tell them about their new leader. Many of the older members whose entire teaching careers were spent at Bowdoin felt as though the college, for a brief moment, was suspended between two worlds. Their mood of solemn constraint was broken as soon as they heard the familiar voice of Kenneth Sills speak of his successor, James Stacy Coles, acting dean of Brown University, whose compelling qualifications had commended him to the Boards. "In these days it is perhaps peculiarly appropriate," K. C. M. S. said, "that an ex-classicist should be succeeded not only by a scientist, but by a scientist who is deeply interested in the humanities and who will be a stout advocate of a liberal education." Although the meeting was informal, there was a slight pause after the president's words, and the members of the faculty remained seated as if awaiting a formal motion for adjournment. No such motion was either offered or needed. Instead, Professor Frederic Tillotson ended the meeting with an epilogue as fitting as it was spontaneous. Turning toward the president, he exclaimed, "We're surely going to miss *you!*"

Forces of continuity and change dominated the 1952 Commencement marking the sesquicentennial of the opening of the college and the closing of the longest Bowdoin presidency on record. "This is Casey's last one," everybody said or thought as Kenneth Sills invoked the ancient formula, *"Candidati pro gradu baccalaureali, assurgite. . . ."* As the academic procession followed the well-worn paths to the gymnasium for the Commencement dinner, the crowds lining the walks to say their "hail and farewell" knew they were witnessing the end of an era. In the line of march, moving into retirement with their chief, were Paul Nixon and Warren Catlin, each ending forty years of teaching at Bowdoin. Sharing the plaudits with her husband was Edith Lansing Koon Sills, wreathed in her new Bowdoin L.H.D. hood and her old Bowdoin graciousness. During the dinner program, K. C. M. S. modestly tried to keep the attention of the 1,200 graduates fixed on the future. He began by reading a telegram to his successor, pledging, in the name of the assembly, loyal and united support. He concluded by voicing his confidence that "the best days for Bowdoin are clearly the days ahead."

Without official planning and without their consent, the entire three-day Commencement program turned into a mounting tribute to Kenneth and Edith Sills. On Thursday afternoon they were the guests of honor at a reception given by the class of 1927; that evening they attended a special production of *Hamlet* by the undergraduate members of Masque and Gown who wished to present the president's favorite play. On Friday the new classroom building was formally named Sills Hall, but K. C. M. S. was dismayed at the size of the bronze plaque. "My mother wanted only one name, *Kenneth*," he protested, "but my grandmother was insistent upon adding *Charles Morton*. That's too long a name to spell out twice on one tablet." Later, he presided at the dedication of Parker Cleaveland Hall, the new chemistry laboratory. In the evening he saw a second production of *Hamlet*, acted by an alumni cast whose members included students from the early days of his deanship. At the graduation dinner, each class brought its own tribute of gratitude and affection. Of all these shining moments, the most memorable came at the end of the Commencement exercises, in the First Parish Church, when Kenneth Sills conferred the honorary degree of doctor of humane letters upon his wife as a "Doctor of Ease and Graciousness." If it was not quite his last official act as president of Bowdoin College, it was the one which brought him the most joy.

# 15

## PRESIDENT EMERITUS

### 1952-1954

Kenneth Sills had often encouraged members of his faculty to spend at least a part of their retirement in Brunswick where their roots were deep and their attachments strong. The Sillses themselves would have been happy to remain there, but K. C. M. S. felt that his permanent residence in town might be awkward for his successor. Portland seemed an ideal solution to the problem, and neither the president nor his wife ever thought seriously of searching for a house anywhere else. Only twenty-eight miles from Brunswick, it was far enough away to provide the sense of physical detachment he sought, yet near enough to permit frequent and casual visits. Portland was also "a Bowdoin town" filled with friends, many of whom he had known since his boyhood days in the deanery on State Street. After much hunting, which proved to be a novel if exhausting adventure, they found the house they were looking for at 134 Vaughan Street. Situated in a pleasantly staid section near the Western Promenade, the tree-canopied street was not unlike the Federal Street they loved. Their old friend, the scholarly William Lawrence, lived nearby.

The pangs of leaving Brunswick were real enough even though they were somewhat lessened by the gradualness of the transition. K. C. M. S. had consented to stay on as president until October 1, but he planned to move out of 85 Federal Street shortly after Commencement. Fondness for the old house had inured the Sillses to some of its inconveniences, but they knew after thirty-four years of continuous occupancy it needed a good deal of refurbishing. When they began housekeeping there in 1918, they had furniture enough for only the essential rooms, but now

their possessions filled three large vans and each item reminded
them of the generosity of alumni and the acquisitions made over
the years by their own patient domestic planning. Until they
could be established on Vaughan Street, they accepted gratefully
the invitation to live in the guest house of Violetta and Harold
Berry at Falmouth Foreside. Meanwhile, Kenneth Sills commuted
to his office four or five times a week to wind up the affairs of
his administration. On July 9 he watched the last van of goods
pull away from 85 Federal Street, and the next morning he returned to the house to walk through each one of the strangely
bare rooms. On his desk pad he noted, "Left at 11:30 a.m. House
empty." A few weeks later, on August 5, he added, "At 134
Vaughan Street—permanently." Old habits, however, were not
easily broken. More than once that summer, after spending the
day in his office in Massachusetts Hall, K. C. M. S. caught himself heading toward Federal Street. "Returning to Portland every
evening," he said, "makes me rub my eyes a bit."

Callers at 134 Vaughan Street were also tempted to rub their
eyes. The floor plan of the new house had enabled the Sillses to
reassemble their furniture, books, and pictures in pretty much
the same old way. The President's study on the second floor was
a virtual replica of his library in the southwest corner of 85 Federal Street. One new luxury, however, was savored only by its
occupant. K. C. M. S. now hoped he would have time enough
to do more than glance hurriedly at recent books before putting
them on his shelves. It would be thrilling, he thought, to be able
to read books through. As of old, there was tea every afternoon
and a constant stream of visitors. Long before their telephone
number was listed in the Portland directory, K. C. M. S. asked
that it be published in the *Alumnus* along with a warm invitation
"to any Bowdoin people who may be passing by and might like
to call." In leaving the new house, Brunswickians half expected
to find themselves at the familiar corner across from the campus.
Forrest Orr's lovely water color of the old house, a parting gift
to the Sillses from the citizens of Brunswick, hung over the fire-

place in the dining room. There were probably times when the president and his wife found it hard to believe they were not still living there.

Since K. C. M. S. feared making any decision which might possibly commit his successor, his last few weeks in office were largely devoted to administrative details. All was not routine, however. On September 2, he presided at the exercises marking the 150th anniversary of the opening of the college. At his suggestion, the simple ceremony was held in front of Massachusetts Hall, which in 1802 had housed the first president, Joseph Mc-Keen, the single tutor, and eight students of the first class. "We today must wage an unceasing war on ignorance and prejudice, the two great foes of freedom," K. C. M. S. said in his last college address as president. "And we must uphold the ideals, not only of free enterprise in business and industry, but of free enterprise in ideas, which is a good definition of academic freedom." In planning the brief program, he sought, as always, to emphasize the town as well as the college, the future as well as the past. Harry Shulman, chairman of the Brunswick Board of Selectmen, told of Bowdoin's services to the community, and Clement Robinson '03, of the Governing Boards, recounted the events between 1794 and 1802 which had delayed the opening of the college. K. C. M. S. reserved the place of honor for the president-elect, Dr. Coles, who praised the terms of the charter enjoining Bowdoin to promote virtue and piety, and the knowledge of languages and the useful and liberal arts and sciences. He promised that "The boards and faculty, the students and alumni, who but temporarily hold that charter and the college in their trust, shall assure that her future may be even greater than her past."

Past and future met symbolically later that afternoon when Ann, Christopher, and Reed, the children of Dr. and Mrs. Coles gathered some acorns from beneath the venerable Thorndike Oak and buried them at widely separated spots on the campus. The youngsters, who had been told how George Thorndike of the class of 1806 had won a measure of Bowdoin immortality by planting a live acorn after the first chapel service on September 2, 1802, decided to have a part in the sesquicentennial themselves. Their gesture, K. C. M. S. thought, was a happy omen of the continuity and growth of the college.

Final exits from the academic stage are no less critical for college presidents than for leading actors in the theater, but Kenneth Sills played his part impeccably. Eager to avoid the slightest break between the old and new administrations, he was always available for assistance to the president-elect who had taken a cottage on the shore near Brunswick during the summer while becoming familiar with the organization of the college. "During August and September, we had several lengthy conversations," Dr. Coles wrote ten years later, "in which he told me much about the College and the people associated with the College, and answered many of my questions. Throughout he was very careful not to suggest his own analysis or views but to be as factual and informational as possible." K. C. M. S. admired his successor's genius for asking precisely the right questions, while Dr. Coles counted himself blessed in having an ideal president emeritus to whom he could go for counsel and encouragement.

K. C. M. S. modestly absented himself from Brunswick on September 30, 1952, the final day of his term of office. In a chapel talk that morning, Professor Fritz Koelln remarked that daily chapel had been one of the most distinctive mediums through which the president kept his personal contact with Bowdoin students. "We should pause for a moment on the last day of his administration," he said, "to reflect upon the Good Spirit that has, for so many years, found an expression in these services, and of which he himself, to all of us, has become a living symbol." The speaker recalled a characteristic instance during the disastrous New England flood in the spring of 1936. The anxious student body had been called together by the president, who spoke briefly before announcing the measures to be taken in the emergency. "It is only natural," Kenneth Sills had said, "that you should all be disturbed as you face this emergency, but let me give you this advice that should make everything much easier. Before you ask the natural question, 'How can I be helped in my particular situation?' remember that the gentleman's first question is, 'How can I help?' "

A desire to be of help prompted the first letter K. C. M. S. wrote in his retirement. It was a greeting to his successor on the morning his new duties began. "I want to send you again on the very first day you take over the presidency of the College my very best wishes for a long and happy administration," he wrote on October 1. "Bowdoin though small is a great college and your office is a very high one. But you will have help and support and loyalty from governing boards, alumni, undergraduates, and friends. . . . I have tried my best to answer questions and to tell you something of my experiences. But I also tried to remember that you have your own convictions and policies—your own way to make, and that I should not try to impose my own views too much. . . . I have great hope and confidence in you—God bless you and yours always."

Except for the welcome honor of introducing President Coles to the alumni and guests at the inauguration dinner on October 13, the official Bowdoin duties of Kenneth Sills were ended. He and Mrs. Sills had booked passage on the *Queen Elizabeth*, sailing two days later, and they planned an extended trip abroad, staying until spring. Their timing, as it happened, was perfect. The new president's inaugural address not only fulfilled his predecessor's expectations, but exceeded his hopes. Although K. C. M. S. had refused to take any responsibility in the selection of his successor, the Boards were aware that their choice would win the president's approval only if he were a scholar committed to sound learning, free inquiry, and a conviction that a small college of liberal arts could make a unique and necessary contribution to the common good. "No one who listened to President Coles's words in the First Parish Church this morning,"

K. C. M. S. said, "can doubt for a moment that Bowdoin's destiny is in the right hands. The best days of Bowdoin College are clearly the days ahead."

Kenneth Sills's mind was so completely occupied by thoughts of Bowdoin's future and the happy auspices under which the new administration was beginning that it had little room for anything else. The speakers representing the state, Bowdoin's sister colleges, the alumni, faculty, and undergraduates quite properly pointed confidently to the years ahead, but the hundreds of alumni and delegates would not allow the president emeritus to forget his own unprecedented role in shaping the modern Bowdoin. When he rose to introduce his successor, the entire company stood up in a single motion and applauded for five minutes. During the ovation, K. C. M. S. exhausted the entire repertory of his characteristic gestures of embarrassment. He brushed fancied specks of dust from his lapels, patted down his necktie, thrust his hands deep in his hip pockets, rocked back and forth on his heels, and finally, in quiet desperation, signaled the assembly to sit down. On this occasion he did not say *consedite*. After the prolonged applause, his quiet remarks seemed startlingly brief. He noted the fine appropriateness of a new president beginning his administration at the start of Bowdoin's 151st year. "You will find," he assured President Coles, "the governing boards and alumni loyal, intelligent, and devoted. I have never known the members of the faculty to be stronger or more devoted to their work. They will be one of the abiding pleasures of your life. As I step down, I look forward eagerly to serving in the ranks."

The retiring president's performance in the last scene of the day was conducted with an equanimity unbroken by sentimentality or the least touch of histrionics. "You showed all the calm self-possession of the village blacksmith locking his shop with something accomplished, something done, and looking forward to a night's repose," Ronald Bridges '30 told K. C. M. S. afterwards. As the crowds scattered following the inaugural dinner, and as the late afternoon shadows lengthened on the campus, a young alumnus saw the president emeritus and Mrs. Sills wave gaily to friends before leaving for Portland. He kept his eyes fixed steadily on their car until it disappeared from view and then said to himself, "Bowdoin *must* be in good hands. Why within the next day or two the Sillses are sailing for Europe and they won't be back for almost a year!"

Now that their actual presence and their diffidence in the face of praise could no longer check their friends' expressions of affection, the Sillses were nearly swamped with letters of grateful regard. "As far as I know," wrote Professor Albert Abrahamson '26, "there is nothing in the bylaws that prevents a faculty member from making a President Emeritus blush." So many friends took advantage of this privilege that the *Queen Elizabeth* docked at Southampton before either K. C. M. S. or Mrs. Sills had been able to read or acknowledge all the bon voyage messages, a pleasant duty they completed with their usual conscientiousness at the Goring Hotel during their first few days in London. Leaves of absence for the president had been comparatively short and never completely without the cares of office, but now he was ready to revel unashamedly in his new leisure with no twinge of conscience. He was amused to learn that he was reported on the *Elizabeth* passenger list, along with Bob Feller of the Cleveland Indians, as "an international lecturer," but he vowed if any lecturing were to be done, the star pitcher would have to do it. More than once during the next six months, he said quietly to his wife, "For the first time since 1917, I feel entirely free."

A generous retirement allowance and substantial checks from a number of alumni clubs also enabled the travelers to enjoy snatches of unaccustomed luxury. Whenever K. C. M. S. hesitated before registering at a first-class hotel, he was reminded by Mrs. Sills of the words of Dr. William Holt '12 in presenting a check from the Portland Bowdoin Club: "Charity begins at home, that is, wherever the Sillses make their home, here or abroad." Actually they seldom used such gifts for themselves. Alumni in England and on the Continent in 1952–53 learned that the hospitality of 85 Federal Street extended to London, Paris, Rome, Florence, and Athens. The president emeritus and his wife needed no better reason for a dinner party than the pleasure of entertaining sons of the college. Mrs. Sills's expertise as a hostess perhaps had its greatest European triumph in Rome where, an hour after arriving at the Hotel Hassler, she solved the mysteries of the Italian telephone exchange to invite eight Bowdoin graduates to dinner, and even managed to locate a Bowdoin soldier, Donald Philbrick, Jr. '44, somewhere in the city on a forty-eight-hour leave from duty in North Africa.

K. C. M. S. told his classmate Roland Clark that their itinerary would depend on the way the spirit moved them, with leisurely stays in London and Rome, and, in the spring, a motor trip through Spain with Violetta and Harold Berry before returning to New York from Gibraltar in mid-April. Without forcing their comfortable pace, they also managed to get exciting, if limited, glimpses of life in India and the Near East. After six weeks in London, they sailed on the *Strathaird* for a fortnight in India, arriving at Bombay on December 20, and spending Christmas in New Delhi, with trips to Agra and Jaipur. Although unused to air travel, they enjoyed a 1,400-mile night flight from Delhi to Madras on December 28, and, two days later, by this time seasoned fliers, took another plane to Colombo for a visit on the island of Ceylon. By January 6 they were on their way west to Marseilles and the Riviera. Ideal weather induced them to linger in Nice before proceeding to Rome in the last week of January. They spent February in the Near East, sailing from Naples on the *Excambion* on January 29, and visiting Alexandria, Cairo, Damascus, and Beirut, with a three-day sojourn in Athens before returning to Naples. Promise of warmer weather and a long-cherished wish to study the Greek theater in Taormina, next drew the travelers to Sicily, but by March 6 they were back in Rome, their favorite European city, this time for a stay of ten days, followed by two days in Florence. On March 19 they left by train for Genoa, where they embarked for Barcelona to begin the last part of their journey.

The joyous reunion with the Harold Berrys in southern Spain was followed by excursions to Madrid, Segovia, Toledo, Cordova, Seville, and Granada. Full of the latest news about the college, their old friends brought reassuring reports of the first months of the new administration. The Sillses had never really been out of touch with Bowdoin affairs and had encountered Bowdoin men and associations at almost every point in their travels. They were welcomed to London by Kendall Niven '46, a C. B. S. news correspondent, who briefed them on current British politics and introduced them to the press corps in the Houses of Parliament. Dr. Robert Lightfoot, fellow of New College, who had held the Tallman professorship at Bowdoin in 1937–38, was their Oxford host, and in London they dined with the Herbert Fleures, who had spent a happy year in Brunswick in 1944–45 when Dr. Fleure had occupied the Tallman chair in the last year of the war. During the Christmas season in India, the Sillses were the guests of another Bowdoin family, the Arthur Bartletts; Arthur Bartlett '22, as head of the U.S. Information Service in New Delhi, put K. C. M. S. in touch with several leaders in education. In Rome the travelers were met at the station by Norman Seagrave '37, legal attaché of the American embassy. "If I had been an influential United States Senator on an important mission, I could not have been shown more hospitality," K. C. M. S. said. The Seagraves put their car at the visitors' disposal and arranged trips to Ostia Antica, Tivoli, and Hadrian's Villa, while Leonard Tennyson '42, in the Rome office of the Economic Cooperation Association, enabled the president emeritus to see at first hand some of the problems faced by the E. C. A. in Italy. Amid all their sightseeing, the Sillses found time to call upon Dr. Enrico Bompiani, a visiting professor of mathematics at Bowdoin in 1930–31 and now teaching at the University of Rome.

university in 1910 after his retirement, and K. C. M. S. admired Lowell for his refusal to be a candidate for a seat in the corporation of Harvard in 1933. By midsummer in 1953, however, two months after President Coles's first Bowdoin Commencement, the president emeritus decided that his occasional presence in Brunswick could not possibly be an inconvenience to his successor. The end of his self-imposed exile delighted his friends. "The best news is that the period in which you purposely abstained from going to and from Brunswick is nearly over," Chauncey Goodrich wrote on August 8. "You have been greatly missed, yet many have commented to me with appreciation on the wisdom and discernment which led you to adopt this policy." President Coles rejoiced at the prospect of seeing K. C. M. S. return to the campus again: "Even though I am very reluctant to impose upon you," he wrote, "I feel it is important for the students of Bowdoin College to have you speak in the Chapel on at least one Sunday of the year." The undergraduates also urged him to return, and it was in response to their invitation that he made his first formal appearance when he addressed the Bowdoin political forum on October 23 on "India and World Politics."

Demands upon his energy and counsel increased rather than diminished with his retirement. In January, three months before his return to the United States, he was notified of his election as warden of the Cathedral Church of Saint Luke. A month later he was named to the board of the Maine General Hospital, and in April he accepted Mrs. Eleanor Roosevelt's invitation to serve as state chairman of the American Association for the United Nations. Within a week of his arrival in Portland, he was called upon by Bishop Appleton Lawrence of Massachusetts to prepare an agenda for a discussion of the relation of the provincial synod to the Church, and in June he was named a trustee of the Portland Public Library. Some of his activities he had foreseen. He continued to serve on important committees of the Carnegie Foundation for the Advancement of Teaching with which he had been identified since 1921 through his influential study, with

William S. Learned, of education in the maritime provinces of Canada. He remained an active member of the boards of the World Peace Foundation, Wellesley and Athens colleges, the Episcopal Theological Seminary, Portland Junior College, Waynflete School, and Hebron Academy. He was, however, surprised at the number of other organizations which enlisted his support. The Federal Home Loan Bank of Boston appointed him public interest director for a second four-year term in 1953, and he was unable to refuse the request of the International Brotherhood of Boilermakers and Iron Ship Builders to act as impartial arbitrator in a pending negotiation with the Bath Iron Works.

Schools, colleges, churches, and societies showered him with invitations to speak, perhaps unmindful that their demands might be heavy for a man in his seventy-fourth year. Managers of fund drives eagerly sought his endorsement and, more often than not, received his active help. When K. C. M. S. called for a chat with William Lawrence in the autumn of 1953, his friend offered a mild remonstrance. "What is it tonight—the Boy Scouts, the Y. M. C. A., or the Salvation Army?" he asked. "While you were President, philanthropic agencies seemed to think they had a claim on half your time; now that you are *emeritus*, they must believe you owe them all of it." Yet each request had its peculiar appeal which he found difficult to resist. In December his enthusiasm for President Nathan Pusey's efforts to revitalize the Harvard Divinity School induced him to share the leadership of the campaign in Maine. His engagement calendar also indicated promises to speak to the Phi Beta Kappa chapter at the University of Vermont, to the first graduating class of the school of nursing at the Maine Medical Center, and at the sesquicentennial of Hebron and Lincoln academies. He also discovered that honorary membership in the Portland and Brunswick Rotary clubs conferred no immunity in the eyes of program chairmen. To the Reverend Bradford Johnson '29, who had inquired about the joys of retirement, K. C. M. S. replied in his usual understatements. "Somehow or other time does not seem to hang on my hands," he wrote on February 3, 1954. "As far as the Church goes, I am still on the Standing Committee, the Diocesan Council, and the Department of Christian Education. I am also the lay delegate for Maine to the Anglican Conference next summer. Locally I am on the Parish Council which the new Dean here has established. . . . I am also in charge of the Red Cross drive for Portland . . . so that although I am no longer working hard, I am busy."

Throughout his trip abroad, Kenneth Sills had been deeply concerned about a painful crisis in St. Luke's Parish. He was distressed to learn that differences between Bishop Oliver Loring and Dean William Hughes had resulted on January 9, 1953, in the Bishop's request for his Dean's resignation. When the Dean refused to resign, and four days later when the lesser chapter or vestry did not vote to declare the office of dean vacant, K. C. M. S. hoped that it would be possible for a committee of Christian churchmen, clerical and lay, to resolve the differences for the welfare of the parish. Before the committee could be organized, however, the Bishop's position was sustained, and Dean Hughes was dismissed by a vote of the lesser chapter on February 10. Kenneth Sills's unhappiness was heightened by his feeling of helplessness. Yet it is unlikely, even though he had been in Portland and used all his powers of reasonableness and skillful compromise, that he would have been able to reconcile the differences. The whole situation evoked memories of his father's resignation as Dean of St. Luke's more than fifty years ago. K. C. M. S. realized again the need of a clearer definition of the authority of a Dean in the spiritual guidance of a parish. He shared William Lawrence's conviction that the issues were fundamental: Is a Dean to have the authority to administer the affairs of the cathedral as the Bishop's delegate, or is the Bishop, as Rector of the cathedral, to be free to exercise ultimate authority, and to change deans at his election?

The deanship was still vacant when K. C. M. S. returned to Portland, where he promptly volunteered his services in the search for promising candidates. "Personally I would prefer one who has had experience in a parish," he wrote Bishop Loring on May 14, "—and while good preaching is important, I feel good hard pastoral work is even more important. Since the Cathedral has both traditions to maintain and relations with the Diocese to regard, I feel strongly that the new Dean should be a good middle-of-the-road Prayer Book Churchman—neither an Anglo-Catholic nor a 'liberal.' As you know, I think the Book of Common Prayer should be the rule and guide, and personally I like neither extempore prayers nor additions not covered by the rubrics." Kenneth Sills's words not only defined his own position; they also summoned up a clear image of his father as Canon and Dean of St. Luke's for more than twenty years.

K. C. M. S. was not a man who ever talked much about his religious feelings. "We Episcopalians are by nature reticent," he said in 1954, "and it is true that I have no reason, intellectual or emotional, for changing my steadfast belief in the principles of the Christian religion." On May 18, however, at the diocesan convention in Portland, when he was presented with a medal for "extraordinary service to the Church," he spoke with touching frankness. His remarks were induced by an impressive recital of his half-century of devoted work as a Maine layman, beginning in 1903 with his appointment as a lay reader by Bishop Codman. During his forty-seven years in Brunswick he served St. Paul's Church as vestryman, and he had now become warden of St. Luke's Cathedral. Since 1921 he was a member of the diocesan council and a delegate to the diocesan conventions. Twice he had been a delegate to the World Convention on Faith and Order —in 1927 in Lausanne and in 1937 in Edinburgh. For six years he was appointed to the national council of the church, and as a council member in 1941 conducted a survey of the missionary district of Honolulu. Eleven times he was elected a lay delegate to general conventions. "He is beyond question," wrote Bishop Henry Knox Sherrill, "one of the most distinguished laymen of our Church in this generation."

"Such service," Kenneth Sills said simply, "was quite natural to me because the Church has so long been a part of my life. All my forebears were Churchmen. My grandfather, father, uncle, and father-in-law were priests. I think the Christian religion, which regards everyone as a child of God, and democracy which regards the individual as worthy of dignity, are my two guiding stars. And the first is more important than the second, which is the outcome of the first. Yet I doubt—and it is a humiliating experience to confess it—if I have ever brought a soul into the fellowship of the Church. I cannot remember taking any one to church or influencing directly any one to become a member of the Christian family. I confess this to show how derelict a supposedly good Churchman can be in Christian duty." The speaker alone seemed unaware that his life as a Christian gentleman was in itself the best witness and that, in Bishop Sherrill's words, his "greatest contribution has been himself, in his wisdom, simplicity, reality, and consecration."

Kenneth Sills's activities during the spring and summer of 1954 kept him almost as busy as he had been before his retirement. In March he accepted the presidency of the Board of Trustees of the Waynflete School in time to ensure a smooth transition between an old and new headmaster and to give fresh impetus to a campaign for funds. "I am flabbergasted to hear what you are doing for Waynflete," wrote Judge Sidney Thaxter, "—more than many others whose children have benefitted by many years there." K. C. M. S. also found time to help organize the statewide campaign for the Boy Scouts and to continue his work in behalf of the Harvard Divinity School. "Can't you drop yourself out of new jobs? When are you going to learn what joys leisure can bring?" asked his former dean, Paul Nixon. "Why not allow me to teach you really how to retire?" Yet K. C. M. S. kept hammering away in half a dozen addresses for the need of a constitutional convention in Maine to abolish the governor's executive council. "I read another speech of yours in which you said that we should do away with the Council," wrote Ernest M. Dodge.

"I heartily agree. . . . Certainly it does not seem right to elect a Governor and then to have seven men elected by the legislature—often with behind-the-scenes manipulation—who can tell the Governor what he can and cannot do."

As one who described himself as a "non-political but politically interested friend who believes in the program of the Democratic Party," Kenneth Sills was cheered in the spring of 1954 by the vigorous leadership of Edmund Muskie and Frank Coffin which promised to restore responsible two-party government to the state. In March he wired "the united and unterrified democracy of Maine" at their convention in Lewiston, pledging his support. Impressed by the party platform and the stature of Muskie and Professor Paul Fullam, the candidates for governor and U. S. senator, K. C. M. S. declared, "I am proud to be a Maine Democrat." On June 16, in accepting the honorary chairmanship of the Democratic Maine Advisory Council, he told reporters, "The present state election campaign affords a very real opportunity, not only for Maine Democrats, but for other interested citizens to work for a two-party government in Maine, in the belief that such a policy will be of a very great benefit to good government." Remembering his own campaign for the U. S. Senate in 1916, with its thinly attended rallies and the difficulty in traveling to all parts of the large state, K. C. M. S. appealed for enough funds to provide television and radio programs. "We wish that every citizen in the length and breadth of Maine could see and hear our candidates," he said. "In their case, seeing really amounts to believing." The election of Muskie and the unprecedented vote for Professor Fullam in September renewed Kenneth Sills's hope for his party. Although he minimized his efforts, they won the gratitude of his fellow Democrats. "It was your kind of support which gave us the courage to go on when the road seemed rough," the governor-elect wrote K. C. M. S. in October, while Frank Coffin, the state chairman, declared, "I can only say that you spiritually sustained me during our entire efforts to bring better government to this State through the medium of the party which we both cherish. I keep your photograph in our headquarters as a constant reminder of what you mean to us."

Kenneth Sills's last formal, public appearance at Bowdoin was in the First Parish Church on October 20, 1954, when he gave the address at the annual James Bowdoin Day exercises in honor of the ranking scholars of the college. The occasion was especially pleasant for the president emeritus, who had presided at the institution of the exercises in 1941. "This recognition of scholarship," he said, "is a reassertion by the College of its central purpose." He chose as his subject, "Some Bowdoin Heroes," three graduates of the College—William Pitt Fessenden, Thomas Brackett Reed, and Edwin Upton Curtis—whose conduct during crises in their careers illustrated "something that is both the cause and result of sound scholarship, and something that in her long history Bowdoin has always endeavored to cultivate—the quality of intellectual integrity. . . . And it must never be forgotten that this fine courageous virtue can only flourish where there is freedom of inquiry, freedom of expression, freedom of mind."

After President Coles had awarded books bearing a replica of the earliest bookplate of the college to the undergraduates who had maintained an "A" record through two consecutive semesters, he surprised the guest of honor by adding his name to the list and presenting him with one of the volumes. "This award is a trifle late," Dr. Coles apologized, "since you were graduated fifty-three years ago, but somehow you managed to achieve 'A's,' not only for two semesters, but throughout all four years of your college course." Characteristically enough, the president emeritus felt uneasy about his prize. "I never looked up my record," he wrote President Coles the day after the ceremony, "but I always thought there was a 'B' or two in it somewhere."

K. C. M. S. had never seemed to be in better health or more vigorous. Paul Nixon, who tried unsuccessfully to see his old chief after the address, mailed him a card later that afternoon, inscribed to "Dr. K. C. M. Sills, Emeritus and Eternal." "Tried to find you in the vestry, at the Union, and at Massachusetts Hall to tell you how much I enjoyed your address today," Nixon wrote. "If you feel as well as you look and act, you're a grand example for Cicero to use." Rolliston Woodbury '22 also thought K. C. M. S. was looking well when they met more than two weeks later on November 6 at the Alumni Day luncheon before the football game with the University of Maine. Unrecognized by the doorman, the president emeritus had slipped inconspicuously into a seat at a table in the rear of the gymnasium. "This is something I've wanted to do for years," he said happily. An hour later when he took his place in the stands on Whittier Field there was a burst of applause in which K. C. M. S. joined heartily, thinking that the acclaim was intended for the Bowdoin team.

It was his last appearance in Brunswick except for a virtually unnoticed visit after dark in the following week when, quite impulsively, the Sillses decided to drive out from Portland after dinner. At a meeting of the fraternity club on November 8, K. C. M. S. had told a friend, "While Mrs. Sills and I are devoted to Portland where we have so many associations, we shall always think of Brunswick as home and always be a bit homesick when we are away from it." A day or two later, they thought it would be pleasant merely to ride around town and see the college without anyone knowing of their presence. A former colleague happened to see their car move slowly up Federal Street, pause for a moment in front of their old house, and then turn into Sills Drive. He was pleased that the cupola was brightly lighted. It must have reminded them, he thought, of their pleasure in escorting hundreds of town and faculty children up the steep stairs to the crown of the house for a view of the college from above the tree tops. As he lost sight of the car, he wondered whether it would follow the familiar route the Sillses had so often taken on foot when each year they left Christmas wreaths at the homes of their friends. "I don't believe I will ever see a wreath of holly at Christmas time," wrote Elizabeth Whitman, "without thinking of it as a Sills' wreath." The sole observer of the Sillses' last visit could only imagine their thoughts as he watched the car disappear in the shadows of the Bowdoin pines.

Kenneth Sills devoted the last week of his life to the institutions he loved best: school, college, country, and church. On Monday he discussed with Frank Coffin plans for a conference to implement the legislative reforms proposed by the Democratic party after Governor-Elect Muskie's inauguration in January. That evening he attended a meeting of the fraternity club to which he had been elected when he moved to Portland. The following day he traveled to Cambridge for a session with the trustees of the Episcopal Theological School, where Dean Charles Taylor recalled that K. C. M. S. was especially effective in interpreting faculty problems with an authority which carried great weight with the laymen on the board. On Thursday, November 11, the president emeritus gave the address at the naturalization ceremony for ninety-one new citizens of fifteen nationalities, sharing the bench in the Federal Courthouse with his former student, Judge John D. Clifford '10. Noting that the majority of the new citizens were Canadians, K. C. M. S. remarked that he was born in Halifax, had been brought to Portland when he was five months old, and had become a citizen of the United States more than fifty years ago. "The best way to maintain our freedom is to exercise the right to vote," he said. "Register at once and vote so that you may do your part to maintain the liberties granted to you. . . . Strike a blow at anything which interferes with the extension of freedom." K. C. M. S. was moved when three members of the naturalization class, a Russian, a Japanese war bride Shisue Thomas, whose husband had served in Korea, and Mrs. Mordecai Chertoff, remained after the ceremony to thank him for his words. The next morning, he spoke to the students of Gorham High School on the value of those liberal studies which free men from narrow prejudices and develop intellectual resourcefulness in a firm Christian character.

Before the Sunday service at St. Luke's Cathedral on November 14, Dean Leopold Damrosch and one of his parishioners noticed K. C. M. S. directing a small boy to a room where the confirmation class was being held. "That is what he has done all his life," the Dean remarked. "He has shown people the way." That evening, Dr. and Mrs. Sills worshipped at the Church of St. Mary the Virgin in Falmouth Foreside. "Of one thing I am reasonably sure," President Sills had once told the members of the Bowdoin Christian Association, "The religious life can be sustained and strengthened by constant practice, by regular worship and prayer."

Early the following afternoon, on his way to a meeting of the standing committee of the diocese of Maine, Kenneth Sills called at the law office of Louis Bernstein '22 to leave the records of the Bowdoin Club of Portland. "I chided him on the fact that I was his successor as President of the Club," Bernstein recalled. "He was warm and happy, declaring that he had become quite accustomed to relinquishing the cares of office and that he enjoyed it thoroughly." Later, during the session of the standing committee, Dean Damrosch was impressed by the vigor of the president emeritus, and observed again his deep concern with church problems and his remarkable skill in reconciling divergent points of view. It was six o'clock when he returned to 134 Vaughan Street. Before dinner, he and Mrs. Sills talked about plans for an "at home" for the Bowdoin alumni of Portland and their families on December 5, his seventy-fifth birthday. "He was anxious to have this reception on that day as a token of his and mine—our appreciation of all the many acts of kindness shown us," Mrs. Sills wrote. "We had 600 invitations printed and he had already directed seventy-five and had suggested to me—almost his last words—that perhaps I could direct some while he was to be out at the Fraternity Club meeting on Monday night." An hour later, while talking with his wife about college and church affairs, he was suddenly stricken with a cerebral hemorrhage and died almost instantly at seven o'clock on the evening of November 15, 1954.

The funeral service was held in St. Luke's Cathedral at two

o'clock on Thursday afternoon, November 18. The throng of more than 1,200 mourners included the faculty, the Trustees, the Overseers, and many alumni and undergraduates. There were representatives of the many state and national organizations he had served, the sister colleges of the state, the institutions from which he had received honorary degrees, learned societies, and the armed services. The varied attendance included former Governor Percival Baxter '98 with whom K. C. M. S. had shared a room in Appleton Hall in 1897, and Governor-Elect Edmund Muskie, in whose behalf Kenneth Sills had headed a citizens' committee during the campaign in September. There were those in humble walks of life for whom the loss was personal rather than institutional. Typical of scores of these was Eddie Cummings, captain of the Red Caps in the Portland Union Station. "He was just as nice to me," he said, "as if I had been President of the United States."

Kenneth Sills had left complete instructions for the conduct of the simple, half-hour service led by the Right Reverend Oliver Loring, Episcopal Bishop of Maine, and the Very Reverend Leopold Damrosch, Dean of the Cathedral. As the procession moved down the central aisle, Dean Damrosch read John 11, "I am the resurrection, and the life: he that believeth on me shall never die." The congregation and the men's and boys' cathedral choirs, augmented by the Bowdoin chapel choir, joined in singing "Lead Kindly Light." Dean Damrosch read Psalm 90, "Lord, thou hast been our dwelling-place in all generations. . . . And let the favor of the Lord our God be upon us; and establish thou the work of our hands upon us; yea, the work of our hands establish thou it." Following the hymn, "O, Lamb of God Still Keep Me," Dean Damrosch led the recitation of "The Apostles' Creed." Bishop Loring read prayers from the burial office and, after the final hymn, "The Strife is O'er, the Victory Won," the Bishop gave the committal prayer and benediction.

The honorary pallbearers were Harold Lee Berry and Roland Clark, college classmates of the president emeritus; William

Witherle Lawrence '98, the lifelong friend who had been the best man at Kenneth Sills's wedding and was now a trustee emeritus; Philip Greely Clifford '03, the overseer who in 1918 had notified Kenneth Sills of his election to the presidency of the college; Nathaniel Cooper Kendrick, dean of Bowdoin, and President James Stacy Coles, Kenneth Sills's successor in office. Burial was in the Pine Grove Cemetery, Brunswick, a short distance from the house in which he had lived for many years and near the grave of his predecessor, William DeWitt Hyde. As the funeral procession entered Brunswick, all business halted, the flag on the Town Hall was at half-mast, and college classes were canceled. While the cortege moved slowly past the First Parish Church, Massachusetts Hall, and the pines bordering Sills Drive, the chapel bell tolled slowly seventy-four times, to count the seventy-four years of Kenneth Sills's life. Following the committal service, the college chimes played his favorite hymns, "Abide With Me" and "Lead Kindly Light." His grave is marked by a granite cross bearing the simple inscription: Kenneth Charles Morton Sills, 1879–1954.

Early that evening, William Lawrence called at Vaughan Street to leave a sonnet he had written when he had learned of the death of his friend:

> His voice was kindly and his brow serene
> And such a friendliness shone in his face
> We felt that, as it were by special grace
> A finer spirit in our midst had been.
> No more beneath the elms will he be seen,
> The hearth-fire sinks in its accustomed place,
> And only memories remain to trace
> What his devotion through the years can mean.
> We should not wholly grieve, but think of him
> As of a traveller, his journey done,
> Sturdy of sinew and of sight not dim,
> Who comes to port with setting of the sun,
> And lies asleep in well-earned rest at last,
> All wandering over, and all striving past.

# INDEX

Since this is a Bowdoin book about a Bowdoin subject, entries such as "academic freedom," "athletics," and "chapel" refer to Bowdoin College. Only biographical topics are listed under "Sills, Kenneth Charles Morton." President Sills's activities and opinions will be found under a variety of headings.